CONSTITUTIONAL CHANGE THROUGH EURO-CRISIS LAW

Constitutional Change Through Euro-Crisis Law contains a comparative constitutional analysis of the impact of a very broad range of euro-crisis law instruments on the EU and national constitutions. It covers (i) contrasting assessments of the impact of euro-crisis law on national parliaments; (ii) various types of criticism on the EU economic governance framework; (iii) different views on what is needed to improve the multi-level system of economic governance and (iv) valuable insights into the nature of emergency discourse in the legislative arena and of the spillover from the political to the judicial sphere. In addition, it deals with how bailout countries, even if part of the same group of euro-area Member States subject to a programme, have reacted differently to the crisis.

THOMAS BEUKERS is Jean Monnet Fellow at the European University Institute and Senior Legal Advisor for the Dutch Ministry of Foreign Affairs. His research interests include the relationship between law and politics, as well as the constitutional law of the European Union. Since he joined the EUI in 2012, his research focuses on the constitutional development of EMU. He is editor of the *European Constitutional Law Review*.

BRUNO DE WITTE was Professor of European Law at Maastricht University from 1989 to 2000 and at the European University Institute in Florence from 2000 to 2010. He currently combines part-time positions at both these institutions. His main areas of research include constitutional reform and treaty revision in the European Union, protection of fundamental rights in Europe, and decision-making and legal instruments of EU law.

CLAIRE KILPATRICK is Professor of International European and Social Law at the European University Institute, Florence, and Co-Director of the Academy of European Law. Her interests lie mainly in the law and policy construction of Social Europe. A focus of her recent work is EMU and Social Europe with a particular focus on sovereign debt loan arrangements and legal challenges to those arrangements from those within debtor EU states.

CONSTITUTIONAL CHANGE THROUGH EURO-CRISIS LAW

Edited by

THOMAS BEUKERS

European University Institute, Florence

BRUNO DE WITTE

European University Institute, Florence

CLAIRE KILPATRICK

European University Institute, Florence

CAMBRIDGE
UNIVERSITY PRESS

CAMBRIDGE
UNIVERSITY PRESS

University Printing House, Cambridge CB2 8BS, United Kingdom

One Liberty Plaza, 20th Floor, New York, NY 10006, USA

477 Williamstown Road, Port Melbourne, VIC 3207, Australia

4843/24, 2nd Floor, Ansari Road, Daryaganj, Delhi – 110002, India

79 Anson Road, #06–04/06, Singapore 079906

Cambridge University Press is part of the University of Cambridge.

It furthers the University's mission by disseminating knowledge in the pursuit of education, learning, and research at the highest international levels of excellence.

www.cambridge.org
Information on this title: www.cambridge.org/9781107184497
DOI: 10.1017/9781316877135

First published 2017

Printed in the United Kingdom by Clays, St Ives plc

A catalogue record for this publication is available from the British Library.

Library of Congress Cataloging-in-Publication Data
Names: Beukers, Thomas, 1979- editor. | Witte, Bruno de, editor. | Kilpatrick, Claire, editor.
Title: Constitutional change through Euro-crisis law / edited by Thomas Beukers, European University Institute, Florence; Bruno de Witte, European University Institute, Florence; Claire Kilpatrick, European University Institute, Florence.
Description: Cambridge [UK] ; New York : Cambridge University Press, 2017. | Includes bibliographical references and index.
Identifiers: LCCN 2016046847 | ISBN 9781107184497 (hardback : alk. paper)
Subjects: LCSH: Constitutional law–European Union countries. | Constitutional amendments–European Union countries. | European Union countries–Economic policy. | Financial institutions–Law and legislation–European Union countries. | European Union countries–Politics and government.
Classification: LCC KJE4445 .C66 2017 | DDC 343.2407–dc23
LC record available at https://lccn.loc.gov/2016046847

ISBN 978-1-107-18449-7 Hardback

CONTENTS

TABLES

CONTRIBUTORS

THOMAS BEUKERS is Senior Legal Advisor at the Dutch Ministry of Foreign Affairs and a Jean Monnet Fellow at the European University Institute.

STEPHEN COUTTS is a lecturer at the School of Law and Government, Dublin City University.

BRUNO DE WITTE is Professor of European Law at Maastricht University, The Netherlands, and part-time Professor of Law at the European University Institute.

LETICIA DÍEZ-SANCHEZ is a PhD researcher at the European University Institute Law Department.

DIANE FROMAGE is Assistant Professor in EU Law at Utrecht University's Law Faculty.

CLAIRE KILPATRICK is Professor of International and European Labour and Social Law in the European University Institute Law Department.

PÄIVI LEINO-SANDBERG is Adjunct Professor of EU Law at the University of Helsinki.

AFRODITI MARKETOU is a PhD researcher at the European University Institute.

LEONARDO PIERDOMINICI is a postdoctoral researcher at the Alma Mater Studiorum Università di Bologna School of Law, and a Research Associate at the Robert Schuman Center for Advanced Studies at the European University Institute.

JAN-HERMAN REESTMAN is Associate Professor of Public Law in the Department of Constitutional and Administrative Law at the University of Amsterdam.

VIOLETA RUIZ ALMENDRAL is Associate Professor of Tax and Finance Law at Universidad Carlos III de Madrid.

JANNE SALMINEN is Senior Lecturer in the Faculty of Law, University of Turku.

MARIJN VAN DER SLUIS is Assistant Professor in EU Law at Erasmus University, Rotterdam.

PREFACE

This book is one of the fruits of a larger research project of the European University Institute (EUI) Law Department and funded by the EUI Research Council from January 2013 to December 2015. As such, it has benefited from the work of a large number of people, most of whom are researchers, Max Weber Fellows or professors in the law department of the EUI. We are extremely grateful to the EUI Research Council for their support, which has helped create not just the project but also a new generation of European Monetary Union (EMU) law scholars at the EUI.

The funded project entailed a study of the impact of euro-crisis law (by which we mean the legal instruments adopted at European or international level in reaction to the Eurozone crisis) on the national legal and constitutional structures of the 28 Member States of the European Union. Scholarly debate on euro-crisis law has mainly focused on the European legal dimension, and on normative issues of democratic legitimacy, legality and the balance between austerity and growth policies. Contributions also exist on the impact of euro-crisis law on specific national constitutional orders, but a comprehensive study is so far lacking. The project set out to fill this gap. Its goal was to provide an open-access research tool, based on a set of reports for each Member State that would constitute an excellent basis for further, especially comparative, studies of the legal status and implementation of euro-crisis law at the national level, the interactions between national legal systems and euro-crisis law and the constitutional challenges that have been faced. That open-access tool is available at http://eurocrisislaw.eui.eu/. This edited volume draws on the project's findings to develop further, especially comparative studies, of euro-crisis law.

Key to the project's success were its three co-ordinators: Thomas Beukers (2013–present), Cristina Fasone (2014–15) and Marijn van der Sluis (2013–14). The reports were based on a detailed questionnaire and on a wider range of sources, including minutes of parliamentary debates, national laws ratifying and implementing euro-crisis law and case law of national constitutional or supreme courts. Thomas Beukers and Marijn van der Sluis were the main authors of the original questionnaire and played an important role in co-ordinating the large team of researchers, many based at the EUI, who authored the country reports. Those reports were then subject to editing and updating. Cristina Fasone, alongside Thomas Beukers, played a central role in editing the reports. Central to the project is the quality of the country reports. We wish to thank, in order of country: Daniela Jaros (Austria); Werner Vandenbruwaene (Belgium); Mihail Vatsov (Bulgaria); Mateja Djurovic (Croatia); Ekaterina Pantazatou (Cyprus); Tomas Dumbrovsky (Czech Republic); Marja-Liisa Laatsit (Estonia); Päivi Leino-Sandberg and Janne Salminen (Finland); Robin Gadbled and Diane Fromage (France); Sabine Mair and Malte Koeger (Germany); Afroditi Marketou and Michail Dekastros (Greece); Dalma Dojcsák (Hungary); Stephen Coutts (Ireland); Leonardo Pierdominici (Italy); Zane Rasnača (Latvia); Loreta Šaltinytė (Lithuania); Malte Kroeger (Luxembourg); Malte Kroeger (Malta); Jotte Mulder (Netherlands); Katarzyna Granat (Poland); Rita Gião Hanek and Daniele Gallo (Portugal); Viorica Viță (Romania); Tomas Dumbrovsky (Slovakia); Urska Petrovcic (Slovenia); Mireia Estrada Cañamares, Germán Gomez Ventura and Leticia Díez Sánchez (Spain); Anna Södersten (Sweden) and Emily Hancox (UK).

The website design involved displaying a map of Europe in which each report was coded according to a traffic light system so that users could search by country which euro-crisis instruments had been controversial. We wish to thank Lorenzo Giuntini for his help with website design and maintenance. Project dissemination and updates via newsletters and the news section of the project's website were in the capable and proactive hands of Viorica Viță and Thomas Beukers.

Cristina Fasone helped Marise Cremona and Claire Kilpatrick to organize a conference at the EUI in October 2014 out of which many of the contributions to this volume developed. Nick Lee played an invaluable role in meticulous editing of both the language and the substance of submitted chapters. His comments and suggestions significantly improved the quality of the volume.

Giorgio Monti, currently Head of Department at the EUI, played a central role throughout the entire life of the project. Loïc Azoulai, Marise Cremona, Stefan Grundmann and Hans Micklitz, professors in the EUI Law Department, all played important roles at various stages.

1

Constitutional Change through Euro-Crisis Law: Taking Stock, New Perspectives and Looking Ahead

THOMAS BEUKERS, BRUNO DE WITTE AND CLAIRE KILPATRICK

This chapter serves as a general introduction to the theme of this book. We will do this in two parts followed by a conclusion. In Section 1, we offer a succinct reconstruction of what has happened at the European Union (EU) level in euro-crisis law. After over half a decade of legal measures and prolific commentary on those measures, it is helpful to stand back and take stock. In Section 2, we present the particular perspective adopted by this book. Its core argument is that an overall and ongoing assessment of euro-crisis measures, especially by including the national level, is an important and distinctive contribution to euro-crisis legal scholarship. In the conclusion, we will consider whether euro-crisis law, although a fitting label to capture the conditions of its production and some parts of its application, has by now mainly become simply the macroeconomic law of the EU.

1 Taking Stock: The Staging-Posts of Euro-Crisis Law

In certain respects, the peaks of production of euro-crisis law by the EU and its Member States acting intergovernmentally are likely to be over. By euro-crisis law we mean the wide-ranging overhaul of macroeconomic law, institutions and governance triggered when the banking and financial crisis from 2007 onwards became interlinked with sovereign debt crises in euro area states. In this regard, it is somewhat poignant to note that the European Council Conclusions of December 2009 strike a note of optimism by welcoming the entry into force of the Lisbon Treaty and noting that 'the economic situation is now showing signs of stabilization and confidence is increasing'. Moreover, the European

Council's agreement on Europe 2020 in March 2010, while linked to the severe downturn caused by the banking crisis of 2007 onwards, was not yet connected to a developed euro-crisis agenda, although it asked for a Task Force to be set up, the recommendations of which proved highly influential in the first phase of euro-crisis law.[1] We can accordingly trace the euro-crisis measures as they emerge from this date.

Three key strands, with different staging posts, of euro-crisis law production can be identified.[2] Two were seen by the EU institutions and the Member States as part of a linked package: first, sovereign debt loan assistance and the accompanying conditionality; and second, an overhaul of the macroeconomic governance regime in the Economic and Monetary Union (EMU). Europe's initial action on sovereign debt loans for Greece in May 2010 was followed by an intense period of EU action on a package of measures to deal with what were seen as the causes and consequences of the euro crisis. The third strand concerns new actions by, and institutional competences for, the European Central Bank (ECB).

With regard to the first two strands, two pivotal drivers of that euro-crisis action can be identified. The first is the follow-up given from June 2010 to December 2011 by the European Council and the EU legislature to the suggestions and recommendations of the Task Force set up in March 2010.[3] This led to the Six-Pack of EU legislation, the Euro-Plus Pact and a first version of the ESM Treaty, which was signed on 11 July 2011.[4] The second is the package agreed at the Euro Summit[5] of 9 December 2011, which led to the Fiscal Compact, the enhanced second version

[1] This is unsurprising when its composition is considered. Headed by Mr Van Rompuy, European Council President, it comprised Mr Olli Rehn, European Commission, Mr Juncker as Eurogroup President, Mr Trichet as ECB President and (mainly) the finance ministers of all EU Member States.

[2] Rather separately and with a different time frame a further strand of actions to reform banks and the financial sector in Europe was developed both for the EU as a whole and for the euro area specifically. While there are important links between this strand and those examined in this volume, we do not consider it here.

[3] So already before the final report of the Task Force appeared in October 2010: 'Strengthening Economic Governance in the EU', Report of the Task Force to the European Council, Brussels, 21 October 2010.

[4] This first version of the ESM Treaty can no longer be traced on the Internet, as it was erased from the websites of the Council and of the EFSF following the signature and the entry into force of the second version of the ESM Treaty. There is a reference to that first treaty in point A.2 of the Frequently Asked Questions page of the ESM website.

[5] The Euro Summit itself is an institutional innovation born out of the banking crisis upon the initiative of French President Sarkozy with its first meeting taking place in 2008. It entails meetings of euro area Heads of State or Government and the Commission

of the ESM Treaty and the further endorsement and outlining of the plans for what became the Two-Pack of legislation of 2013.

A. *Euro-Crisis Strand One: Sovereign Debt Loan Assistance and Conditionality*

Although sovereign debt loan assistance was provided to both non-euro and euro area states, there were significant differences in its provision. The banking crisis beginning in 2007–8 provoked balance of payments difficulties in a number of non-euro area Eastern EU Member States. These were resolved through sovereign debt loan assistance to Hungary, Latvia and Romania, mainly from the International Monetary Fund (IMF), but with a relatively modest EU contribution provided by an existing mechanism with a clear EU Treaty basis.[6] However, the EU went into the crisis with little money available, and no existing EU fund, to grant sovereign debt loans to euro area states. Moreover, the loans needed were on an entirely different scale to those required by the Eastern EU Member States. Through a series of different actions setting out various loan assistance mechanisms, this issue has been addressed. It was resolved, first, by agreeing on 2 May 2010 to loan Greece 80 billion EUR on the basis of bilateral agreements with other euro area states alongside 30 billion EUR from the IMF (known as the Greek Loan Facility). Immediately thereafter (Sunday, 9 May 2010), an EU fund was established relying on the relatively small amounts available in the EU budget, the European Financial Stability Mechanism (EFSM)[7] and a larger sum was made available through the European Financial Stability Fund (EFSF), contemporaneously established by an immediately effective

President. Its status was made 'official' in the Fiscal Compact Treaty of March 2012, Article 12.

6 Article 143 TFEU fleshed out in Regulation 333/2002 establishing a facility providing medium-term financial assistance for Member States' balance of payments. Pre-crisis, the latter made the maximum total available 12 billion EUR. Post-crisis this was increased to 50 billion EUR. The Treaty explicitly envisions such EU assistance being accompanied by IMF assistance as well as bilateral assistance from other States: Article 143(2) TFEU.

7 Article 122(2) TFEU is the legal basis for Council Regulation 407/2010 of 11 May 2010 establishing a European Financial Stability Mechanism: 'Where a Member State is in difficulties or is seriously threatened with severe difficulties caused by natural disasters or exceptional occurrences beyond its control, the Council, on a proposal from the Commission, may grant, under certain conditions, Union financial assistance to the Member State concerned.'

international agreement between the euro area states.[8] This much larger fund, initially 440 billion euros and later extended, operated as a private company established in Luxembourg under the control of the euro area states.[9] Parallel to these unprecedented political initiatives, the ECB Governing Council decided on 10 May 2010 on a number of unconventional monetary policy measures to address the tensions in the financial markets (see Strand Three).

One part of the package finalised at a central European Council meeting of 25 March 2011, following the broad suggestion of the 2010 Task Force to consider this in the medium term, concerned setting up a new more permanent financial assistance mechanism. While the European Council decided, at that meeting, to amend the Treaties so as to include an explicit authorisation in Article 136(3) of the Treaty on the Functioning of the European Union (TFEU) for the euro area Member States to set up such an assistance mechanism,[10] the assistance mechanism itself, the European Stability Mechanism, was agreed only one year later.[11] As noted above, a first version of the ESM Treaty had in fact been agreed already in July 2011 but the unfolding crisis in the financial markets in the summer of 2011 led the euro area governments to

[8] Decision of the Representatives of the Governments of the Euro Area Member States Meeting Within the Council of the European Union, Council Document 9614/10 of 10 May 2010. The EFSF was incorporated on 7 June 2010.

[9] The bulk of Ireland's support scheme, 85 billion EUR (November 2010–December 2013), and Portugal's 78 billion EUR (May 2011–May 2014), came from these two sources. Greece's second loan programme (Greece II) was exclusively EFSF-based: in March 2012 a 130 billion EUR loan was agreed (initially planned to last until December 2014, later extended until the end of June 2015 as a result of the elections bringing Syriza to power in January 2015).

[10] European Council Decision of 25 March 2011 amending Article 136 of the Treaty on the Functioning of the European Union with regard to a stability mechanism for Member States whose currency is the euro OJ 2011, L 91/1 of 6 April 2011. The amendment provides: '3. The Member States whose currency is the euro may establish a stability mechanism to be activated if indispensable to safeguard the stability of the euro area as a whole. The granting of any required financial assistance under the mechanism will be made subject to strict conditionality'. It required the approval by all 27 Member States to enter into force which, after a late Czech approval, finally occurred in April 2013.

[11] ESM Treaty signed on 2 February 2012. Containing a special rule for its entry into force (Article 48), it came into effect on 27 September 2012 after only 16 parties had completed ratification. For details of its lending to date see www.esm.europa.eu. For an unsuccessful legal challenge to the compatibility of the Article 136(3) TFEU amendment and the creation of the ESM with the EMU Treaty provisions, see *Thomas Pringle* v. *Government of Ireland, Ireland and the Attorney General*, Case C-370/12 (27 November 2012).

re-open the negotiations and to enhance the ESM's functions,[12] allowing it not only to lend to states in sovereign debt programmes (Article 16) and purchase their bonds (Article 17) but also to finance recapitalisation of financial institutions through loans to governments even in non-programme countries (Article 15), act on the basis of a precautionary programme (Article 14) and intervene in the secondary bond markets to avoid contagion and safeguard financial stability (Article 18). Designed to have an effective lending capacity of 700 billion EUR, the ESM's first use in full bailout mode was in relation to Cyprus' programme which made up to 9 billion EUR loan assistance available from the ESM (May 2013–March 2016).[13] On 8 July 2015 Greece requested a third round of financial assistance, this time from the ESM. After difficult negotiations, Greece III was agreed and makes up to 85 billion EUR available under the ESM between August 2015–2018.

Although the ESM was said to have superseded both the EFSM and the EFSF,[14] in the passage to Greece III in the summer of 2015, recourse was again made to the EU-based EFSM. While the ESM request which became Greece III was under examination, on 17 July 2015, Greece was granted just over 7 billion EUR in short-term financial assistance under the EFSM in order to meet July 2015 repayment obligations to the ECB (the redemption of bonds) and to settle its arrears with the IMF.[15] The assistance was disbursed in one instalment on 20 July 2015, and was linked to economic policy conditionality. The ESM assistance was, inter alia, to repay that short-term EFSM bridge loan. This EFSM assistance was controversial. Among the non-euro area Member States, the UK and the Czech Republic were most strongly opposed to using an EU, rather than a euro area only, financial instrument to grant the bridging loan to Greece. As the EFSM is an EU-wide fund, backed by the EU budget, disbursements from it need the approval of all of the EU's

[12] Statement by the Heads of State or Government of the Euro Area and EU Institutions of 21 July 2011, http://europa.eu/rapid/press-release_DOC-11-5_en.htm

[13] Between December 2012 and December 2013, 41.3 billion EUR was disbursed from the ESM as a sovereign debt loan to Spain to recapitalise and restructure its banks. As this loan was directed only at a particular sector of the economy, it could not be accompanied by IMF assistance and did not entail, as the other sovereign debt loans did, suspension of the normal EU macroeconomic regime under EMU during the loan assistance period.

[14] See, for example, the European Council Conclusions of 16/17 December 2010 making this assertion. See also Preamble (1) of the ESM Treaty which provides that the ESM 'will assume the tasks currently fulfilled by the EFSF and the EFSM'.

[15] Council Implementing Decision 2015/1181 of 17 July 2015 on granting short-term financial assistance to Greece OJ 2015 L192/15.

28 governments, rather than just the 19 of the euro area. However, decisions in the EFSM are taken by qualified majority voting,[16] which means the UK and the Czech Republic, and even all non-euro states, could be outvoted. The different situations of euro area and non-euro area states were however taken into account in both the Council Decision granting the bridging loan under the EFSM to Greece, and in an amendment to the EFSM regulation itself by providing that 'Union financial assistance under this Decision shall not be made available unless liquid collateral amounting to their exposure has been provided to those Member States whose currency is not the euro under legally binding arrangements such that it is immediately payable to them to the extent required to cover any liability they may incur as a result of any failure by Greece to repay the financial assistance in accordance with its terms.'[17]

Sovereign debt loan assistance to euro area states has since 2010 consistently been accompanied by strict macroeconomic conditionality. While the EFSF and ESM are non-EU Treaties, the loan conditions and disbursements are managed by EU institutions, with the Commission being given the task of negotiator and monitor, in liaison with the ECB. The IMF completes the troika. Political decisions on conditions and disbursements have regularly been taken in the Eurogroup, and occasionally in a Euro Summit, only to be formally adopted by the relevant institutions of the EFSF and ESM (notably the same people). In addition, from 2013, the conditions attached to sovereign debt loan assistance to euro states were given a stronger EU law basis by introduction in one of the Two-Pack Regulations (on which see now Strand Two) of a requirement that they should also be stated in EU law Macro-Economic Adjustment Programmes.[18]

B. Euro-Crisis Strand Two: Reinforcing Fiscal Stability and Macroeconomic Governance

A second strand consisted of reinforcing fiscal stability and macroeconomic governance, especially in the euro area states. The Europe 2020

[16] Article 3(2) EFSM Regulation.

[17] Article 1(2) Council Implementing Decision (EU) 2015/1181 of 17 July 2015 on granting short-term financial assistance to Greece; new Article 3(2a) EFSM Regulation.

[18] Regulation No 472/2013 of 21 May 2013 on the strengthening of economic and budgetary surveillance of Member States in the euro area experiencing or threatened with serious difficulties with respect to their financial stability.

strategy, the successor to the Lisbon strategy of 2000–2010, was launched in March 2010. Aimed at smart, sustainable and inclusive growth, it set targets on employment rates, R&D investment, climate and energy, educational attainment of the young and poverty reduction. This strategy rapidly got caught in the slipstream of the broader overhaul of macroeconomic governance. The recommendations of the Task Force set up in March 2010 provided a blueprint for the design of a new EMU based on increasing fiscal discipline, deepening co-ordination and widening surveillance, which led to the Six-Pack of legislation at the end of 2011. Hence, in June 2010 the European Council first refers to the new nomenclature of the 'European Semester' suggested by the Task Force. The European Semester grouped together each spring, from 1 January 2011, EU review of the broadened macroeconomic regime to allow Member States to fully take these into account in their national budgets and macroeconomic decision-making in the second half of each calendar year. Initially operated with no legislative basis, it was given such a basis in the Six-Pack at the end of 2011. Other changes made stemming from the Task Force report include the Macro-Economic Imbalance Procedure; operationalising debt, rather than just deficits, in the Excessive Deficit Procedure; a shift to Reverse Qualified Majority Voting in making economic governance decisions; additional sanctions for euro area states, including macroeconomic conditionalities in the next iteration of the EU structural and investment funds; and the establishment of independent national fiscal bodies. The Task Force also recommended a fast track to introduce legislation on these matters. These changes were rendered in legislative form in the so-called Six-Pack of five Regulations and one Directive in November 2011.[19]

The central European Council meeting of 25 March 2011 which agreed the Treaty amendment relating to the ESM also agreed the Euro-Plus Pact and its text is annexed to the Conclusions of the European Council. A soft law intergovernmental measure, it was agreed by the euro area

[19] Directive 2011/85 on requirements for budgetary frameworks of the Member States; Regulation 1173/2011 on the effective enforcement of budgetary surveillance in the euro area; Regulation 1174/2011 on the prevention and correction of macroeconomic imbalances; Regulation 1175/2011 amending Council Regulation 1466/97 on the strengthening of the surveillance of budgetary policies and the surveillance and co-ordination of economic policies; Regulation 1176/2011 on the prevention and correction of macroeconomic imbalances; Regulation 1177/2011 amending Regulation 1467/97 on speeding up and clarifying the implementation of the Excessive Deficit Procedure. The Six-Pack is available in OJ 2011 L 301/1-47.

states plus (hence its name) other willing participating states. Its mode of operation required commitments by the heads of state or government on an annual basis to concrete actions, particularly in areas lying within national competence. Those commitments would then be included in the European Semester process and be subject to political monitoring. The Pact sets out four goals at which those commitments should aim: fostering competitiveness (by, e.g., reviewing the degree of centralisation of collective bargaining and wage indexation mechanisms); fostering employment (by, e.g., labour market reforms to promote flexicurity); enhancing the sustainability of the public finances (by committing to translating EU fiscal rules as set out in the Stability and Growth Pact into national legislation) and reinforcing financial stability (by committing to putting into place national legislation for banking resolution).

Although not stemming from the Task Force's report, the need to reinforce national fiscal rectitude was also the force animating what became the Fiscal Compact Treaty (officially entitled the Treaty on Stability, Coordination and Governance in the Economic and Monetary Union). Signed on 2 March 2012, between the 17 euro area countries and eight further EU Member States, it entered into force on 1 January 2013.[20] The reasons for concluding it outside the EU institutional framework are not obvious at first sight. Most of what it contains in terms of economic governance at the European level could have been adopted through EU legislation or by means of a modification of Protocol No. 12 on the Excessive Deficit Procedure. In particular, the obligation to introduce into national law the new budgetary limits defined in Article 3(1) could technically have been achieved by means of EU legislation, if necessary adopted by means of the enhanced cooperation mode of decision-making in which not all EU states must participate. At the same time, it can be questioned whether EU secondary legislation provides sufficient legitimacy to impose an obligation to introduce a Balanced Budget Rule in the national constitution (during the negotiations on the Fiscal Compact Treaty this obligation was weakened to a mere 'preference' to include it in the constitution), national ownership being a central function of the introduction of the rules also at the national level. In any event, it was made very clear by the German government in the course of the autumn of 2011 that the crisis circumstances on the financial markets required nothing less than a 'treaty'. The argument went that a renewed

[20] The text of this treaty can be found on www.consilium.europa.eu/en/european-council/pdf/Treaty-on-Stability-Coordination-and-Governance-TSCG (last visited 18 July 2016).

collective commitment to budgetary stability would sound more convincing and would prove to be more permanent if contained in a treaty that cannot be 'bent' later on, whereas EU legislation was more liable to be 'softened' through later amendments. Therefore, making a treaty seemed to be the appropriate symbolic message of strong resolve which the unruly financial markets required in the autumn of 2011.

The kind of treaty norm that the German government, and later also the French government, had in mind was a formal amendment of the TFEU like the one that was adopted in March 2011 on the financial stability mechanism (the current article 136(3) TFEU). But this would have required the unanimous agreement of all EU Member States and probably a prior debate at a convention, in accordance with the EU's cumbersome ordinary revision procedure. At the December 2011 summit, that process was stopped short from the very start when the UK government refused to agree on such a TFEU amendment given that the (unrelated) conditions it had put forward had not been accepted by the other governments. During the European Council meeting itself, the other governments, led by the French-German tandem, decided instantaneously to 'exit' from the EU institutional framework, and to go for a separate international agreement instead, so as to circumvent the British veto.[21] They did not take time to consider whether, given the impossibility of a TFEU amendment, the wisest course might have been to adopt EU *legislation* through enhanced cooperation, rather than take the risk of engaging in this new and unpredictable treaty game.[22] So, one could say that the states *accidentally* stumbled into the conclusion of a separate international agreement, for a mix of reasons including the rigidity of the TFEU amendment process, the belief (especially on the German side) in the symbolic power of a treaty, and also – admittedly – the wish to avoid going through the cumbersome and lengthy procedures of EU legislation.

The final element of deepened and widened macroeconomic governance came with the Two-Pack of legislation, the foundations of which were also laid in Autumn 2011. The Six-Pack had already introduced additional measures for euro area states only, in particular, sanctions in relation to preventive budget discipline, the Excessive Deficit Procedure

[21] That political decision was embodied in a Statement by the Euro Area Heads of State or Government within the meeting of the European Council of 9 December 2011.

[22] For an evocation of the political circumstances of the December meeting of the European Council that eventually led to the choice for a separate treaty, see 'The European Union and the Euro – Game, Set and Mismatch', *The Economist* 17, December 2011, 43.

and the Macroeconomic Imbalance Procedure. The Two-Pack continues to develop euro area–only obligations and regimes. One of the Regulations (473/2013) focuses on increased control over national budgets and over Member States with excessive deficits. It increases control of national budgets by introducing a fixed common budgetary timeline and granting the Commission the power to ask for draft budgets to be amended and also by increasing the powers of the independent fiscal bodies already required by the Six-Pack Directive for all EU Member States (except the UK). It increases control of euro area states with excessive deficits in two ways: by introducing Economic Partnership Programmes, combining fiscal and structural reforms, in euro area states where the Council has decided, under Article 126(6) TFEU on the existence of an excessive deficit; and by placing more frequent reporting obligations on euro area excessive deficit states.[23]

C. *Euro-Crisis Strand Three: New Actions and Institutional Roles for the ECB*

Although this is best presented as a separate strand, there are of course very strong interactions between the other strands and the ECB's actions and roles during the crisis.[24] A first set of actions concerns the ECB's interactions with the national banking system.[25] An important part of the ECB's activity from the banking crisis onwards concerned providing enhanced liquidity to banks or other credit institutions in the euro area. A further linked activity, with determining effects on the entry of states into sovereign debt loan assistance, concerned its decisions on the provision of Emergency Liquidity Assistance by National Central Banks to euro area banks.

[23] The other half of the Two-Pack (Regulation 472/2013) deals with states in sovereign debt loan programmes (discussed in Strand One) and states at risk of being in such a programme (discussed in Strand Three because of the ECB's involvement).

[24] See for much greater detail and analysis, though differing evaluations, T. Beukers, 'The New ECB and Its Relationship with the Eurozone Member States: Between Central Bank Independence and Central Bank Intervention', 50 *CMLRev* (2013), 1579; C. Kilpatrick, 'Abnormal Sources and Institutional Actions in the EU Sovereign Debt Crisis: ECB Crisis Management and the Sovereign Debt Loans' in L. Azoulai and M. Cremona (eds.), *EU Legal Acts: Challenges and Transformations*, Oxford University Press, forthcoming.

[25] As mentioned above, a further strand of actions to reform banks and the financial sector, the developing European Banking Union with new elements of risk avoidance and risk sharing, with a central role for the ECB, will not be considered here.

A third ECB activity concerned bond-buying programmes formally or informally conditional on policy reforms and asset purchase programmes. Although the ECB mainly interacts with national systems through its tenders to purchase bank assets for money, it can also directly buy and sell marketable instruments. These can include government bonds provided they are purchased on the secondary bond markets and not directly from a national sovereign. Article 18(1) of the ECB Statute allows the ECB to inter alia buy and sell marketable instruments and the purchase of government bonds as such instruments is justified by the ECB to ensure accurate transmission of its monetary policy. The bonds are bought on the secondary market because Article 123 TFEU prohibits the direct purchase by the ECB of Member State debt instruments.[26] The ECB introduced two high-profile bond-buying programmes since the euro area sovereign debt crisis. The first, the Securities Market Programme (SMP),[27] was introduced in May 2010 to accompany the first euro area bailout in Greece. It operated in Greece, Ireland and Portugal as well as in two states not in sovereign debt loan programmes, Italy and Spain, where it operated briefly from August 2011. The second, the Outright Market Transactions (OMT) programme was announced in September 2012,[28] preceded by the famous announcement of ECB President Mario Draghi on 26 July 2012 that 'Within our mandate, the ECB is ready to do whatever it takes to preserve the euro. And believe me, it will be enough'. Both programmes entail purchase by the ECB of government bonds of euro area states on the secondary bond market. A feature of these programmes is that they are directed towards the bonds of particularly vulnerable states and are accompanied by conditionality.[29]

[26] Article 123(1) TFEU provides: 'Overdraft facilities or any other type of credit facility with the European Central Bank or with the central banks of the Member States (hereinafter referred to as "national central banks") in favour of Union institutions, bodies, offices or agencies, central governments, regional, local or other public authorities, other bodies governed by public law, or public undertakings of Member States shall be prohibited, as shall the purchase directly from them by the European Central Bank or national central banks of debt instruments'.

[27] Decision of the ECB of 14 May 2010 establishing a Securities Markets Programme (ECB/2010/5), [2010] OJ L124/8.

[28] Note that OMT was announced only in a press release following the meeting of the ECB Governing Council on 5–6 September 2012. Legal instruments regulating OMT have not to date been adopted. The compatibility of OMT with EU law was the subject of a preliminary reference from the German *Bundesverfassungsgericht*, see *Gauweiler and Others* v. *Deutscher Bundestag*, Case C-62/14 (16 June 2015).

[29] This distinguishes both these programmes from the broader Public Sector Purchasing Programme launched in January 2015: Decision of the ECB of 4 March 2015 on a

The ECB is, fourthly, a member of the troika managing the roll-out of sovereign debt loan assistance. It has an important formal role in devising and monitoring the conditions imposed in return for sovereign debt loan assistance in the euro area. The various different loan instruments all give the ECB roles alongside the Commission. As provided from 2013 in one of the EU Two-Pack Regulations accompanying all euro area bailouts, whatever their source:

> Where a Member State requests financial assistance . . . it shall prepare, in agreement with the Commission, acting in liaison with the ECB, a draft macro-economic adjustment programme.[30]

In addition to drafting the loan conditions, the ECB liaises with the Commission to monitor its implementation and a programme state is placed under a legal obligation to fully co-operate with the Commission and the ECB.[31]

A final function comes from the same Two-Pack Regulation of 2013.[32] This introduced a new regime of enhanced surveillance for euro area states in receipt of precautionary financial assistance requiring policy changes or at risk of entering a sovereign debt programme. In this regime the Commission and ECB have distinct roles, with the Commission deciding whether to place a euro area state in the regime while the ECB's role is linked to its role as a supervisor of the euro-area banking system so that it may, for example, carry out stress tests on banks as part of this regime. The Commission and ECB are empowered to carry out regular review missions.[33]

2 New Perspectives: Constitutional Change at the European and National Levels Combined

Most of the euro-crisis legal measures listed above involved some further action by the participating states at the domestic level. These domestic

secondary-markets public-sector asset purchase programme (ECB/2015/10) [2015] OJ L121/20. This is aimed at all euro area states except those in sovereign debt programmes which are excluded unless they comply with their programmes. Building on smaller earlier programmes, this is a euro-system-wide large-scale purchasing programme of government bonds and EU institutions and government agency securities, designed to combat deflationary tendencies in the euro area. This is usually called quantitative easing.

30 Article 7(1) Regulation 472/2013.

31 Article 7(4) Regulation 472/2013.

32 See further C. Kilpatrick, 'The New E in EMU: A Lawful and Effective Design?' ADEMU Working Paper, EUI, 2016.

33 See, in particular, Article 3 Regulation 472/2013.

actions included parliamentary authorisations for some of the crucial European-level decisions, ratifications of the various intergovernmental treaties and implementation of the obligations contained in the treaties and in EU legislation. This national dimension of euro-crisis law is less fully documented in the scholarly literature. A research project was conducted at the EUI, funded by its Research Council, between 2013 and 2015, in which this national dimension was documented as fully as possible. This *euro-crisis law* project was based on the hypothesis that the national implementation of a wide raft of measures designed to regulate the economic performance of Member States and rescue the euro was likely to prove controversial and give rise to national reactions worthy of detailed evaluation and further comparative analysis. To investigate this, reports for each state were authored by legal scholars on the basis of a specially designed questionnaire. The result is a website that charts the implementation of the various measures in 27 Member States. The website is accessible via this link: http://eurocrisislaw.eui.eu. It is interactive and openly accessible to any stakeholder, policy-maker and researcher as a working tool to identify and study the progress of the euro-crisis treaties and legislation in the Member States. The reaction to particular euro-crisis measures has been colour-coded so that the map of EU states can be searched to find out which measures were controversial in which states. An active news section gives the website ongoing topical relevance.

Building on this foundation, we invited a group of scholars from across the EU to reflect on euro-crisis law through their contributions to the present volume. This is not the first book devoted to euro-crisis law. Some monographs have sought to provide an overall view of the legal dimension of the euro crisis,[34] and a number of edited volumes have explored a cross-selection of issues,[35] not to mention a myriad of

[34] See, in particular: K. Tuori and K. Tuori, *The Eurozone Crisis – A Constitutional Analysis* (Cambridge University Press, 2014); A. Hinarejos, *The Euro Area Crisis in Constitutional Perspective* (Oxford University Press, 2015); F. Fabbrini, *Economic Governance in Europe – Comparative Paradoxes and Constitutional Challenges* (Oxford University Press, 2016); F. Martucci, *L'ordre économique et monétaire de l'Union européenne* (Bruylant, 2016).

[35] See, in particular: B. De Witte, A. Héritier and A. Trechsel (eds.), *The Euro Crisis and the State of European Democracy* (European University Institute, online publication, 2016); M. Adams, F. Fabbrini and P. Larouche (eds.), *The Constitutionalization of European Budget Constraints* (Hart, 2014); U. Neergaard et al. (eds.), *Proceedings of the XXVIth FIDE Congress in Copenhagen, Volume 1: The Economic and Monetary Union* (Djøf Publishing, 2014); F. Fabbrini, E. Hirsch Ballin and H. Somsen (eds.), *What Form of*

periodical publications,[36] but the perspective adopted in this volume distinguishes itself from that literature by a combination of four elements.

First, the contributors to the volume have relied extensively on the detailed country-specific data collected for the euro-crisis law project described above and are thereby able to offer new and deeper insights, especially of the national legal and political dimensions of euro-crisis law.

Second, this book wishes to open for assessment not just the creation of a particular measure but its ongoing significance and relevance as a euro-crisis measure. One way of doing that is to ask whether measures have lasting relevance and continuing effects or whether, after the initial flurry of attention and high drama surrounding their enactment, they have produced limited effects and been quietly abandoned[37] or, on the contrary, had significant though comparatively varying effects at national level. That is to say, we are interested in a focus on law-in-action and, in particular, on the national implementation, uses, assessments, institutional locations and effects of euro-crisis law. Sovereign debt loan assistance and the new macroeconomic regime are often described as a shift from soft to hard law and to the creation of a social straitjacket for the Member States. But the analysis may be very different even between different programme states, depending also on such issue as the specific institutional dynamics between the executive and parliament, the level of permissiveness of national constitutional courts, or the impact on existing (de)centralising forces. And analysing the European Semester requires careful attention to the unfolding of the Country-Specific Recommendations, the Macro-Economic Imbalance Procedure, the preventive and corrective arms of fiscal discipline and whether, how and to which states sanctions are applied in practice.

Government for the European Union and the Eurozone? (Hart, 2015); J. Schmidt, C. Esplugues and R. Arenas Garcia (eds.), *EU Law after the Financial Crisis* (Intersentia, 2016).

[36] For a survey of the periodical literature, see T. Beukers, 'Legal Writing(s) on the Eurozone Crisis', EUI Working Papers, Law 2015/11.

[37] A striking example here is the Euro-Plus Pact (Strand Two discussed above). A 2015 paper analysing the Euro-Plus Pact by the European Commission's in-house think tank, the European Political Strategy Centre, concludes that it is 'largely dormant and receives little attention in Member States, as evidence by poor take-up in the National Reform *Programmes*': *EPSC Strategic Notes*, Issue 3/2015. The Fiscal Compact Treaty is a further good candidate example. Although it did cause legal changes in the domestic law of some participating countries, the question of (non-)compliance of euro area states with its provisions is entirely ignored at the current moment.

Similarly, measures that were seen as no longer in the euro-crisis toolbox may rapidly be brought back into play when circumstances so require, as the example of the use of the 'superseded' EFSM in the passage between the second and third Greek loan packages, discussed in Strand One, exemplifies.

Third, we have, in this volume, sought to stand back from the immediate controversy caused by the unfolding events and to propose instead a more nuanced and contextual interpretation of the legal impact of euro-crisis measures. The novelty, the high drama and stakes of the euro crisis, and the need to make an academic splash, have encouraged bold claims about the nature of the changes engendered by the euro-crisis measures set out in the first part of this chapter. The characterisations (or accusations) of euro crisis have therefore been, albeit for widely differing reasons depending on the authors, ones of EU constitutional and institutional transgression, mutation, imbalance and emergency. Those reasons include, to give just some prominent examples: (i) States 'going outside the Treaties' in making the EFSF, the ESM and the Fiscal Compact; (ii) States breaching the EU Treaties (particularly Article 125 TFEU) in making sovereign debt loan assistance available under the EFSM and EFSF; (iii) the ECB breaching Article 123 TFEU by purchasing bonds on the secondary market in the Securities Market Programme and OMT; (iv) the EU legislature permitting the shift to Reverse QMV by Member States in imposing sanctions or finding non-compliance in macroeconomic governance when the TFEU refers to QM voting or (v) the breaches of the Rule of Law and EU social requirements said to occur in the provision of sovereign debt loan assistance or more broadly in the European Semester. We by no means wish to deny the interest and indeed the persuasiveness of at least some of these claims. Nonetheless, we wish to suggest that a close analysis of how measures have played out in national contexts may identify more clearly the areas where issues of constitutional and institutional concern have arisen, and may provide a sounder basis for the identification and evaluation of change and evolution in euro-crisis law.[38]

[38] See further B. De Witte, 'Euro-Crisis Responses and the EU Legal Order: Increased Institutional Variation or Constitutional Mutation' *EuConst*, 11(3), 2015, 434; C. Kilpatrick, 'Abnormal Sources and Institutional Actions in the EU Sovereign Debt Crisis: ECB Crisis Management and the Sovereign Debt Loans' in L. Azoulai and M. Cremona (eds.), *EU Legal Acts: Challenges and Transformations*, (Oxford University Press, forthcoming).

Fourth, amongst the moments of constitutional high drama sparked by euro crisis, perhaps the greatest attention has been given to the 'high noon' of the first preliminary reference made by the German Constitutional Court on the compatibility with Article 123 TFEU of the ECB's OMT programme.[39] No doubt this is an exceptionally interesting constitutional court episode. Yet a broader constitutional court analysis of euro-crisis measures, in particular, including how the constitutional courts of states in receipt of sovereign debt loans have dealt with legal challenges, reveals a broader and richer range of constitutional issues to consider and analyse.

Such reflections shape the structure and content of this book. Central to Part I is the reconstruction of the European space for economic governance as a result of the financial and euro crisis. This part describes, analyses and critically assesses the various euro-crisis law instruments, their implications for both the European and national level of economic governance, and for the balance between them. It offers contrasting assessments of the impact of euro-crisis law on the role of national parliaments, various types of criticism on the EU economic governance framework and different views on what is needed to improve the multi-level system of economic governance. What emerges is a picture of great variety in the impact on individual Member States, depending among others on whether a Member State is part of the single currency area, on whether it is also a programme country and on the national institutional setting in which euro-crisis law has landed.

In Chapter 2, Violeta Ruiz Almendral assesses the influence of the European Union fiscal consolidation legal framework on national fiscal constitutions and on parliamentary democracy of especially euro area Member States. She argues that there is a general case to be made for fiscal constraints, since disorderly growth of deficit can create a democratic deficit for future generations and because of time consistency issues. There is also a case to be made for fiscal consolidation rules in the European Union, as they serve to fill the design gap of the EMU, minimise moral hazard, select the best normative criteria to minimise inequities and attribute to intergenerational equity. But the current design does leave much to be desired. The link between profligacy and the crisis is dangerous, Member States have lost their economic stabilisers, and the current structure defies the logic of fiscal federalism,

[39] *Gauweiler and Others* v. *Deutscher Bundestag*, Case C-62/14 (16 June 2015).

whereby countercyclical fiscal policy should be done at the central level. Ruiz Almendral is not pessimistic when it comes to the role of national parliaments in the budget. Some of the critics idealise parliaments' role, which in practice was already very limited as budgets are a product of government. With the exception of bailout countries for which the panorama is substantially different, the current EU legal framework has the potential to increase the role of parliaments in the budget. The narrative that budgetary discipline actually undermines the powers of parliaments vis-à-vis the budget, may curb growth and substantially change the economic constitution, is flawed. There is no clear and evident link between the fiscal consolidation legal framework and social expenditure. The narrative leaves out the lion's share of the fundamental problems that the stability legal framework presents, ignores the arguments for balancing budgets and misrepresents what the current rules actually entail.

In Chapter 3, Païvi Leino and Janne Salminen examine the rules on economic governance from the perspective of competence, democracy and effectiveness. Many of the economic governance measures adopted on the basis of Article 136 TFEU stretch the limits of EU competence in the area of economic policy quite considerably. They build on a comprehensive reading of the Member States' obligation to coordinate their economic policies. In fact, many of the measures have relied on legal ambiguity and abstraction, which has had obvious consequences for the accountability of measures both at the EU and national levels and has blurred the division of competence between the two. Three case studies (Finland, France and Portugal) illustrate the impact of the governance framework on different euro area Member States and the use of discretion and degree of conditionality that application of the framework implies. They reveal that externally imposed reforms are most efficiently undertaken, and Member State discretion in economic policy-making most limited, when economic hardship is so deep that the State relies on external funding and is subject to conditionality. Importantly, implementation still presumes a great deal of discretion, which raises questions of political accountability as it is difficult, if not impossible, to scrutinise whether the economic governance rules have been applied correctly. EU rules are difficult to enforce when the Member State concerned feels that they entail unreasonably tight economic policy choices. That time limits are extended, or new soft law documents written in order to find a new interpretation, is a logical consequence of the legitimacy problems identified in the literature. Leino and Salminen argue that these problems cannot be resolved by adding more rules. The direction should perhaps be towards more national rules and fewer, but more credible, EU rules. After all, a policy that is not broadly experienced as legitimate is unlikely to have great impact.

In Chapter 4, Diane Fromage zooms in on one specific element of the European space for economic governance: Independent Fiscal Institutions. In a rich comparative study, she examines how Member States have fulfilled their obligations under international and EU law, as well as the consequences for national constitutional orders. The picture that emerges is one of great variety. Fromage distinguishes four categories of Member States on the basis of the international and European obligations that apply. Member States have adopted different paces in the creation and reform of Independent Fiscal Institutions. The institutional setting in which they have been introduced or adapted is diverse. Independent Fiscal Institutions have been mostly placed within the executive. Some Member States have two or more institutions fulfilling the tasks prescribed by international and EU norms. According to Fromage, these differences in institutional settings are not surprising and should not be seen negatively as local ownership is absolutely crucial. Additional tasks are not to be seen as impairing on their capacity to act as a fiscal watchdog, as long as sufficient resources and independence are formally guaranteed. EU and international norms are rather open in defining only minimum conditions, which permits Member States to create weak institutions. In fact, Fromage argues that the potential benefits of Independent Fiscal Institutions have not been fully exploited. She identifies a need to establish tighter relationships with parliaments, which are relatively weak in the Euro-national budgetary process and whose role has been severely restricted by the adoption at EU level of strict rules. The EU should set minimum standards for involvement of parliaments, ensure a minimum size of Independent Fiscal Institutions, and a minimum period of time for them to prepare reports.

Thomas Beukers and Marijn Van der Sluis conclude this part of the book in Chapter 5 with a perspective on non-euro area Member States. The euro crisis and euro-crisis law have made the differentiated status of European integration in the field of EMU substantially more complex, among ins, between ins and outs, and among the outs. The crisis has confronted outs with challenges related to the potential effects on their legal position in terms of their future membership conditions, immediate new obligations and effects on their substantive interests. A comparative analysis illustrates the main concerns of non-euro area Member States with the recent development of EMU, such as marginalisation from decision-making, and negative effects of euro-crisis law on their substantive interests relating to, for example, the internal market or banking union. It also illustrates their different responses to the political and legal questions raised by the Fiscal Compact and ESM, and identifies future challenges that EMU will confront them with. EMU traditionally blends the constitutional and instrumental differentiation logics, with some Member States simply not interested in joining the euro, and others not considered ready. This distinction between constitutional and instrumental differentiation is being blurred as a consequence of the euro crisis. Some permanent outs have shown surprising commitment to the single currency project, while other temporary outs – that is with an obligation to join the euro in the future – have shown strong disengagement. In between these two extremes, there is also a group of Member States that has found a middle ground, for example, in dealing with the tension between not accepting far-reaching obligations before euro-area membership and an interest to preserve influence on euro-area developments.

Part II examines national constitutional manifestations of economic emergency in four of the euro-area Member States that have been most severely hit by the crisis. It offers valuable insights into the nature of emergency discourse in the legislative arena and of the spillover from the political to the judicial sphere. It illustrates how bailout countries, even if part of the same group of euro-area Member States subject to a programme, have reacted differently to the crisis, with different combinations of emergency procedures and instruments, and with contrasting reactions from the judiciary. This has at times led to a transformation of the constitution without formal amendment.

In Chapter 6, Afroditi Marketou takes the implementation of economic adjustment programmes in Greece to argue that a total transformation of Greek constitutional politics has taken place without formal constitutional change. Emergency discourse has been used to justify an extended deconstruction of constitutional forms. Economic adjustment programmes have found their way into the Greek legal order through emergency procedures, notably through Decree-Laws and through the use of a single article rendering any amendment to specific provisions impossible, leaving no place for parliamentary discussion. In its relationship with both the executive and the troika, the Greek Parliament has been impotent. The economic adjustment programmes have thus operated in the domestic legal order with no respect for constitutional procedures and forms. As a result, legal accountability has been excluded and political accountability considerably limited. While an emergency should be exceptional or temporary, this has not been the case in Greece, as Memoranda of Understanding have progressively ceased to be perceived as exceptional instruments to face the economic emergency and have instead been normalised and institutionalised. Is there then still a place for the Greek Constitution as a valid point of reference in political decision-making? Marketou's last hope is with the Greek supreme courts which, after a period of initial inaction, have finally assumed a more active role.

In Chapter 7, Leticia Díez Sanchez gives a broad overview of the transformation of the Spanish constitutional regime implemented through various emergency instruments. A reform of the labour regime has taken place through Royal Decree-Laws. Regional fiscal powers have been constrained with an Organic Law, with Spanish legislation generally favouring efficient implementation of anti-crisis measures over the respect for regional and local spheres of government. As a result, the autonomy of the local government is now conditional on respect for budgetary stability and financial sustainability. The principle of budgetary stability has been given constitutional status through the reform of Article 135 of the Constitution, notably through a simplified amendment procedure (as opposed to an aggravated procedure), using a combination of two special parliamentary procedures, namely the single reading procedure and the urgency procedure. The overall effect of emergency legislation has been that parliamentary debate was either bypassed or strongly limited, and in fact the (ab)use of the Decree-Law and of the urgency procedure have been criticised. Díez Sanchez notes the contagion of the language of pressing economic circumstances from the political to the judicial sphere. The policy of economic survival has met strong judicial permissiveness from the Constitutional Court, which has been remarkably lenient and has provided unconditional support for euro-crisis measures. In the area of labour rights the Court has engaged in a constitutional change without formal amendment. With regard to territorial entities, it has generally favoured the interests of the central government. Díez Sanchez warns that this permissiveness comes at a price.

The similarities between Spain and Italy are striking. In both countries constitutional reform has been enacted in reaction to a letter from central bankers, and in both cases the relationship between the central and regional or local government has been affected. Moreover, in both countries use has been made of Decree-Laws to quickly respond to the crisis. But there are also differences, notably in the reaction of the Constitutional Courts. In Chapter 8, Leonardo Pierdominici analyses the ongoing process of reform of the Italian constitutional system of territorial decentralisation. In Italy there has been no formal recognition of a 'state of emergency', but there have been evident traces of exceptionality and even a distorted use of legal sources. The letter from Trichet and Draghi broke decades of Italian inertia, and the new technical Monti government tried to comply with the 'condition' of a strong commitment to abolish or merge some intermediate levels of administration. The formal measures used to implement the reform, Decree-Laws, however, were challenged before the traditionally deferential Italian Constitutional Court which struck down parts of them for violation of the Constitution. The Court highlighted the discrepancy between the transient nature of Decree-Laws and the importance of organic constitutional reform.

Among the four countries studied in this part, Ireland stands out for being the only one in which no use has been made of Decree-Laws to respond to the crisis. A special parliamentary procedure allowing the government to guillotine legislative debate to some extent removed the need for this type of legislation. In Chapter 9, concluding this part of the book, Stephen Coutts examines the special position of Ireland. Invoking a legal emergency has not been a feature of the Irish implementation of euro-crisis law, although the concept of emergency was clearly at play both in terms of the extent and the justification for accelerated legislative procedures. Unlike some other Member States, it has not made use of an expressly exceptional legislative procedure. Instead, the case of Ireland is characterised by the adaptation of traditional methods to meet the requirements of urgency and flexibility deemed necessary in a state of emergency. Part of the legislation was passed in remarkably short time frames; part of it has granted relatively wide-ranging powers to both government ministers and other bodies. The Irish Courts have fitted the language and justification of emergency into existing legal tests, with the judicial review framework being sufficiently flexible to accommodate considerations of a general economic nature.

Part III on constitutional judicial challenges to euro-crisis law confirms the picture of predominant judicial restraint that emerges from the preceding part. The focus of Chapters 10 and 11, with which the book concludes, is perfectly complementary in terms of the broad range of euro-crisis law. A comparative analysis of national highest court approaches to constitutional legal questions emerging from the ESM treaty and the Fiscal Compact is followed by a comparative analysis of the judicial approaches to Memoranda of Understanding and to their national implementing legislation.

Jan Herman Reestman discusses judicial strategies with regard to the ESM Treaty and the Fiscal Compact in a great number of Member States, including Slovenia, Estonia, Ireland, Germany, Austria and France. These treaties, as well as the simplified revision procedure of the EU Treaties related to the ESM Treaty, have raised several procedural and substantive constitutional issues. Reestman presents national constitutional perspectives on the relationship between the ESM Treaty and the Stability Treaty on the one hand, and issues such as EU law in general, national budgetary powers and sovereignty on the other hand. He argues that the courts had no alternative to approving the treaties due to the interests at stake, which does not, however, mean that the judgments were not convincing. The courts have all found their own way of showing judicial restraint, skilfully dismantling potentially constitutionally explosive content of treaty provisions, or taking the edge off arguments that the ESM undermines national parliamentary democracy. Their judgements have helped to legitimise the ratification of the treaties, and thus a major shift in the functioning of EMU, by ending discussions on legality, by limiting the national constitutional impact of the treaties and by indicating limits to further EMU integration.

In Chapter 11, Claire Kilpatrick investigates the constitutional court reactions to bailouts and social rights in the seven sovereign debt loan Member States. A cluster of cases decided by the constitutional courts of several of these states dealing with the social implications of euro-crisis law present a rich new terrain for EU lawyers, for comparative constitutional lawyers and for scholars interested in the justiciability of economic and social rights alike. The findings of unconstitutionality of sovereign debt measures by, in particular, the Portuguese Constitutional Court, provoked an intense negative response, both from the troika and in academic scholarship. Kilpatrick critiques such responses and develops alternative readings and further questions. For instance, she explains why juristocracy critiques are not compelling in times of EU sovereign debt crisis and how particular developments in constitutional social scholarship have led to the judgements being read through a specific, and questionable, set of lenses. She further argues that this set of constitutional judgements cannot be explained through existing paradigms of EU constitutional law of explicit constitutional interaction through dialogue, co-operation or conflict. Instead, there is an avoidance of undesired EU judicialisation of constitutional conflict between bailout sources and national constitutional rights. The judgements also raise interesting questions for work on comparative constitutional court dialogues in Europe.

3 Conclusion: Euro-Crisis Law or the New EU Macroeconomic Constitution?

To conclude this introductory chapter, we submit that the very term of 'euro-crisis law', which we have adopted in this volume, may soon have run its course. Some of the measures enacted in the midst of the crisis have already fallen into oblivion (such as the Euro-Plus Pact and maybe even the Fiscal Compact); others have been replaced (such as the EFSF). What has remained is the ESM, the enhanced role of the ECB and the new macroeconomic governance regime enacted by means of the Six-Pack and the Two-Pack. The latter has acquired a routine character, which is well rendered by the notion of an ever-recurring 'European Semester'. Although some of the elements of the economic governance regime are still uncertain and untested (e.g. as to whether any financial sanctions will ever be inflicted on countries that step out of line), most of it has become the 'new normal' of a shared multi-level budgetary process. The ESM, from its side, is now well established; it will, admittedly, never become a routine mechanism like the European Semester, since it is triggered only in emergency situations threatening the euro area's financial stability, but its institutional mechanism and decision making rules are now well settled, and there are no signs indicating that it will soon be absorbed into mainstream EU law. However, its deployment, currently only in Greece, will continue to raise significant constitutional, institutional and social questions about, in this case, very long-term, EU crisis management. The expanded role of the ECB has withstood economic and legal challenge, and is now stabilised. The national constitutional fallout of the euro crisis has been reflected in some constitutional texts and in the case law of a number of national constitutional courts. In a few years' time, the term 'macroeconomic constitution',[40] with its suggestion of permanence and entrenchment, may well sound more appropriate as a way to denote this complex multi-level legal regime than the term 'euro-crisis law'.

It is still too early to tell how the prospect of a Brexit may affect this 'normalisation' of euro-crisis law. Although the UK has not adopted the euro and is not a party to a number of euro-crisis legal instruments, the referendum in favour of Brexit of 23 June 2016 may nevertheless have effects on the strands of substantive law discussed in this volume. Should

[40] As proposed, for example, by K. Tuori and K. Tuori, *The Eurozone Crisis – A Constitutional Analysis* (Cambridge University Press, 2014) chap. 6.

Brexit occur, it will in any event change the balance between EU euro 'ins' and 'outs' by removing the most influential 'out', and it may eventually lead to a more uniformly applicable EU law of macroeconomic governance.

Similarly, it is too early to tell what effect the prospect of a Brexit will have on the future development of EMU, the European Banking Union and also the Capital Markets Union. This is true for any immediate impact on the various initiatives proposed by the Commission in the first 'Deepening by Doing' stage following the presentation of the Five Presidents' report in June 2015, and even more so for the long-term impact on more far-reaching issues related to the second 'Completing EMU' stage, for which the Commission is expected to present a white paper in spring 2017. The impact will to a great extent depend on the following factors: (i) the outcome of the reflection period announced by the '27' including their analysis of the causes of the Brexit vote and the extent to which these are more commonly present in other EU Member States; (ii) the balance struck between calls for more Europe, less Europe, and for a Europe focused on results; (iii) the results of upcoming national general elections in Europe, including in France and Germany; (iv) potential crises related to the stability of the banking sector; (v) and the extent to which Europe's energy is absorbed by other crises, such as migration and, not least, the aftermath of the Brexit referendum itself.

It is hoped that the claims made in, and lessons drawn from, this book will prove useful in analysing this process. Among the former are the importance of credible rules, of national ownership, and of respect for national constitutions. Among the latter is the great variation and differentiation witnessed not only at the EU level, but even more so when euro-crisis law interacts at the national level. While common dichotomies used for analysing EMU and the EU in general, such as euro versus non-euro area, north versus south, debtor versus creditor, are no doubt powerful, the picture emerging from this book is one of much greater variety among the Member States of the Union.

PART I

Reconstructing the European Space for Economic Governance

2

The European Fiscal Consolidation Legal Framework: Its Impact on National Fiscal Constitutions and Parliamentary Democracy

VIOLETA RUIZ ALMENDRAL*

1 Introduction

In the following pages, I will assess the consequences of the European Union fiscal consolidation legal framework from two perspectives: its influence on fiscal constitutions and its impact on parliamentary democracy; in particular, from the perspective of its deemed restrictive impact on the financing of social rights.

It has been argued that the current legal framework stunts the growth of welfare policies and that it limits democracy by unduly restricting the role of parliaments with regard to the budget, which would particularly affect social expenditures. To assess the current legal framework from these perspectives, I will examine the rules adopted at the EU level together with some examples of the legal reforms actually undertaken by EU Member States.[1] Although there have been tangible implications for all EU Member States, in this paper I will mostly draw examples from Member States of the EU using the euro (euro area), where budgetary discipline rules have had (and still have) greater consequences.

* I would like to thank Thomas Beukers, Bruno De Witte and Alain Cuenca for reading different versions of this paper and substantially contributing to its improvement. The usual disclaimer applies.

[1] I have employed some of the available data here: http://eurocrisislaw.eui.eu/. An accurate and detailed summary of all fiscal rules adopted can be found at the 'Database on numerical fiscal rules', which includes data tracked since 1990, as well as a 'fiscal rule strength index'. See European Commission, 'Numerical Fiscal Rules in the EU Member States', http://ec.europa.eu/economy_finance/db_indicators/fiscal_governance/fiscal_rules/index_en.htm.

Examination of the legal reforms undertaken by Member States offers a limited perspective. The actual laws enacted represent only a fraction of the story. Most of them are quite recent, so it is too early to assess their consequences. In some cases, the new laws and institutions created may look sophisticated and yet be just for show. That will often be the case in countries without a tradition of controlling budgetary discipline. Also (and this is particularly the case when examining the available data), it is too early to adequately distinguish correlation from causation. The deficit and debt indicators have substantially improved in the past two years (2014–15), but so has the economic climate.

The terms employed need to be clarified. By 'fiscal consolidation legal framework', I refer to the Stability and Growth Pact (SGP), as well as the subsequent legal reforms undertaken to fortify it (i.e. the 'Six Pack', 'Fiscal Compact' and 'Two Pack'). By 'fiscal constitution', I refer to the laws governing how a country is financed: that is, the set of rules, primarily of constitutional nature (where there is a written constitution), that lists the sources of public revenue (mainly taxes) and determines the structure of the budget and its control.[2] By 'economic constitution', I refer to the constitutional rules governing the basic elements of the economic system (such as the right to property, freedom to conduct business, rules governing the stability of the market, etc.).[3]

2 Have Fiscal Consolidation Rules Transformed EU Member States' Fiscal Constitutions?

A. *The (General) Case for Fiscal Constraints*

Until very recently, most EU Member States' constitutions did not have a balanced-budget rule or an otherwise specific rule to limit the deficit and public debt. This is both the consequence of, and explains the fact that, in

[2] I follow the concept employed in H. Blöchliger and J. Kantorowicz, 'Fiscal Constitutions: An Empirical Assessment', OECD Economics Department, Working Papers, No. 1248 (23 July 2015) (Paris: OECD Publishing), www.oecd-ilibrary.org/economics/fiscal-constitutions-an-empirical-assessment_5jrxjctrxp8r-en.

[3] The term 'economic constitution' is well established in continental Europe. On its German (Weimar Republic) origin see C. Joerges, 'What Is Left of the European Economic Constitution?', EUI Working Paper, LAW 2004/13 (2004), http://cadmus.eui.eu/bitstream/handle/1814/2828/law04-13.pdf?sequence=1, pp. 10ff.

most of them, the debate on this type of rule and on the issue of public indebtment and deficit has too often been absent in constitutional law discussions.[4]

Furthermore, the establishment of legally binding fiscal rules, loosely defined as rules that impose a constraint on fiscal policy (by controlling debt and/or public deficit) is still a relatively new phenomenon. According to the International Monetary Fund (hereinafter IMF) database,[5] in 1985–86, only Austria, Germany, Indonesia, Japan, Malaysia, Singapore and the United States had some form of Fiscal Rules. In 2013, only a few countries do *not* have one (Argentina, Canada, Iceland, India and Maldives).

Nevertheless, the need to curb deficit (and debt) is, in general terms, largely uncontested in the realm of public finance scholars. High public debt levels do curb growth, which eventually poses sustainability issues.[6]

Finally, disorderly growth of deficit can create a democratic deficit for future generations. They are then 'subject to "taxation without representation", because today's politicians can vote to implement programmes to benefit today's voters but to be paid for in part by tomorrow's tax payers'[7]. Sustained deficits do entail a sort of ghost tax upon future generations. Intergenerational equity is one of the most persuasive arguments to curb deficit and public debt. Yet, it is hard to address for obvious political reasons (the main stakeholders have not been born yet). Policies to mitigate or reserve climate change are the clearest current example of this issue.

[4] This is consistent with the fact that, with some rare exceptions, the study of the 'financial constitution' (revenues and spending rules) is usually not a fundamental part of constitutional law handbooks. Equally, constitutional law does not occupy a central role in tax and finance law books.

[5] See T. Kinda, C. Kolerus, P. Muthoora and A. Weber, 'Fiscal Rules at a Glance: Country Details from a New Dataset', IMF Working Paper, WP/12/273 (October 2013), www.imf.org/external/pubs/ft/wp/2012/wp12273.pdf and the accompanying Fiscal Rules Dataset (1985–2013).

[6] This not contested in the literature, although disagreement does remain as to where the growth deterrent figure lies. See C. Reinhart and K. Rogoff, 'Growth in a Time of Debt', *American Economic Review: Papers and Proceedings*, 100(2), 2010, 573–8; P. De Grauwe, 'The Governance of a Fragile Eurozone', *Australian Economic Review* 45(3), 2012, 255–68. See, for an alternative view, U. Panizza and A. Presbitero, 'Public Debt and Economic Growth: Is There a Causal Effect?', Money and Finance Research Group, Working Paper No. 65/2012 (2 April 2012), http://docs.dises.univpm.it/web/quaderni/pdfmofir/Mofir065.pdf.

[7] E. Elliott, 'Constitutional Conventions and the Deficit', *Duke Law Journal*, 6, 1985, 1077–111, 1092.

There are political incentives to spend more across the board, as well as to reduce the tax burden.[8] Budgeting methods, as well as lobby groups, facilitate the resilience to change public spending (once budgeted, it will never move). Budgetary allocations reflect the power of the organs in charge of their management. In many instances, it will be hard to avoid political incentives to increase public spending and finance it with debt operations, rather than with new taxes.[9] Increasing public debt has, if any, a much lower political cost than introducing new taxes or increasing the tax pressure in another way.

As public budgets grew larger (mainly after the Second World War), deficits were revealed as a structural element of democracies, as is a structural growth of public spending. In fact, public debt grew substantially in the final decades of the last century.[10]

Two unrelated phenomena contributed to stressing the importance of establishing some type of rules to tip the balance towards controlling the deficit. On the one hand, the relative deregulation of financial markets, whose consequences on the current financial crisis are now well known, contributed to facilitating emissions of public debt. On the other hand, there was a decrease in tax revenues in relation to the public expenditure, in particular deriving from income taxes (both on individuals and legal entities).[11] From this last perspective, it has been argued that fiscal constraints or budgetary discipline rules may, as a side-effect at least, have the virtuous consequence of changing the debate in tax law. Resources are intrinsically scarce, but fiscal rules reinforce that view and may at least indirectly help redesign a tax system.

Therefore, the underlying rationale for establishing such rules is that fiscal policy suffers from time-inconsistency issues. This is why central banks exist in the first place, and it is both a rationale for hardbound rules, as well as for an institutional design to control fiscal rules.[12]

[8] Vested interests or lobby groups may resist the introduction of new taxes. See ibid., 1080.

[9] As the main critics of Keynesianism point out. See J. Buchanan and R. Wagner, *Democracy in Deficit: The Political Legacy of Lord Keynes* (New York: Academic Press, 1977), pp. 93–154.

[10] For OECD countries, the time series (1980–2010) can be viewed at https://stats.oecd.org/index.aspx?queryid=8089.

[11] D. Cameron, 'Taxes, Spending and Deficits: Does Government Cause Inflation?', in L. Lindberg and C. Maier (eds.), *The Politics of Inflation and Recession* (Washington DC: Brookings Institution, 1985), pp. 224–79; in particular, 234–9 and 252–9. See, for criticism, D. Wolfe, 'Politics, the Deficit and Tax Reform', *Osgoode Hall Law Journal*, 26 (2), 1988, 347–66, 351ff.

[12] See, with regard to the need to introduce independent fiscal institutions, European Commission, 'Report on Public Finances in EMU', European Economy 9 (2014), http://

Thus, enshrining fiscal constraints, together with a culture of budgetary discipline, may, if well designed, actually help end the perverse (political) separation between the revenue and the expenditure sides.[13]

B. *The Case for Introducing Fiscal Consolidation Rules in the European Union, and the Difficulty in Designing Them*

The question on whether or not (and how) to enact budgetary constraint rules in the constitution acquires a different character in the European Union.

It has become commonplace to state that the design of the European Monetary Union (EMU) is a unique experiment, which separates economic and monetary union *contra natura*, as has often been pointed out.[14] This was not the initial plan, which was to develop a more integrated union.[15] In this context, the underlying logic of reinforcing budgetary supervision by developing a fiscal consolidation legal framework is that it will serve to fill the design gap of the EMU, thus guaranteeing that the Union would be in a position to back up its currency. The reasons are well known (mainly, to minimise 'inflationary debt bail-outs' and other spillover effects derived from uncoordinated economic and fiscal policies).

Fiscal constraints would then, the theory goes, minimise 'moral hazard', which arises when governments may feel protected by the rest

ec.europa.eu/economy_finance/publications/european_economy/2014/pdf/ee9_en.pdf, pp. 54–66. On the different options, see C. Wyplosz, 'Fiscal Policy: Institutions versus Rules', *National Institute Economic Review*, 191(1), 2005, 64–78, 67ff.; C. Wyplosz, 'Europe's Quest for Fiscal Discipline', European Commission, Economic Papers 498 (April 2013), p. 24.

13 E. Elliott, 'Regulating the Deficit after *Bowsher* v. *Synar*', *Yale Journal of Regulation*, 4(2), 1987, 317–62, 352; D. Cameron, 'On the Limits of the Public Economy', *The Annals of the American Academy of Political and Social Science*, 459, 1982, 46–62, 50ff.

14 I. Maher, 'Economic Governance: Hybridity, Accountability and Control', *Columbia Journal of European Law*, 13(3), 2007, 679–702, 682; V. Hatzopoulos, 'Why the Open Method of Coordination Is Bad for You: A Letter to the EU', *European Law Journal*, 13(3), 2007, 309–42, 322f; F. Snyder, 'EMU Revisited: Are We Making a Constitution? What Constitution Are We Making?', in P. Craig and G. De Bùrca (eds.), *The Evolution of EU Law*, 1st edn (Oxford University Press, 1999), pp. 417–77, at 434ff.

15 See C. Joerges, 'The Market without a State? The "Economic Constitution" of the European Community and the Rebirth of Regulatory Politics', *European Integration Online Papers*, 1(19), 1997.

of the Union and incur higher debts than they otherwise would. This can have disastrous consequences, as Member States 'fish from the same pool of financial capital'.[16]

However, this rationale may also be a reason not to limit beforehand all room for manoeuvre. In this regard, it has been rightly argued that the more limited and myopic the rules, the less leeway Member States will have to develop their own cooperation mechanisms. That, in turn, may actually decrease the effectiveness of the rules from the beginning, as they will be perceived as something external and there will be less of an incentive to develop their own rules to achieve fiscal consolidation.[17]

The problem of course lies in the design of fiscal consolidation rules, which are relatively new to the constitutional law tradition. Judging by the scholarly work produced in the past five years, there is a tendency in academic writing to assume that fiscal consolidation rules limit spending. In a classic confusion of correlation and causation, the fact that the actual application of such rules has resulted in budgetary cuts in many EU Member States has served to often dismiss these rules out of hand.

As explained earlier, one of the objectives should be to minimise intergenerational inequality by avoiding an excessive burden on future generations. The problem then is to select the best normative criteria to minimise said inequities. Roughly put, what indebtedness will finance is a fundamental element of the intergenerational analysis.[18] This idea is encapsulated in the so-called 'golden rule' of deficit spending, according to which public debt shall only be incurred for investment, but not current spending.[19] The idea is relatively simple but harder to execute: typical handbook examples of investment are infrastructures (a highway), while an example of current spending would be salaries of public servants.

However, in practice, the 'golden rule' (debt for investment only) is controversial.[20] Among other reasons not to enshrine it in a binding

[16] See, on the basic models, P. De Grauwe, *Economics of Monetary Union*, 9th edn (Oxford University Press, 2012), pp. 218ff.

[17] W. Schelkle, 'EU Fiscal Governance: Hard Law in the Shadow of Soft Law?', *Columbia Journal of European Law*, 13(3), (2007), 705–31, 707ff.

[18] D. Shaviro, *Do Deficit$ Matter?* (The University of Chicago Press, 1997), pp. 114ff.

[19] M. Artis, 'The Stability and Growth Pact: Fiscal Policy in the EMU', at F. Breuss, G. Fink and S. Griller (eds.), *Institutional, Legal and Economic Aspects of EMU* (Vienna: Springer, 2003), pp. 111ff.; M. Buti and D. Franco, *Fiscal Policy in Economic and Monetary Union. Theory, Evidence and Institutions* (Northampton: Edward Elgar, 2005), pp. 6ff.

[20] R. Bird, 'Evaluating Public Expenditures: Does it Matter How They Are Financed?', *International Tax Program*, University of Toronto, Paper 0506; B. Eichengreen,

rule (constitutional or similar) is that once established there will be accounting *gimmickry* to conveniently 'repackage' current spending as investment.[21] Of course, a large part of the problem lies in correctly defining 'investment' and 'current spending', which is much harder than it may seem. Furthermore, exactly which type of expenditures can pass the intergenerational equity test is debatable. Building a highway may seem like a good investment today as it constitutes an asset that may be enjoyed by future generations. There is then, in theory, a clear (future) correlation between that expenditure projected in the future (through debt) and its cost. But this will depend on the marginal utility of that asset through its lifetime, which can only be roughly estimated.

To complicate matters further, the traditional golden rule, which limited deficit spending to financing investment, has usually justified the financing of infrastructures (roads, airports). However, current spending also may have an intergenerational impact, as will be the case of research and education investment, which may facilitate a change in the economic model. Ultimately, the development of well-designed welfare policies also increases economic output and has an intergenerational effect.

The intergenerational equity test is, then, as easy to define as it is hard to implement in a formula. For it to work, different elements would need to be thrown into the formula, such as whether 'public' deficit is dependent on who generates it (the government, its agency, a strictly regulated public-private corporation, etc.), the time frame taken as a reference point, which elements integrate it or the causes for it (structural or not).[22] The formula would then become too complex and create new opportunities to avoid it.

Nevertheless, the current design of the EU legal framework does attempt to take into account the golden rule, and therefore pays particular attention to public investment (and so, to intergenerational equity).

'Institutions for Fiscal Stability', Institute for European Studies, University of Berkeley, Working Paper PEIF-6 (2003), 9ff.

21 V. Koen and P. van den Noord, 'Fiscal Gimmickry in Europe: One-off Measures and Creative Accounting'. OECD, Economics Department Working Papers, n. 417 (2005), www.oecd-ilibrary.org/docserver/download/5lgsjhvj757f.pdf?expires=1458910284&id=id&accname=guest&checksum=3E1EFB529A8FAD161461AB116B4C521C, pp. 13ff.; Buti and Franco, *Fiscal Policy in Economic and Monetary Union*, p. 35.

22 Shaviro, *Do Deficit$ Matter?*, pp. 153ff.

Article 2a of Council Regulation (EC) No. 1466/97,[23] on the medium-term budgetary objectives, states that these 'shall ensure the sustainability of public finances or a rapid progress towards such sustainability while allowing room for budgetary manoeuvre, considering in particular the need for public investment'. Public investment must be part of the stability and convergence programmes (Articles 3(2)(b) and 7(2)(b). Also, Article 5 provides that 'the Council and the Commission shall take into account the implementation of major structural reforms which have direct long-term positive budgetary effects, including by raising potential sustainable growth'. Monitoring public investment is also a part of the macroeconomic imbalance procedure. There is, however, evidence to suggest that public investment has been reduced excessively, particularly in crisis countries such as Greece, but also in Ireland, Italy, Portugal and Spain.[24]

The need for some form of budgetary coordination (with this model or another) in a monetary union may seem self-evident, at least in theory. Another matter is whether the current design is actually desirable. Mounting evidence suggests that it is not:

- First, looseness of fiscal policy did not cause the sovereign debt crisis, so it is dangerous to establish a link between 'profligacy' and the crisis. Such link may in fact worsen the fiscal crisis, as financial markets may punish deficit countries and end up making the situation much worse.[25] The link between budgetary rules and the credibility of the currency, biased as it is, has nevertheless perversely permeated the Member States' internal debates. Thus, for example, the reform of Article 135 of the Spanish Constitution and Austria's Stability Pact of 2012 were fundamentally motivated by a need to reassure financial markets.[26]

[23] Council Regulation (EC) No. 1466/97 of 7 July 1997 on the strengthening of the surveillance of budgetary positions and the surveillance and coordination of economic policies (OJ L 209, 2.8.1997, p. 1).

[24] See European Commission, 'Making the Best Use of the Flexibility within the Existing Rules of the Stability and Growth Pact', COM (2015) 12 final, http://ec.europa.eu/economy_finance/economic_governance/sgp/legal_texts/index_en.htm.

See also European Council, 'Conclusions', EUCO 79/14 (27 June 2014), www.consilium.europa.eu/uedocs/cms_Data/docs/pressdata/en/ec/143478.pdf.

[25] See, for criticism, P. De Grauwe and J. Yuemei, 'How Much Fiscal Discipline in a Monetary Union?', *Journal of Macroeconomics*, 39, (2014), 348–60.

[26] In the case of Austria, the motivation was not to lose the AAA rating on its debt. In the case of Spain, the situation was much direr, with bond yields eventually hitting close to 10 per cent in 2012.

- Second, the very design of EMU, and in practice the process by which Member States have lost their economic stabilisers – namely, the Central Bank's role as lender of last resort – has very likely aggravated the crisis, with a solvency crisis being followed by austerity policies that worsened the situation.[27]
- Finally, the structure as it is defies the logic of fiscal federalism, whereby countercyclical fiscal policy should be done at the central level.[28] Of course, the only way to do that is for the EU to have fiscal capacity.[29]

C. Brief Overview of the Current Fiscal Consolidation Legal Framework

The initial stability legal framework, which basically consisted of the 1997 SGP and the two Council Regulations,[30] gave a very specific shape to the loose principle that 'Member States shall avoid excessive government deficits' (formerly enshrined in Article 104 Treaty Establishing the European Community; now rooted in Articles 121 and 126 Treaty on the Functioning of the European Union), including rigid deficit and debt thresholds, often deemed arbitrary.

The introduction of budgetary stability rules was shaped by previous attempts to introduce stricter and enforceable budgetary discipline (the German Constitutional Court's Maastricht Opinion, the Waigel Plan and, further back, the Werner Plan sought to establish the fundamental elements of a monetary union and were much more ambitious than the current form).[31] The current design is further shaped by the particular

[27] P. De Grauwe, 'Design Failures in the Eurozone – Can They Be Fixed?', European Commission, Economic Papers 491 (April 2013), p. 9.

[28] P. Van Malleghem, '(Un)balanced Budget Rules in Europe and America', in M. Adams, F. Fabbrini and P. Larouche (eds.), *The Constitutionalisation of European Budget Constraints* (Oxford: Hart Publishing, 2014), pp .151–80, at 174.

[29] See European Commission, 'A Blueprint for a Deep and Genuine Economic and Monetary Union. Launching a European Debate', COM (2012) 777 final/2 (30 November 2012), http://ec.europa.eu/archives/commission_2010-2014/president/news/archives/2012/11/pdf/blueprint_en.pdf.

[30] Council Regulation (EC) No. 1466/97, above n. 23, and Council Regulation (EC) No. 1467/97 on speeding up and clarifying the implementation of the excessive deficit procedure (OJ L 209, 2.8.1997, p. 6).

[31] Bundesministerium der Finanzen, 'Stabilitätspakt für Europa: Finanzpolitik in der Dritten Stufe der WWU', Pressemitteilung des Bundesministerium der Finanzen (10 November 1995), 6–9. See, for a summary, H. Hahn, 'The Stability Pact for European Monetary Union: Compliance with Deficit Limit as Constant Legal Duty', *Common Market Law*

institutional architecture of price stability supervision and the mono-mandate of the European Central Bank.[32]

After the 2005 reform, the SGP has been substantially modified by the so-called 'Six Pack' (five Regulations and a Directive adopted on November 2011). The strengthening of the rules is based on Article 136 of the TFEU.

To reinforce the Six Pack, an international treaty was also adopted: the Treaty on Stability, Coordination and Governance in the Economic and Monetary Union (hereinafter the Fiscal Compact) with specific, and complicated, links to European Law. In 2013, two further regulations were adopted (the Two Pack), to further coordinate public budgets.

The fiscal consolidation rules have thus been reinforced during the crisis, taking advantage of the momentum given by the assistance programmes,[33] which were conditioned, inter alia, on compliance with fiscal consolidation. Legal instruments to establish financing ('bailout') mechanisms – the European Financial Stability Facility (EFSF) and the European Financial Stability Mechanism (EFSM) – are thus intertwined with the fiscal consolidation legal framework. Assistance and oversight have become, under this logic, two sides of the same coin of budgetary governance, in that the former has reinforced the latter. They are, as has been pointed out, 'joined at the hip'.[34]

The link of the fiscal consolidation to the bailout programmes is in itself problematic for a number of reasons. The most obvious one is that too much stress on fiscal consolidation will backfire in the middle of a

Review, 35(1), 1998, 77–100, 80ff. See also V. Ruiz Almendral, *Estabilidad presupuestaria y gasto público en España* (Madrid: La Ley-Wolters Kluwer España, 2008), pp. 33ff.

[32] See C. Zilioli and M. Selmayr, 'The European Central Bank: An Independent Specialised Organisation of Community Law', *Common Market Law Review*, 37(1), 2000, 591–643, 592ff. See, for alternative perspectives, R. Torrent, 'Whom Is the Central Bank the Central Bank of? Reaction to Zilioli and Selmayr', *Common Market Law Review*, 36(6), 1999, 1229–41, 1232ff.; F. Amtenbrink and H. De Haan, 'The European Central Bank: An Independent Specialised Organisation of Community Law – A Comment', *Common Market Law Review*, 39(1), 2002, 65–76, 68ff.; B. Dutzler, 'Institutional Framework of the EMU: Is the ECB a Fourth Pillar?', Breuss, Fink and Griller (eds.), *Institutional, Legal and Economic Aspects of EMU*, pp. 5ff.

[33] On the financial assistance mechanisms, see A. de Gregorio Merino, 'Legal Developments in the Economic and Monetary Union During the Debt Crisis: The Mechanisms of Financial Assistance'. *Common Market Law Review*, 49(5), 2012, 1613–45, 1613; P. Craig, 'Economic Governance and the Euro Crisis: Constitutional Architecture and Constitutional Implications', in Adams, Fabbrini and Larouche, *The Constitutionalisation of European Budgetary Constraints*, pp. 19–40.

[34] Craig, 'Economic Governance and the Euro Crisis', p. 23.

crisis (as has happened), as it will further weaken an already weak internal demand, thereby aggravating the fiscal crisis and delaying economic recovery.

Now, as before, general government deficit may not exceed 3 per cent of gross domestic product (GDP), while public debt must not exceed 60 per cent of GDP without being on a diminishing path. These figures are debatable and have been questioned since the first SGP.[35] From that perspective, the current framework has been improved in that it pays substantially more attention to the overall sustainability position of the Member States' finances by means of controlling also the structural deficit. Still, most Member States do not comply with them, and in fact, in historical terms, the 3 per cent of GDP deficit threshold has only been met occasionally.[36]

The current system intends to reinforce prevention, to monitor different elements of public finance, not just the outcomes (deficit and debt), and to force Member States to internalise the rules.

This requires a much higher level of sophistication of the legal framework, to adequately assess exactly what the cyclically adjusted balance is.[37] Such sophistication remains a work in progress. For example, to date, there is no legal definition of how exactly the notion of structural deficit should be calculated.[38] The methods are published and discussed, but they are not enshrined in law. This is problematic, as the numerical

[35] See, for early criticism, B. Eichengreen, 'Should the Maastricht Treaty Be Saved?', Princeton Studies in International Finance, No. 74 (December 1992); Craig, 'Institutions for Fiscal Stability'. See also G. Majone, *Dilemmas of European Integration: The Ambiguities and Pitfalls of Integration by Stealth* (Oxford University Press, 2005), p. 169; Artis, 'The Stability and Growth Pact: Fiscal Policy in the EMU'.

[36] See H. Burret and J. Schnellenbach, 'Implementation of the Fiscal Compact in the Euro Area Member States', German Council of Economic Experts, Working Paper 08/2013e (2013, partially updated 2014), p. 2.

[37] The system rests on the European System of National and Regional Accounts (ESA), established by Regulation (EU) No. 549/2013 of the European Parliament and of the Council of 21 May 2013 on the European system of national and regional accounts in the European Union (OJ L 174, 26.6.2013, p.1). The specific rules to determine the statistics employed in the EDP are provided by Council Regulation (EC) No. 479/2009 of 25 May 2009 on the application of the Protocol on the excessive deficit procedure annexed to the Treaty establishing the European Community (OJ L 145, 10.6.2009, p.1). The ESA was amended in May 2013, which had consequences for the budget balance and debt calculations. See European Commission, 'Report on Public finances in EMU', pp. 49ff.

[38] The method has recently been amended, see G. Mourre, G. Isbasoiu, D. Paternoster and M. Salto, 'The Cyclically-Adjusted Budget Balance Used in the EU Fiscal Framework: An Update', European Commission, Economic Papers 478 (March 2013), http://ec.europa.eu/economy_finance/publications/economic_paper/2013/pdf/ecp478_en.pdf.

value of such deficit has direct consequences, which can ultimately entail the imposition of sanctions, possibly without sufficient legal certainty. Sanctions would deserve another chapter. They have never been credible and still are not. Currently, the main novelty (after the Six Pack and the Fiscal Compact)[39] is that they may now also be imposed in the preventive phase, not only in the corrective phase.[40] The Fiscal Compact establishes a set of rules in Articles 3–8 known as the Fiscal Compact, which apply in parallel to the Six Pack. It reinforces the existing balanced-budget rule and, in general, follows the same concepts for tracking fiscal consolidation (in particular, medium-term objectives, the notions of 'significant deviation' and 'exceptional circumstances'). The Fiscal Compact intends to make the eventual application of sanctions easier by applying reverse qualified majority voting to all stages of the excessive deficit procedure (EDP). The control is mostly formal and regulates what the numbers are, what explains them, what the plans are and how they are planned (time-framed). General advice is provided on the main areas of expenditure (and revenue), as can be seen in the country-specific reports. However, specific policies are left for Member States to devise and implement. Sanctions are, at least in theory, easier to impose by way of reverse qualified majority voting, introduced in the Six Pack for most sanctions. As a consequence of reverse qualified voting, any recommendation by the Commission will be deemed adopted in the Council unless a qualified majority of Member States votes against it. This is, of course, the theory. Even with reverse majority, sanctions are unlikely to be imposed and lack credibility, as has often been pointed out.[41]

Overall, the legal framework is tilted towards prevention, by way of analysing two areas: general outcomes (deficit as a percentage of GDP, general spending areas and their percentage equivalences) and budgetary

[39] I agree with Paul Craig that, in essence, there is no substantial variation to the existing EU Law framework. See P. Craig, 'The Stability, Coordination and Governance Treaty: Principle, Politics and Pragmatism', *European Law Review*, 37(3), 2012, 231–48, 235.

[40] Regulation (EU) No. 1173/2011 of the European Parliament and of the Council of 16 November 2011 on the effective enforcement of budgetary surveillance in the euro area (OJ L 306, 23.11.2011, p. 1) establishes sanctions 'for enhancing the enforcement of the preventive and corrective parts of the Stability and Growth Pact in the euro area'. Sanctions include not only infractions regarding the preventive and corrective phase (Arts. 4–7), but also manipulation of statistics (Art. 8), done 'intentionally or by serious negligence' with the result of misrepresenting deficit and debt data.

[41] See Burret and Schnellenbach, 'Implementation of the Fiscal Compact in the Euro Area Member States', pp. 7ff.; International Monetary Fund, 'Toward a Fiscal Union for the Euro Area', Discussion Note SDN/13/09 (September 2013), 11.

procedures. The focus on economic policies can be seen in the macroeconomic imbalance procedure (also part of the European Semester). It does so by monitoring and showing, the idea being to avoid real estate bubbles or excessive indebtment growing unnoticed. At the same time, it focuses on lack of investment. In its current stage, it does not dictate economic policies, although it could in the future, for example, as has already been proposed, in order to encourage structural reforms.[42]

D. *Impact on the Fiscal Constitutions of Euro Area Member States*

Both the Fiscal Compact and Council Directive 2011/85 establish the need for Member States to establish their own fiscal consolidation legal framework.[43] There is ample leeway as to what type of rules will fit the requirements, as long as the rules are of 'binding force and permanent character, preferably constitutional' (Fiscal Compact).

The idea is for Member States to acquire a stability culture and control it through their legal system. For the rules to be credible, they must be a part of the internal fiscal constitution. Furthermore, rules, or in general the deficit/debt debate, needs to be part of the political culture, which entails, among other things, electorates supporting a debate on what to finance and how. To date, a brief overview of the reforms undertaken shows very different types of domestic fiscal rules (budget balance, debt, expenditure and revenue rules/constitutional or legal, etc.).

It is not easy to assess whether the reforms undertaken have meant that Member States have internalised the fiscal consolidation legal framework. Only three years after the Fiscal Compact made it mandatory for Member States to establish their own budgetary discipline provisions, the only possible analysis is a purely descriptive one.

[42] See the 'Five Presidents' Report': J. Juncker, D. Tusk, J. Dijsselbloem, M. Draghi and M. Schulz, 'Completing Europe's Economic and Monetary Union' (June 2015), p. 8.

[43] Council Directive 2011/85/EU of 8 November 2011 on requirements for budgetary frameworks of the Member States (OJ L 306, 23.11.2011, p. 41) requires Member States to adopt 'numerical fiscal rules which are specific to it and which effectively promote compliance with its obligations deriving from the TFEU in the area of budgetary policy over a multiannual horizon for the general government as a whole' (Art. 5) and specifically describes the content of such rules (Art. 6). Art. 3.2 of the TSCG specifically requires Member States (in this case, signatories of the TSCG) to introduce binding and permanent law, preferably of constitutional nature, adopting the country-specific MTOs. The rules are similar, as has been often pointed out. See Craig, 'The Stability, Coordination and Governance Treaty', 236.

There is substantial information on which countries have adopted which rule, within which time frame and after what type of public debate. There is also information (in the press) on what type of public debate, if any, has surrounded the adoption of the rules. But for a full assessment of the constitutional or legal internal rules, Member States' own legal set of concepts must first be analysed. A mere transplant of a debt brake into a legal system with no procedures or even tradition of assessing the budget will be nothing more than a rare exotic plant that may or may not take root in the legal environment to which it is transplanted. It quite evidently follows that the actual consequences of the constitutional reforms will depend on the existing culture, as migration of constitutional concepts does occur, but it is questionable whether forcing such migration in a centralised manner attains the intended result.

In a limited way, there is at least some data to analyse to see what has happened.

Since the 1990s the Commission (DG ECFIN) has monitored fiscal rules, taking into account the different levels of government (central and subnational – regional or local; general government and social security). With the compiled data a 'fiscal rule strength index' is construed, which provides additional information on the institutional elements of fiscal rules.

The 'index of strength' results from information derived from these five factors:[44]

(i) the statutory base of the rule,
(ii) room for setting or revising its objectives,
(iii) the body in charge of monitoring respect and enforcement of the rule,
(iv) the enforcement mechanisms relating to the rule and
(v) the media visibility of the rule.

This fiscal strength index is then employed as a basis for the Fiscal rule index (FRI), which provides a snapshot of the evolution of fiscal rules. The weight given is determined both by the fiscal strength of the rule and its coverage.

Table 2.1 shows the FRIs for euro area countries for selected years. The closer to 3, the better the rule. Minus figures imply lack of compliance

[44] The information is available at European Commission, 'Numerical Fiscal Rules in the EU Member States', http://ec.europa.eu/economy_finance/db_indicators/fiscal_governance/fiscal_rules/index_en.htm.

Table 2.1 *Fiscal Rules Index (FRI)*

Country	1990	2000	2010	2011	2012	2013	2014
Austria	−1,0081	0,0533	**0,6110**	0,6969	0,8942	0,8942	0,8942
Belgium	−0,5519	−0,0375	−0,0375	−0,0375	−0,0061	−0,0061	**1,5480**
Cyprus	−1,0081	−1,0081	−1,0081	−1,0081	−1,0081	**0,2656**	0,5117
Estonia	−1,0081	0,7805	**0,9011**	0,9011	0,4443	0,7618	0,7618
Finland	−1,0081	0,8365	0,0896	**0,3271**	0,2547	0,2547	0,2514
France	−0,6812	−0,0879	0,5734	1,2059	1,2059	**3,1400**	3,0472
Germany	0,2781	0,2781	0,5633	**1,0017**	1,0017	**2,8274**	2,8274
Greece	−1,0081	−1,0081	−1,0081	−1,0081	**0,7091**	0,7091	0,8175
Ireland	−1,0081	−0,9850	−0,7824	−0,7824	−0,7904	**2,4094**	2,4094
Italy	−1,0081	−0,5585	−0,2893	−0,2799	−0,2784	−0,2615	**2,8547**
Latvia	−1,0081	−0,0725	−0,0725	−0,0725	−0,0725	**2,1437**	2,8405
Lithuania	−0,7542	−0,1039	**0,5402**	0,5402	0,5595	0,5595	0,5595
Luxembourg	−0,8508	0,7510	1,0088	1,0088	1,0175	1,4598	**2,1531**
Malta	−1,0081	−1,0081	−1,0081	−1,0081	−1,0081	−1,0081	**1,4360**
Netherlands	−1,0081	1,4338	1,4338	1,4338	1,4999	1,4999	**2,9776**
Portugal	−1,0081	−1,0081	−0,1720	−0,1720	−0,0251	**1,5086**	1,5497
Slovakia	−0,8068	0,2430	0,2584	0,3591	**−0,8242**	−0,8242	−0,8242
Slovenia	−1,0081	−1,0081	0,0895	0,0895	**2,1516**	2,1516	2,9496
Spain	−0,3946	−0,3946	**1,2096**	**2,0790**	2,6901	2,6901	3,0439

with the (somewhat limited) criteria analysed in the FRI. Substantial changes in the index have been signalled in bold.

Most euro area Member States have adopted specific fiscal consolidation rules. Most of them did so via legal rules but not through constitutional reform, some of them even via a political commitment.[45] They have also modified their budgetary cycle to adapt timelines (like Portugal),[46] as well as set up specific institutions to control compliance or reinforced the existing ones.

So far, five members of the euro area have modified their constitutions: Italy, Spain, Slovakia, Germany and Slovenia.[47] In the case of Germany and Spain (which partially follows the German reform), the reforms took place before the Fiscal Compact required them to.

The changes in the *strength index* can, at least in some cases, be explained by the actual reforms undertaken. As Table 2.1 shows, in 11 countries there were substantial changes in the index in the years 2013 and 2014.

In 2013 Cyprus, France, Germany, Ireland, Latvia and Portugal all experienced substantial changes in the index. The reforms undertaken partly explain them.

Thus, for example, while France has not yet had a constitutional amendment, the Organic Law on the Programming and Governance of Public Finances has redefined the function of Programming Acts and aims at fulfilling the requirements of the Fiscal Compact as interpreted by the Constitutional Council.[48] Furthermore, a new institution, the High Council of Public Finance (to assess the macroeconomic forecasts projected by the government in financial acts), pre-assesses draft budgetary laws before they are sent to the Council of State and to the parliament. It also requires the government to explain deviations from the deficit.

In Ireland the impact has been focused more on the government, given the already limited role of parliament with regard to the budgetary process, which is informal and centralised in the government. It has

[45] For a full summary of fiscal rules, see ibid.

[46] See the report on Portugal prepared by R. De Brito Gião Hanek, D. Gallo, M. Lourenco and B. Queiroz for the 'Constitutional Change through Euro Crisis Law' project of the EUI Law Department. All the country reports referred to in this paper are part of the same project and are available on its website http://eurocrisislaw.eui.eu.

[47] A. Cuenca and V. Ruiz Almendral, 'Budgetary Stability in the Autonomous Regions: Beyond Constitutional Reform', *Spanish Economic and Financial Outlook*, 3(4), 2014, 53–62.

[48] See the Report on France prepared by R. Gadbled and D. Fromage.

adopted legislation to adapt the timeline.[49] Also, a new institution was created, the Irish Fiscal Advisory Council (IFAC), which was given a statutory footing in the Fiscal Responsibility Act 2012.

The case of Germany is different, and the jump can be attributed to an improvement of the information process. Germany has extensive experience with fiscal constraints, having introduced a specific rule in 1967.[50] Currently the German rule is embedded in Article 109 and, as is well known, it has served as a blueprint for the Fiscal Compact. Germany's regions (*Länder*) are not allowed to run a deficit after 2020. One salient element of Germany's model is the creation, directly in the constitution, of a Stability Council. By contrast, until 2012 Cyprus had neither fiscal rules nor a binding medium-term budgetary framework. There was no fiscal council either.

Estonia, to name just another example, adopted some budgetary adjustments (enactment of the State Budget and Rules of Procedure and Internal Rules Act) as a reaction to the European Stability Mechanism Treaty.[51] It has also created a Fiscal Council. Latvia's budgetary legal framework was already in line with the new rules (Articles 66 and 73 of the Constitution of Latvia).[52] It was reinforced by the Law on Fiscal Discipline (LFD) in early 2013 and the Fiscal Discipline Council, which was also established.

In 2014, Belgium, Italy, Luxembourg, Malta and the Netherlands saw their index change too. The case of Italy stands out, as it has also substantially changed its rules.[53] From this perspective only (as the deficit is quite different) the Italian case shows some similarities with Spain. The financial crisis had a strong impact on the reorganisation and reform of its budgetary process, likewise affecting the regions. Italy modified Articles 81, 97, 117 and 119 of the Constitution (Constitutional Law 1/2012) and Article 119 specifically provides a no bailout rule for the regions. Constitutional Law 1/2012 also creates a Fiscal Council. In addition, the harmonisation of public budgets is now an exclusive competence of the centre (Article 117).

Finally, two countries changed their index in 2011 (Finland, moderately and Spain) and another three in 2012 (Greece, Slovakia and Slovenia). The reforms undertaken vary considerably.

49 See the Report on Ireland prepared by S. Coutts.

50 Gesetz zur Förderung der Stabilität und des Wachstums der Wirtschaft, June 1967; then codified in Art. 115 of the German Constitution.

51 See the Report on Estonia prepared by M. Laatsit.

52 See the Report on Latvia prepared by Z. Rasnača.

53 See the Report on Italy prepared by L. Pierdominici.

The 2011 jumps in the index are quite different in nature. Finland has a typical budgetary cycle, which centres on the government and, in particular, the Ministry of Finance, which plays a key role in the elaboration of policy.[54] In fact, in Finland, the aim of the Fiscal Compact was not seen to require an amendment to the Constitution. The balanced budget rules of the Treaty on Stability Coordination and Governance (TSCG) were introduced in a regular Act of the Parliament (n. 869/2012). There was no constitutional amendment. The correction mechanism consisted of reporting duties between the government and the parliament. The provisions of the Fiscal Compact limit the budgetary powers of the parliament and these limitations were considered significant by the Constitutional Law Committee of the Parliament (PeVL 37/2012 vp of 4 of December 2012), but no more than those resulting from the SGP. There already was a National Audit Office.

Spain was one of the early adopters, due to the substantial increase of its bond yields in the summer of 2011 (which actually paled in comparison with 2012 skyrocketing bond yields, *after* the reform). On 27 September 2011, Article 135 of the Constitution was amended for the purpose of introducing deficit and debt rules. The provision is further developed in Organic Law 2/2012 (Law on Budgetary Stability and Financial Sustainability).[55]

As for the 2012 change group, Slovenia undertook a constitutional change in 2013 (which shows as a 'jump' in the table for 2014).[56] Article 148 of the Slovenian Constitution now determines that 'All revenues and expenditures of the state and local communities for the financing of public spending must be included in their budgets. If a budget has not been adopted by the first day it is due to come into force, the beneficiaries financed by the budget are temporarily financed in accordance with the previous budget'. Article 149 provides that 'State borrowings and guarantees by the state for loans are only permitted on the basis of law'.

In Slovakia, the most significant change is the establishment of the Council for Budget Responsibility.[57] Parliament gained a new competence to elect members of the Council for Budget Responsibility, acting

[54] See the Report on Finland prepared by P. Leino-Sandberg and J. Salminen.

[55] See V. Ruiz Almendral, 'The Spanish Legal Framework for Curbing the Public Debt and the Deficit'. *European Constitutional Law Review*, 9(2), 2013, 189–204.

[56] See the Report on Slovenia prepared by U. Petrovcic.

[57] See the Report on Slovakia prepared by T. Dumbrovsky.

on the basis of proposals by the government, the President of Slovakia and the Governor of the National Bank of Slovakia (one each).

In the case of Greece, the increase of strength can be attributed in part at least to the introduction of new legislation in order to balance the budget in structural terms.[58] Greece now has a very complex budgetary cycle and has undertaken a very impressive list of reforms, including a detailed calendar for the budget. Inter alia, Statute 4270/2014 incorporated this timeline into the new budgetary process that it instituted and further harmonised domestic law with the 'European semester'.

The index does not, of course, clearly reflect all the reforms. The information gathered so far refers to the changes undertaken by Member States after the fiscal consolidation legal framework was put in place (2011 and thereafter). While informative, this provides very limited information on how the fiscal rules are actually being applied. The actual effectiveness will largely depend on the previous existing culture and the different institutional make-up surrounding the rule.

For some EU Member States, the Six Pack/Two Pack legal framework has substantially altered the budgetary legal framework, even without constitutional reform. Such is the case of Austria, which has a balanced budget rule based on the German model.[59] It was adopted in 2011. Previously (2008–9), Austria had undertaken a thorough reform of the Federal Budget Law, including spending limits for the different groups of the budget (i.e. law and security, etc.). The Federal Budget Law was reformed in 2013 to improve the structure of the budget. This does not show as a jump in the table, however. A more limited reform was undertaken by Belgium, mainly altering the timeline of the budget.[60] There already existed independent fiscal councils, in charge among other of publishing macro-economic forecasts. There has not been a real change in the institutional balance. Nevertheless, unlike Austria, Belgium does have a significant jump in the index (for 2014). There is not yet sufficient information on Lithuania, where the reforms are more recent.[61]

Finally, a comparison between the index and the debt to GDP and deficit ratios is still inconclusive (see Table 2.2). To date, there is no obvious link between the deemed strength of the index and the actual

[58] See the Report on Greece prepared by A. Marketou and M. Dekastros.
[59] See the Report on Austria prepared by D. Jaros.
[60] See the Report on Belgium prepared by W. Vandenbruwaene.
[61] See the Report on Lithuania prepared by L. Šaltinytė.

Table 2.2 *Euro Area Excessive Deficit Procedures and Deficit Indicators*

MS	EDP (deadline)	FRI	Debt to GDP	Deficit to GDP	Structural balance
Austria	2009–2014 (Closed)	0,8942	81.2	-2.9	−1.3
Belgium	2010–2014 (Closed)	1,5480	104.5	−3.0	−2.7
Cyprus	**Open (2016)**	0,5117	102.2	−4.9	−2.1
Estonia	–	0,7618	10.1	−0.6	−1.1
Finland	2010–2013 (Closed)	0,2514	56.0	−2.9	−1.1
France	**Open (2017)**	3,0472	92.2	−4.5	−3.3
Germany	2002–2007 2009–2012 (Closed)	2,8274	76.9	0.0	0.6
Greece	**Open (2016)**	0,8175	174.9	−12.2	1.6
Ireland	2009–2015 (Closed)	2,4094	123.3	−5.7	−4.8
Italy	2005–2008 2009–2013 (Closed)	2,8547	127.9	−3.0	−0.9
Latvia	2009–2013 (Closed)	2,8405	38.2	−1.2	−1.6
Lithuania	2009–2013 (Closed)	0,5595	39.0	−2.6	−2.2
Luxembourg	2010 (Closed)	2,1531	23.6	−0.4	0.4
Malta	2013–2015 (Closed) 2009–2012 2004–2007	1,4360	69.8	−2.7	−2.9
Netherlands	2010–2014 2002–2005	2,9776	68.6	−2.5	−0.8
Portugal	**Open (2016) 2002; 2005–2008 (Closed)**	1,5497	128.0	−4.9	−1.9
Slovakia	2010–2014 (Closed 2004–2008	−0,8242	54.6	−3.0	−2.1

Table 2.2 (*cont.*)

MS	EDP (deadline)	FRI	Debt to GDP	Deficit to GDP	Structural balance
Slovenia	**Open (2015)**	2,9496	70.4	−14.6	−2.5
Spain	**Open (2016)**	3,0439	92	**−6.8**	**−2.3**

Source: Eurostat (2013–2014).
I include all cases where at least one step of Article 126 TFEU has been undertaken. In some cases, the procedure has stopped there (such as Luxembourg, in 2010). The only two countries to whom the procedure has never been started are Estonia and Sweden.

balance. Of course, in most cases the substantial changes took place between 2012 and 2014 so it is too early to judge the level of internalisation of the rules.

3 The Consequences of the Budgetary Discipline Legal Framework on the Role of Parliaments

In this section, I will attempt a general assessment of the consequences for parliamentary democracy that the adoption of budgetary rules has had in the euro area countries.

A. *The Actual Role of Parliaments in the Budget*

The general idea that parliaments allocate and control the public money is one of the oldest principles in democracy, rooted in the separation of powers. These principles shaped the budget as both a fundamental political document and an Act of Parliament. One of these principles was the notion of equilibrium. Thus, the idea of balancing the budget, that is, controlling the resulting debt and deficit during the budget cycle and establishing some predetermined rules to be legally binding, is far from new.[62]

Budgets are, however, much more complex today, and less controllable by parliament. It was not until the mid-20th century that budgets

[62] A. Fozzard, 'The Basic Budgeting Problem: Approaches to Resource Allocation in the Public Sector and Their Implications for Pro-Poor Budgeting', Overseas Development Institute, Centre for Aid and Public Expenditure, Working Paper 147 (2001), 21ff.

acquired their present form, that of lengthy complicated documents summarising all public economic policy. The game change, and subsequent increase of public spending that took place mainly after the Second World War (New Deal, Welfare State) transformed public budgets into documents both difficult to manage and to discuss in a public forum such as the parliament. The chambers still approved the document, but they were growingly incapable of fully discussing its complicated content. To a certain extent, there is a trade-off between the size of the public sector and the possibility that the budget that encapsulates its financing can be democratically discussed. Furthermore, most large expenditure areas (such as pensions, social security funds) will normally already be set for a multiyear period, which of course also implies parliaments will not have much leeway to fully change a budget in one given fiscal year.

In fact, the very size of the budget fostered a certain reallocation of spending decisions. Thus, to ease the management of public funds, new techniques such as the creation of independent agencies resulted in chunks of public funds being decided and controled completely outside the parliament, whose role was limited to approving their overall budget.[63]

Because budget laws were no longer fully democratically debated laws but executive documents that flew through parliament, and precisely in order to partially minimise the democratic deficit, some areas were excluded from budget laws, such as those not directly related to the estimation of revenues and the authorisation of expenditures. The purpose was to prevent parliaments from being swamped with macro-laws impossible to discuss.[64] This was embedded in some constitutions or became part of the rules governing the budget.[65] There are many other examples of budgetary rules that specifically limit the role of parliaments in the budget.[66]

[63] See ibid. for a good summary of this evolution of budgeting techniques. See also OECD, 'Budgeting Practices and Procedures in OECD Countries', OECD Publishing (2014); J. Wehner, 'Legislative Arrangements for Financial Scrutiny: Explaining Cross-National Variation', in R. Pelizzo, R. Stapenhurst and D. Olsen (eds.), *The Role of Parliaments in the Budget Process* (Washington DC: World Bank Institute, 2005), pp. 3–19; C. Forestiere and R. Pelizzo, 'Does the Parliament Make a Difference? The Role of the Italian Parliament in Financial Policy', in Pelizzo, Stapenhurst and Olsen (eds.), *The Role of Parliaments in the Budget Process*, pp. 32–41.

[64] Such as budget 'riders' in the US.

[65] Such as Art. 81 of the Italian Constitution, or Art. 134 of the Spanish Constitution.

[66] On the actual role of parliaments (and their idealised role), see Forestiere and Pelizzo, 'Does the Parliament Make a Difference?'. One of the conclusions of their 89-country survey is that 'the executive is more likely to be accountable to the legislature for its spending in parliamentary systems than in presidential systems', p. 29.

The objective to avoid extra budgetary matters, also known as '*cavaliers budgétaires*', is usually linked to maintaining the rule of law and the democratic principle. Budgets are complicated documents discussed in parliament, within an often impossibly short time frame. The actual debate is then, in practice, quite limited as is the role of parliament in controlling the budget in the approval phase.

Furthermore, the role of parliaments is severely limited due to other circumstances; for instance, the possibility to alter the effective impact of the budget or parts of it by way of executive orders and decrees.[67]

Therefore, before analysing the democratic impact of the current EU legal framework, it should be borne in mind first that parliaments in practice have a very limited role in the budget, so that some of the critics may be actually idealising the role or parliaments[68]. Parliaments can of course veto it and create a government crisis, but they are mainly designed and applied by governments.

Budgets have a double nature; they are, so to speak, a 'hybrid' document of legal form and political action. The double nature of the budget is evident when we analyse its life cycle, which in most Member States goes basically like this:

Phase 1: Elaboration. Budgets are elaborated by the executive power, the government, which normally will have the sole legislative initiative in this matter.

Phase 2. Approval. Budgets are discussed and eventually approved by parliament.

Phase 3. Execution. Budgets are a document designed for the executive, who must then apply it (i.e. spend the monies).

Phase 4. Control. Budgets, or rather their execution, will be *ex post facto* controlled by parliament, through a Court of Auditors. There are other forms of control, such as internal government base control mechanisms, as well as specific budgetary offices.

In all Member States, the parliaments approve the national budgets. This is a consequence of the basic rule of law and the 'no taxation without

67 See, on these trends, J. von Hagen and I. Harden, 'Budget Processes and Commitment to Fiscal Discipline', IMF Working Paper No. 96/78 (1996). In Spain, there were 29 Royal Decrees in 2012, 17 in 2013; 17 in 2014 and a total of 12 in 2015 (see www.congreso.es).

68 As Cristina Fasone points out in her well-balanced article on this matter, governments also lost powers. See C. Fasone, 'Taking Budgetary Powers Away from National Parliaments'. EUI Working Paper, LAW 2015/37, http://cadmus.eui.eu/handle/1814/36658, pp. 11ff.

representation' principle. However, actual powers of parliaments vary a lot, depending on the democratic tradition. The way budgets are structured, approved and executed depends on the political structure of the country as well as the specific procedure to approve laws. Some countries do not have a written constitution, while others define the entire budgetary process in the constitution (such as Article 134 of the Spanish Constitution, or, more impressively as to its detail, Articles 110ff. of the German Constitution).[69] Other countries, such as the United States, do not even have 'a budget' but have many different laws covering aspects of the budget. This translates into parliaments having wildly different powers in the budgetary process to start with.[70]

Fundamentally, budgets are political action in numbers, in that they mirror the executives' plans. For this reason and despite country differences, budgets are a product of government, not a product of parliament. A government outlines and directs fiscal policy mainly through the budget. One of many consequences of this double nature of budgets is quite tangible: failing to have the budget approved is one way of losing confidence in parliament.[71]

B. Brief Assessment of the EU Legal Framework for Budgetary Coordination

One distinctive element of the current legal framework is the establishment of a budgetary coordination procedure. Under the current regime, more information is requested from Member States, including, in particular, their budgetary draft law proposals, and there are more control procedures following the 'comply or explain' logic. Budgetary positions are analysed and controlled in the 'European Semester', defined as a 'framework' for 'economic policy coordination',[72] while new sanctions are set up to enforce 'budgetary surveillance in the euro area'.[73]

[69] See ibid., pp. 4ff.

[70] See OECD, 'The Legal Framework for Budget Systems: An International Comparison', *OECD Journal on Budgeting*, 4(3), Special Issue 2004, at 28–30.

[71] The US is a special case, where the executive power actually has much less power (a salient example is the possibility of a foreclosure). In continental systems the executive power has more leeway and may even partially circumvent a veto by parliament via Decree.

[72] Regulation (EU) No. 1175/2011 of the European Parliament and of the Council of 16 November 2011 amending Council Regulation (EC) No. 1466/97 on the strengthening of the surveillance of budgetary positions and the surveillance and coordination of economic policies (OJ L 306, 23.11.2016, p. 12).

[73] Regulation (EU) No. 1173/2011.

Council Directive 2011/85/EU on requirements for budgetary frameworks of the Member States requires budgets to be put in a temporary context of at least three years (Article 9). This implies that budgets must provide information on the projected evolution of the main areas of revenue and spending. The information thus conveyed will be based in economic projections, which must be 'realistic'. The wording of the provision is softened by a reminder of who makes decisions, thus Article 11 clarifies that 'No provision of this Directive shall prevent a Member State's new government from updating its medium-term budgetary framework to reflect its new policy priorities'. However, the new government must provide information on the new policies. The Directive also establishes the need for independent bodies or bodies endowed with functional autonomy that would ensure and monitor compliance with country-specific numerical fiscal rules (the debt and deficit thresholds among others). The main aim of the Directive is to substantially coordinate budgetary frameworks, so that all Member States speak the same (budgetary) language.

The Two Pack further reinforces surveillance by taking into account the whole budgetary process.[74] Regulation (EU) No. 473/2013[75] provides 'enhanced monitoring of budgetary policies in the euro area', in order to determine whether national budgets are consistent with the fiscal consolidation legal framework (namely, the SGP and the European Semester for economic policy coordination). Member States are expected to introduce legislation to ensure a common timeline to draft budgets and approve them (Article 4). It also intends, among other things, to prevent Member States from adopting their budgets based on 'biased and unrealistic macroeconomic and budgetary forecasts', partially with the help of 'Independent bodies monitoring compliance with fiscal rules' (Article 5). Budgets must be drafted in compliance with the fiscal consolidation legal framework and provide sufficient information to determine said

[74] This surveillance will be substantially more intense should the Member State be either experiencing or threatened with serious financial difficulties, as laid out in Regulation (EU) No. 472/2013 of the European Parliament and of the Council of 21 May 2013 on the strengthening of economic and budgetary surveillance of Member States in the euro area experiencing or threatened with serious difficulties with respect to their financial stability (OJ L 140, 27.5.2013, p. 1).

[75] Regulation (EU) No. 473/2013 of the European Parliament and of the Council of 21 May 2013 on common provisions for monitoring and assessing draft budgetary plans and ensuring the correction of excessive deficit of the Member States in the euro area (OJ L 140, 27.5.2013, p. 11).

compliance, which will be closely monitored. Member States must submit their budgetary plans or drafts to the Commission before approving them in parliament (Article 6), which will be then assessed (Article 7). The Regulation also deals specifically with the problem of unrealistic economic forecasts in the budget.[76]

This legal framework has the potential to be game changing with regard to the very meaning of 'national' budgets. For example, according to Regulation (EU) No. 473/2013, in order to avoid spillover effects Member States must consult 'the Commission and each other before adopting any major fiscal policy reform plans with potential spill-over effects', allowing assessment of the possible impact that such a reform may have. The Regulation does not provide examples but the general way in which this is formulated practically allows for any major policy change to become subject to consultation.

The mere submission of budgetary drafts may also have consequences under the new Two Pack regime. Should the Commission identify 'particularly serious non-compliance with the budgetary policy obligations laid down in the SGP', it will request a revised draft of the budgetary plan. That will be the case 'where the implementation of the draft budgetary plan would put at risk the financial stability of the Member State concerned or risk jeopardising the proper functioning of the economic and monetary union, or where the implementation of the draft budgetary plan would entail an obvious significant violation of the recommendations adopted by the Council under the SGP'. The Commission's opinion on the plan must be adopted in November at the latest. The national parliament is then given an opportunity to request that the Commission present its opinion directly in the Chamber, once such opinion has been made public (Article 7(3) of Regulation (EU) No. 473/2013). In this regard, the game change is primarily directed to the executive power. It can be argued that, in a way, the Regulation may actually strengthen the role of national parliaments, at least not in comparison with their ideal role but with the actual role in the context of complicated documents that are difficult to fully discuss.

The traditional 'preventive arm', (including the 'country-specific medium-term objective') remains in place with the following tweaks. First, there is now a quantitative definition of what exactly will be considered a significant deviation of the country-specific medium-term objective.

[76] Regulation (EU) No. 473/2013, Preamble, para. 10.

Second, this micromanaging of the consolidation path is completed with the existing medium-term budgetary frameworks, which is part of the budgetary coordination and basically obliges the country to place its budget in a multiyear context, as provided by Article 9 of Directive 2011/85/EU, so that national fiscal planning follows a multiannual fiscal planning perspective (by providing a 'credible, effective medium-term budgetary framework providing for the adoption of a fiscal planning horizon of at least 3 years', Article 9.1).

Further provision of information is expected from Member States subject to an EDP. Thus, the so-called partnership programme outlined in Article 9 of Regulation (EU) No. 473/2013 is designed to ensure that Member States undertake the structural reforms necessary to ensure a correction of the excessive deficit. Should the Member State be part of an EDP the reporting requirements will be of much greater scope (see Article 10 of Regulation (EU) No. 473/2013) which basically consists of substantially enhanced reporting obligations, outlining all the different elements of the budget.

Finally, for countries in a dire situation, the monitoring will be particularly intense, as laid out in Regulation (EU) No. 472/2013.[77] This specifically means that more information will need to be provided and more recommendations will be received for the Member State to implement. In this scenario, the sovereignty of the Member State will be substantially limited, at least from a legal perspective. Economically, of course, dire situations de facto undermine the sovereignty of the country, so the comparison terms should be chosen carefully.

The current budgetary process (or, rather, the cycle) is encapsulated in the so-called European Semester, in which Member States' budgetary cycles become European budgetary cycles by means of permanent connection with the EU institutions (Table 2.3).

It is (again) too soon to determine the real effect that the Two Pack has had on how national budgets are designed. However, given the content of the regulation, the impact is, again, mostly formal, in the sense that it addresses how the information, the budgetary decisions, have to be reflected on the budget.[78]

[77] Regulation (EU) No. 472/2013.

[78] The current legal framework has been self-evaluated in the Commission reports of February and November 2014. The evaluation does not provide much information on the actual functioning of the system, which is consistent with the fact that it is quite new.

Table 2.3 *Budgetary Cycle*

Phase	Participating institutions
0. Pre-budgeting	National Governments/Commission
1. Elaboration (law project)	National Governments/Supervision by Independent Councils Commission opinion on draft budget
2. Approval	National Parliaments
3. Execution (spending phase)	National Governments
4. Control	National Government (internal control mechanisms) National Parliaments (Fiscal Councils) Commission/Council (assessment of end results). European Court of Justice
5. Controlling the results	Deficit/debt: - Commission/Council - ECJ

In fact, it can be argued that the current regime also has the potential to increase the role of parliaments in the budget, by providing new tools for them to be more actively involved in the process. As seen above, Member States are now required to better outline their policy measures and place them in the economic context. Examination of the outline of the policies, via analysis of the general spending units, is precisely part of the parliament's role when assessing the budget – at least in theory. In the current context, the need to comply with the medium-term budgetary objective,[79] that must be monitored, together

See European Commission, 'Communication from the Commission to the European Parliament and the Council on the application of Regulation (EU) No. 472/2013', COM (2014) 61 final (6 February 2014), p. 6. See also European Commission, 'Economic governance review. Report on the application of Regulations (EU) No. 1173/2011, 1174/2011, 1175/2011, 1176/2011, 1177/2011, 472/2013 and 473/2013', COM (2014) 905 final (28 November 2014), 11ff.

[79] The medium-term budgetary objectives are not a new idea: See, on the so-called Medium Term Expenditure Framework (MTEF), A. Fozzard and M. Foster, 'Changing Approaches to Public Expenditure Management in Low Income Aid-Dependent Countries', UNWIDER, Discussion Paper No. 2001/107 (2001), www.od.org/sites/odi .org.uk/files/odi-assets/publications-opinion-files/2209.pdf.

with insertion of the budget into a previously specified context ('medium-term budgetary framework'), provides a very useful navigation tool for parliaments.[80]

C. *Implications of the EU Budgetary Coordination Legal Framework for National Parliaments*

The current EU budgetary coordination legal framework has a myriad of implications, as has been pointed out by many commentators,[81] but it does not substantially change the way parliaments deal with the budget.

In fact, the executive power may often be the most affected (i.e. draft budgets are submitted by governments, not parliaments), while the actual role of parliaments will be enhanced as they may use the opportunity to monitor reforms more closely. In this regard, Regulation (EU) No. 1177/2011, amending Regulation (EC) No. 1467/97 on speeding up and clarifying the implementation of the excessive deficit procedure, also enhances coordination by means of including the European Parliament (Article 2a), as well as establishing new communication avenues to ensure a permanent coordination process (a 'permanent dialogue', according to Article 10a).

One useful tool to establish the type of changes undertaken by the legal reforms is the monitoring of the medium-term budgetary objectives, undertaken by the Commission since 2006.[82] By requiring Member States to outline how decisions are adopted in the construction of the budget and how medium-term budgetary objectives are designed (what time frame, etc.) or when they can be revised and how, the framework 'prods' Member States to both provide information and (maybe) reflect on their own budgetary processes and possibly improve accountability.

[80] See the database (Excel doc) at European Commission, 'Medium term budgetary framework in the EU Member States', http://ec.europa.eu/economy_finance/db_indicators/fiscal_governance/framework/index_en.htm.

[81] See Craig, 'Economic Governance and the Euro Crisis', pp. 26ff.

[82] There is currently data available for the years 2006, 2008–2014. See above n. 82 for the database.

See, for example, Question 3.10 of the Commission questionnaire (the same questionnaire is employed every year since 2006):

> In terms of the revision of budgetary objectives/targets, please select which of the following applies:
> The medium-term budgetary framework can be revised at any time
> The medium-term budgetary framework can be revised once per year
> The medium-term budgetary framework cannot be revised
> The government has to publicly justify why the budgetary objectives/targets are revised
> An independent fiscal institution has to be consulted/has to endorse any revision
> Other

By answering such specific questions, Member States provide an X-ray of the budgetary decision-making process, as well as information on the democratic quality of the process; for instance, Question 6.15 addresses media coverage of the stability and convergence programme in place and its changes. Other questions refer to the coordination of the different surveillance/benchmark mechanisms in place, such as Question 6.6: 'How are the fiscal objectives specified in the SCP related to the fiscal targets established by the medium-term budgetary framework?'

One of the dimensions assessed in the medium-term budgetary objectives database is the actual involvement of the national parliament in the preparation of the medium-term budgetary plans.[83]

For the fiscal years 2012 and 2014, the assessment showed the following results:

In most cases (16 out of 28), there was no vote (score 1). In three cases, there was no formal presentation of the objectives to the national parliament. In nine cases, there was a vote of the parliament on the main medium-term objectives, in the context of a national medium-term budgetary framework or of the stability and convergence programmes (score 2).

For the fiscal year 2014 there is a slight change, as in most cases there was actually a vote on the main medium-term objective (14 cases, up from 9 in 2012). In 11 cases (down from 16) there was at least a formal presentation of the objectives, while also in 3 (different from 2,012) cases there was no formal presentation at all (Table 2.4).

[83] See ibid., Box 2 'Scores . . .', Dimension 2.

Table 2.4 *Involvement of National Parliaments in the Preparation of 'Medium-Term Budgetary Frameworks' (MTBF)*

Country	Involvement of national parliaments in the preparation of MTBF (2012)	Involvement of national parliaments in the preparation of MTBF (2014)
Austria	No vote but formal presentation of the objectives to the national parliament	Vote of the parliament on the main medium-term objectives (in the context of a national MTBF or of the SCP)
Belgium	No vote but formal presentation of the objectives to the national parliament	No vote but formal presentation of the objectives to the national parliament
Bulgaria	**No formal presentation of the objectives to the national parliament**	No vote but formal presentation of the objectives to the national parliament
Croatia	Vote of the parliament on the main medium-term objectives (in the context of a national MTBF or of the SCP)	Vote of the parliament on the main medium-term objectives (in the context of a national MTBF or of the SCP)
Cyprus	No vote but formal presentation of the objectives to the national parliament	No vote but formal presentation of the objectives to the national parliament
Czech Republic	Vote of the parliament on the main medium-term objectives (in the context of a national MTBF or of the SCP)	Vote of the parliament on the main medium-term objectives (in the context of a national MTBF or of the SCP)
Denmark	Vote of the parliament on the main medium-term objectives (in the context of a national MTBF or of the SCP)	No vote but formal presentation of the objectives to the national parliament
Estonia	No vote but formal presentation of the objectives to the national parliament	No vote but formal presentation of the objectives to the national parliament
Finland	No vote but formal presentation of the objectives to the national parliament	No vote but formal presentation of the objectives to the national parliament

Table 2.4 (*cont.*)

Country	Involvement of national parliaments in the preparation of MTBF (2012)	Involvement of national parliaments in the preparation of MTBF (2014)
France	Vote of the parliament on the main medium-term objectives (in the context of a national MTBF or of the SCP)	Vote of the parliament on the main medium-term objectives (in the context of a national MTBF or of the SCP)
Germany	No vote but formal presentation of the objectives to the national parliament	**No formal presentation of the objectives to the national parliament**
Greece	No vote but formal presentation of the objectives to the national parliament	Vote of the parliament on the main medium-term objectives (in the context of a national MTBF or of the SCP)
Hungary	No vote but formal presentation of the objectives to the national parliament	**No formal presentation of the objectives to the national parliament**
Ireland	**No formal presentation of the objectives to the national parliament**	No vote but formal presentation of the objectives to the national parliament
Italy	No vote but formal presentation of the objectives to the national parliament	Vote of the parliament on the main medium-term objectives (in the context of a national MTBF or of the SCP)
Latvia	No vote but formal presentation of the objectives to the national parliament	Vote of the parliament on the main medium-term objectives (in the context of a national MTBF or of the SCP)
Lithuania	No vote but formal presentation of the objectives to the national parliament	No vote but formal presentation of the objectives to the national parliament
Luxembourg	No vote but formal presentation of the objectives to the national parliament	Vote of the parliament on the main medium-term objectives (in the context of a national MTBF or of the SCP)
Malta	No vote but formal presentation of the objectives to the national parliament	No vote but formal presentation of the objectives to the national parliament

Table 2.4 (*cont.*)

Country	Involvement of national parliaments in the preparation of MTBF (2012)	Involvement of national parliaments in the preparation of MTBF (2014)
Netherlands	Vote of the parliament on the main medium-term objectives (in the context of a national MTBF or of the SCP)	Vote of the parliament on the main medium-term objectives (in the context of a national MTBF or of the SCP)
Poland	**No formal presentation of the objectives to the national parliament**	**No formal presentation of the objectives to the national parliament**
Portugal	Vote of the parliament on the main medium-term objectives (in the context of a national MTBF or of the SCP)	Vote of the parliament on the main medium-term objectives (in the context of a national MTBF or of the SCP)
Romania	Vote of the parliament on the main medium-term objectives (in the context of a national MTBF or of the SCP)	Vote of the parliament on the main medium-term objectives (in the context of a national MTBF or of the SCP)
Slovakia	No vote but formal presentation of the objectives to the national parliament	Vote of the parliament on the main medium-term objectives (in the context of a national MTBF or of the SCP)
Slovenia	No vote but formal presentation of the objectives to the national parliament	No vote but formal presentation of the objectives to the national parliament
Spain	Vote of the parliament on the main medium-term objectives (in the context of a national MTBF or of the SCP)	Vote of the parliament on the main medium-term objectives (in the context of a national MTBF or of the SCP)
Sweden	No vote but formal presentation of the objectives to the national parliament	Vote of the parliament on the main medium-term objectives (in the context of a national MTBF or of the SCP)
United Kingdom	Vote of the parliament on the main medium-term objectives (in the context of a national MTBF or of the SCP)	No vote but formal presentation of the objectives to the national parliament

D. *The Impact on Expenditure: The Case of Social Expenditures*

Member States are still relatively free to design their budgets and, in particular, to tax and spend, although there is now an obligation to coordinate the budgetary processes, the data on which it is based and the timeline of approval.

There is, in particular, no clear and evident link between the fiscal consolidation legal framework and social expenditures. The EU legal framework does not determine the need to decrease expenditure.

The 'expenditure benchmark', introduced in the Six Pack, does not specifically require a reduction in spending but rather seeks to contain the growth of public spending by matching any increases with revenue measures, that the Member States are quite free to establish.

However, reducing spending, namely on investment, has often proved the quickest way to reduce the deficit in a limited time frame. Furthermore, some possibly mistaken 'austerity' policies, as well as the link of budgetary constraints to bail out programs, has reinforced the idea that budgetary discipline actually undermines the powers of parliaments vis à vis the budget, may curb growth and substantially change the economic constitution, also endangering the very survival of what is left of the European welfare system.

This persuasive narrative is not new but is currently more widespread. There is of course truth in this general explanation of budgetary rules, but it leaves out the lion's share of the fundamental problems that the stability legal framework presents. By focusing on the harm inflicted by *austericide* policies, this narrative minimises or even often ignores the arguments for balancing budgets. It also vastly misrepresents what the current rules actually entail, by confusing their mandatory provisions with the actual policy decisions undertaken 'in the name of' such provisions. Budgetary discipline is then often equated with the reduction of social expenditures.

The first issue to bear in mind when assessing the impact of the fiscal consolidation legal framework on social protection spending is that this type of expenditure acts as an automatic stabiliser, which is why it increases as GDP drops.[84] In a recession, the rations of social spending to GDP will increase as the need for social support programs increases (namely, unemployment funds). The correlative decrease in GDP also contributes to the growth of social expenditures, as the data shows; on

[84] See Eurostat, 'Issue 14/2012' (In 2009 a 6.5 per cent rise in per capita social protection expenditure matched a 6.1 per cent drop in EU-27 GDP – Issue no. 14/2012), http://ec.europa.eu/eurostat/web/products-statistics-in-focus/-/KS-SF-12-014.

average, public social spending-to-GDP ratios in countries in the Organisation for Economic Co-operation and Development (OECD) went from 18.9 per cent in 2007 to 21.9 per cent in 2009.[85]

Also, and to further complicate the analysis, there is not one but several models of social expenditure. In fact, what exactly is the European Social Model is of course the subject of much debate.[86] For the purpose of this article, I refer to the so-called welfare state policies, as defined by Eurostat under 'social protection', which is the financing risks and needs associated with disability, old age, parental responsibilities, unemployment, housing or social exclusion.[87]

Table 2.5 shows the vast differences in the level of social expenditure between the different Member States.

There are also vast differences in the capacity of the tax systems. Table 2.6 also shows that the impact of the crisis has been quite different depending on the country. While most countries saw a decrease in their revenue between 2007 and 2009, the differences among them are substantial.

The year-on-year analysis presents a clearer picture, particularly when examining the growth rate of total revenues (per GDP) in the pre- and crisis years (which plummeted 7.3 points in 2009 alone for the euro area).[88]

The crisis had an obvious impact in fiscal consolidation, as tax revenues plummeted and public spending – especially social spending (in particular, unemployment contributions) – increased. Deprived of monetary policy instruments (i.e. interest rates and currency devaluation), most affected Member States had to undertake internal devaluation policies, that is, budgetary cuts. The need to reduce social expenditure can be explained by the weight they have in the budget.[89] In the midterm at least the largest expenditure areas will need to be evaluated (such as pensions, due to the ageing of the population).[90]

85 See, specifically, OECD, 'Social Expenditure Update', OECD Social Expenditure Database (November 2014), www.oecd.org/els/soc/OECD2014-Social-Expenditure-Update-Nov2014-8pages.pdf, p. 2.

86 See P. Whyman, M. Baimbridge and A. Mullen, *The Political Economy of the European Social Model* (Abingdon: Routledge, 2012).

87 See Eurostat, 'Glossary: Social Protection', http://ec.europa.eu/eurostat/statistics-explained/index.php/Glossary:Social_protection.

88 See total tax revenue by country, 1995–2014 (year-on-year growth rates) at ibid.

89 See F. Costamagna, 'The Impact of Stronger Economic Policy Co-ordination on the European Social Dimension: Issues of Legitimacy' in Adam, Fabbrini and Larouche (eds.), *The Constitutionalisation of European Budgetary Constraints*, pp. 359–78, p. 372.

90 This idea is present in the 'Five Presidents' Report', n. 41, which clearly stresses the need to 'align the retirement age with life expectancy', an idea which has become almost anathema for a good part of the European left, pp. 8f.

Table 2.5 *Expenditure on Social Protection, 2002–2012 (per cent of GDP)*

	2002	2007	2008	2009	2012
EU-28	:	:	26,7	29,5	29,5
EU-27	:	26,1	26,7	29,6	29,5
Euro area (EA-18)	27,3	26,8	27,5	30,3	30,4
Austria	28,9	27,9	28,5	30,7	30,2
Belgium	26,8	26,9	28,3	30,6	30,8
Bulgaria	:	14,1	15,5	17,2	17,4
Croatia	:	:	18,7	20,8	21,2
Cyprus	16,3	18,2	19,5	21,1	23,1
Czech Republic	19,4	18,0	18,0	20,3	20,8
Denmark	29,7	30,7	30,7	34,7	34,6
Estonia	12,7	12,1	14,9	19,0	15,4
Finland	25,7	25,4	26,2	30,4	31,2
France	30,5	30,9	31,3	33,6	34,2
Germany	30,4	27,7	28,0	31,5	29,5
Greece	24,0	24,8	26,2	28,0	31,2
Hungary	20,4	22,7	22,9	23,4	21,8
Ireland	16,4	18,0	21,2	26,2	32,5
Italy	25,2	26,6	27,7	29,9	30,3
Latvia	14,3	11,3	12,7	16,9	14,0
Lithuania	14,0	14,4	16,1	21,2	16,5
Luxembourg	21,6	19,3	21,4	24,3	23,3
Malta	17,2	17,7	18,1	19,6	19,4
Netherlands	27,6	28,3	28,5	31,6	33,3
Poland	21,1	18,5	19,4	20,6	18,1
Portugal	22,8	23,9	24,3	26,8	26,9
Romania	13,6	13,6	14,4	17,2	15,6
Slovakia	19,1	16,1	16,1	18,8	18,4
Slovenia	24,3	21,3	21,4	24,2	25,4
Spain	20,0	20,8	22,0	25,2	25,9
Sweden	31,3	29,2	29,5	32,0	30,5
United Kingdom	25,6	24,7	25,6	28,3	28,8

The problem, of course, is the perception of an imbalance between economic integration and the pursuit of social agendas. However, to fully assess the impact the narrative cannot be limited to listing the budgetary cuts undertaken by Member States. Crucial issues

Table 2.6 *Total Tax Revenue by Country, 2000–2014 (per cent of GDP)*

	2000	2007	2008	2009	2010	2011	2012	2014
EU-28	:	**39,3**	39,2	**38,5**	38,5	38,9	39,6	40,0
EA-19	40,8	**40,0**	39,6	**39,3**	39,2	39,7	40,7	41,5
Austria	43,6	**41,5**	42,4	**42,0**	41,8	41,9	42,5	43,8
Belgium	46,1	**45,2**	45,8	**45,2**	45,5	46,2	47,3	47,9
Bulgaria	30,9	**31,4**	30,6	**27,2**	26,3	25,5	26,6	27,8
Croatia	:	**37,1**	36,8	**36,4**	36,1	35,2	35,9	36,7
Cyprus	27,4	**36,4**	35,1	**32,1**	32,2	32,2	31,6	34,2
Czech Republic	32,5	**34,4**	33,1	**32,1**	32,6	33,7	34,2	34,1
Denmark	48,6	**47,7**	46,1	**46,5**	46,6	46,6	47,2	50,8
Estonia	31,2	**31,4**	31,6	**35,1**	33,5	31,7	31,7	32,5
Finland	46,0	**41,6**	41,3	**41,1**	40,9	42,2	42,8	44,0
France	44,6	**44,3**	44,3	**43,9**	44,1	45,2	46,5	47,9
Germany	41,5	**38,8**	39,2	**39,6**	38,2	38,7	39,3	39,5
Greece	34,9	**33,5**	33,7	**32,9**	34,2	36,1	38,3	39,0
Hungary	39,2	**39,7**	39,7	**39,2**	37,5	36,9	38,6	38,4
Ireland	32,0	**32,1**	30,4	**29,0**	28,6	28,2	29,1	30,5
Italy	40,2	**41,6**	41,5	**42,0**	41,7	41,7	43,7	43,7
Latvia	29,5	**28,4**	28,1	**27,5**	28,0	27,9	28,7	29,2
Lithuania	30,8	**30,4**	30,9	**30,6**	28,7	27,6	27,3	28,0
Luxembourg	38,0	**37,4**	38,1	**40,0**	39,0	39,2	40,2	39,4
Malta	28,3	**34,2**	33,4	**33,8**	32,5	33,2	33,3	35,0
Netherlands	38,1	**36,6**	36,9	**35,9**	36,7	36,4	36,5	38,0
Poland	33,8	**35,5**	35,2	**32,3**	32,0	32,5	32,8	33,0
Portugal	33,6	**35,0**	34,9	**33,4**	33,7	35,5	34,5	36,9
Romania	30,4	**29,6**	28,3	**27,0**	26,9	28,1	27,9	27,7
Slovakia	33,9	**29,3**	29,1	**28,9**	28,2	28,7	28,4	31,2
Slovenia	36,8	**37,3**	36,8	**36,7**	37,4	37,0	37,4	37,0
Spain	34,1	**37,1**	32,9	**30,6**	32,1	32,0	33,0	34,4
Sweden	49,7	**45,8**	44,9	**45,1**	44,1	43,5	43,5	43,7
United Kingdom	36,3	**36,2**	37,7	**34,9**	35,5	35,9	35,2	34,4

Source: Eurostat, 'Tax Revenue Statistics'.
This table shows the total receipts from taxes and social contributions (incl. imputed social contributions) after deduction of amounts assessed but unlikely to be collected in per cent of GDP.

are how they were being financed before and the actual fall in public revenues.[91]

This debate has been shaped by the link between fiscal consolidation and bailout programs, which has proved poisonous, as it has created a link between the austerity policies undertaken in the framework of the bailout programs (which were often ill-designed, and actually undermined growth, as official reports acknowledge)[92] and the fiscal consolidation legal framework as a whole. Furthermore, country-specific recommendations do often insist on the need to review spending.[93] This focus on spending has further shaped the debate, which is not always objective.

The role of constitutional courts when analysing budgetary cuts is still unfinished, as there are still pending cases. The available data suggest that some of them have managed to strike a balance between the need to reduce spending and the protection of social rights, such as the Italian or the Spanish Constitutional Court.[94] Others, such as the Portuguese Constitutional Court, have actually struck down some of the measures (such as public workers' pay cuts), without taking into account the general economic context, and therefore ignored that other sectors (private-sector workers) may have fared worse.[95]

[91] See updated EU tax revenue data at Eurostat, 'Tax Revenue Statistics'.

[92] See the report by the European Court of Auditors, 'Financial Assistance Provided to Countries in Difficulties', No. 18 (2015), www.eca.europa.eu/Lists/ECADocuments/SR15_18/SR_CRISIS_SUPPORT_EN.pdf;

European Parliament, 'Report on Employment and Social Aspects', Committee on Employment and Social Affairs, A7-0135/2014,

www.europarl.europa.eu/sides/getDoc.do?pubRef=-//EP//NONSGML+REPORT+A7-2014-0135+0+DOC+PDF+V0//EN. On Spain, see European Commission, 'Evaluation of the Financial Sector Assistance Programme for Spain, 2012–14', Institutional Paper 19 (January 2016),

http://ec.europa.eu/economy_finance/publications/eeip/ip019_en.htm.

[93] See, for example, Council Recommendation of 14 July 2015 on the 2015 National Reform Programme of France and delivering a Council opinion on the 2015 Stability Programme of France (2015/C 272/14) (OJ C 272, 18.8.2015, p. 51).

[94] D. Tega, 'Welfare Rights and Economic Crisis before the Italian Constitutional Court', *European Journal of Social Law*, 4(1), 2014, 63–74. The author names many examples of the Court's 'balancing test' (*bilanciamento*), which preserves legislative discretion on the distribution of public resources. To a certain extent, this is also the view of the Spanish Constitutional Court (see, inter alia, its Opinion 49/2015, 5 March 2015).

[95] For further discussion, see in this book Chapter 11 'Constitutions, Social Rights and Sovereign Debt States in Europe: A Challenging New Area of Constitutional Inquiry' by Claire Kilpatrick.

Absent from the debate is a thorough analysis of the opportunity costs of financing some social programs against other social expenditures. All rights have costs, if only because rights entail a system of guarantees and remedies that must operate if they are breached, which is why there needs to be a publicly financed court system.[96] From this perspective, as Holmes and Sustein explain, third-generation rights (such as health, education, pension funds) are not necessarily costlier than fundamental rights (due process, the right to property, freedom of speech).[97]

The 'cost of rights' debate should be at the centre of any public debate on fiscal restrictions. There is a spending ceiling, but there is also a revenue floor, which is harder to maintain in light of declining tax revenues. There is a cultural impediment. Evaluating the cost of rights is often welcomed with a great amount of suspicion, as it is usually identified with restricting such rights. Quite surprisingly, no constitutional law handbook mentions this issue (to the best of my knowledge). This is part of the reason why a debate on the cost remains partly hidden even though there are daily, tangible examples that show how some things are financed and others are not. Budgetary cuts receive wildly different public responses depending on the sector that is affected by them. In a limited patchwork way there is a Europe-wide debate on the cost of euro-crisis law, but it has mainly focused on what bailouts actually cost (although with little debate of the cost of not financing bailouts).

4 Conclusions

Most euro area Member States have adopted some form of budgetary constraints, which have a democratic rationale, rooted in time inconsistency issues and the need to preserve intergenerational equity. It is too soon to determine whether they have been also fully internalised, as this depends on the previously existing culture (the general beliefs on the merits of controlling public spending) and institutional practice. It is,

96 Constitutional lawyers and scholars have an intriguing tendency to ignore this, as beautifully explained, with US examples, by S. Holmes and C. Sustein, *The Cost of Rights: Why Liberty Depends on Taxes* (London: W. W. Norton & Company, 2000); in particular, pp. 87ff.

97 All rights are positive. See ibid., pp. 37ff. on the futility of the dichotomy between positive and negative rights.

however, much too early to reach a conclusion, as most of the substantial reforms have taken place between 2012 and 2014.

The existing data suggest that the fiscal consolidation legal framework has not substantially transformed the fiscal constitutions of EU Member States, as the general revenue and expenditure areas remain largely untouched.

In an imperfect monetary union, there is a case for some type of fiscal discipline. However, it should be done as a result of an amendment of the European Treaties and with careful wording so as to not restrict the necessary leeway for Member States. Of course, enshrining constitutional rules limiting the debt and deficit implies a petrification of political options, but so does enshrining fundamental rights, which can then evolve as all constitutional options do (the constitution as a living tree). In fact, the case for fiscal constraints and their introduction in the constitution is not so different from the case for establishing the building blocks of a revenue system. Western constitutions do have a preference for a revenue system based on taxes, which in euro area countries represent 90 per cent of public revenue.

An entirely different matter is just what the specific wording of the constitutional clause should be. It can be argued that the way the European fiscal consolidation legal framework has adopted, and adapted, the existing economic wisdom is suboptimal and is the result of a sketchy unorganised process, where general principles have transformed into one-size-fits-all strict rules, whose sanctions are neither clear nor credible.

The need for fiscal 'discipline', 'surveillance' or the adoption of 'automatic' measures and correction paths derives from the legal framework in a very obvious way. The patchwork legal system builds on the previous legal framework in that it established specific debt and deficit ratio thresholds, as well as an institutional design to control compliance levels. But the enhanced permanent supervision adds significant complexity to the budgetary cycle. It also conveys the impression of an automatic process, of complicated machinery where every step of building the budget is (formally) monitored.

This sense of control is misleading. There is no control (nor can there be) on the specific economic policy of Member States. Revenues and spending programs are left largely untouched, and the content of the budget is left unsupervised, except for the general recommendations provided by the Council. This is problematic, as conveying the idea that all possible elements of public finances are actually being controlled may create perverse incentives, as the feeling of control fosters moral hazard. Because the budget cycle is being monitored externally, there may seem to be no need to internally monitor it, for instance, by substantially revising the expenditure/revenue structure of the country. As long as a Member State is complying, or in the process of complying with the external framework, there will be less pressure to fully revise its spending structure.

The assessment of the consequences for parliamentary democracy is not easy given how recent the reforms are. With that caveat, I think the fiscal consolidation legal framework has not undermined parliamentary democracy, but it has provided a tool kit for reviving the – often defunct – role of parliaments in the budget. This leaves out the bailout countries for which the panorama is substantially different. For them, specific directives are given as to how to cut spending and boost public revenue, which logically imposes tangible limits to parliaments (although it can be argued that sovereign debt issues undermine democracy too, as dependency on markets increases).

The fiscal consolidation legal framework does not necessitate a reduction of the welfare state (whatever model each country has). On the other hand, the current legal framework has also been moderately successful in introducing a much-needed debate about the cost of rights.

3

A Multi-Level Playing Field for Economic Policy-Making: Does EU Economic Governance Have Impact?

PÄIVI LEINO-SANDBERG AND JANNE SALMINEN*

1 Introduction

In recent years the European Union rules on economic governance have been developed in great haste.[1] The 'Six Pack' and 'Two Pack'[2] were

* Janne Salminen gratefully acknowledges the financial support granted by the Niilo Helander Foundation. We thank Marketta Henriksson and Ilkka Kajaste for a number of thoughtful comments on an earlier draft. All web pages visited 21 March 2016.

1 Concerning the development in general, see P. Leino and J. Salminen, 'Should the Economic and Monetary Union Be Democratic After All? Some Reflections on the Current Crisis', *German Law Journal*, 14(7), 2013, 844–68.

2 The Six Pack was adopted in November 2011 to improve budgetary discipline and economic surveillance. It is composed of five Regulations and one Directive: 1) Regulation (EU) No. 1175/2011 of the European Parliament and of the Council of 16 November 2011 amending Council Regulation (EC) No. 1466/97 on strengthening the surveillance of budgetary positions and the surveillance and coordination of economic policies (OJ L 306, 23.11.2011, p. 12); 2) Council Regulation (EU) No. 1177/2011 of 8 November 2011 amending Regulation (EC) No. 1467/97 on speeding up and clarifying the implementation of the excessive deficit procedure (OJ L 306, 23.11.2011, p. 33); 3) Regulation (EU) No. 1173/2011 of the European Parliament and of the Council of 16 November 2011 on the effective enforcement of budgetary surveillance in the euro area (OJ L 306, 23.11.2011, p. 1); 4) Regulation (EU) No. 1176/2011 of the European Parliament and of the Council of 16 November 2011 on the prevention and correction of macroeconomic imbalances (OJ L 306, 23.11.2011, p. 25); 5) Regulation (EU) No. 1174/2011 of the European Parliament and of the Council of 16 November 2011 on enforcement measures to correct excessive macroeconomic imbalances in the euro area (OJ L 306, 23.11.2011, p. 8); 6) Council Directive 2011/85/EU of 8 November 2011 on requirements for budgetary frameworks of the Member States (OJ L 306, 23.11.2011, p. 41). The 'Two Pack', adopted in 2013, includes Regulation (EU) No. 472/2013 of the European Parliament and of the Council of 21 May 2013 on the strengthening of economic and budgetary surveillance of Member States in the euro area experiencing or threatened with serious difficulties

adopted in swift succession, without sufficient observation of how such rules were functioning in practice or a comprehensive vision of the future framework. The same applies to the Fiscal Compact, an international agreement between most EU Member States,[3] which partly overlaps with instruments of secondary law.[4] The result is a maze of treaty provisions and secondary legislation specifying Member States' obligations and the roles of the institutions in the two main procedures created under Articles 121 and 126 of the Treaty on the Functioning of the European Union (TFEU): respectively, the multilateral surveillance procedure and the Excessive Deficit Procedure (EDP). These provisions have the primary aim of ensuring trust in good economic governance at the EU level through new rules, stronger control and greater harmonisation of statistical requirements. In addition, the Fiscal Compact has created an obligation to introduce Independent Fiscal Institutions[5] and automatic correction mechanisms in Member States' national legislation, preferably backed up by constitutional guarantees. These reforms, together with the budgetary framework directive included in the Six Pack, aim to ensure the achievement of jointly defined economic policy objectives as well as a level playing field at the national level. These measures illustrate the multi-level approach that has been deemed necessary to tackle the crisis.[6]

The frameworks within which the Member States operate are not identical. While all EU Member States are subject to some economic

with respect to their financial stability (OJ L 140, 27.5.2013, p. 1) and Regulation (EU) No. 473/2013 of the European Parliament and of the Council of 21 May 2013 on common provisions for monitoring and assessing draft budgetary plans and ensuring the correction of excessive deficit of the Member States in the euro area (OJ L 140, 27.5.2013, p. 11).

[3] The Fiscal Compact signifies the obligations set out in Title III of the Treaty on Stability, Coordination and Governance in the Economic and Monetary Union (TSCG).

[4] See also J. Salminen, 'Sopimus talous – ja rahaliiton vakaudesta – tie fiskaaliunioniin', *Lakimies*, 111(6), 2013, 1076–98, at 1082–4.

[5] For further discussion on the establishment of Independent Fiscal Institutions through euro-crisis law, see in this book Chapter 4, 'Creation and Reform of Independent Fiscal Institutions in EU Member States: Incomplete and Insufficient Work in Progress?' by Diane Fromage.

[6] For a discussion on the general idea of the compound character of the Union in the context of the Eurocrisis, see I. Pernice, 'Domestic Courts, Constitutional Constraints and European Democracy: What Solution for the Crisis?' in M. Adams, F. Fabbrini and P. Larouche (eds.), *The Constitutionalisation of European Budget Constraints* (Oxford: Hart Publishing, 2014), pp. 297–318. Concerning the multi-level constellation and its requirements in this particular field, see F. Amtenbrink, 'Integration, Coordination or Fragmentation in Economic Policy Matters? A Comment on the René Smits Contribution', in D. Obradovic and N. Lavranos (eds.), *Interface between EU Law and National Law* (Amsterdam: Europa Law Publishing, 2007), pp. 171–84, at 181–4.

governance rules, a number of stricter requirements and additional procedural stages apply to euro area Member States. The Fiscal Compact, ratified by all Member States except the UK, the Czech Republic and Croatia[7] introduces additional obligations for the Contracting Parties. However, the greatest dividing line caused by the crisis relates to the way in which the measures have divided Member States into creditors and debtors and the role of conditionality in this process. Programme countries have been subject to a number of additional procedures and requirements within and outside the EU framework. It is evident that, in a setting involving strict conditionality, the impact of EU level measures is fundamentally different, since its function is specifically to ensure compliance. For the creditors, conditionality has been deemed a necessary safeguard to avoid moral hazard, especially because the EU rules relating to economic governance have not operated in a credible manner. If the granting of financial assistance presumes strict conditionality, thus effectively reducing the recipient state's room for manoeuvre, these states are likely to do their utmost to avoid being subject to it. Whether this is experienced as unfair or not depends on your position as either debtor or creditor in the crisis.

Our focus will be on the impact of the mainstream framework of economic governance (the Six Pack, Two Pack and the Fiscal Compact) and conditionality will be considered to the extent relevant in this context.[8] The strengthened rules of economic governance specifically aim at preventing Member States from running bad economic policies. But while the Member States have felt compelled to subject each other to stricter Commission scrutiny, they have a strong preference for maintaining national autonomy in their *own* economic policy choices – something that Dawson has described as 'asymmetric sovereignty transfer'.[9] At the same time, it has been necessary to achieve these outcomes without amending the Treaties, where currently the primary

[7] In the Czech Republic, approval of the Fiscal Compact is pending in the Parliament.

[8] The measures adopted under EU law also include conditions based on Council Regulation (EU) No. 407/2010 of 11 May 2010 establishing a European financial stabilisation mechanism (OJ L 118, 12.5.2010, p. 1). See, for example, Council Implementing of 7 December 2010 on granting Union financial assistance to Ireland (Decision 2011/77/EU) (OJ L 30, 4.2.2011, p. 34), as amended by Council Implementing Decision of 22 October 2013 amending Implementing Decision 2011/77/EU on granting Union financial assistance to Ireland (2013/525/EU) (OJ L 282, 24.10.2013, p. 71).

[9] See M. Dawson, 'The Legal and Political Accountability Structure of "Post-Crisis" EU Economic Governance', *Journal of Common Market Studies*, 53(5), 2015, 976–93.

responsibility for such policies remains with the Member States. It is obvious that these objectives are not only challenging in economic terms, but also filled with legal complications.[10] Many of the measures have relied on legal ambiguity and abstraction.[11] This has had obvious consequences for the accountability of measures both at the EU and national levels and, as will be shown below, blurred the division of competence between the two. Reform has not only centred on the EU legal system, but has (through an instrument of public international law) required reform of the Member State legal system, with considerable variation among Member States as a result.

After a brief description of the new economic governance framework, we examine the recent legal developments and their possible impact from two intertwined angles: those relating to EU constitutional law, focusing in particular on the scope and effects of EU competence in economic policy, and national constitutional law, through three case studies of euro area Member States (Finland, France and Portugal). The 'impact' that we address is mainly legal – even constitutional – or political. We assess this impact primarily through examination of the effects of these measures on the division of competence between the EU and its Member States, the effects of EU surveillance on Member States and the eventual diminishing of national discretion in making policy choices. Finally, we argue that accountability and legitimacy-related challenges also affect the impact and effectiveness of policies.

2 The New Framework for Economic Governance

A. *EU Economic Policy Competence*

The two pillars of the EMU rely on different modes of integration. While Monetary Union is based on Union exclusive competence and is largely

[10] Or, as Sonja Bekker and Ivana Palinkas put it, the 'new measures are also increasingly mingling with matters of national competences'. See S. Bekker and I. Palinkas, 'The Impact of the Financial Crisis on EU Economic Governance: A Struggle between Hard and Soft Law and Expansion of the EU Competences?', *Tilburg Law Review*, 17(2), 2012, 360–6. Similar findings can also be found in R. Bieber, 'The Allocation of Economic Policy Competences in the European Union', in L. Azoulai (ed.), *The Question of Competence in the European Union* (Oxford University Press, 2014), pp. 86–100.

[11] See Leino and Salminen, 'Should the Economic and Monetary Union be Democratic After All?'.

run by the ECB, the Economic Union has been built around a mode of soft coordination of Member State economic policies, building on a vague conception of 'common concern'. The Lisbon Treaty maintained the specific character of economic policy among EU policies.[12] It establishes the categories of EU competence (exclusive, shared and competence to support, coordinate or supplement the actions of the Member States) and the nature of competence in different areas of EU action.[13] But economic policy is of a sui generis character as it is not covered by any of these provisions but has received its own paragraph in Article 5 TFEU, which leaves the exact nature of this competence and its effects on the Member States formally undefined.[14] The specific Treaty provisions on economic policy illustrate these choices. The Treaties provide for a number of possibilities to coordinate and even supervise Member States' economic policies and to adopt relevant secondary legislation, if deemed necessary. They also place the Member States under an obligation to consider their economic policies as a 'matter of common concern' (Article 121(1) TFEU) and thus take into account the spillover effects of their national choices on other euro area Member States. But even if the Treaty provisions affect the primary responsibility of the Member States for their economic policies, they ultimately leave the responsibility for such policies with the Member States. As the Court of Justice of the European Union (CJEU) acknowledged in its ruling in *Pringle*, 'Articles 2(3) and 5 (1) TFEU restrict the role of the Union in the area of economic policy to the adoption of coordinating measures' (para. 64).[15]

The choices made when defining EU competence in the area of economic policy are a natural reflection of various national, even constitutional, ideologies concerning the democratically acceptable way of

[12] See J. Louis, 'Economic Policy under the Lisbon Treaty', in S. Griller and J. Ziller (eds.), *The Lisbon Treaty: EU Constitutionalism without a Constitutional Treaty?* (Vienna: Springer, 2008), pp. 285–98, at 291ff.; U. Häde, 'The Treaty of Lisbon and the Economic and Monetary Union', in H. Blanke and S. Mangiameli (eds.), *The European Union after Lisbon: Constitutional Basis, Economic Order and External Action* (Vienna: Springer, 2012), pp. 412–39.

[13] Art. 3 TFEU includes a list of policy areas in which the Union has exclusive competence, Art. 4 TFEU includes a list of the 'principal areas' in which the Union and the Member States have shared competence and Art. 6 TFEU defines the areas where the Union has competence to support, coordinate or supplement the actions of the Member States.

[14] Art. 5(1) TFEU: 'The Member States shall coordinate their economic policies within the Union. To this end, the Council shall adopt measures, in particular, broad guidelines for these policies. Specific provisions shall apply to those Member States whose currency is the euro.'

[15] *Thomas Pringle* v. *Government of Ireland, Ireland and the Attorney General*, Case C-370/12.

economic and fiscal policy-making. The most well-known and authoritative example of the statements concerning the 'essential areas of democratic formative action', which belong to the national sphere and where the room for constitutionally accepted transfers of power is limited, is found in the decisions of the German Federal Constitutional Court (*Bundesverfassungsgericht*). The Federal Constitutional Court has established that 'revenue and expenditure including external financing and all elements of encroachment that are decisive for the realisation of fundamental rights' are among such issues. For the *Bundesverfassungsgericht*, the key questions concern the extent of the powers to be transferred, the degree of independence that EU-level decision-making enjoys and its (lack of) democratic guarantees. The German concerns thus relate especially to the substantial influence that national parliaments should enjoy in the field of economic policy to guarantee the democratic nature of decision-making.[16] The Finnish Parliament has also stressed that economic policy needs to be examined with a much broader legal and political approach, taking into account its effects on citizens and their rights and the requirements set by democratic legitimacy:

> Fiscal power, the power to tax citizens and decide on how to spend the money, has been one of the most important subjects of citizens' right to participate ever since the democratic revolutions of the eighteenth century. As long as nation states remain the prime object of citizens' allegiance, it is hard to see how budgetary power could be transferred to the Union without a loss of democratic legitimacy ... The committee concludes that the principles of democracy require that member states retain their primacy in economic policy.[17]

In the view of the Parliament's Grand Committee, the requirement of democratic legitimacy constitutes the main challenge for the plans for the future development of the EMU.

[16] German Federal Constitutional Court, Case No. 2 BvE 2/08, 30 June 2009 (Lisbon), paras. 244 and 249. For an analysis, see P. Huber, 'The Rescue of the Euro and its Constitutionality', in W. Ringe and P. Huber (eds.), *Legal Challenges in the Global Financial Crisis: Bail-outs, the Euro and Regulation* (Oxford: Hart Publishing, 2014), pp. 9–26, and M. Wendel, 'Judicial Restraint and the Return to Openness: The Decision of the German Federal Constitutional Court on the ESM and the Fiscal Treaty of 12 September 2012', *German Law Journal*, 14(1), 2013, 22–52.

[17] Grand Committee of the Finnish Parliament, 'Banking Union and the Future of EMU', Statement SuVL 4/2012 vp, 13 December 2012. Unofficial translation available from the European Parliament, www.europarl.europa.eu/webnp/webdav/users/malfons/public/week%202013/Contribution%20ECON%20ICM%20Finnish%20Parliament.pdf.

Economic Union has been built around a number of general principles. The Member States are to conduct their economic policies with a view to conforming to a number of rather broadly defined Union objectives and to regard their economic policies as a matter of common concern. However, their obligations have been largely limited to a duty to coordinate such policies, based on broad guidelines adopted through recommendations by the Council (Article 121 TFEU) and to avoid excessive deficits (Article 126 TFEU). These Treaty provisions and the secondary legislation adopted on the basis of them will be considered in detail below.

A third legal basis for the development of economic policy rules can be found in Article 136 TFEU, which was added by the Treaty of Lisbon and concerns the euro area Member States. This legal basis has been used jointly with Article 121 or 126 TFEU when measures concerning euro area Member States have been adopted. It is a particularly loosely defined provision, which enables both measures aimed at addressing a specific situation and those with a more general scope, provided that these serve the proper functioning of the EMU. Its implementation is subject to the general provisions described above. In particular, Article 136 TFEU cannot be used to expand Union competence, to change its nature, or to replace Member State competence in the area of economic policy. It gives no powers to amend the budgetary obligations of the Member States included in a separate Protocol No. 12. And yet, as we will see, many of the measures adopted on the basis of Article 136 TFEU stretch the limits of EU competence in the area of economic policy quite considerably.

B. Article 126 TFEU: Excessive Deficit Procedure

Article 126 TFEU places the Member States under an obligation to avoid excessive government deficits and report on their actions. The Commission monitors, reports, and, if needs be, addresses an opinion on the matter to the Council for the purpose of making recommendations and, ultimately, imposing fines on the Member State concerned under the Excessive Deficit Procedure, which is the most established economic governance procedure at EU level.[18] The reference values are set out in

[18] Art. 126 TFEU also provides a specific exception to the implementation of the Arts. 258 and 259 TFEU procedures, preventing the Commission and Member States from bringing cases against a Member State suspected of breaching their obligations under Art. 126 TFEU.

Protocol No. 12 on the EDP, which establishes 3 per cent for the ratio of the planned or actual government deficit to gross domestic product (GDP) and 60 per cent for the ratio of government debt to GDP – figures that were determined based on the economic situation in the early 1990s. Although these figures play a key function in the Treaty framework, their implementation involves complicated and detailed calculations and entails a great deal of discretion.[19] In addition, Article 3 of the Protocol stipulates that the governments of the Member States are responsible for the deficits of general government. The Member States are to ensure that national budgetary procedures enable them to meet their Treaty obligations.

Article 126 TFEU also includes a legal basis for the Council to adopt detailed rules and definitions for the application of Protocol No. 12 on a proposal from the Commission and after consulting the European Parliament. This provision has been used to adopt the so-called 'corrective' arm of the Stability and Growth Pact (SGP) and Directive 2011/85/EU on budgetary frameworks.[20] Even if the approximate debt level in the euro area now is around 92 per cent of GDP, no procedures have been launched solely on the basis of the debt criterion, even though the Treaty would enable this, and the debt criterion has been further functionalised in the Six Pack.[21] The fact that no procedures have been launched based on debt alone has been justified with reference to how the Member States already have an excessive budgetary deficit procedure, or because they still benefit from a transitional period of three years from an EDP decision that was in force when the Six Pack entered into force.[22] Several reports adopted on the basis of Article 126(3) have considered whether the debt criterion is met, but the conclusion has always been that it is

[19] The implementation of these provisions and the problems encountered in enforcing them are explained in detail in M. Henriksson and P. Leino-Sandberg, 'Talouspolitiikan koordinaatio EU:ssa: lohduton labyrintti vai tie talouspoliittiseen täyttymykseen?', *Kansantaloudellinen aikakausikirja*, 110(4), 2014, 521–48.

[20] Council Regulation (EC) No. 1467/97, amended by Regulations 1056/2005 and 1177/2011 and Council Regulation (EC) 479/2009, as amended by Regulation 679/2010.

[21] See Council Regulation (EC) No. 1467/97 of 7 July on speeding up and clarifying the implementation of the excessive deficit procedure (OJ L 209, 2.8.1997, p. 6), as amended by Council Regulation (EC) No. 1056/2005 of 27 June 2005 amending Regulation (EC) No. 1467/97 on speeding up and clarifying the implementation of the excessive deficit procedure (OJ L 174, 7.7.2005, p. 5) and Council Regulation (EU) No. 1177/2011. The latter Regulation forms part of the Six Pack (see above n. 2).

[22] In greater detail, see Henriksson and Leino-Sandberg, 'Talouspolitiikan koordinaatio EU:ssa: lohduton labyrintti vai tie talouspoliittiseen täyttymykseen?'.

fulfilled and opening an EDP is not warranted.[23] A significant difference with the deficit criterion is that opening an EDP on a breach of the debt criterion is only possible based on observed data.

C. *Article 121 TFEU: Multilateral Surveillance Procedure*

The multilateral surveillance procedure is regulated by Article 121 TFEU. This is a procedure for coordinating Member State economic policies in the Council, which monitors and evaluates whether national policies comply with the jointly agreed broad objectives. Monitoring is based on information produced by the Member States and by Commission reporting. If Member State policies are found to depart from the broad economic guidelines, the Council may address recommendations to the concerned Member State, based on a recommendation from the Commission. Unlike the Article 126 TFEU procedure described earlier, this procedure, as the Treaty defines it, has a soft character: The Article 121 TFEU procedure builds on recommendations and makes no provision for sanctions.

In addition to establishing the main parameters of the multilateral surveillance procedure, Article 121 TFEU includes a legal basis for the adoption of regulations laying down detailed rules for the said procedure. This legal basis has been used various times during the past years through the Six Pack and Two Pack legislation to strengthen the preventive arm of the SGP[24] and to establish the new Macroeconomic Imbalances Procedure (MIP).[25] This procedure also builds on the final stage of the

[23] For example, the Art. 126(3) TFEU Reports on Finland, Belgium and Italy. See European Commission, 'Finland', COM(2015) 803 final (16 November 2015), http://ec.europa.eu/economy_finance/economic_governance/sgp/pdf/30_edps/126-03_commission/2015-11-16_fi_126-3_en.pdf; 'Belgium', COM(2015) 112 final (27 February 2015), http://ec.europa.eu/economy_finance/economic_governance/sgp/pdf/30_edps/126-03_commission/2015-02-27_be_126-3_en.pdf; 'Italy', COM(2015) 113 final (27 February 2015), http://ec.europa.eu/economy_finance/economic_governance/sgp/pdf/30_edps/126-03_commission/2015-02-27_it_126-3_en.pdf.

[24] See Regulation (EC) No. 1466/97 of 7 July 1997 on the strengthening of the surveillance of budgetary positions and the surveillance and coordination of economic policies (OJ L 209, 2.8.1997, p. 1), as amended by Regulation (EC) No. 1055/2005 of 27 June 2005 amending Regulation (EC) No. 1466/97 on the strengthening of the surveillance of budgetary positions and the surveillance and coordination of economic policies (OJ L 174, 7.7.2005, p. 1) and Regulation (EU) No. 1175/2011. The latter Regulation forms part of the Six Pack (see above n. 2).

[25] See Regulation (EU) No. 1174/2011 and Regulation (EU) No. 1176/2011.

multilateral surveillance procedure under Article 121 TFEU. In addition, Article 121 TFEU acts as a second legal basis together with Article 136 TFEU for four Regulations that concern only the euro area Member States. These Regulations form part of the Six Pack and Two Pack and further strengthen effective enforcement of budgetary surveillance by introducing common provisions for monitoring and assessing draft budgetary plans and ensuring the correction of an excessive deficit of a euro area Member State.[26] As a result of these measures, the original Article 121 TFEU procedure focusing on the adoption of broad economic guidelines has become largely obsolete.

Instead, Article 121 TFEU today forms a basis for three separate procedures: the preventive arm of the SGP and both the preventive and corrective arm of the MIP.[27] When studying the impact of the new legislation on Member States and their competence, it is specifically the Regulations based partly on Article 136 TFEU that are of interest. In particular, these measures develop the multilateral surveillance procedure far beyond measures of coordination. Regulations have not only been used to regulate the Article 121 TFEU procedure in greater detail (as the legal basis provides), but, as will be explained below, secondary legislation has added a number of new stages to the procedure. Secondary legislation has expanded and amended the roles of the EU institutions beyond those defined in the Treaty-based economic policy framework and introduced significant legal consequences for Member States unwilling to follow the recommendations issued in the course of the procedure, through the adoption of sanctions (for which Article 121 TFEU itself does not expressly provide).

A key change brought by secondary legislation concerns the choice of instrument. While the Council instrument specified in Article 121 TFEU is a recommendation, secondary legislation also provides for the use of Council decisions, which are used to establish that certain Member State measures have been insufficient or to impose interest-bearing deposits or fines.[28] This choice bears clear legal consequences. Recommendations have 'no binding force' (Article 288 TFEU) and fall outside the legal

[26] Regulation (EU) No. 1173/2011, Regulation (EU) No. 1174/2011, Regulation (EU) No. 472/2013, and Regulation (EU) No. 473/2013.

[27] In greater detail, see Henriksson and Leino-Sandberg, 'Talouspolitiikan koordinaatio EU:ssa: lohduton labyrintti vai tie talouspoliittiseen täyttymykseen?'.

[28] See Regulation (EU) No. 1174/2011, Art. 3; Regulation (EU) No. 1173/2011, Arts. 5 and 6.

control carried out by the Court of Justice, to the extent they are not intended to produce legal effects *vis-à-vis* third parties (Article 263 TFEU). According to the Court's jurisprudence, 'recommendations are not intended to produce binding effects and are not capable of creating rights that individuals can rely on', but are still not entirely 'without any legal effect'.[29] This seems to correspond to their function in the Treaty-based economic policy framework. Recommendations are generally adopted by the institutions when 'they do not have the power under the Treaty to adopt binding measures or when they consider that it is not appropriate to adopt more mandatory rules'.[30] But the Court has also stressed that even when non-binding instruments are used, the institutions must duly take account of the division of powers and the institutional balance established by the Treaty in that particular field.[31] It seems doubtful that the mandate under Article 121 TFEU, even when read jointly with Article 136 TFEU, includes the possibility to change the applicable instrument from a non-binding to a binding one.[32]

The changed nature of the instrument contributes to blurring the division of competence between the EU and Member States and has turned the soft coordination procedure into one with rather hard edges. First, a Council decision is 'binding in its entirety' and its legality can be reviewed by the Court of Justice. Therefore, for example, the legality of a Council decision establishing an excessive macroeconomic imbalance in a Member State should in principle be possible to submit to the Court for review. The use of Council decisions is particularly prominent in the context of the Two Pack. Based on Regulation (EU) No. 472/2013, the Council also adopts implementing decisions approving the update of the relevant Member States' macroeconomic adjustment programme.[33]

Second, secondary legislation has introduced the possibility of imposing sanctions on a euro area Member State that does not follow recommendations. It is evident that this reform aims at turning recommendations into something that is binding in practice. Sanctions are intended to have implications for the character of the procedure by limiting the Member States' room for manoeuvre in deciding whether to

[29] *Altair* Case C-207/01, para. 41. [30] *Grimaldi* Case C-322/88, para. 13.

[31] *France* v. *Commission* Case C-233/02.

[32] See Arts. 82(2), 83(2) and 168(6) TFEU, which all include limitations concerning the applicable instrument.

[33] For a recent decision concerning Portugal, see Council Implementing Decision of 23 April 2014 approving the update of the macroeconomic adjustment programme of Portugal (2014/235/EU) (OJ L 125, 26.4.2014, p. 84).

follow these recommendations. Therefore, the introduction of sanctions can hardly be justified with the mandate that is given by Article 136 TFEU to adopt more detailed procedural rules.[34]

Finally, many of the measures relating to economic governance have contributed to a significant strengthening of the role of the Commission. This is especially related to the introduction of reverse qualified majority voting (RQMV) in many of the procedures, under which the Council is assumed to have adopted a Commission recommendation unless it rejects it by a qualified majority.[35] The use of RQMV is intended to make the adoption of decisions more automatic. In the Preamble of Regulation (EU) No. 1174/2011, for example, the use of RQMV is justified by the fact that the 'Commission should have a stronger role in the enhanced surveillance procedure' and by the general need to strengthen economic governance. It is evident that the introduction of RQMV buttresses, in particular, the position of the Commission in relation to the Council since its recommendation is likely to be adopted, and it limits the possibility of a Member State to prevent adoption of the decision.[36]

In general, the Six Pack legislation was welcomed by the Member State governments, even if some concerns relating to subsidiarity and changed institutional balance through secondary law were expressed.[37] Since all institutions ultimately agreed on the introduction of the procedure, the Court has not addressed its compatibility with the Treaties.[38] There has

[34] See on this R. Palmsdorfer, 'The Reverse Majority Voting under the "Six Pack": A Bad Turn for the Union?', *European Law Journal*, 20(2), 2014, 186–203. However, since Art. 126 TFEU includes a reference to sanctions, their use cannot be automatically incompatible with the nature of EU economic policy competence.

[35] See Regulation (EU) No. 1173/2011, Arts. 4(2), 5(2) and 6(2); Regulation (EU) No. 1466/97, as amended by Regulation (EU) No. 1175/2011, Arts. 6(2) and 10(2); Regulation (EU) No. 1173/2011, Arts. 4(2), 5(2) and 6(2), Regulation (EU) No. 1176/2011, Art. 10(4); Regulation (EU) No. 1174/2011, Art. 3. The Fiscal Compact also includes provisions stipulating the use of RQMV.

[36] For a discussion of possible effects, see D. Chalmers, 'The European Redistributive State and a European Law of Struggle', *European Law Journal*, 18(5), 2012, 667–93, at 691.

[37] See the national reports of the Constitutional Change through Eurocrisis Law project, organised by the European University Institute, available at http://eurocrisislaw.eui.eu/topic/six-pack/. These demonstrate how the reform was largely supported by governments. However, in Finland the use of Art. 136 TFEU as legal basis was problematised because of its loose formulation.

[38] The Court has addressed a Council decision-making procedure with a similar character in *Eurocoton*, but this decision predates the Treaty of Lisbon and relates to competition

been surprisingly little legal discussion concerning this development.[39] Some criticism has been directed at the way in which RQMV amends the decision-making procedure under Article 121(4) TFEU and the main principle of qualified majority voting under Article 16(3) TFEU. Even if direct proceedings against the legislative acts including this procedure can no longer be initiated before the Court,[40] the compatibility of the Council's decision-making procedure with the Treaties may be raised if the validity of its subsequent decisions is challenged. Unlike Article 126 TFEU, Article 121 TFEU includes no limitation concerning Court jurisdiction.

Since entry into force of the Six Pack in May 2013, the Council position concerning a Member State's failure to take action in response to a Council recommendation to adjust to, and maintain, the medium-term budgetary objective in the preventive part of the SGP[41] manifests as a Council decision. It is well within the bounds of possibility that the national measures adopted subsequent to such decisions could be considered to constitute situations where a Member State is implementing Union legislation, thus bringing these situations within the scope of implementation of the Charter of Fundamental Rights.[42] At the same time, it is clear that if the decisions adopted at EU level have binding implications for the Member States, these decisions should be capable of being subjected to a legality check. This is especially the case in light of how many of the euro-crisis related measures have proved difficult to challenge before the CJEU due to lack of clarity regarding who, in fact, is legally or politically responsible for them.[43] For example, the Court has accepted that the Memoranda of Understanding cannot be seen to originate with the Commission or the ECB but need to be traced back to the European Stability Mechanism (ESM), which is not a Union body

law, where institutional roles and competence are different from those applicable in economic policy. See *Eurocoton* Case C-76/01 P.

[39] See, however, Palmsdorfer, 'The Reverse Majority Voting under the "Six Pack"'.

[40] See Art. 263 TFEU, final paragraph: 'The proceedings provided for in this Article shall be instituted within two months of the publication of the measure, or of its notification to the plaintiff, or, in the absence thereof, of the day on which it came to the knowledge of the latter, as the case may be'.

[41] See Regulation (EU) No. 1173/2011.

[42] See Article 51(1) of the Charter of Fundamental Rights.

[43] See C. Kilpatrick, 'Are the Bailouts Immune to EU Social Challenge Because They Are Not EU Law?', *European Constitutional Law Review*, 10(3), 2014, 393–421.

whose acts the Court has jurisdiction to assess.[44] And since the Euro Group cannot be regarded as a decision-making body either, its statements cannot be seen to produce legally binding effects that could be assessed by the Court.[45] And yet, Regulation (EU) No. 472/2013, forming a part of the Two Pack, is closely linked with the stability mechanisms: it allocates tasks to bodies outside the EU institutions ('where appropriate, the IMF') and becomes applicable specifically in the situation where a euro area Member State either experiences or is threatened with serious difficulties, or requests or receives external financial assistance, including from the ESM. The failed attempts to judicially challenge euro-crisis measures demonstrate not only the complex institutional structure created to maintain stability in the euro area, but also the existence of legitimacy-related challenges. There have also been claims based specifically on the Council decisions being ultra vires, in reaching beyond EU competence in economic policy by dictating specific outcomes in a Member State.[46] The cases are still pending.

The economic governance measures adopted through secondary legislation build on a comprehensive reading of the Member States' obligation to coordinate their economic policies.[47] With some goodwill, one can argue that the roles of the institutions are not extended beyond their usual constitutional mandate framed in the Treaties. After all, the Commission still proposes and supervises while the Council adopts the final measures[48] (which can be understood as falling under 'implementation') and formally takes the necessary decisions, even if its threshold for amending the Commission recommendations is, in practice, set high.[49]

[44] See, for example, *Ledra Advertising Ltd* v. *Commission and ECB* Case T-289/13; *Ledra Advertising Ltd* v. *Commission and ECB* Case T-289/13 and *Konstantinos Mallis ja Elli Konstantinou Malli* v. *Commission and ECB* Case T-327/13.

[45] Ibid. [46] See *Sotiropoulou and (67) Others* v. *Council* Case T-531/14.

[47] See R. Smits, 'The Impact of EMU Law on National Budgetary Freedom', in Obradovic and Lavranos (eds.), *Interface between EU Law and National Law*, pp. 131–68, p. 133, and C. Calliess, 'From Fiscal Compact to Fiscal Union? New Rules for the Eurozone', in C. Barnard et al. (eds.) *Cambridge Yearbook of European Legal Studies 2011–2012*, Vol. 14 (Oxford: Hart, 2012), pp. 101–17.

[48] See M. Maduro, 'Opening Statement', in A. Kocharov (ed.), 'Another Legal Monster? An EUI Debate on the Fiscal Compact Treaty', EUI Working Papers, Law 9/2012 (2012), pp. 3–6, p. 3.

[49] For an example of slightly similar 'implementing' decisions in another context, see Art. 9 (4) of Council Regulation (EC) No. 1225/2009 of 30 November 2009 on protection against dumped imports from countries not members of the European Community (OJ L 343, 22.12.2009, p. 51).

However, it is evident that the reforms affect institutional balance in the area of economic policy-making and have implications for the clarity of the division of competence between the EU and the Member States. For the Court, specifically, the principle of institutional balance has been of crucial significance when evaluating what kind of procedural changes might be compatible with the Treaties. While the gravest concerns of the Court have often related to the prerogatives of the European Parliament, the principle also has a wider purpose and function. The Court has generally stressed that 'the rules regarding the manner in which the Community institutions arrive at their decisions are laid down in the Treaty and are not at the disposal of the Member States or of the institutions themselves'.[50] Following this, the 'Treaty alone may empower an institution to amend a decision-making procedure established by the Treaty'.[51] For the Court:

> The Treaties set up a system for distributing powers among the different Community institutions, assigning to each institution its own role in the institutional structure of the Community and the accomplishment of the tasks entrusted to the Community. Observance of the institutional balance means that each of the institutions must exercise its powers with due regard for the powers of the other institutions.[52]

In addition to the new institutional balance between the Commission and the Council, the reforms have affected the impact of the exercise of EU economic policy competence. Do the reforms make EU economic policy guidance more binding and its effects on Member State discretion more significant than what the Treaties might imply? This is partly a rhetorical question, since this effect is exactly the one that was aimed at. The division of competence between the Union and the Member States is further blurred by the linkages to 'strict conditionality', which is a crucial element in many of the new economic governance instruments; in

[50] *UK* v. *Council* Case 68/86, para. 38.

[51] *European Parliament* v. *the Council* Case C-133/06, paras. 54–5, which concerns the use of so-called secondary legal bases. The Court referred to ex-Art. 67(2) TEC, which included a specific *passerelle* for the amendment of the applicable decision-making procedure. However, at the same time, Council Regulation (EC) No. 1/2003 of 16 December 2002 on the implementation of the rules on competition laid down in Articles 81 and 82 of the Treaty (OJ L 1, 4.1.2003, p. 1) develops the Procedure included in (now) Arts. 101 and 102 TFEU quite significantly. See Art. 103 TFEU for the legal basis for the Regulation.

[52] See *European Parliament* v. *the Council* Case C-70/88, paras. 21–2. See also *European Parliament* v. *the Council* Case C-133/06, para. 57.

particular, the ESM, but also in the macroeconomic adjustment programmes adopted under Regulation (EU) No. 472/2013, which also involve 'strict policy conditionality'.

The European Semester serves today as an umbrella concept covering economic and fiscal policy coordination within the EU. Its objective is to ensure that the Member States align their budgetary and economic policies with the EU objectives and rules. In addition to the MIP, described earlier, the European Semester includes structural reforms, which focus on promoting growth and employment in line with the Europe 2020 strategy, and Member States' fiscal policies. The Country Specific Recommendations adopted under the European Semester are intended to offer advice to guide national policies every year through a set of concrete, targeted and measurable recommendations concerning measures that can realistically be achieved in the next 12 to 18 months.[53] Such recommendations are given to all Member States with the exception of the programme countries. Country Specific Recommendations often take a very comprehensive approach and involve comprehensive reform agendas that are difficult (impossible) to achieve in a year. However, since the Member States have the possibility to comment on the recommendations before their adoption, these can be expected to largely reflect their own reform agendas. At the same time, the general usefulness of these recommendations remains unclear. Data about their implementation is revealing: a major part of Country Specific Recommendations given to the Member States demonstrate no or only limited progress.[54]

D. *Fiscal Compact and Six Pack Directive: Creating National Guarantees for Sound Economic Policy-Making*

The reformed governance framework has contributed to a need for the Member States to adjust their budgetary procedures to EU requirements. Directive 2011/85/EU, part of the Six Pack',[55] requires national implementing legislation concerning the systems of budgetary accounting and

[53] See the website of DG ECFIN http://ec.europa.eu/europe2020/making-it-happen/index_en.htm.

[54] See, for a very useful compilation of data, European Parliament, 'Country Specific Recommendations (CSRs) for 2014 and 2015: A Comparison and an Overview of Implementation', www.europarl.europa.eu/RegData/etudes/STUD/2015/542659/IPOL_STU(2015)542659_EN.pdf.

[55] Directive 2011/85/EU.

statistical reporting, rules and procedures governing the preparation of budgetary planning forecasts and the adoption of fiscal rules, such as debt or deficit limits and medium-term budgetary frameworks.[56] The European University Institute's (EUI) national reports (part of the Constitutional Change through Euro-crisis Law project) indicate how some Member States considered that their national legislation and practices required no changes and were already in line with the Directive.[57] Possible Member State concerns related to the organisation of budgetary coordination between the different administrative levels. Some Member States have traditionally had strikingly minimalist or low-level legislation on budgetary matters. This relates to how such rules have mainly concerned how budgetary decisions are made, not the substance of economic policy.

The Fiscal Compact strengthens the aims of the amended SGP.[58] It met with surprisingly little political opposition. For many, it mainly appeared to be political theatre. However, from a legal point of view, the Compact has been a source of endless interest,[59] especially as regards Member State competence to conclude the Treaty on Stability, Coordination and Governance in the Economic and Monetary Union and to use Union institutions for its purposes.[60] The Fiscal Compact itself specifies that it is to be applied and interpreted in line with the EU Treaties, and its core substance should be incorporated into the legal framework of the

[56] Some other EU legislative acts also include provisions affecting Member States' national arrangements. See, for example, Art. 5 of Regulation (EU) No. 473/2013 on independent bodies monitoring compliance with fiscal rules.

[57] See above n. 36.

[58] See C. Ohler, 'Treaty Change, Fiscal Union and the ECB', in Ringe and Huber (eds.), *Legal Challenges in the Global Financial Crisis: Bail-outs, the Euro and Regulation*, pp. 121–30, p. 128.

[59] See, for example, the sharp critique in C. Joerges, 'Europe's Economic Constitution in Crisis and the Emergence of a New Constitutional Constellation', *German Law Journal*, 15(5), 2014, 985–1027, at 1002ff. For a more general examination of the Fiscal Compact, see P. Craig, 'The Stability, Coordination and Governance Treaty: Principle, Politics and Pragmatism', *European Law Review*, 37(3), 2012, 231–48. See also S. Peers, 'The Stability Treaty: Permanent Austerity or Gesture Politics?', *European Constitutional Law Review*, 8 (3), 2012, 404–41; Calliess 'From Fiscal Compact to Fiscal Union? New Rules for the Eurozone' and Salminen, 'Sopimus talous- ja rahaliiton vakaudesta – Tie fiskaaliunioniin'.

[60] However, under so-called Bangladesh case law, it is possible to allocate duties to the EU institutions under legal arrangements other than the EU Treaties. See *European Parliament* v. *the Council and European Parliament* v. *the Commission* Joined Cases C-181/91 and C-248/91; *Thomas Pringle*, paras. 68 and 158–9.

EU in the near future[61] – an objective included among the long-term objectives of the 'Five Presidents' Report' published in June 2015.[62] But since the presumption is that this would require a Treaty change, it is not evident that the plan will hold. Sensitivities relating to the exercise of economic and fiscal policy competence are unlikely to be overcome in the near future.

As regards substance, the Fiscal Compact has required the introduction of the balanced budget rule, preferably at constitutional level, strengthened numerical fiscal rules, provisions relating to medium-term budgetary planning, rules on budgetary coordination between different levels of government, the introduction of national fiscal councils,[63] budget monitoring and macroeconomic and budget forecasting.[64] The Fiscal Compact stresses the so-called balanced budget rule: general government budgets shall be 'balanced' or in surplus. It further includes a debt brake rule, as per the SGP, and provisions concerning an automatic correction mechanism, which is triggered in case the balanced budget rule or the debt brake rule is not followed. Article 3 is not only the material core provision of the Treaty, but also sets requirements for national implementation measures. According to Article 3(2), the Fiscal Compact's main provisions:

> shall take effect in the national law of the Contracting Parties – through provisions of binding force and permanent character, preferably constitutional, or otherwise guaranteed to be fully respected and adhered to throughout the national budgetary processes.

The Fiscal Compact further establishes that the correction mechanism is to fully respect the prerogatives of national Parliaments. The introduction of the balanced budget rule into national law, be it as a constitutional provision or something else, has been the most obvious and straightforward reason for formal constitutional amendment or national legal

[61] Art. 16 of the Fiscal Compact.

[62] See the 'Five Presidents' Report': J. Juncker, D. Tusk, J. Dijsselbloem, M. Draghi and M. Schulz, 'Completing Europe's Economic and Monetary Union' (June 2015).

[63] For further discussion on the establishment of Independent Fiscal Institutions through euro-crisis law, see in this book Chapter 4, 'Creation and Reform of Independent Fiscal Institutions in EU Member States: Incomplete and Insufficient Work in Progress?' by Diane Fromage.

[64] In greater detail, see European Central Bank, 'The Importance and Effectiveness of National Fiscal Frameworks in the EU', *ECB Monthly Bulletin* (February 2013), www.ecb.europa.eu/pub/pdf/other/art1_mb201302en_pp73-88en.pdf, pp. 73–88.

change brought about by the crisis.[65] The Fiscal Compact is a mixture of national modes of enforcing budgetary discipline. It facilitates recourse to sanctions and is backed up by the Court of Justice's involvement.

The obvious assumption behind the Fiscal Compact is that provisions included in a national constitution provide a strong guarantee for their actual implementation.[66] Member States would agree to introduce debt brakes in their national constitutions and allow the EU Commission to monitor their policies.[67] The main architects of this agreement were Germany and France. The introduction of the 'golden rule' (and possibly even the demands concerning its obligatory inclusion into national constitutions) was straightforward from the German perspective, since the German Constitution provides for a similar rule at both the Federal and *Länder* level.[68] The idea of incorporating the balanced budget rule into the national constitutions or, where this would be impossible due to practical difficulties related to amending the constitution, in special domestic sources of law that are hierarchically superior to the ordinary acts of parliament, was a crucial element of the plan. After all, ordinary legislation can typically be altered through a simple majority in the parliament. Additionally, typical meta-rules such as *lex specialis* or *lex posterior* function as 'business as usual' in relation to more general or older ordinary legislation. The new constitutional rule would then operate as a ground for constitutional review of budgetary laws, and its implementation would be ensured on the national level by national courts.[69] Both of these objectives, however, proved to create additional hurdles for the ratification of the agreement. Amendments to national

[65] See L. Besselink and J. Reestman, 'Editorial: The Fiscal Compact and the European Constitutions: "Europe speaking German"', *European Constitutional Law Review*, 8(1), 2012, 1–7.

[66] For further discussion, see in this book Chapter 2, 'The European Fiscal Consolidation Legal Framework: Its Impact on National Fiscal Constitutions and Parliamentary Democracy' by Violeta Ruiz Almendral.

[67] See Besselink and Reestman, 'Editorial: The Fiscal Compact and the European Constitutions: "Europe speaking German"'.

[68] German legislation after the 2009 constitutional reform has served as the model for drafting the balanced budget rule in the Fiscal Compact. The German design of the budget rules is, in its turn, largely based upon Swiss debt brakes, which had already been implemented in the early 1920s in some of the Swiss cantons.

[69] F. Fabbrini, 'The Fiscal Compact, the 'Golden Rule', and the Paradox of European Federalism', *Boston College International & Comparative Law Review*, 36(1), 2013, 1–38, at 32ff. See also K. Tuori, 'The European Financial Crisis: Constitutional Aspects and Implications', EUI Working Papers, Law 2012/28 (2012), http://cadmus.eui.eu/handle/1814/24301, pp. 19ff.

constitutions require elections or referenda in some EU Member States, which in this context would most presumably have become challenges to the European Union at large and/or to participation in the euro. In some Member States, the constitution also establishes a certain time interval between amendments.[70] However, the inclusion of specific constitutional provisions relating to fiscal discipline was still tempting: the existence of such rules would create a constitutional commitment that would be binding on future governments, thus limiting their policy choices. This links with another key function of the Fiscal Compact: to offer governments EU-related arguments to rely on in budgetary debates with the national parliament.

While the inclusion of an intergovernmental agreement can be seen to represent an anti-federalist act stressing sovereign rights, the agreement itself relies on heavy centralisation, which is deeper than that, for example, found in the US.[71] In the literature, the idea of placing constitutional limitations on the discretion of political decision-making through specific clauses adopted under great time pressure and in response to external motivation is typically linked to rule-making during crisis.[72] When provisions are adopted because of the demands of an international treaty, they are usually discussed through the source of that rule (the agreement itself), and consequently perceived as a sovereignty question. Less consideration is given to the consequences of those rules and their potential impact at national level. Therefore, in times of urgency, greater weight is placed on the symbolic constitutionalisation of the balanced budget rules and not, for example, on their applicability and future purpose and function, or the institutional or other consequences of their constitutional status.[73]

[70] See, from a comparative perspective in relation to constitutional change and amendment procedures in EU states, X. Contiades, *Engineering Constitutional Change. A Comparative Perspective on Europe, Canada and the USA* (London: Routledge, 2013).

[71] Fabbrini, 'The Fiscal Compact, the "Golden Rule", and the Paradox of European Federalism', pp. 32–38. See also M. Humphery-Jenner, 'Balanced Budget Rules and Expenditure Limits: Lessons from the US and Australia and Implications for the EU', *German Law Journal*, 13(6), 2012, 607–36. From the less formalistic perspective of the United Kingdom, see J. McEldowney, 'Debt Limits in Constitutional Law: A UK Perspective', in Ringe and Huber (eds.), *Legal Challenges in the Global Financial Crisis: Bail-outs, the Euro and Regulation* (Oxford: Hart, 2014), pp. 63–78.

[72] X. Contiades and A. Fotiadou, 'How Constitutions Reacted to the Financial Crisis', in X. Contiades (ed.) *Constitutions in the Global Financial Crisis: A Comparative Analysis* (Farnham: Ashgate, 2013), pp. 9–59, pp. 28–30.

[73] Ibid.

The Fiscal Compact does not specify in exact terms what kind of balanced budget rules or correction mechanisms it entails, but these have been elaborated on by the Commission in its 2012 Communication on common principles on national fiscal correction mechanisms.[74] The Commission is in the process of evaluating national implementation measures under Article 8(1) of the Fiscal Compact. The report is to be presented to the Contracting Parties 'in due time' after having given them the opportunity to submit observations; a procedure that was started already some time ago and which, if previous experiences from the framework are anything to go by, is likely to include a great deal of interpretation, bargaining and negotiation. This is particularly so considering that a negative finding may bring about consequences: in case the Commission ultimately finds a failure to comply with the Fiscal Compact, the Treaty stipulates that 'the matter will be brought' before the Court of Justice by one or more Contracting Parties. Failure to comply with a ruling may lead to the imposition of a lump sum or a penalty payment. The findings concerning compliance with the Fiscal Compact are also of relevance for the application of the Treaty Establishing the European Stability Mechanism, since the granting of new financial assistance programmes is conditional on the ratification of the Fiscal Compact and compliance with its requirements.[75]

The EUI euro-crisis project reports on individual Member States demonstrate variation in the implementation of the Fiscal Compact. At least Spain (2011), Italy (2012), Slovakia (2011) and Slovenia (2013) have adopted the required reforms at the constitutional level.[76] The Portuguese budget rule also has a superior legal status.[77] In some other Member States, the governments have contemplated constitutional

[74] European Commission, 'Common Principles on National Fiscal Correction Mechanisms', COM(2012) 342 final, 20 June 2012, http://eur-lex.europa.eu/LexUriServ/LexUriServ.do?uri=COM:2012:0342:FIN:En:PDF.

[75] See the Preamble to the TSCG. The linkages between the ESM and the Fiscal Compact are underlined in the literature. See, for example, Calliess, 'From Fiscal Compact to Fiscal Union? New Rules for the Eurozone' and Salminen, 'Sopimus talous- ja rahaliiton vakaudesta – Tie fiskaaliunioniin'.

[76] See the Report on Spain prepared by M. Estrada-Cañamares, G. Gomez Ventura and L. Díez Sánchez for the 'Constitutional Change through Euro Crisis Law' project of the EUI Law Department. All the country reports referred to in this paper are part of the same project and available on its website: www.eurocrisislaw.eui.eu., http://eurocrisislaw.eui.eu/spain/; The Report on Italy prepared by L. Dominici; The Report on Slovakia prepared by T. Dumbrovsky; the Report on Slovenia prepared by U. Petrovcic.

[77] See the Report on Portugal prepared by R. De Brito Gião Hanek, D. Gallo, M. Lourenco and B. Queiroz.

amendments[78] and in some Member States the situation remains under consideration.[79] Due to the fact that the golden rule and the other key provisions of the Fiscal Compact are based on an international treaty, they enjoy a special constitutional status in the Netherlands.[80] Interestingly, the Czech Republic, one of the opponents of the Treaty and ultimately outside the Compact, has introduced a Fiscal Constitutional Act.[81] Comparisons between the Member States' legal doctrines and theoretical debate in this field reveal that the requirement of the balanced budget rule was sometimes believed to constitute one of the recognised legal principles of constitutional law, predating the requirements of the Fiscal Compact.[82] This has eased the process of incorporating the rule into the text of some national constitutions. The Greek Constitution establishes a mandatory time interval between two consecutive amendments; therefore, a regulatory act was used.[83] Belgium implemented the Compact on several levels, on federal level and on the levels of Regions and Communities.[84]

The choices made in Spain and Italy are of a particular interest keeping in mind the broader historical background of their constitutional amendments.[85] While the Spanish Constitution of 1978 is known to be extremely difficult to amend and had been amended only once before, it was now amended in a very hasty process in order to incorporate the balanced budget rule. The symbolic force of constitutional amendment, and a very quick one, was intended as a message to the international markets.[86] The balanced budget rule was also introduced into the

[78] See, for example, the Report on Bulgaria prepared by M. Vatsov; the Report on France prepared by R. Gadbled and D. Fromage; the Report on Malta prepared by M. Kroeger.

[79] See the Report on Hungary prepared by D. Dojcsák; the Report on Latvia prepared by Z. Rasnaca.

[80] See the Report on the Netherlands prepared by J. Mulder.

[81] See the Report on the Czech Republic prepared by T. Dumbrovsky.

[82] For example, the French, Estonian and Hungarian constitutions already contained variation of a balanced budget rule. See the Report on France prepared by R. Gadbled and D. Fromage; the Report on Estonia prepared by M. Laatsit; the Report on Hungary prepared by D. Dojcsák. For Italy, the rule was recognised in the constitutional jurisprudence. See T. Groppi et al., 'The Constitutional Consequences of the Financial Crisis in Italy', in X. Contiades (ed.), *Constitutions in the Global Financial Crisis: A Comparative Analysis* (Farnham: Ashgate, 2013), pp. 89–113, at pp. 96–99.

[83] The Report on Greece prepared by A. Marketou and M. Dekastros.

[84] See the Report on Belgium prepared by W. Vandenbruwaene.

[85] See Contiades and Fotiadou (2012) especially at pp. 23, 28–30 and 47–48.

[86] See A. Ruiz Robledo, The Spanish Constitution in the Turmoil of the Global Financial Crisis, in Contiades (ed.), *Constitutions in the Global Financial Crisis: A Comparative Analysis*, pp. 141–65 at 158–63.

1948 Italian Constitution through a fast-track procedure. This reform of the Italian Constitution has been notable for the consensus it demonstrates in a country which is otherwise characterised by polarised political elites, thus demonstrating constitutional adaptation in the face of the crisis.[87] In both countries, there seems to have been discussion on the extent to which the constitutional law doctrine would have included such a rule, even before its formal introduction through the new amendments, and the pre-existing doctrine can be expected to have contributed to their easier adoption.[88]

The incorporating acts of the Fiscal Compact demonstrate great variation in how its contents are understood. In some Member States it was seen to introduce significant and new obligations, while in others, for example in Finland, the Fiscal Compact was not considered to establish any significant new competences at the European level.[89] The substantive implementation of the Fiscal Compact also shows a great variation: many nationally implemented balanced budget rules actually seem to be – as black letter law – rather weak ones. Almost all the national implementation laws have incorporated the Fiscal Compact exceptions, allowing deviations in emergency situations which then increases discretion in implementing them. Likewise, there seems to be a great deal of variation in the ways in which the balanced budget rule covers different levels of government in the Member States. It is not evident that the national implementation measures of the Fiscal Compact always live up to the key criteria relating to the design of fiscal rules in being well-defined, encompassing all levels of government, strictly binding and fully enforceable. Additionally, the ECB has voiced concern that the implementation measures of the Fiscal Compact and the budgetary framework directive include clear loopholes, providing generous escape clauses and a correction mechanism that is not quite as automatic as it should be.[90] However, a relevant question is whether it is realistic to speak of automatic mechanisms in a policy area where every calculation presumes interpretation and uncertainty.

[87] Groppi et al., 'The Constitutional Consequences of the Financial Crisis in Italy', 94–6. See also Fabbrini 'The Fiscal Compact, the "Golden Rule", and the Paradox of European Federalism'.

[88] See Contiades and Fotiadou, 'How Constitutions Reacted to the Financial Crisis', pp. 23, 28–30 and 47–48.

[89] See P. Leino and J. Salminen, 'The Euro Crisis and Its Constitutional Consequences for Finland: Is There Room for National Politics in EU Decision-Making?', *European Constitutional Law Review*, 9(3), 2013, 451–79.

[90] See European Central Bank, 'The importance and effectiveness of national fiscal frameworks in the EU'.

3 The Impact of Economic Governance and the Issue of Discretion: Three Case Studies

As a consequence of the Six Pack and Two Pack reforms, the EU surveillance mechanisms have received a more formal structure and cover a broader area in a more detailed manner than before. As a result, detailed and enforceable budgetary and economic surveillance increasingly extends beyond the imposition of objectives, to requiring particular reforms to achieve those objectives.[91] In the following, we present three case studies with the purpose of discussing the impact of the governance framework on three different euro area Member States and the use of discretion and degree of conditionality that application of the framework implies.

A. *Finland*

The Finnish example is of interest because it demonstrates how flexibly many of the key criteria can be interpreted by adding new factors to be considered and how difficult it is to realise many Country Specific Recommendations within the expected time frame of a year. During the Six Pack and Two Pack negotiations, the Finnish economy was still in relatively good shape and problems in the distant corners of Europe were not really seen to involve it, other than in the capacity of a creditor, putting it in a position to make demands of others.[92] The amendments made to national legislation as a consequence of the EU reforms have been limited. Since it would have been difficult to introduce the Fiscal Compact rules into the Constitution of Finland, the correction mechanism is based on ordinary, parliamentary legislation and is built on duties of reporting and informing between the Government and the Parliament at three successive stages depending on the Union reaction.[93] The legislation underlines the responsibilities of the Government under the basic doctrines of parliamentary democracy and the prerogatives of the Parliament in the area of budgetary powers. However, the correction

[91] A. Hinarejos, 'Fiscal Federalism in the European Union: Evolution and Future Choices for EMU', *Common Market Law Review*, 50(6), 2013, 1621–42, at 1631.

[92] See, for detailed discussion, Leino and Salminen, 'Should the Economic and Monetary Union Be Democratic After All?'.

[93] Ibid.

mechanism is far from being automatically activated.[94] The choices may be understood as reflecting an understanding that there would not be a serious need for these mechanisms; after all, the economy was in good shape. However, the situation has changed rapidly due to many separate factors such as a long economic downturn, loss of significant industry and the sanctions against Russian, together with the difficulties encountered when pressing through vital structural reforms.

Finland has so far not been subject to procedures, but the need to initiate one has been under consideration several times. An EDP was opened for Finland in 2010 due to an expected breach of the deficit benchmark. However, the actual figures showed that the deficit was under 3 per cent and the EDP decision was abrogated. The Commission has assessed fulfilment of the debt criterion in Finland in March 2013, May 2014 and February 2015. Its reports concluded that Finland was in compliance with the debt criterion even though the 60 per cent reference value would be exceeded in 2015. This was, however, deemed acceptable with reference to Finland's participation in various solidarity operations on the one hand and the difficult cyclical position on the other. After all, Regulation (EC) No. 1467/97, as amended by the Six Pack places the Commission under an obligation to:

> give due and express consideration to any other factors which, in the opinion of the Member State concerned, are relevant in order to comprehensively assess compliance with deficit and debt criteria.[95]

Needless to say, this provision introduces a strong discretionary element to the evaluation. The fact that Finland would most likely breach the debt rule in 2015 was also highlighted by the National Audit Office, which independently monitors and evaluates fiscal policy for Fiscal Compact purposes. In 2014, it stressed that the observance of the deficit objective would not alone ensure that government debt would remain within the limits of the SGP.[96]

[94] In fact, it remains to be seen whether this manner of implementation fulfils the criteria of the Fiscal Compact. See the Report on Finland prepared by P. Leino-Sandberg and J. Salminen and ibid., 474.

[95] See Regulation (EC) No. 1467/97, Art. 3(3).

[96] See National Audit Office of Finland, 'Fiscal Policy Audit and Monitoring Report on the 2011–2014 Parliamentary Term', R 20/2014 vp (16 December 2014), www.vtv.fi/files/5022/R_202014_vp_National_Audit_O_ffice_s_Fiscal_Policy_Audit_and_Monitoring_Report_on_the_2011_2014_Parliamentary_Term.pdf.

In spring 2015 it became apparent that the Finnish budgetary deficit had exceeded the benchmark of 3 per cent in 2014 and would continue to be in excess also in the years ahead. The Commission's report of May 2015 concluded that Finland was in breach of both the deficit and the debt criterion.[97] This coincided with parliamentary elections and the writing of the new Government Programme. The Commission reassessed the situation after completion of the new Government Programme and considered that the full implementation of the adjustment measures envisaged in the Government Programme would be adequate to push the deficit below 3 per cent in 2016. Hence, the Commission argued that the deficit criterion could be deemed to be fulfilled. According to the Commission, the excess over the 3 per cent of GDP reference value could be considered close and temporary, so that the excess over the reference value could be qualified as 'exceptional'. All relevant factors considered, the conclusion could be drawn that the deficit criterion 'should be considered as currently complied with'. As regards the debt criterion, the Report argued that while the planned breach of the debt criterion could be fully explained by Finland's financial contribution to safeguarding financial stability in the euro area in 2015, this would no longer be the case in 2016. While the debt ratio reflects the effects of Finland's current cyclical position, this factor could not, by itself, explain the excess over the 60 per cent of GDP reference value in 2016. However, based on other relevant factors, Finland could be expected to broadly comply with the required adjustment path towards the medium-term objective in 2015 and 2016, which should help ensure that debt decreases at a sufficient pace in the medium term. On this basis, the Commission argued, even the debt criterion should be considered as currently complied with. However, the Commission urged Finland to adopt pension and other structural reforms increasing productivity and supply of labour.[98] The same matters have frequently figured in the Country

[97] European Commission, 'Report from the Commission, Finland, Report prepared in accordance with Article 126(3) of the Treaty', COM (2015) 246 final (13 May 2015), http://ec.europa.eu/transparency/regdoc/rep/1/2015/EN/1-2015-246-EN-F1-1.PDF. See also European Commission, 'Country Report Finland 2015: Including an In-Depth review on the prevention and correction of macroeconomic imbalances', SWD (2015) 45 final (26 February 2015) http://ec.europa.eu/europe2020/pdf/csr2015/cr2015_finland_en.pdf.

[98] European Commission, 'Finland', COM (2015) 803 final (16 November 2015), http://ec.europa.eu/economy_finance/economic_governance/sgp/pdf/30_edps/126-03_commission/2015-11-16_fi_126-3_en.pdf.

Specific Recommendations and proved difficult to achieve.[99] However, many of these reforms have proved painful to negotiate and have not advanced within the time frame envisaged in the Government Programme.

In its report on fiscal policy monitoring to the 2015 Parliament, the National Audit Office stated that compliance with the fiscal rules embedded in the preventive arm of the SGP and the processes under the SGP had not ensured that Finland could meet the EU Treaties' general government reference values. The Report also points out that the flexibility elements of the SGP that can be invoked in a prolonged economic downturn might entail, in practice, that compliance with the preventive arm will not guarantee compliance with the corrective arm.[100] While the EU framework may be considered to have some impact on national discussions, since politicians including the Prime Minister have publicly justified the need for structural reforms with the wish to avoid closer scrutiny by the Commission and the International Monetary Fund (IMF), the Finnish example demonstrates how structural reforms are still a matter for the national political process, in which the impact of external factors is secondary to national political considerations. The reactions of the Commission demonstrate that this is a fact that it is prepared to accept.

B. France

The French example also demonstrates the difficulties of the Commission to enforce the rules on a large Member State that, even more clearly than Finland, has persistently breached the rules. The French debate stressed the role of France in proposing the golden rule to be introduced in national legislation.[101] However, instead of an actual constitutional amendment, reform at the level of the so-called organic laws, *lois organique*, is used. As the balanced budget rule belonged to the program of the French conservative party, the changes in the government after the election of 2012 have ensured the end of any prospect of constitutional

99 For example, in 2014 Finland received a number of recommendations relating to sound public finances, administrative reforms relating to the structure of municipalities and social and healthcare services, the labour market, competition and labour market segmentation. See Council Recommendation of 8 July 2014 on the National Reform Programme 2014 of Finland and delivering a Council opinion on the Stability Programme of Finland, 2014 (OJ C 247, 29.7.2014, p. 127).

100 National Audit Office of Finland, 'National Audit Office's Separate Report to Parliament: Fiscal Policy Monitoring Report 2015', R 17/2015 vp (8 September 2015).

101 See the Report on France prepared by Gadbled and Fromage.

reform and the *Conseil Constitutionnel* has established that a constitutional amendment was not, in any case, necessary to comply with the requirements of the Fiscal Compact.[102] Nevertheless, following a constitutional amendment in 2008, Article 34 of the Constitution already provided an "objective of a balanced budget".

With France, the key consideration relates to the implementation of the EDP procedure. Its example demonstrates how, in practice, instead of using sanctions, Member States have been given a more flexible time frame for addressing the observed problems; something that has not always contributed to overcoming them. The Council Decision establishing an excessive deficit was adopted in April 2009.[103] The same year the Council recommended that the French authorities should put an end to the excessive deficit situation by 2013.[104] The deadline for correcting it has been extended numerous times. Regulation (EC) No. 1467/97, as amended by the Six Pack, makes express provision for the possibility to extend a deadline for the correction of the excessive deficit, but establishes 'one year as a rule',[105] while France has received the extension several times and also for significantly longer periods of time.

France was requested to present an economic partnership programme by 1 October 2013.[106] However, the Council argued the measures presented in the partnership programme 'will be insufficient to address fiscal and structural imbalances and little detail on planned reforms to further respond to the Council Recommendation of 9 July 2013 has been provided'. Subsequently, the Council recommended a number of swift measures and concluded that the Commission and the Council would monitor the implementation of the reforms in the context of the European Semester.[107] The latest Country Report demonstrates that

[102] Conseil Constitutionel decision no. 2012-653 DC, 9 August 2012. See ibid. for discussion, as well as Chapter 10 in this book, 'Legitimacy through Adjudication: The ESM Treaty and the Fiscal Compact before the National Courts' by Jan-Herman Reestman.

[103] Council Decision of 27 April 2009 on the existence of an excessive deficit in France (2009/414/EC) (OJ L 135, 30.5.2009, p. 19).

[104] Council Recommendation to France with a view to bringing an end to the situation of an excessive government deficit, Council Doc. 15762/09 (30 November 2009), http://ec.europa.eu/economy_finance/economic_governance/sgp/pdf/30_edps/104-07_council/2009-12-02_fr_126-7_council_en.pdf.

[105] Council Regulation (EC) No. 1467/97, Art. 3(5).

[106] See Regulation (EU) No. 473/2013, Art. 9(4) and the Council Opinion on the Economic Partnership Programme of France (2013/C 368/02).

[107] Council Opinion of 10 December 2013 on the Economic Partnership Programme of France (2013/C 368/02) (OJ C 368, 17.12.2013, p. 4).

France has made only limited progress in addressing its 2014 Country Specific Recommendations.[108]

In October 2014, questions relating to institutional powers under the EDP, discretion and scrupulous budget discipline re-surfaced as the media reported on the possibility that the Commission might, under Regulation (EU) No. 473/2013, ask France to amend its 2015 budget draft and submit a new one that would better reflect the French deficit reduction obligations in the EDP.[109] France had been given a two-year extension in 2013. In September 2014, the French Government announced that it would not meet the 2015 deadline and that its budget deficit would only fall below 3 per cent in 2017, with a debt level estimated at 95.6 per cent GDP for 2014 and 96.6 per cent GDP for 2015.[110] After discussions with the French government, the Commission announced that it had found no instances of 'particularly serious non-compliance'.[111] The current deadline expires in 2017. At the same time, the Commission Economic Forecasts foresee the French public debt-to-GDP ratio increasing further, albeit at a slower pace, to 97.1 per cent of GDP in 2017.[112] Therefore, it is evident that the impact of the new rules has been limited and further diminished by the repeated decisions to allow France more time to bring its policies in line with the EU budgetary rules. The French case also illustrates that despite attempts to depoliticise and automatise the application of the SGP, this remains highly political in practice.

C. *Portugal*

The Portuguese example offers a study of a country which – in addition to being subject to the general framework of economic governance (even

[108] European Commission, 'Country Report France 2015: Including an In-Depth Review on the Prevention and Correction of Macroeconomic Imbalances, SWD (2015) 29 final (26 February 2015), http://ec.europa.eu/europe2020/pdf/csr2015/cr2015_france_en.pdf.

[109] See Regulation (EU) No. 473/2013, Art. 7. See also R. Gadblad, 'Brussels, French Politics and the 'Macron' Law' (31 March 2015), http://eurocrisislaw.eui.eu/news/brussels-french-politics-and-the-macron-law-by-robin-gadblad/ .

[110] See the Commission European Economic Forecast Spring 2014, available at http://ec.europa.eu/economy_finance/publications/european_economy/2014/pdf/ee3_en.pdf.

[111] See Commission Vice-President Jyrki Katainen, 'Statement on the Draft Budgetary Plans' (29 October 2014), http://europa.eu/rapid/press-release_STATEMENT-14-344_en.htm.

[112] See European Commission, 'European Economic Forecast, Winter 2016', Institutional Paper 020, February 2016, http://ec.europa.eu/economy_finance/publications/eeip/pdf/ip020_en.pdf.

though only to a more limited extent since it is a programme country and as such subject to particular surveillance) – has also been under programme conditions. Thus, the Portuguese example offers additional avenues for an examination of the impact of EU measures through conditionality, to which Finland and France have not been subject. After all, the whole governance framework now builds on the idea that the degree of your national discretion depends on your fiscal health. In the basic divide created by the euro crisis, Portugal is a debtor. At the same time, its example demonstrates the difficulties involved in enforcing a reform agenda that has been largely imposed from the outside but depends on implementation at the national level. Even when a sufficient majority could be found in the Parliament to adopt the necessary legislative reforms, these have been challenged before the Constitutional Court, which has blocked them as being contrary to the Portuguese Constitution.[113]

The Portuguese Government supported the adoption of the Fiscal Compact. Portugal was also among the first countries to ratify the Treaty, which was implemented through incorporation in the budgetary framework law, which is an organic law and prevails over ordinary laws. In addition, the Portuguese Constitution enshrines a certain idea concerning the balanced budget rule.

Portugal was subject to an EDP procedure in 2005–8. The current EDP procedure has been ongoing since 2009,[114] but, between May 2011 and June 2014, Portugal also received support from an economic adjustment programme, which involved surveillance of imbalances and monitoring of corrective means.[115] These procedures are separated from the general coordination framework and linked to the broad conditionality framework relating to the stability mechanisms. An Economic Adjustment Programme was negotiated in May 2011 between Portugal and the

[113] Relating to reforms in the area of labour law, see the rulings of the Portuguese Constitutional Court in Judgments 353/2012, 5 July 2012; 187/2013, 5 April 2013; 474/2013, 29 August 2013; Judgment 602/2013, 20 September 2013; 794/2013, 21 November 2013; 862/2013, 19 December 2013 and 413/2014, 30 May 2014. These decisions and the jurisprudence of the Portuguese Constitutional Court are discussed in detail by Claire Kilpatrick in this book in Chapter 11 'Constitutions, Social Rights and Sovereign Debt States in Europe: A Challenging New Area of Constitutional Inquiry'.

[114] Council Decision of 19 January 2010 on the existence of an excessive deficit in Portugal (2010/288/EU) (OJ L, 21.5.2010, p. 44).

[115] Council Implementing Decision on granting Union financial assistance to Portugal (2011/344/EU) (OJ L 159, 17.6.2011, p. 88).

Commission, the ECB and the IMF, and formally adopted in May 2011 at a Eurogroup/ECOFIN meeting in Brussels. The Memorandum of Understanding (MoU) and the Loan Agreement were signed thereafter. Many of the implementing decisions adopted by the Council relating to the granting of aid have entailed deep guidance of its economic policy choices, since Council implementing decisions have been used to place Portugal under a set of incredibly detailed obligations reaching into most areas of society, based on the 'Two Pack' legislation combined with the requirements of the stability mechanisms.[116] These implementing decisions have continued to take stock of progress and to guide the reform processes underway in Portugal, specifying the measures to adopt 'in line with specifications in the Memorandum of Understanding'.[117] The relevant question becomes whether such requirements relating to macroeconomic assistance programmes can be justified under the multilateral surveillance procedure that it is formally built on.

As in many crisis countries, the role of the Constitutional Court has become central. The Portuguese Constitutional Court has built on its earlier jurisprudence, which illustrates the Court's own role as a guarantor of the democratic state and the need to set limits on the political institutions, or even to sanction (sometimes disputably and not always in cooperation with the legislator) the action of political institutions whenever they have overstepped the constitutional limits set in the case law.[118] Constitutional judgments on euro-crisis law in Portugal have concerned a more weighted balancing between social rights, financial resources, legitimate expectations and, as in all crisis countries, the pre-eminence of constitutional principles in the constitutional adjudication of rights.[119] But also the Court of Justice has delivered preliminary rulings regarding the compatibility of Portuguese national legislation to cut holiday and Christmas pay with the Charter of Fundamental Rights. The preliminary rulings predated the Two Pack and the Court of Justice was not

[116] Ibid.

[117] See Council Implementing Decision 2014/234/EU of 23 April 2014 amending Implementing Decision 2011/344/EU on granting Union financial assistance to Portugal (OJ L 125, 26.4.2014, p. 75).

[118] See in this book Chapter 11 'Constitutions, Social Rights and Sovereign Debt States in Europe: A Challenging New Area of Constitutional Inquiry' by Claire Kilpatrick for further discussion.

[119] See for a deep, comparative analysis, C. Fasone, 'Constitutional Courts Facing the Euro Crisis. Italy, Portugal and Spain in a Comparative Perspective', EUI Working Paper, MWP 2014/25 (2014), http://cadmus.eui.eu/handle/1814/33859.

convinced that the requests for a ruling indicated concrete factors demonstrating that the national legislation aimed at implementing Union law.[120] This illustrates how difficult it is to challenge euro-crisis measures affecting programme countries in the Court of Justice.[121]

Portugal exited its Economic Adjustment Programme in June 2014 and is now under post-Programme Surveillance (PPS) until at least 75 per cent of the financial assistance has been repaid. Under the PPS, the Commission, together with the ECB, continue to organise regular review missions and make semi-annual assessments, which may recommend further measures. The latest country report demonstrates that while Portugal has made some progress in addressing its Country Specific Recommendations, many of the recommendations remain partly or wholly unaddressed.[122] The Commission alerts that despite significant progress during the programme, Portugal is experiencing excessive macroeconomic imbalances, which require decisive policy action and specific monitoring.[123] The debt level continues to be high: from 130.2 per cent at the end of 2014, the gross public debt-to-GDP ratio is expected to have only slightly fallen to 129.1 per cent by year-end 2015. The Commission expects the ratio to fall only slightly, to 128.5 per cent, in 2016 and more pronouncedly in 2017, to 127.2 per cent.[124]

D. *Evaluation*

The case studies discussed above demonstrate several issues. First, externally imposed reforms are most efficiently undertaken, and Member State discretion in economic policy-making most limited, when economic hardship is so deep that the State relies on external funding and

[120] See the Order of the Court in *Sindicato dos Bancários do Norte* v. *BNP – Banco Português de Negócios SA* Case C-128/12 and in *Sindicato Nacional dos Profissionais de Seguros e Afins* v. *Fidelidade Mundial – Companhia de Seguros SA* Case C-264/12.

[121] See, for example, *Ledra Advertising Ltd v. Commission and the ECB*, Case T-289/13 and *Konstantinos Mallis and Elli KOnstantinou Malli* v. *Commission* v. *the ECB* Case T-327/13.

[122] European Commission, 'Country Report Portugal 2015: Including an In-Depth Review on the Prevention and Correction of Macroeconomic Imbalances', SWD (2015) 41 final (26 February 2015), http://ec.europa.eu/europe2020/pdf/csr2015/cr2015_portugal_en.pdf.

[123] European Commission, '2015 European Semester: Assessment of growth challenges, prevention and correction of macroeconomic imbalances, and results of in-depth reviews under Regulation (EU) No. 1176/2011', COM (2015) 85 final (26 February 2015), http://ec.europa.eu/europe2020/pdf/csr2015/cr2015_comm_en.pdf.

[124] See European Commission, 'European Economic Forecast, Winter 2016'.

is subject to conditionality. Second, while the key procedures have been specified further in secondary legislation and various soft law documents, their implementation still presumes a great deal of discretion. The amount of soft law, consisting of guidelines, recommendations and codes of conduct in the area of economic governance, is striking, and much use of it has been made, for example, in the Finnish and French cases discussed above. A key example of soft law used in this context is the application manual called the Vade Mecum intended to explain how the Commission applies the rules of the Stability and Growth Pact,[125] another is the Commission's 2015 Communication on 'Making the best use of the flexibility within the existing rules of the Stability and Growth Pact',[126] which builds on the invitation by the European Council to make 'best use of the flexibility that is built into the existing Stability and Growth Pact rules'.[127] This interpretative Communication was intended to provide additional guidance 'without changing or replacing the existing rules'. Soft law of this kind has been deemed necessary, in particular, by the Member States, in order to limit the discretion of the Commission and ensure equal treatment. At the same time, it contributes to the further complexity of the framework and its lack of transparency, since it is difficult to predict how a rule will be applied in an individual case. Under economic governance, the adoption of reports and recommendations often falls under Commission discretion. The methodologies used for evaluating successful measures are complex and the evaluations have proved difficult to predict or repeat.[128] Even the concept of 'structural deficit', which forms the core of the preventive arm of the SGP, is difficult to measure and includes a great risk of error. This also stresses the risk of incorrect policy recommendations. Such a wide room for discretion in the exercise of administrative power in a key policy area and with it, even a possibility to misuse the power, raises obvious questions relating to political accountability. As Dawson has found, we

[125] European Commission, 'Vade Mecum on the Stability and Growth Pact' (2016 edition), European Economy, Institutional Paper 021 (March 2016), http://ec.europa.eu/economy_finance/publications/eeip/pdf/ip021_en.pdf.

[126] European Commission, 'Making the Best Use of the Flexibility within the Existing Rules of the Stability and Growth Pact', COM (2015) 12 final (13 January 2015), http://eur-lex.europa.eu/legal-content/EN/TXT/PDF/?uri=CELEX:52015DC0012&from=EN.

[127] European Council, 'Conclusions of 26/27 June 2014', EUCO 79/14 (27 June 2014), www.consilium.europa.eu/uedocs/cms_data/docs/pressdata/en/ec/143478.pdf.

[128] On the scope of Commission discretion, see Henriksson and Leino-Sandberg, 'Talouspolitiikan koordinaatio EU:ssa: lohduton labyrintti vai tie talouspoliittiseen täyttymykseen?'.

now experience a discretionary system that lacks clearly delineated rules, which makes it difficult if not impossible to scrutinise whether they have been applied 'correctly'.[129]

If used to the maximum, the current mechanisms would certainly come close to the 'red lines' of the exercise of competence in economic policy, as stipulated by the German Constitutional Court, for example. However, in practice, many of the relevant procedures have remained in reserve and their key function has been to operate as a deterrent. No decisions have been taken by reversed qualified majority and no sanctions adopted. This demonstrates the political difficulties in the Commission and the Council when applying the new powers and questions their usefulness and added credibility. Instead, another methodology has been discovered, enabling the Commission to carry out new calculations, which have then enabled the possibility of granting the concerned Member States more time to carry out the necessary reforms.

In its 2014 Six Pack and Two Pack review, the Commission evaluated that 'the current rules are effective and generally operate to satisfaction'. This is justified with reference to how:

> [t]he various pieces of governance legislation have been at the core of this evolution and have significantly bolstered the existing governance setup. Overall, deficits have declined with many countries having exited the Excessive Deficit Procedure and imbalances are being corrected.[130]

Others point out that the framework has increased the number of indicators and the complexity of procedures, which is an odd combination of rules and principles.[131] In June 2014, the IMF published a Selected Issues Paper[132] arguing that while the recent reforms have introduced many positive elements to the framework, a number of problems persist. In particular, the new rules have not prevented a steady deterioration in public accounts:

[129] Dawson, 'The Legal and Political Accountability Structure of "Post-Crisis" EU Economic Governance'.

[130] European Commission, 'Communication of the Commission, Economic Governance Review, Report on the Application of Regulations (EU) No. 1173/2011, 1174/2011, 1175/2011, 1176/2011, 1177/2011, 472/2013 and 473/20131. 28.11.2014', COM (2014) 905 final (28 November 2014), http://register.consilium.europa.eu/doc/srv?l=EN&f=ST%2016236%202014%20INIT.

[131] On this, see K. Tuori and K. Tuori, *The Eurozone Crisis: A Constitutional Analysis* (Cambridge University Press, 2014).

[132] International Monetary Fund. 'Euro Area Policies'. 2014 Art. IV Consultation, IMF Country Report No. 14/199 (26 June 2014), www.imf.org/external/pubs/ft/scr/2014/cr14199.pdf.

> Under the SGP, noncompliance has been the rule rather than the exception. Currently, nearly all euro area economies have breached at least one of the fiscal rules.[133]

As far as the design of the framework is concerned, the IMF refers to the growing complexity of the system and the incomplete separation of powers. In its assessment, this contributes to rule design problems and governance failures, which in turn may have contributed to poor enforcement of the SGP. The EDP may have contributed to a certain stabilisation of Member State economies. Debt levels in some individual Member States are approaching dangerously high levels. This contributes to a low level of confidence in the existing enforcement mechanisms embedded in the SGP.[134] This is problematic, keeping in mind the original ambition of the framework of economic governance, which related specifically to the need to create trust and peer pressure.

Constitutional or other legislative amendments will not alone guarantee more effective implementation of budget rules. Domestic legal effects depend on various institutional features and government structures. The key consideration relating to the requirements of the Fiscal Compact concerns how particular provisions serve their function in a particular Member State. In a system that is based on the implementation of the balanced budget rule, there is an expectation that the executives propose and parliaments ultimately approve annual budget laws that are either at a surplus or on balance or have a deficit that does not exceed the limits set by the Fiscal Compact. At the political-cultural level, this might have an impact on the budgetary policies of various EU Member States.[135] After all, governments that propose heavy budget cuts are seldom in power after the next general election. From a constitutional point of view, the Spanish and Italian developments are of particular interest. They have introduced strong constitutional rules in this field. However, in the Commission European Economic Forecast Winter 2016, Spanish debt continues to circle at around 101 per cent in 2016–7. While Italy is not subject to an EDP procedure, its debt is evaluated at 132.4 per cent in

[133] Ibid., pp. 93ff.

[134] See C. Allard et al., 'Toward a Fiscal Union for the Euro Area', IMF Staff Discussion Note 13/09 (September 2013), www.imf.org/external/pubs/ft/sdn/2013/sdn1309.pdf, p. 11.

[135] Fabbrini, 'The Fiscal Compact, the "Golden Rule", and the Paradox of European Federalism', 19; K. Lenaerts, 'EMU and the European Union's Constitutional Framework', *European Law Review*, 39, 2014, pp. 753–69, 765–6; Salminen, 'Sopimus talous- ja rahaliiton vakaudesta – Tie fiskaaliunioniin', 1094–6.

2016 and 130.6 per cent in 2017. These figures illustrate how in Europe 'speaking German' is not necessarily 'acting German'.[136] The new national budgetary provisions also illustrate the effect of these rules on institutional politics, since they contribute to strengthening the position of some national institutions against other institutions. These effects are also context-specific. Besides cultural factors, the role of national parliaments varies greatly. Some of them are real decision-makers in the budgetary processes while some are clearly ex-post supervisors of the government. For example, in the Italian political-constitutional context the rule may give the government new means to force Parliament to vote in a particular way, as far as the budget is concerned.[137] The balanced budget rule could have either empowering or constraining effects on the executive branches in the German and Spanish political-constitutional setting. In the context of semi-presidential France, the balanced budget rule might, instead of strengthening the position of the executive, provide instruments for parliamentary opposition.[138] In addition, the existence of a constitutional balanced budget rule makes the provision justiciable in some Member States. This strengthens the role of courts as the guardians and controllers of fiscal discipline, and the position of the national Constitutional Courts, assuming that they enjoy jurisdiction based on the golden rule.[139] Even if the central role of courts in interpreting loose provisions is in some ways a traditional solution in the EU constitutional framework, the relevant question should be whether it is appropriate that key decisions on economic policy are pushed to the courts – the Portuguese discussion is a good example of this.

4 Conclusions: Towards More National and Fewer but Credible European Rules

The new framework for economic governance can be seen as a balancing exercise between risk assessment and risk management, with the Commission assessing domestic performance and the Council taking formal

[136] Besselink and Reestman, 'Editorial: The Fiscal Compact and the European Constitutions: "Europe speaking German"'.

[137] Fabbrini, 'The Fiscal Compact, the "Golden Rule", and the Paradox of European Federalism', 20.

[138] Ibid., 21. [139] Ibid., 18–22.

decisions based on its assessments.[140] However, framing economic governance as a regulatory process is not honest: it is 'political in economy terms, namely that it is a significant part of the process for organising a State's economy and budget'.[141] Economic policies involve numerous national sensitivities closely related with the sovereignty of Member States. The EU institutions, in particular the Commission, would at least, to a certain extent, benefit from clear rules that would be easy to enforce in a politically challenging situation. However, the more detailed the rules become, the more problematic they become from the point of view of EU competence. Ambiguity has in many ways been intentional, but it also contributes to blurring responsibilities between the EU and national level. But economic governance also highlights many fundamental questions relating to power. The power to take economic policy decisions seems to be something many players are keen to possess, but – when things get rough – it turns into power that many feel reluctant to use and would gladly see the responsibility for taking difficult decisions redirected somewhere else. The importance of these questions is stressed by how many of these decisions are based on uncertain facts and are made without a clear knowledge of the outcome. Responsibility for decisions also involves responsibility for possible policy mistakes.

The Commission has proposed solving many of these challenges by suggesting a move towards a fully fledged fiscal union, which would also presume some fundamental Treaty changes amending the division of competence between the EU and its Member States and reformulating the nature of EU competence in economic policy.[142] Establishing a framework of stricter coordination and governance within EMU is widely seen as a cornerstone on which systems of risk-sharing and joint liability between Member States can be built. In particular, Mario Draghi, President of the ECB, has repeatedly stressed the case for the joint exercise of sovereignty over relevant economic policies, involving in particular structural reforms. For Draghi, this should in the longer-term also involve a shift 'from coordination to common decision-making, and from rules to institutions', both of which are to have a binding nature,

[140] Chalmers, 'The European Redistributive State and a European Law of Struggle'.

[141] Ibid., 691.

[142] European Commission, 'Communication from the Commission: A Blueprint for a Deep and Genuine Economic and Monetary Union, Launching a European Debate', COM (2012) 777 final (30 November 2012), http://ec.europa.eu/archives/commission_2010-2014/president/news/archives/2012/11/pdf/blueprint_en.pdf.

justified not only with economic arguments, but also how 'sharing a single currency *is* political union'.[143] The 'Five Presidents' Report' argues for an increased sharing of decision-making and a shift from a system of rules and guidelines for national economic policy-making to a system of further sovereignty sharing within common institutions, including on issues relating to their national budgets and economic policies.

However, the 'Five Presidents' Report' does not discuss how a further strengthening of EU powers might overcome the problems that the Commission already experiences in applying its current powers. Serious question marks exist as to whether the most fundamental fault is with the current rules, their implementation or their background assumptions. Scharpf's well-known thesis builds on a distinction between democratic input legitimacy and result-based legitimacy, originating in its performance and delivery.[144] While democracy still only exists at the national level, Scharpf argues that European competencies need to be narrowly construed and continue to depend on the agreement of democratically accountable national governments in the Council.[145] While the EU can legitimately act on questions that involve a range of common interests that are sufficiently broad and stable to justify common actions,[146] EU-level decisions cannot legitimately deal with highly controversial issues or with problems that require zero-sum redistribution: 'the success of positive integration depends mainly on the ability of European policy makers to identify solutions that will not provoke massive opposition'.[147] The fundamental lesson for the current contribution is that the EU 'will not be capable of positive action on issues where national governments, and the interests they represent, are in conflict'.[148] These theoretical dimensions seem to be supported by the findings of our three case studies. EU rules are difficult to enforce when the Member State concerned feels that they entail unreasonably tight economic policy choices. That time limits are extended, or new soft law documents written in order to find a new interpretation, is a logical consequence of the legitimacy problems Scharpf raises. These problems cannot be resolved by adding more rules.

[143] M. Draghi, 'Stability and Prosperity in Monetary Union', Speech given at the University of Helsinki (27 November 2014), www.ecb.europa.eu/press/key/date/2014/html/sp141127_1.en.html.

[144] F. Scharpf, *Governing in Europe: Effective and Democratic?* (Oxford University Press, 1999).

[145] Ibid., p. 10. [146] Ibid., p. 11. [147] Ibid., pp. 22–4. [148] Ibid., p. 26.

While the institutional thinking is strongly moving towards a further strengthening of EU-level mechanisms, academic commentators are divided on the potential of national mechanisms. Maduro argues that the current problems are already related to too great a reliance on national politics.[149] The creation of Fiscal Councils and correction mechanisms at the national level contribute to a certain overlap between the EU and national levels.[150] Once the national mechanisms are in place and fully functional, they could be used to replace EU coordination to the extent that there are overlaps between the two. It might be worthy of consideration whether national rules enforced by national institutions could have greater potential than externally imposed ones. Others stress that, while the crisis requires European solutions, their success relies on the employment of legitimacy resources of the Member States:[151]

> Solutions will still have to be Europe-wide, but they will not be ideated, designed and crafted using the classical 'community method' but will be negotiated and validated by the member states.[152]

In Scharpf's view, the difficulties involved in the current economic governance framework also link to legitimacy considerations and the distrust of European policy-makers for democratically accountable national governments and parliaments as regards their ability to adopt and implement good policies.[153] As a result, mechanisms building on national democratic legitimacy have been undermined, while the European governing functions cannot convincingly rely on their own legitimacy.[154] While (probably) no one seriously suggests getting rid of the EU economic governance framework altogether, the direction should perhaps be towards more national rules and fewer, but more credible, EU rules. The exact formulation of comprehensive and effective rules for

[149] M. Maduro, 'A Governance for the European Union and the Euro: Democracy and the Justice', RSCAS Policy Papers 2012/11 (2012), http://cadmus.eui.eu/handle/1814/24295.

[150] See also Tuori, 'The European Financial Crisis: Constitutional Aspects and Implications', 45 and Lenaerts, 'EMU and the European Union's Constitutional Framework', 757. See, further, in this book Chapter 4, 'Creation and Reform of Independent Fiscal Institutions in EU Member States: Incomplete and Insufficient Work in Progress?' by Diane Fromage.

[151] J. Weiler, 'In the Face of Crisis: Input Legitimacy, Output Legitimacy and the Political Messianism of European Integration', *Journal of European Integration*, 34(7), 825–41, at 826.

[152] Ibid., p. 827.

[153] Scharpf, *Governing in Europe: Effective and Democratic?*, p. 24.

[154] Ibid., p. 26.

fiscal policy could be left to the Member States, building on the Directive 2011/85/EU, and covering the whole of general government with all of its subsectors. They should guarantee the Union's reference value for public debt while being flexible to different means of stabilisation and sustainability of the economy.[155] This kind of system might have greater potential for legitimacy, which is important also from an economic point of view.[156] After all, a policy that is not broadly experienced as legitimate is unlikely to have a great impact.

[155] These could consist of a fiscal policy benchmark of the Union for a Member State's general government debt-to-GDP ratio and debt reduction for a period assessed to go beyond the business cycle, e.g. five years. See Ministry of Finance of Finland, 'Improving the Resilience of Europe's Economic and Monetary Union', Economic Policy 37b/2015 (18 September 2015), vm.fi/dms-portlet/document/0/399130.

[156] On this, see P. Leino, 'Further Development of the EMU – Should Legitimacy Come First or Last?', *EU Law Analysis* (1 November 2015), http://eulawanalysis.blogspot.be/2015/11/further-development-of-emu-should.html.

4

Creation and Reform of Independent Fiscal Institutions in EU Member States: Incomplete and Insufficient Work in Progress?

DIANE FROMAGE*

1 Introduction

The Maastricht Treaty marked the creation of the Economic and Monetary Union (EMU) in the European Union (EU) framework. With the aim of preparing for the introduction of the common currency, deficit and debt limits were introduced in the Treaty: up until today, government deficits shall not exceed 3 per cent of GDP while public debt shall remain below 60 per cent. A few years later, in 1997, the Stability and Growth Pact was approved in order to 'strengthen the monitoring and coordination of national fiscal and economic policies to enforce the deficit and debt limits established by the Maastricht Treaty'.[1] Yet, in 2003, both France and Germany failed to respect the limits prescribed by the Pact without being sanctioned. As is well known, this flexibility was one of the factors that led to the still ongoing Eurocrisis. This crisis has evidenced the need to approve stricter measures constraining Member States contained in the 'Six Pack', the 'Two Pack' and the Treaty on Stability, Coordination and Governance (TSCG, or – when referring to Title III of the Treaty – the 'Fiscal Compact'), also generally referred to as 'euro-crisis law'.[2]

* I would like to thank warmly the editors for their insightful comments.

[1] European Commission, 'Stability and Growth Pact', http://ec.europa.eu/economy_finance/economic_governance/sgp/index_en.htm.

[2] See the editors' Introduction to this book as well as Chapter 11, 'Constitutions, Social Rights and Sovereign Debt States in Europe: A Challenging New Area of Constitutional Inquiry' by Claire Kilpatrick for a definition and discussion of the concept of euro-crisis

With these developments, the need for more independent information regarding fiscal and economic data became more pressing and, additionally, more important, as the effects of measures and sanctions imposed by the application of European rules can have dramatic consequences for the Member States, as illustrated by the Greek and Portuguese cases. Perhaps most importantly, the gap between Brussels and the EU Member States had to be reduced in allowing the latter to interiorise these rules as their own.[3]

It is to this end that all EU Member States with the exception of the United Kingdom (UK) have since been requested to create (or reform pre-existing) Independent Fiscal Institutions, or Fiscal Councils. Their task is, generally, to monitor compliance with national fiscal rules, monitor the balanced-budget rule and produce or endorse the macroeconomic forecasts used in annual budgets and medium-term fiscal plans. However, this does not mean that all Independent Fiscal Institutions have to assume all of these competences and their tasks differ among Member States. The Independent Fiscal Institutions' tasks may also go beyond what is entailed by their EU and international obligations and duties and, in fact, their tasks differ among Member States of the EU, as we will see in the present chapter. This may require that they be split into different organisational units.

Actually, although these provisions were introduced recently, the idea of the creation of Independent Fiscal Institutions in EU Member States is by no means new: it had previously been advocated by the Organisation for Economic Cooperation and Development (OECD), the International Monetary Fund (IMF) and the European Central Bank (ECB).[4] This is also part of a broader recent trend towards the generalisation of Independent Fiscal Institutions around the world: their worldwide number has grown sharply over the past 10 years[5] and even the EU itself now has its own Independent Fiscal Institution. Yet this European Fiscal Board (EFB) and Member States' Independent Fiscal Institutions are deemed to fulfil very different functions: the EFB is not meant to monitor the EU's own fiscal policy, but to help the Commission in monitoring the Member States.

law. As a concept, it encompasses EU relevant to the crisis and international agreements entered into by subsets of EU Member States and administered by EU institutions.

[3] European Central Bank, 'Monthly Bulletin June 2014', www.ecb.europa.eu/pub/pdf/mobu/mb201406en.pdf, pp. 95–100.

[4] L. Calmfors and S. Wren-Lewis, 'What Should Fiscal Councils Do?', *Economic Policy*, 26 (68), 2011, 649–95, 652.

[5] X. Debrun and T. Kinda, 'Strengthening Post-Crisis Fiscal Credibility: Fiscal Councils on the Rise – A New Dataset', IMF Working Papers, WP/14/58 (April 2014), pp. 13 and 58.

The deadlines for the implementation of both European and international obligations concerning Independent Fiscal Institutions expired at the end of 2013. Against this background, this chapter aims at examining how Member States have fulfilled their obligations and the consequences for their constitutional orders. This analysis is particularly needed: the implementation process by the Member States has taken numerous forms, has taken several years (in fact it is still ongoing) and has attributed these Independent Fiscal Institutions different powers and tasks. Their relationship with the domestic legislatures is of particular importance. The latter are responsible for ensuring the democratic legitimation of the budgetary procedure, while parliaments' role has been severely restricted by the adoption at EU level of strict rules in this domain.[6]

I argue that, thus far, the potential benefits that Independent Fiscal Institutions could bring for Member States and, in particular, for their national parliaments, as well as for the EMU in general, have not been fully exploited. There does not appear to be a strong political will to remedy these shortcomings; in particular, where the creation of an Independent Fiscal Institution solely responds to EU obligations.[7]

This chapter is organised as follows. It first identifies the obligations of EU Member States in the area of Independent Fiscal Institutions (Section 2). It then examines how Member States have adapted to these new obligations; in particular, as regards the pace of their adaptation, the institutional setting chosen for the creation of their Independent Fiscal Institution and the quality and appointment procedures of their members (Section 3). Following this analysis, though with caution given that many of the Independent Fiscal Institutions have been in operation

[6] The view of marginalisation of parliament is not, however, unanimously supported. See for opposite views: C. Fasone, 'Taking Budgetary Powers Away from National Parliaments?: On Parliamentary Prerogatives in the Eurozone Crisis', EUI Working Paper, LAW 2015/37, http://cadmus.eui.eu/handle/1814/36658, p. 7. See, for further discussion, in this book Chapter 2, 'The European Fiscal Consolidation Legal Framework: Its Impact on National Fiscal Constitutions and Parliamentary Democracy' by Violeta Ruiz Almendral. In addition, the importance of Independent Fiscal Institutions for legislatures has been recognised by the OECD Principles for independent fiscal institutions (see n. 31).

[7] The consequences from an economic perspective remain outside the scope of the present chapter, since it adopts a legal perspective. For studies from an economic perspective see, inter alia, R. Beetsma and X. Debrun, 'Fiscal Councils: Rationale and Effectiveness', CEPR Discussion Paper Series, DP11140 (February 2016), www.cepr.org/active/publications/discussion_papers/dp.php?dpno=11140 and G. Kopits, *Restoring Public Debt Sustainability: The Role of Independent Fiscal Institutions* (Oxford University Press, 2013).

for a very short time, some of the difficulties faced by Independent Fiscal Institutions are underlined (Section 4). Some preliminary conclusions are drawn as to the consequences of their introduction for the constitutional order of the Member States (Section 5). Finally, the concluding remarks contain some indications as to what can be expected in this field in the medium-term and what might be the shortcomings of the current EU and international rules in this field (Section 6).

2 The International and European Legal Framework Regarding Independent Fiscal Institutions: Varying Obligations for Member States

As mentioned, the idea of EU Member States having Independent Fiscal Institutions is not new. However, the obligation was introduced only recently and, in fact, rests upon several EU and international legal provisions which imply the existence of different categories of Member States: euro area Member States, non-euro area Member States bound by the Fiscal Compact, non-euro area Member States not bound by the Fiscal Compact and the UK.

A. *Directive 2011/85/EU and the Need for Fiscal Rules Based on 'Reliable and Independent Analysis'*

As regards the obligations contained in EU documents, they were first laid out as part of the Six Pack of legislation in 2011. According to Article 6(1)(b) of Directive 2011/85/EU on requirements for budgetary frameworks of the Member States, all the Member States' fiscal rules, excluding the UK's, have to be based on 'reliable and independent analysis carried out by independent bodies or bodies endowed with functional autonomy vis-à-vis the fiscal authorities of the Member States'.[8] The features or the prerogatives of these institutions are not further detailed, however.

B. *Regulation (EU) No. 473/2013: Independent Fiscal Institutions' Characteristics and Automatic Correction Mechanism*

Regulation (EU) No. 473/2013 on common provisions for monitoring and assessing draft budgetary plans and ensuring the correction of

[8] Council Directive 2011/85/EU of 8 November 2011 on requirements for budgetary frameworks of the Member States (OJ L 306, 23.11.2011, p. 41)

excessive deficit of the Member States in the euro area,[9] approved as part of the 'Two Pack' of legislation in 2013, provides more information in this regard. Article 2(1)(a) of Regulation (EU) No. 473/2013 defines the Independent Fiscal Institutions' characteristics, in order for their independence to be ensured:

> [they shall be] structurally independent or bodies endowed with functional autonomy vis-à-vis the budgetary authorities of the Member State, and which are underpinned by national legal provisions ensuring a high degree of functional autonomy and accountability, including:
>
> (i) a statutory regime grounded in national laws, regulations or binding administrative provisions;
> (ii) not taking instructions from the budgetary authorities of the Member State concerned or from any other public or private body;
> (iii) the capacity to communicate publicly in a timely manner;
> (iv) procedures for nominating members on the basis of their experience and competence;
> (v) adequate resources and appropriate access to information to carry out their mandate.

A high degree of 'functional autonomy' and accountability must therefore be guaranteed. Note the choice of the terms 'functional autonomy', which implies that this autonomy may not necessarily require full institutional autonomy as well. Rather, it depends on 'the elimination of any political interference, in the sense that such bodies must not "take instructions" and their activity must be marked by an absolute non-partisanship'.[10] As will be illustrated by some examples below, only a minority of the Independent Fiscal Institutions that exist in EU Member States are institutionally independent. In fact, and quite counterintuitively given their functions, many of them are placed under government structures.[11] But these choices for a certain institutional setting may be

[9] Regulation (EU) No. 473/2013 of the European Parliament and of the Council of 21 May 2013 on common provisions for monitoring and assessing draft budgetary plans and ensuring the correction of excessive deficit of the Member States in the euro area (OJ L 140, 27.5.2013, p. 11).

[10] P. Magarò, 'Independent Fiscal Institutions: A Comparative Analysis', *Transylvanian Review of Administrative Sciences*, 9(39), 2013, 66–90, 72.

[11] See, on the relationship between Independent Fiscal Institutions and governments and Independent Fiscal Institutions and parliaments and the need to separate Independent Fiscal Institutions from governments, C. Fasone and E. Griglio, 'Can Fiscal Councils Enhance the Role of National Parliaments in the European Union? A Comparative Analysis' in B. de Witte, A. Héritier and A. Trechsel (eds.), *The Euro Crisis and the State of European Democracy* (European University Institute, 2012), pp. 264–305, 270f.

explained by the fact that 'the design of [the Independent Fiscal Institutions] should take into account the existing institutional setting and the administrative structure of the Member State concerned. In particular, it should be possible to endow a suitable entity of an existing institution with functional autonomy provided that such an entity is designated to carry out specific monitoring tasks, has a distinct statutory regime and complies with the other principles referred to in this recital'.[12] This last point is with no doubt of particular importance: it can be particularly challenging for a brand-new institution to establish its authority. Being attached to, or placed within, a pre-existing institution may contribute to rendering this process smoother and can also be useful in providing a venue and non-specialised staff.

Additionally, Article 5 of Regulation (EU) No. 473/2013 defines the functions that Independent Fiscal Institutions should assume, being in charge of monitoring compliance with numerical fiscal rules incorporating the Member State's medium-term budgetary objective in the national budgetary process. They should also:

> where appropriate, provide public assessments with respect to national fiscal rules, inter alia relating to:
>
> (a) the occurrence of circumstances leading to the activation of the correction mechanism for cases of significant observed deviation from the medium-term objective or the adjustment path towards it . . .;
> (b) whether the budgetary correction is proceeding in accordance with national rules and plans;
> (c) any occurrence or cessation of circumstances referred to in the tenth subparagraph of Article 5(1) of Regulation (EC) No. 1466/97 [i.e. 'unusual event outside the control of the Member State concerned which has a major impact on the financial position of the general government or in periods of severe economic downturn for the euro area or the Union as a whole'] which may allow a temporary deviation from the medium-term budgetary objective or the adjustment path towards it, provided that such a deviation does not endanger fiscal sustainability in the medium term.

The function of Independent Fiscal Institutions in this respect is particularly delicate as the definition provided for these 'exceptional circumstances' is far from straightforward: these 'unusual event[s] outside of the control of the Member State concerned' leave considerable leeway for

[12] Regulation (EU) No. 473/2011, Preamble, para. 17

interpretation. Note, additionally, that Independent Fiscal Institutions can only 'provide public assessments' and in no way limit the Member State governments' margin of action.

C. *Fiscal Compact: Independent Fiscal Institutions, Automatic Correction Mechanism and Judicial Review*

Next to these EU law instruments, Independent Fiscal Institutions are also governed by an intergovernmental agreement, the Fiscal Compact. Article 3(2) of the TSCG refers to their role in the activation of the Automatic Correction Mechanism in stating that 'The Contracting Parties shall put in place at national level the correction mechanism … on the basis of common principles to be proposed by the European Commission, concerning in particular the nature, size and time frame of the corrective action to be undertaken, also in the case of exceptional circumstances, and the *role and independence of the institutions responsible at national level for monitoring compliance with the rules set out in paragraph 1*' [emphasis added].

Not all provisions of the TSCG apply to all contracting parties, though.[13] Article 3(2) binds all except Hungary, Poland and Sweden as it is part of Title III (the Fiscal Compact).[14]

Interestingly, this article is also the only provision of the TSCG eligible for judicial review by the European Court of Justice in accordance with Article 8(1):

> The European Commission is invited to present in due time to the Contracting Parties a report on the provisions adopted by each of them in compliance with Article 3(2). If the European Commission, after having given the Contracting Party concerned the opportunity to submit its observations, concludes in its report that such Contracting Party has failed to comply with Article 3(2), the matter will be brought to the Court of Justice of the European Union by one or more Contracting Parties. Where a Contracting Party considers, independently of the Commission's report, that another Contracting Party has failed to comply with Article 3 (2), it may also bring the matter to the Court of Justice.

[13] Euro area Member States must be contracting parties whereas non-euro area Member States may adhere voluntarily. In January 2016, all EU Member States except for Croatia, the Czech Republic and the UK had ratified the Fiscal Compact.

[14] See also in this book Chapter 5, 'Differentiated Integration from the Perspective of Non-Euro Area Member States' by Thomas Beukers and Marijn van der Sluis.

Furthermore, Article 8(2) of the TSCG foresees a second procedure should the non-complying Member State not abide by the Court of Justice's decision:

> Where, on the basis of its own assessment or that of the European Commission, a Contracting Party considers that another Contracting Party has not taken the necessary measures to comply with the judgment of the Court of Justice referred to in paragraph 1, it may bring the case before the Court of Justice and request the imposition of financial sanctions following criteria established by the European Commission in the framework of Article 260 of the Treaty on the Functioning of the European Union.

However, as illustrated below, this possibility of judicial review appears to be rather remote and formal.

The obligations contained in the Fiscal Compact were further detailed in the Communication from the Commission on Common Principles on National Fiscal Correction Mechanisms, approved in June 2012 as part of the implementation of the Fiscal Compact.[15] In this document, the Commission underlined the need for 'Independent bodies or bodies with functional autonomy acting as monitoring institutions [to] support the credibility and transparency of the correction mechanism'. Apart from requiring the publicity of their role in this framework, this Communication also introduces the critical 'comply or explain principle' according to which the 'concerned Member State shall be obliged to comply with, or alternatively explain publicly why they are not following the assessments of these bodies'. It further insists on the need to take into account pre-existing institutional settings and the country-specific administrative structure at the time of designing new Independent Fiscal Institutions. Finally, some conditions are set in order to guarantee independence. We observe that Regulation (EU) No. 473/2013 approved almost one year later, in May 2013, anchored these principles in EU legislation while only slightly making them more precise as regards the legal document in which Independent Fiscal Institutions are to have their statutory regime grounded. Nevertheless, it did not take up the 'comply or explain' principle which may be problematic as the Independent Fiscal Institutions' opinions are not deemed to be binding by the EU and international rules.

[15] European Commission, Common Principles on National Fiscal Correction Mechanisms, COM(2012) 342 final, http://eur-lex.europa.eu/LexUriServ/LexUriServ.do?uri=COM:2012:0342:FIN:En:PDF, Principle 7, Annex.

Although Member States had until 31 December 2013 to implement the provisions of Article 3(2) of the TSCG as well as Directive 2011/85/EU, the Commission presented its report on this topic only in February 2017. As could be expected, the European Commission was particularly careful in considering whether a Member State has failed to comply with its obligations in relation to the Independent Fiscal Institutions' independence, for it is bound to respect Member States' constitutional identity enshrined in Article 4(2) of the Treaty of the European Union.[16]

In its report on the implementation by the Member States regarding their Independent Fiscal Institutions, the Commission was indeed particularly careful and lenient, which confirms that the Commission is not seeking to attract judicial review of the Member States for their implementation of this sensitive provision of the TSCG. Still, Member States could be assessed for their compliance with their EU obligations as the deadline for transposing Directive 2011/85/EU expired at the end of December 2013 and Member States had to comply with Article 5 of Regulation (EU) No. 473/2013 by the end of October of the same year. Assessing the implementation of this Directive might be easier, especially regarding technical matters such as the necessary endorsement of macroeconomic forecasts by an Independent Fiscal Institution. However, the question of the 'independence' itself is a more delicate and subjective one. The ECB considered in 2014 that 'not all fiscal councils in the euro area countries seem to have mandates that are fully in line with the requirements set out in the two-pack'.[17]

[16] Article 3(2) TSCG also addresses the introduction of the balanced budget rule in the legal systems of the Member States, and it is unlikely that any case will be brought to the Court of Justice on this basis. This provision, and the Fiscal Compact as a whole, should rather be seen as a solution to calm the financial markets during the peak of the crisis. See, on the Fiscal Compact's adoption and judicial review under Art. 8 TSCG, P. Craig, 'The Stability, Coordination and Governance Treaty: Principle, Politics and Pragmatism', *European Law Review*, 37(3), 2012, 231–48 and R. Barratta, 'Legal Issues of the 'Fiscal Compact': Searching for a Mature Democratic Governance of the Euro' in De Witte, Héritier and Trechsel (eds.), *The Euro Crisis and the State of European Democracy*, pp. 31–62, esp. 47ff.

[17] ECB, 'Monthly Bulletin June 2014', p. 98.

D. *Conclusion*

From the above the following picture emerges. Whereas Directive 2011/85/EU simply required that Member States' fiscal rules be based on independent and reliable analysis, the Fiscal Compact linked Independent Fiscal Institutions to the Automatic Correction Mechanism and introduced the possibility for judicial review if Member States fail to have functioning Independent Fiscal Institutions. Later on, the Commission's Communication introduced the 'comply or explain' principle whereas Regulation (EU) No. 473/2013 anchored in EU law and detailed further the content of the Communication in which the Commission detailed the Independent Fiscal Institutions' main features following the entry into force of the Fiscal Compact. It also defined their tasks further; in particular, in relation to the activation of the Correction Mechanism.

It results that euro area Member States are under the strictest obligations.[18] Additionally, although membership of the TSCG was primarily important for euro area Member States, eventually only the Czech Republic and the UK decided not to be party to this international Treaty.[19] This means that some non-euro area Member States are also parties to the TSCG and, in particular, to the Fiscal Compact.[20] This is true for Bulgaria and Romania who are therefore bound by both the TSCG provisions and by those contained in Directive 2011/85/EU. However, not all Member States are bound by the provisions concerning Independent Fiscal Institutions in Article 3(2) of the TSCG, placed under the Fiscal Compact. Hungary, Poland and Sweden are not, as long as they do not join the euro. Bearing in mind that Regulation (EU) No. 473/2013 concerns only euro area Member States, it results that Croatia, the Czech Republic, Hungary, Poland and Sweden only have to comply with Directive 2011/85/EU, whereas Bulgaria and Romania are bound by this Directive and by Article 3(2) of the TSCG. On the other hand, the UK is the only State not bound by any of the relevant provisions and did not need to create an Independent Fiscal Institution as it is excluded from the

[18] This is only logical as sharing a common currency implies a higher level of risk for these Member States collectively. They consequently have a stronger interest in promoting sound fiscal policies. Moreover, this is all the more necessary as the EMU is neither complete nor strong enough to prevent further crises.

[19] Croatia is not a signatory to the TSCG either. It entered the EU after the TSCG was already in force and has not acceded.

[20] See in this book also Chapter 5, 'Differentiated Integration from the Perspective of Non-Euro Area Member States' by Thomas Beukers and Marijn van der Sluis.

scope of Directive 2011/85/EU.[21] The UK is not a party to the TSCG either and Regulation (EU) No. 473/2013 only applies to euro area Member States. Nevertheless, this does not mean that the UK has no Independent Fiscal Institution. Actually, its Office for Budgetary Responsibility was created in 2010 ('to provide independent and authoritative analysis of the UK's public finances')[22] under Section 3 of the Budget Responsibility and National Audit Act 2011. But this decision was made independently from any EU or international obligation.

3 Member States' Implementation and the Resulting Independent Fiscal Institution Patchwork

Before proceeding to analyse how Member States have implemented their obligations, it should be duly noted that the definition of what Independent Fiscal Institutions are and which institutions should be considered as falling under this category is not uncontroversial and may vary depending on which institution performs such assessment. In fact, the EU Commission itself acknowledges that the definition it has been using to compile the information contained in its Independent Fiscal Institutions database[23] 'has been used since 2006 for the purpose of selecting institutions present in the database and as a result [. . . still] differs in certain respects from the definition of independent fiscal institutions that emerged from the new EU legal requirements gradually put in place since 2011'.[24] The EU Commission has now published its report on the implementation of their obligations by the Member States but it only contends the TSCG. Against this background, though other national institutions have been taken into account, particular attention is devoted in this chapter to the institutions categorised as Independent Fiscal Institutions by the ECB in its monthly bulletin of June 2014. Institutions

21 Directive 2011/85/EU, Preamble, para. 17: 'The obligation to have in place numerical fiscal rules that effectively promote compliance with the specific reference values for the excessive deficit, and the related obligation for the multiannual objectives in medium-term budgetary frameworks to be consistent with such rules, should . . . not apply to the United Kingdom'.

22 Office for Budgetary Responsibility, 'What We Do', http://budgetresponsibility.org.uk/about-the-obr/what-we-do/.

23 European Commission, 'Independent Fiscal Institutions in the EU Member States', http://ec.europa.eu/economy_finance/db_indicators/fiscal_governance/independent_institutions/index_en.htm.

24 Ibid.

introduced or reformed recently also receive particular attention. The present study is therefore neither exhaustive nor final but suffices to draw preliminary conclusions as to the adaptation by the Member States to their new obligations and the consequences for the Member States' constitutional framework.

To this end, the pace at which Member States have changed their institutions to comply with the EU and international norms or have created new Independent Fiscal Institutions will first be examined, though it does not necessarily mean that in doing so they have fully complied with their obligations (a). Second, the different institutional settings chosen are analysed (b). Following this, the tasks attributed to Independent Fiscal Institutions are compared (c) and so are the quality and designation procedures of their members (d).

A. *Pace of the Creation and Reform of EU Member States Independent Fiscal Institutions*

Even if Independent Fiscal Institutions in some Member States may be relatively young institutions, only six Member States (Austria, Belgium, Denmark, Hungary, Sweden and the UK) had Independent Fiscal Institutions in 2010.[25] In reality the Member States adopted different paces, and some met their obligations only recently, whereas others, such as Germany, still have to fully complete their reforms in order to comply with their EU obligations.[26] These differences can be explained by the fact that even those Member States that already had Independent Fiscal Institutions may have needed to reform them to guarantee compliance with EU norms. Or they may have had or wished to create a new institution that exists in parallel to the previously established one. Some States, such as Italy and Spain, indeed opted for creating new institutions

[25] ECB, 'Monthly Bulletin June 2014', p. 97.

[26] Of course, this evaluation will be subject to the Commission's final assessment. Some lack of compliance, such as the one observed for Germany, is nonetheless undisputed and clearly underlined in the Commission's opinion on Germany's draft budgetary plan for 2016: 'Regulation (EU) No. 473/2013 requires the draft budget to be based on independently endorsed or produced macroeconomic forecasts. The macroeconomic forecasts underlying the Draft Budgetary Plan have not been endorsed or produced by an independent body. Germany should ensure that an independent body in charge of producing or endorsing macroeconomic forecasts is in place as a matter of urgency'. See European Commission, Opinion of 16.11.2015 on the Draft Budgetary Plan of Germany, C(2015) 8101 final, http://ec.europa.eu/economy_finance/economic_governance/sgp/pdf/dbp/2015/de_2015-11-16_co_en.pdf, para. 6.

even where they could have reformed pre-existing bodies.[27] The creation of the Italian Parliamentary Budgetary Office was preceded by lengthy discussions as to whether the pre-existing Court of Auditors may be able to comply with the basic requirements defined in the EU documents and perform the tasks attributable to Independent Fiscal Institutions. The Court of Auditors is indeed a constitutionally established body with a strong reputation of independence and autonomy, and it can rely on a long tradition as it was established as early as 1862.[28] Nevertheless, Constitutional Law n.1/2012, which also introduced the balanced-budget rule in the Italian Constitution, strictly defined that a new independent body established within the two parliamentary chambers had to be established 'in compliance with their constitutional autonomy, to whom the task to analyse and check the trends in public finance and to assess the respect of budgetary rules are assigned'.[29] In Spain, too, the pre-existing Budgetary Office of the Parliament could have been revived or transformed and used in the implementation of the European and international obligations.[30] But a new body was created instead by Organic Law 6/2013 on the creation of the Independent Authority of Fiscal Responsibility and it was (structurally) placed within the Ministry of Budget and Public Administrations, though the law clearly recalls that 'this secondment will in no way affect its autonomy and functional independence'.[31]

Additionally, the creation of some Independent Fiscal Institutions may have coincided with the adoption of the EU obligations but originated from a national resolution, as was, for instance, the case in Slovakia,

[27] See, on these two Member States' Independent Fiscal Institutions, C. Fasone and D. Fromage, 'Fiscal Councils: Threat or Opportunity for Democracy in the Post-Crisis Economic and Monetary Union?' in L. Daniele, P. Simone and R. Cisotta (eds.), *Democracy in the EMU in the Aftermath of the Crisis* (Springer, 2017), pp. 161–178.

[28] Constitution of Italy, Arts. 100 and 103. An official parliamentary translation of the Constitution of Italy is available at www.senato.it/documenti/repository/istituzione/costituzione_inglese.pdf.

[29] Constitutional Law n. 1/2012, Art. 5

[30] This Office was created by Law 37/2010, following several failed attempts to create parliamentary and governmental budgetary offices. It also faced numerous difficulties following its creation, when it was not in a position to function properly. See, on this failure to function adequately, F. Bornstein, 'Réquiem Por un Parlamento Inútil: Nacimiento y Muerte de su Oficina Presupuestaria', *Cuarto Poder*, (14 May 2013), www.cuartopoder.es/luzdecruce/requiem-por-un-parlamento-inutil-nacimiento-y-muerte-de-su-oficina-presupuestaria/6239.

[31] Organic Law 6/2013, Art. 7.

where a working paper of the National Bank was at the origin of the introduction of an Independent Fiscal Institution in 2011.[32]

Another category of Member State is further formed by those States that had to create an Independent Fiscal Institution in order to be granted financial assistance: Ireland[33] and Portugal,[34] for instance,[35] whereas the lack of an effective Independent Fiscal Institution in Greece was one of the crucial points in the discussions regarding its third bailout in July 2015.[36] Moreover, although it is beyond doubt that the creation of an Independent Fiscal Institution by Ireland was required for it to be granted financial assistance, the creation of a fiscal council was already part of the measures the government planned to improve Ireland's financial situation in 2010.[37]

As regards the Member States that already had an Independent Fiscal Institution and therefore had to reform a pre-existing body, some of them were very prompt in taking the necessary steps and creating a functioning institution that ensures the required independent expertise. Denmark set

[32] See OECD, 'Principles for Independent Fiscal Institutions and Country Notes', Draft for Discussion, 7th Annual Meeting of OECD Parliamentary Budget Officials and Independent Fiscal Institutions, p. 174. Available on the Austrian parliament's website: www.parlament.gv.at/ZUSD/BUDGET/Principles_for_Independent_Fiscal_Institutions_and_Country_Notes_x_Draft_for_Discussion_xOECD_Secretariatx.pdf. Note that in spite of these origins, the Slovakian institution introduced in 2011 complies with the TSCG.

[33] See Council of the European Union, Council Recommendation with a view to bringing to an end the situation of an excessive deficit in Ireland, 17210/10, 7 December 2010.

[34] The creation of the Portuguese Fiscal Council was contained in the Memorandum of Understanding on specific economic policy conditionality of 17 May 2011, http://ec.europa.eu/economy_finance/eu_borrower/mou/2011-05-18-mou-portugal_en.pdf, para. 3.12–6. This creation was, however, part of a broader package of reforms to improve budgetary management launched in 2010. See OECD, 'Principles for Independent Fiscal Institutions and Country Notes', p. 162.

[35] In the Spanish case, the requirement to have a functioning Independent Fiscal Institution was contained in the Memorandum of Understanding approved to save its banking sector. See M. Martínez Lago, 'La Autoridad Fiscal Independiente', *E-prints Complutense* (2014), http://eprints.ucm.es/24379/1/EPrintMAML201401.pdf, p. 16.

[36] See European Council, Euro Summit Statement, 12 July 2015 (SN 4070/15), www.consilium.europa.eu/en/press/press-releases/2015/07/pdf/20150712-eurosummit-statement-greece/, p. 2. However, it appears that Greece had already foreseen the creation of an Independent Fiscal Institution in Art. 2 of Law 4270/2014 transposing Directive 2011/85/EU, but that it was never set up in practice.

[37] OECD, 'Principles for Independent Fiscal Institutions and Country Notes', p. 103. See in this book Chapter 9, 'Ireland: Traditional Procedures Adapted for Economic Emergency' by Stephen Coutts for further discussion of how post-'bailout law' in Ireland built substantially on measures already initiated.

up its Economic Council in compliance with the rules contained in the Fiscal Compact in a particularly swift manner, as it already conducted the necessary reforms in 2012.[38] In Austria, the Government Debt Committee had existed since 1970 and was replaced by the Fiscal Advisory Council in 2013 to comply with the EU requirements.[39] Following this reform, the Austrian body was made more independent and, interestingly, a Parliamentary Budgetary Office was created too. Also the Belgian High Council of Finance, in place since 1936, was reformed in 2013 to comply with the reformed European fiscal framework.[40]

Concerning the Member States that had to create a new institution, France was among the first to have a functioning Independent Fiscal Institution. Italy and Spain were also on schedule with their transposition, but their institutions were functioning later than the French Council. Indeed, the French High Council of Public Finances was introduced by Organic Law 2012/1403 on the programming and the governance of public finances of December 2012.[41] It started to function in March 2013, which means that the first (early) renewal of its members took place in autumn 2015, which was the opportunity to make the first assessment of its activities.[42] The Italian Office by contrast was created in December 2012 but has been in place since April 2014. Spain approved the Organic Law creating the Independent Authority of Fiscal Responsibility in extremis in November 2013 and it started to function in the spring of 2014. Other countries complied after the deadline for transposition of the Directive had expired. This is, for example, true for Estonia, where an Independent Fiscal Institution was created in February 2014 within the Bank of Estonia, and for Bulgaria, where the bill creating the Independent Fiscal Institution was approved in February 2015.[43]

[38] Law no. 167 of 2012. See OECD, 'Principles for Independent Fiscal Institutions and Country Notes', p. 74.

[39] OECD, 'Principles for Independent Fiscal Institutions and Country Notes', p. 32. The Federal Law on the Establishment of the Government Debt Committee was amended to formally establish an independent Fiscal Advisory Council.

[40] See OECD, 'Principles for Independent Fiscal Institutions and Country Notes', p. 47.

[41] On the French Council and the consequences of its introduction, see D. Fromage, 'Le Haut Conseil des Finances Publiques: Quelles conséquences deux ans après sa création?', *Revue du Droit Public*, 4, 2015, 1107–25.

[42] See HCFP, 'Activity Report 2013–2015' (17 December 2015), www.hcfp.fr/Avis-et-publication/Actualites/The-2013-2015-Activity-Report-of-the-High-Council-of-Public-Finance.

[43] 'Bulgaria's Gov't Approves Bill on Establishing Fiscal Council', *Novinite* (4 February 2015), www.novinite.com/articles/166343/Bulgaria per centE2 per cent80 per cent99s +Govt+Approves+Bill+on+Establishing+Fiscal+Council.

According to the European Central Bank, in June 2014, roughly six months after the expiry of the deadlines provided for by Directive 2011/85 and Regulation (EU) No. 473/2013 but six months before the end of the deadline defined in the Fiscal Compact, 19 Member States had Independent Fiscal Institutions, six had drafts and two (Czech Republic and Poland) were reported as not discussing any draft legislative proposal at that point.[44] All in all, in the Commission's view, in July 2015 all Member States but Slovenia had adopted the necessary legislation for the creation of independent monitoring institutions although five Member States had not effectively set up their Independent Fiscal Institution at that time (Bulgaria, Czech Republic, Greece, Poland and Slovenia).[45] Since then, however, the Slovenian Independent Fiscal Institution was created on 11 February 2016 and its members designated by the Slovenian government,[46] although eventually no agreement could be found. The members of the Bulgarian Independent Fiscal Institution were also elected in November 2015.[47] Poland, on the other hand, still does not have an Independent Fiscal Institution and its Minister of Finance recently expressed an opinion that it is not deemed necessary. In fact, the Polish *Sejm*'s website clearly states that the Supreme Audit Office fulfils the EU obligations anchored in Directive 2011/85/EU, which are the only ones applicable to Poland.[48] There might therefore be some discrepancies between the Polish and the European Commission's interpretations. Also, the Czech Republic – which is bound solely by Directive 2011/85/EU – still does not have an Independent Fiscal Institution.[49] This is consistent with the Estonian Independent Fiscal Institution's website, which finds that no plan exists to set up an Independent Fiscal

[44] ECB 'Monthly Bulletin June 2014', p. 96.

[45] See the presentation by Stefan Ciobanu, Head of Unit, Fiscal Governance and Fiscal Statistics, European Commission, at European Commission,'Fiscal frameworks, Fiscal Compact and Independent Fiscal Institutions' (8 July 2015), http://ec.europa.eu/slovenia/documents/2015-0708-stefan_ciobanu.pdf.

[46] 'Gov't nominates fiscal council members', *STA* (11 February 2016), https://english.sta.si/2230173/govt-nominates-fiscal-council-members.

[47] 'Bulgaria parliament elects chair, members of Fiscal Council', *FOCUS Information Agency* (25 November 2015), www.focus-fen.net/news/2015/11/25/390560/bulgaria-parliament-elects-chair-members-of-fiscal-council.html.

[48] Sejm, 'Nawyższa Izba Kontoli', www.sejm.gov.pl/sejm7.nsf/BASLeksykon.xsp?t=s&id=8715C9B98714EDCEC1257E06002D0D51&q=regu%C5%82y.

[49] Polish Ministry of Finance, 'To Save or to Spend? Interview with Mateusz Szczurek', *WBJ Observer* (May 2015), www.warszawa.scelna.gov.pl/en/web/bip/ministry-of-finance/for-the-media/interviews/articles.

Institution either in Poland or in the Czech Republic.[50] Greece only recently set up its Independent Fiscal Institution, although, interestingly, its Parliamentary Budget Office had already adhered to the Network of EU Independent Fiscal Institutions.

In conclusion, few Member States were particularly prompt in creating an Independent Fiscal Institution but, three years after the expiry of the deadlines, almost all of them have one. This obviously does not mean that they were created or reformed in compliance with EU and international norms. Only a future Commission assessment will be able to confirm or deny this.

B. *Institutional Setting*

Another major point of difference among the EU Member States in this field regards the institutional setting they chose for their Independent Fiscal Institutions.

These are particularly varied, ranging from a parliamentary office (Italian Parliamentary Budget Office) or a body placed under the statutory authority of parliament (Finnish National Audit) to a Council placed within the Court of Auditors (French High Council of Public Finances) and including bodies that are functionally placed within the government (Spanish Independent Authority of Fiscal Responsibility and Dutch Bureau for Economic Policy Analysis). The Slovak Council for Budget Responsibility is placed within the central bank, and the Austrian Fiscal Advisory Council is staffed by the Austrian central bank. Nevertheless, most Independent Fiscal Institutions have been placed within the executive. Being closely linked to the government and therefore having limited institutional independence from this budgetary authority does not mean, however, that an Independent Fiscal Institution cannot be 'functionally independent' as requested by the EU obligations if the criteria listed in Regulation (EU) No. 473/2013 and in the aforementioned Commission Communication are fulfilled.

It should furthermore be borne in mind in this context that some Member States also have two or more institutions fulfilling the tasks Independent Fiscal Institutions are deemed to perform according to EU norms, where each may be operating in a different setting. For instance, in Germany the Council of Academic Experts is, on the one hand, in charge of 'describ[ing] the current economic situation and its foreseeable

[50] Fiscal Council, 'Fiscal Councils in the European Union', http://eelarvenoukogu.ee/about-the-council/other-fiscal-councils.

development [and of . . .] investigat[ing] the possibilities of simultaneously assuring, within the framework of the free market economy, stability of the price level, a high rate of employment and equilibrium in foreign trade and payments', though it may not recommend the adoption of any specific policy.[51] On the other hand, the Stability Council is an institution common to both the Federation and the Länder, constitutionally anchored in Article 109a of the Basic Law, responsible for contributing to avoiding budgetary emergency by supervising budgetary management at both Federal and Länder levels. It is not only related to the executive but also composed of their representatives as it is formed by the Federal Ministers of Finance and for Economic Affairs and Energy and the Länder Finance Ministers. Additionally, an independent advisory board to the Stability Council was introduced by the reform of the Fiscal Council Act of 15 July 2013 following which this new independent body (i.e. not composed of federal and regional ministers) shall 'monitor the Federal and Länder budgets on a regular basis and . . . carry out the budget rehabilitation procedure [. . . and] monitor compliance with the upper limit for the general government structural deficit under Section 51 subsection (2) of the Budgetary Principles Act'.[52] Also, in Belgium, the traditional functions of Independent Fiscal Institutions are fulfilled by more than one institution, namely the High Council of Finance, the National Accounts Institute and the Federal Planning Bureau.[53] In Luxembourg, the mandate and organisation of the National Statistical Office were revised by the law of 10 July 2012 and its Directorate *Etudes, Prévisions et Recherche* (Studies, forecasts and research) is

[51] Act on the Appointment of a Council of Experts on Economic Development, Art. 2.

[52] Stability Council Act, Art. 2.

[53] Again, as mentioned, the classification of one institution or the other as an Independent Fiscal Institution in the European sense is not uncontroversial. For instance, the OECD report on 'Principles for Independent Fiscal Institutions and Country Notes' contemplated these three institutions, whereas the report on Belgium prepared by Werner Vandenbruwaene analyses the Court of Auditors and the High Council of Finance. See the Report on Belgium prepared by W. Vandenbruwaene for the 'Constitutional Change through Euro Crisis Law' project of the EUI Law Department, Section VII.5. All the country reports referred to in this paper are part of the same project and available on its website: http://eurocrisislaw.eui.eu. By contrast, a European Parliament Briefing refers to the role played by the Federal Planning Bureau in, inter alia, the production of the medium-term economic outlook. See European Parliament, 'Involvement of Independent Fiscal Bodies in 2016 DBP and 2014 and 2015 SCP', PE 528.747 (9 February 2016), www.europarl.europa.eu/RegData/etudes/note/join/2014/528747/IPOL-ECON_NT(2014)528747_EN.pdf.

in charge of producing Luxembourg's macroeconomic forecast.[54] However, Luxembourg also created a National Council of Public Finance in July 2014 entrusted with the monitoring of compliance with the rules related to the medium-term budgetary objective and with the application of the correction mechanism as well as with the evaluation of the macroeconomic and budgetary forecasts.[55]

The differences in the institutional settings of the various Independent Fiscal Institutions are unsurprising and not necessarily to be perceived as something negative. The former is because the European norms themselves prescribe that 'The design of those monitoring bodies should take into account the existing institutional setting and the administrative structure of the Member State concerned.'[56] The latter is because local ownership is absolutely crucial to the Independent Fiscal Institutions having any positive effect on the Member States' fiscal sustainability at all. The Independent Fiscal Institutions' opinions are, in most cases, not binding, and hence their impact solely depends on their publicity and on the prestige of their analyses and of their members or the institution they are related to.[57] Moreover, even their role in the activation of the Automatic Correction Mechanism can be easily reduced to nothing by national governments as will be illustrated below.

Yet the choice for the one institutional setting or the other is not devoid of any consequences, in particular, for parliaments.[58] In Spain, for instance, at the time of the creation of the Independent Authority of Fiscal Responsibility, the then-opposition party PSOE (socialist party) advocated that this Authority should be closer to parliament and led by a collegial body. Instead, the Independent Authority for Fiscal Responsibility was set up in 2013 under the Ministry of the Budget and Public Finances. As a matter of fact, the parties PSOE, Izquierda unida (United Left), Convergència i Unió (centre-right alliance of Catalan parties),

[54] European Commission, 'Report on Public Finances in EMU', European Economy 9 (2014), http://ec.europa.eu/economy_finance/publications/european_economy/2014/pdf/ee9_en.pdf, p.63. The ECB solely contemplates the High Council of Finance ECB, 'Monthly Bulletin June 2014', p.97.

[55] Law of 12 July 2014 on the coordination and governance of public finances, Art. 8.

[56] Regulation (EU) No. 473/2013, Preamble, para. 17.

[57] In the euro area Member States, at least. Outside the euro area, the Croatian Independent Fiscal Institution has a certain degree of leverage. See ECB, 'Monthly Bulletin June 2014', p. 99.

[58] See further, Fasone and Griglio, 'Can fiscal councils enhance the role of national parliaments in the European Union?'.

Partido nacionalista vasco (Basque nationalist party) and the Grupo Mixto (Mixed Group) voted against the Organic Law that instituted the Authority on the ground of the lack of independence.[59] The fact that the Authority is placed within this ministry and not within parliament has had strong consequences for the Members of Parliament, in particular those from the opposition parties. Organic Law 6/2013 foresees very limited relationships between the Independent Fiscal Institution and the parliamentary chambers. Article 24(8) simply states that 'the President of the Independent Authority for Fiscal Responsibility shall appear, at least once a year, before the appropriate Commission of the Congress of Deputies and the Senate'.[60] And indeed only this minimum obligation has been complied with: its President has appeared once before the Finance and Public Administrations Committee of the Congress of Deputies in March 2015 and once before the Budgets Committee of the Senate in September 2015.[61] However, requests had been filed for more hearings which could not be organised, as – also in this context – the majority rule applies. This explains why, in spite of four successfully registered requests, the President appeared only once before the Congress. Had the Independent Fiscal Institution been established as a parliamentary body as advocated by the main opposition party at the time, it can reasonably be assumed that the parliamentary opposition would have had easier access to the Authority's independent expertise, as it would not have been fully dependent on the majority's agreement to communicate with its members.

Nevertheless, the assumption that placing the Independent Fiscal Institution within parliament might be a guarantee for more democratic legitimacy, by allowing for better control by parliament, may not always prove to be the most appropriate setting. Being placed under parliament did not prevent the Hungarian Independent Fiscal Institution from being replaced by a much weaker body in 2011 after the centre-right government gained a two-thirds majority in parliament. The Hungarian Fiscal Council created in 2008 originally benefited from a very positive

[59] 'PSOE, IU-ICV, CiU, PNA, ERC y BNG rechazan la nueva Autoridad Fiscal Independiente por su falta de independencia', *Europa Press* (4 September 2013).

[60] An official translation of Organic Law 6/2013 is available at www.slideshare.net/airefcomunicacion/2-lo-6-2013-de-14nov-de-creacin-airef-entrad.

[61] *Diario de sesiones del Congreso,* no. 760, 10 March 2015, www.congreso.es/public_oficiales/L10/CONG/DS/CO/DSCD-10-CO-760.PDF, and *Diario de sesiones del Senado*, no. 531, 23 September 2015, www.senado.es/legis10/publicaciones/pdf/senado/ds/DS_C_10_531.PDF.

reputation, but its independence and capacities have since been strongly questioned, and rightfully so.[62] It is in fact this example that dissuaded Slovakia to create its new Independent Fiscal Institution under parliament as originally planned, in order to protect its independence.[63] Instead, it opted for a new body fully independent from any other institution and whose budget is dependent on the central bank. This solution might be beneficial, as budgetary resources can indeed be a source of conflict with the government (as we will see later).

In any event, the possibility left open by the European rules to take the pre-existing institutional framework into account has been embraced by Member States whose Independent Fiscal Institutions undoubtedly exist in very different settings. Only an analysis of actual practice can confirm whether political independence and functional autonomy can still be fully guaranteed. Furthermore, it follows from the different settings chosen by Member States that placing an Independent Fiscal Institution under the government is an option that was not only chosen for the older Independent Fiscal Institutions (i.e. when Independent Fiscal Institutions were created on the initiative of the Member States themselves and not as a result of the introduction of European and international obligations) but also for many of the more recently created ones. Yet, Independent Fiscal Institutions have to monitor compliance with certain fiscal rules during the budgetary cycle, in which the government plays an important role. Therefore, it may seem quite surprising that so many Member States who created their Independent Fiscal Institutions to comply with their new obligations opted for placing them within the executive.

C. *Tasks and Powers*

Like the choice of institutional setting for the Independent Fiscal Institutions, the tasks and powers these institutions have been granted also differ from one Member State to the other.[64] This holds true for tasks foreseen by the European and international rules themselves, which have

[62] See, for example, Swedish Fiscal Policy Council, 'Swedish Fiscal Policy 2013' (27 August 2013), www.finanspolitiskaradet.com/download/18.1b89d9140c56bc4c73b70/1378219272657/Swedish+Fiscal+Policy+2013.pdf, pp. 111–3. Note that among the various obligations regarding Independent Fiscal Institutions described in Section II, Hungary is only bound by Directive 85/2011/EU.

[63] OECD, 'Principles for Independent Fiscal Institutions and Country Notes', p. 175.

[64] See further on this: Debrun and Kinda, 'Strengthening Post-Crisis Fiscal Credibility', pp. 16–17 and European Commission, 'Report on Public Finances in EMU', p. 57.

been more or less extended in the implementation, and for the tasks that Independent Fiscal Institutions generally perform outside of this framework. This is, of course, because the list of powers contained in the EU and international provisions only provides a minimum, so their powers may still be further extended. As will be developed in the conclusion, perhaps one of the shortcomings of the European norms is precisely that they provide only a minimum that leaves Member States too large a margin. Member States are free to define their Independent Fiscal Institutions' powers which, in turn, will influence the impact the Independent Fiscal Institutions will have once they are in operation.

Some of the Independent Fiscal Institutions have seen their attributions limited to this EU and international minimum. This is the case in France where the High Council is not entitled to produce any reports apart from those foreseen in the Organic Law 2012/1403[65] and which merely cover the EU requirements. This limited capacity to express its opinion appears to define its influence even more strongly, as its opinions are strictly consultative and do not bind the government in any way (although they may be used by the Constitutional Council, should it examine a budgetary law's respect for the principle of sincerity).[66] In fact, the High Council's president has criticised its limited and precisely defined role, which does not include the production of macroeconomics forecasts,[67] and the 'minimal fulfilment of the European obligations'.[68] By contrast, the Spanish Council has a more extended role. For example, although it does not produce the macroeconomic forecasts itself, it produces a report on the methodology to calculate the forthcoming expenditures and incomes and the growth rate.[69] It may also be entrusted

[65] Organic Law 2012/1403, Art. 21.

[66] See Constitutional Council, Decision 2012-658 DC, 13 December 2012, para. 19. However, no yearly budgetary law has been struck down on this ground so far and the Council has adopted a rather lenient interpretation in this context. See, further, Fromage, 'Le Haut Conseil des Finances Publiques', pp. 1118ff.

[67] Some Member States have opted for having their Independent Fiscal Institution produce these forecasts whereas others have attributed them their mere endorsement; for example, Austria, Belgium, Luxembourg, the Netherlands and Slovenia have opted for an institution independent from the Ministry of Finance to produce these forecasts, whereas Estonia, Spain, France, Ireland, Italy, Malta, Portugal and Slovakia have opted for one that only provides an endorsement of these forecasts. See European Commission, 'Report on Public Finances in EMU', pp. 62–3.

[68] Transcript of the session of 1 October 2014. Finance Committee of the French National Assembly, 9, www.assemblee-nationale.fr/14/cr-cfiab/14-15/c1415003.asp.

[69] Organic Law 6/2013, Art. 15.

with the duty to produce other opinions by law.[70] The Swedish Fiscal Policy Council's remit further comprises the task to 'analyse the effects of fiscal policy on the distribution of welfare in the short and the long run'[71] and the Belgian Federal Planning Bureau may assess the costs of the electoral programmes proposed by political parties during the elections to the Chamber of Representatives.[72]

These examples illustrate the fact that Independent Fiscal Institutions having more extended tasks than the minimum defined at EU level is not necessarily the result of their having already been in place when the EU and international obligations were adopted. Rather, these different situations appear to be the consequence of differences in the national context related for instance to the political culture and tradition. Yet, as long as Independent Fiscal Institutions have sufficient resources and their independence is formally guaranteed, the fact that they perform additional tasks should not be seen as impairing their capacity to act as 'fiscal watchdogs'.

D. Quality and Appointment Procedure of Independent Fiscal Institutions' Members

Whereas independence is a criterion common to all members of Independent Fiscal Institutions, the requirements to be appointed vary and so do the appointment procedures themselves. These different features and, in particular, the involvement of a diversity of institutions – among which parliaments should arguably play a special role due to their providing democratic legitimacy – shall allow for the appointment of independent persons. The procedure for their appointment deserves attention as it may allow for the guarantee of independence or at least for a balance of the political orientations represented. For example, in France, six bodies are involved in the appointment of the members of the High Council: the President of the Court of Auditors (who himself presides over the High Council and is appointed by the President of the Republic), the Presidents of the Senate and the National Assembly and those of both their finance committees and the President of the Economic, Social and Environmental Council.[73] The parliamentary opposition may in this way be represented through the involvement of

[70] Ibid., Art. 23.

[71] Ordinance with Instructions for the Fiscal Policy Council, SFS 2011:446, Art. 7(4)

[72] Law 2014, 0722.

[73] Organic Law 2012/1403, Art. 11.

the presidents of both chambers and their finance committees, as the presidency of the finance committees is traditionally assumed by a senator or a deputy of the opposition.[74] By contrast, the members of the Irish Council are nominated by the Minister of Finance[75] and those of the Latvian Fiscal Discipline Council are nominated according to either a joint proposal of the Governor of the Bank of Latvia and the Minister of Finance or a proposal made by at least 10 members of the Latvian Parliament.[76] Although it is difficult to design a 'one size fits all' process, it seems that parliament – opposition and majority – should be involved and that the more institutions involved the higher the chances to have truly independent members.

In addition to the bodies involved in the designation procedure, the issue of the appointment of foreigners as members of Independent Fiscal Institutions is also the subject of diverging interpretations. Some have indeed considered that appointing foreigners was synonymous with a guarantee of independence, whereas others specifically prohibit the nomination of non-nationals. Austria establishes in this regard, for example, that the Fiscal Council's members must be eligible for election to the National Council, which means that they must be Austrian nationals.[77] By contrast, the law governing the Latvian fiscal council specifically states that its members shall be '[s]pecialists of the field of finances and economics from Latvia or other Member State of the European Union who have experience in fiscal policy issues'.[78] The Portuguese Public Finance Council currently has a German professor as vice-president.[79]

Furthermore, the size of Independent Fiscal Institutions is particularly varied, ranging from 3 to 16 members. This is of particular importance, as it may in the end influence the impact of the Independent Fiscal Institutions. According to Article 2 of Regulation (EU) No. 273/2013, Independent Fiscal Institutions should have sufficient resources. Admittedly, such assessment is likely to vary from one Member State to the other depending on its size or the tasks the Independent Fiscal Institution

[74] M. Lascombe, 'La Nouvelle Gouvernance Financière', *Actualité Juridique Droit Administratif*, 4, 2013, 228–35, 235.

[75] Fiscal Responsibility Act, Section 7(1).

[76] Fiscal Discipline Law, Art. 22(1).

[77] Federal Law Establishing the Fiscal Advisory Council, Art. 1(4).

[78] Fiscal Discipline Law, Art. 22(2).

[79] Portuguese Public Finance Council, 'Conselho Superior', www.cfp.pt/about-us/composition/board/.

has to fulfil.[80] In any case, a minimum is needed both for the Independent Fiscal Institution to be truly functional and influential and for a certain diversity of opinions – and hence independence – to be guaranteed.

Another feature that differs from one Independent Fiscal Institution to the other is the involvement of academics, usually economics professors, or its absence. Also, the fact that some members are simultaneously members of other public institutions; for example, in France, the President of the Court of Auditors is ex officio also the President of the High Council, whereas two out of six members of the Estonian Fiscal Council currently also represent the Bank of Estonia. The composition is particularly important as it can influence the Independent Fiscal Institutions' independence.[81]

Finally, the issue of gender is worth mentioning. Following the adoption of a parliamentary amendment put forward by Senators Gattolin and Placé,[82] gender balance is guaranteed in the Organic Law establishing the French High Council.[83] Gender balance is also an aim for the members of the Swedish Council.[84] By contrast, all six members of the Estonian council nominated in 2014 are men,[85] and this is also the case of the six members of the Latvian council.[86]

In sum, the preceding analysis has shown that Independent Fiscal Institutions in EU Member States constitute a group of very different entities even after the introduction of EU and international rules in this domain and despite the fact that most of them were created following the introduction of these obligations. This is precisely because EU and international norms are rather open in defining only minimum conditions and, therefore, sometimes leave too much room for Member State adaptation. To a certain extent, such openness is justified and welcome; for example, when it allows Member States to take into account their size, actual needs and institutional settings. But it also permits them to create weak institutions, which can be detrimental to the aim pursued by the introduction of requirements in this domain in EU and international norms.

[80] For instance, the roles which Independent Fiscal Institutions are called to play by the Fiscal Compact and Regulation (EU) No. 473/2013 and the monitoring of fiscal rules thus entailed require more permanent structures. European Commission, 'Report on Public Finances in EMU', p. 58.

[81] Calmfors and Wren-Lewis, 'What Should Fiscal Councils Do?', 666.

[82] Amendment 42 ter. [83] Organic Law 2012/1403, Art. 11(4).

[84] Ordinance with Instructions for the Fiscal Policy Council, SFS 2011:446, Art. 11.

[85] Estonian Fiscal Council, 'About the Council', http://eelarvenoukogu.ee/about-the-council.

[86] Latvian Fiscal Discipline Council, 'Council', http://fiscalcouncil.lv/council.

4 Difficulties Encountered Thus Far by Independent Fiscal Institutions

Against this background, some of the difficulties encountered thus far by the Independent Fiscal Institutions will be described. They are linked to their information (a), the time frame in which they operate (b) and their budgetary constraints (c).

A. *Access to Information*

One crucial factor for the correct operation of Independent Fiscal Institutions lies in their access to all the information they need in due time as laid down in Regulation (EU) No. 473/2013.[87] Even where some protective provisions exist in the Independent Fiscal Institutions' favour, governments or their bodies do not always fully respect them.

The President of the French Council, for instance, complained about some shortcomings in this domain when the High Council had to examine the stability programme for 2013–7[88] and when it had to evaluate the budgetary law for 2014.[89] He would, for instance, have considered it preferable to receive preliminary information on the macroeconomic framework before the Council actually had to produce its report on the stability programme.

In Spain, the problem was even more serious. The President of the Independent Authority of Fiscal Responsibility sued the Spanish Ministry of Finance in November 2015 for failing to guarantee its 'appropriate access to information' and thus being in breach of European obligations anchored in Regulation EU (No) 473/2013. More precisely,

[87] This was underlined by the OECD: 'There is often asymmetry of information between the government and the Independent Fiscal Institution – no matter how well an Independent Fiscal Institution is resourced. This creates a special duty to guarantee in legislation ... that the Independent Fiscal Institution has full access to all relevant information in a timely manner, including methodology and assumptions underlying the budget and other fiscal proposals.' See OECD, 'Recommendation of the Council for Principles for Independent Fiscal Institutions' (February 2014), www.oecd.org/gov/budgeting/OECD-Recommendation-on-Principles-for-Independent-Fiscal-Institutions.pdf, Principle 6.

[88] Minutes of the hearing of the High Council's President before the Finance Committee of the National Assembly, 16 April 2013, 3, www.assemblee-nationale.fr/14/cr-cfiab/12-13/c1213079.asp.

[89] Minutes of the hearing of the High Council's President before the Finance Committee of the National Assembly, 25 September 2013, 3. www.assemblee-nationale.fr/14/cr-cfiab/12-13/c1213122.asp.

the issue was related to the fact that, like the Organic Law, a ministerial order[90] approved in June 2015 with the aim of defining the information to be transmitted by the Ministry to the Authority (and the procedure for transmission) established that the provision of said information should 'preferably' be conducted through the Ministry and not directly from one public administration to the Authority. The latter possibility would only arise at a later stage if the information provided was 'insufficient, incomplete or requires further explanations'. It seems that this battle between the two institutions has been settled but the Authority took the government before court indeed and it seems that the decisive element in the resolution of this conflict was the report adopted by the European Commission in February 2017. This lengthy battle illustrates that, in spite of its institutional link to the government, the Authority's first president is acting on his promise to run it in an independent manner.[91]

These two examples show that the Independent Fiscal Institutions' access to information is certainly not always perceived as neutral, nor as part of the State's obligations. They also highlight that, where sufficient legal safeguards are not in place, the Independent Fiscal Institutions' capacity to perform their tasks in an appropriate manner ultimately depends on the quality of the person(s) involved (in the Spanish case, the strength of the Authority's president). However, this lack of information is not common to all Member States: the secretariat of the Austrian Fiscal Council notes that it 'does not recall instances where the government has threatened or attempted to limit its access to relevant information'.[92] In this context, again, political culture and tradition play an important role in ensuring the good functioning of Independent Fiscal Institutions.

B. *Timing*

In addition to information, time is also crucial for Independent Fiscal Institutions to perform their analysis successfully. In some occasions and

[90] Orden HAP/1287/2015 of 23 June 2015.

[91] See 'La Autoridad Fiscal denuncia a Montoro ante la Audiencia Nacional', *El Mundo* (12 November 2015), www.elmundo.es/economia/2015/11/12/5643b187ca474198528b45c5.html.

[92] OECD, 'Principles for Independent Fiscal Institutions and Country Notes', p. 38.

in some Member States, Independent Fiscal Institutions only have an extremely limited amount of time to present their opinions. In Estonia, for example, the Independent Fiscal Institution has two weeks to present its report after the publication of the Ministry of Finance's forecasts.[93] The same deadline applies to the newly created Bulgarian council. In France, by contrast, this deadline is as short as one week and has been deemed insufficient, especially where the government does not provide the High Council with relevant information beforehand or where the High Council must produce two reports at the same time. This was the case in 2014 when it had to prepare a report on the programming act for 2014–19 and on the budget act and the act on the financing of the social security for 2015.[94]

Therefore, Independent Fiscal Institutions should be guaranteed a reasonable amount of time to prepare their reports and it is desirable that the information flow between Independent Fiscal Institution and government is continuous at the time when Independent Fiscal Institutions have to prepare their evaluations.

C. *Budgetary Constraints*

Finally, the available budget may be an issue in ensuring the correct operation and the independence of Independent Fiscal Institutions.[95] Whereas Regulation EU (No.) 473/2013 foresees that Independent Fiscal Institutions need to have sufficient resources, some of them have not been provided with a sufficient budget.[96] The Spanish Authority, for example, faced budgetary difficulties and threatened to resign if it did not receive a higher budget.[97] In fact, this issue is problematic not only because the Authority cannot comply with all the tasks assigned to it by the Organic Law – it insisted, for instance, that it only had one person to

93 Fiscal Council of Estonia, 'Report for 2014' (April 2015), http://eelarvenoukogu.ee/files/Fiscal%20Council%20Report%202014.pdf, p. 4.

94 On the absence of exchanges of information beforehand and the obligation of High Council to conduct this analysis within one week under the Organic Law, see the High Council President's speech during its hearing before the finance committee of the National Assembly, 1 October 2014, www.assemblee-nationale.fr/14/cr-cfiab/14-15/c1415003.asp.

95 Calmfors and Wren-Lewis, 'What Should Fiscal Councils Do?', pp. 665ff.

96 Regulation (EU) No. 473/2013, Art. 2.

97 See 'La autoridad fiscal pide a Montoro una paga extra por exceso de trabajo', *El País* (12 November 2015).

check on the expenditures of all Spanish municipalities.[98] It is also problematic because due to its embeddedness within the Spanish Ministry of Finance it depends on the latter's willingness to assign its resources. Also in Sweden the resources of the Fiscal Policy Council are too limited.[99] In Austria on the other hand, the budget for the operation of the Fiscal Advisory Council is secured through the National Bank, which is obliged by law to provide it with sufficient resources, although the amount is not public.[100] This does not seem to be an obstacle to it receiving a sufficient budget though, as its secretariat regards it as sufficient for carrying out its activities.[101]

These examples illustrate that it is absolutely critical for Independent Fiscal Institutions to have their own budget directly originating from the general state budget and that the government must have no means of pressure whatsoever.

5 Consequences of the Creation and Reform of Independent Fiscal Institutions at Member State Level

Since most of these institutions have only been created recently, their independence, credibility and effectiveness will have to be confirmed by practice in the coming years. It can already be noted that despite their recent creation, some Independent Fiscal Institutions have already positively assessed their own role. The Estonian Independent Fiscal Institution, for instance, declared in its (first) annual report for the year 2015 that: 'To sum up the year, it can be said that the Fiscal Council stepped successfully into the fiscal policy of Estonia. Previous experience has shown that the opinions of the Fiscal Council have weight and resonance.'[102]

The lack of a long institutional practice of many of the Independent Fiscal Institutions does not prevent the drawing of (preliminary) conclusions as to the consequences, at Member State level, of the creation of new Independent Fiscal Institutions and of the reform of older

98 See 'Sólo tenemos a una persona para evaluar a todos los Ayuntamientos', *El País* (19 June 2015), http://economia.elpais.com/economia/2015/06/19/actualidad/1434717430_796344.html.

99 L. Calmfors, 'Sweden: Watchdog with a Broad Remit' in G. Kopits (ed.), *Restoring Public Debt Sustainability: The Role of Independent Fiscal Institutions* (Oxford Scholarship Online, 2014), p. 11.

100 OECD, 'Principles for Independent Fiscal Institutions and Country Notes', p. 36.

101 Ibid. 102 Fiscal Council of Estonia, 'Report for 2014', p. 3.

Independent Fiscal Institutions. Their relation to the budgetary authorities will be examined: governments, first, (a) and then parliaments (b).

A. Relationship to Government: Only Publicity and Reputation Matter

As noted earlier, Independent Fiscal Institutions do not have any binding power over governments according to EU and international norms;[103] they are advisory and not decision-making bodies.[104] Yet their reports and assessments – which are always public – may constitute a threat for the government that does not want to see its forecasts or budget plans denounced publicly. Consequently, governments may seek to establish informal exchanges with Independent Fiscal Institutions beforehand or may preventively adjust their fiscal plans to avoid attracting any blame.[105]

The tasks with which Independent Fiscal Institutions have been entrusted may also influence the potential governmental accountability entailed by their creation (or reform). This is, for example, the case where Independent Fiscal Institutions have to endorse macroeconomic forecasts prepared by the government (instead of preparing them directly), as their intervention will invite the government to be realistic or prudent in its forecasts.[106] Nevertheless, this also requires that Independent Fiscal Institutions have important specialised resources. Additionally, the Independent Fiscal Institution's control is not always dissuasive. In France, for instance, the High Council of Public Finances has deemed the government's growth forecasts to be non 'prudent' but still 'achievable, should growth be fuelled by domestic and European demand'[107] and the

[103] This does not mean that national laws cannot grant them such powers.

[104] Granting Independent Fiscal Institutions with decision-making powers would be incompatible with 'basic tenets of fiscal policy-making'. See European Commission, 'Report on Public Finances in EMU', p. 55.

[105] These effects may be weaker during the Independent Fiscal Institutions' first years of operation, when they do not have authority and may be reluctant to be too critical. Ibid., pp. 56–7.

[106] Ibid., p. 59.

[107] HCFP, 'Opinion of the High Council of Public Finance on the Budget Bill for 2016' (30 September 2015), www.hcfp.fr/Avis-et-publication/Avis/Avis-n-2015-03-relatif-aux-projets-de-lois-de-finances-et-de-financement-de-la-securite-sociale-pour-2016.

growth forecast to be 'optimistic'.[108] Also, the Spanish Independent Authority for Fiscal Responsibility considered the macroeconomic forecasts of the budgets of the regions of Madrid and Murcia to be 'little probable' in 2014.[109]

Beyond this, the main issue regards the impact Independent Fiscal Institutions can have. As stated, unless national norms provide otherwise, their assessments do not bind the governments. Only the 'comply or explain' principle applies and the Independent Fiscal Institutions' potential impact solely depends on the publicity of their assessments and the authority they may have themselves as reliable and independent 'fiscal watchdogs'. Additionally, their capacities are further limited by the fact that even the Automatic Correction Mechanism can easily be circumvented by national governments. Even when it is triggered neither the EU norms nor the Fiscal Compact prevent Member States from adopting a new programming act which will automatically lift the correction mechanism. This is what happened in France in 2014 when a new programming Act for 2014–19 was approved, despite the fact that the previous programming Act covered the period 2012–17. Through the adoption of the new law the correction mechanism activated in May 2014 de facto ceased to be in force.[110] Even after this new Act was adopted, the government has used yet again other values for its public finances and these changes have been criticised by the High Council.[111]

In sum, the constraining power Independent Fiscal Institutions can have on governments is limited to their capacity to 'name and shame' them.

[108] HCFP, 'Opinion of the High Council of Public Finance on the Budget Bill for 2015', www.hcfp.fr/content/download/231/1323/version/1/file/English+summary_Avis_nHCFP201405_PLF_PLFSS.pdf.

[109] Informe sobre las previsiones macroeconómicas de los presupuestos para 2015 de las Comunidades Autónomas, 1, www.airef.es/system/assets/archives/000/000/796/original/1_-_Informe_sobre_las_Previsiones_Macroecon%C3%B3micas_de_los_Presupuestos_para_2015_de_las_Comunidades_Aut%C3%B3noma.pdf?1436977340.

[110] See further Fromage, 'Le Haut Conseil des Finances Publiques: quelles conséquences deux ans après sa création?', 1124–5.

[111] 'Even if the 17th December 2012 [the organic law] allows the Government to do so, the HCFP reiterates its reservation of principle . . . on such a review of the assumptions on potential growth of the programming law. A review beyond the scope of the programming law makes it harder to analyse the evolution of the structural component of general government balance and hampers the transparency of fiscal policy.' See HCFP, 'Opinion of the High Council of Public Finance on the Budget Bill for 2016', p. 2.

B. *Relationship to Parliament: Too Loose in Many Cases?*

Independent Fiscal Institutions may still be useful for parliaments in providing them with information which they, in turn, can use to control the government's actions and hold them to account. This is particularly helpful, as acquiring fiscal information requires certain expertise they do not necessarily have and it is time-consuming.[112]

In fact, the adaptation to the European norms has in some cases allowed for a reinforcement of the relationship between Independent Fiscal Institutions – or their predecessors – and legislatures. In Austria, for instance, whereas the Government Debt Committee had no direct relationship to parliament, the reformed Fiscal Council does, as a representative of the newly created Parliamentary Budget Office can participate in all meetings held by the Fiscal Council in an advisory capacity.[113] However, neither chamber of the Austrian Parliament is involved in the designation of the Council's members as this responsibility rests on the federal government, the Austrian Chamber of Commerce in agreement with the Presidium of the Chambers of Agriculture, the federal Chamber of Labour, the Austrian Association of Municipalities, the Association of Austrian Cities and the Conference of Provincial Governors. Furthermore, its annual report is to be presented by the federal Minister of Finance to both the federal government and the National Council; no delay for this is defined though.[114]

In France, there is a strong relationship between the Independent Fiscal Institution and parliament, even if when the Organic Law establishing the High Council was approved '[s]ome members of parliament did speak out ... to condemn what they saw as a new technocratic framework divesting the parliament of its prerogatives in the budget process'.[115] The President of the High Council is to be heard at any time at the request of the committees of the National Assembly and the Senate[116] and, in fact, a close relationship was established during the first two-and-a-half years; the President has already attended 13 hearings in parliament.[117]

The Slovak Independent Fiscal Institution, which, as mentioned, was originally intended to be placed under parliament but was finally created

[112] European Commission, 'Report on Public finances in EMU', p. 55.
[113] OECD, 'Principles for Independent Fiscal Institutions and Country Notes', p. 33.
[114] Federal Law establishing the Fiscal Advisory Council, Art. 1(5).
[115] OECD, 'Principles for Independent Fiscal Institutions and Country Notes', p. 95.
[116] Organic Law 2012/1403, Art. 20. [117] HCFP, 'Activity Report 2013–2015', p. 5.

independently of any pre-existing institution, nonetheless has close ties with parliament as well. The latter is involved in the nomination of its members and regularly receives the Council's reports.[118]

In other cases, such as that of the Belgian High Council of Finance, there are still no formal relationships to the federal nor to the sub-national parliaments.[119] In 2014, for example, the High Council of Finance's reports were not debated in parliamentary committees nor did any of these committees invite High Council of Finance's representatives to appear before them, although this possibility exists.[120]

Given the relative weakness of parliaments in the Euro-national budgetary process, it would be highly desirable for Independent Fiscal Institutions and parliaments to establish tight(er) relationships, especially given the consequences faced by Member States when they do not respect the rules of the Stability and Growth Pact through the Excessive Deficit Procedure.

6 Concluding Remarks

As the preceding analysis has shown, it is particularly difficult to draw conclusions on the constitutional implication of the creation (or reform) of Independent Fiscal Institutions in the EU Member States, because it is both work in progress and an undefined subject. Yet, some preliminary conclusions can be formulated.

As has been highlighted, the EU and international obligations establish a minimum framework within which Member States still have quite some room for their own interpretation which in turn allows them to limit significantly the Independent Fiscal Institutions' impact, though it also permits them to take their national institutional features into account. Additionally, these obligations differ between Member States depending, for instance, on whether they belong to the euro area or on whether they are bound by the Fiscal Compact. As a consequence, Member States have created institutions whose variety in terms of length of existence, size, institutional features and powers, to give but a few examples, is particularly large. Also, the reason for the Independent

118 OECD, 'Principles for Independent Fiscal Institutions and Country Notes', p. 175.
119 OECD, 'Principles for Independent Fiscal Institutions and Country Notes', p. 48.
120 Ibid.

Fiscal Institutions' creation varies and may have an impact on their authority and general acceptance by the Member States' budgetary authorities.

Against this background, the question remains as to whether EU obligations will be sufficient for Independent Fiscal Institutions to make a real difference for Member States. The examples given above, where there is total absence of parliamentary involvement, suggest that the EU should have set minimum standards for the involvement of parliaments or a minimum size for the Independent Fiscal Institution, as many appear to be facing difficulties due to their overly limited size. Furthermore, EU rules could (and probably should) have ensured a minimum period of time for Independent Fiscal Institutions to prepare their reports; of two weeks, for example. Arguably, it would have intruded into the institutional autonomy of the Member States. However, EU law (and the Fiscal Compact) already invaded this when demanding that all Member States introduce a new institution into their institutional system. Additionally, these minimum requirements appear to be harmless if compared to what may happen to Member States if they fail to comply with their obligations contained in euro-crisis law and become subject to the Excessive Deficit Procedure.

As regards the difference Independent Fiscal Institutions can make for the EMU, and without seeking to assess this issue from an economic point of view, it appears that Independent Fiscal Institutions may invite Member States' governments to be more virtuous and respectful of their EU obligations if they do not want to face public blame. Given the fact that the Independent Fiscal Institutions' role is solely advisory, it is mostly in this sense that Independent Fiscal Institutions can be conceived as a sort of Sword of Damocles for governments and represent added value for the EMU as a whole.

Finally, perhaps one additional way to provide remedy to some of these shortcomings is also through exchanges between Independent Fiscal Institutions, as has happened in the past for national parliaments through their cooperation with each other and with the European Parliament. Independent Fiscal Institutions created an EU independent fiscal institutions network (EU Independent Fiscal Institutions)[121] in September 2015 on the basis of pre-existing informal exchanges between

[121] See www.euifis.eu/.

Independent Fiscal Institutions.[122] These 'inter-Independent Fiscal Institutions' relationships are further complemented by another forum of exchanges headed by the European Commission and bilateral relationships; for example, a visit to the Estonian Independent Fiscal Institution by their Latvian equivalent in December 2014, a few months after its creation.[123] These horizontal exchanges can be very fruitful given the limited constraining capacities possessed by Independent Fiscal Institutions, the opportunity for the more recently established to benefit from the expertise of older institutions and the important role played by Independent Fiscal Institutions in the Euro-national budgetary procedure (through the certification of budgetary forecasts or the activation of the Correction Mechanism). This is also the reason why their direct relationship with the European Commission is a development that needs monitoring in the future. Likewise, to determine whether these new 'fiscal watchdogs' will have any impact at all, it will be necessary to observe how the Commission assesses the Member States' compliance with their implementation duties and how national parliaments interact with Independent Fiscal Institutions in practice.

[122] An informal network was launched in 2013 on the initiative of the Slovak institution and it was formalised through the designation of a president and a vice-president in 2015. See HFCP, 'Activity Report 2013–2015', p. 28. Interestingly, although the UK is under no obligation to have an Independent Fiscal Institution according to EU and international rules, it is part of this network and the EUIFIS. See Office for Budgetary Responsibility, 'International Engagement', http://budgetresponsibility.org.uk/topics/international-engagement/. Prior to these developments, the OECD had already launched its own Network of Parliamentary Budget Officials and Independent Fiscal Institutions (PBO). However, membership of this network is not clearly defined as all institutions falling within this category in the OECD member states may – and, in fact, do – participate. However, no exhaustive list of the participating institutions is available.

[123] Fiscal Council of Estonia, 'Report for 2014', p. 7.

5

Differentiated Integration from the Perspective of Non-Euro Area Member States

THOMAS BEUKERS AND MARIJN VAN DER SLUIS

1 Introduction

Economic and Monetary Union (EMU) and differentiated integration were already a fascinating combination long before the Eurocrisis. This is not only because EMU can be seen as the paradigm of differentiated integration,[1] or as the field in which differentiated integration is most relevant and complex.[2] It is also because EMU blends the constitutional and instrumental differentiation logics.[3] According to the logic of constitutional differentiation, differentiation originates from treaty revisions that transfer national competences to the Union (deepening) and is motivated by concerns about national sovereignty and identity.[4] This logic explains why the United Kingdom and Denmark still have their own currencies, as they negotiated an exemption from the legal obligation to join the euro. To a lesser extent, this also explains the position of Sweden. According to the logic of instrumental differentiation, it has its origins in enlargement rounds (widening) and is motivated by efficiency and distributional concerns.[5] This can explain why the 10 new Member States that joined the Union in 2004 and 2007 were not allowed into the

[1] S. Van den Bogaert and V. Borger, 'Differentiated Integration in EMU', in B. De Witte, E. Vos and A. Ott (eds.), *Between Flexibility and Disintegration: The State of EU Law Today* (Cheltenham: Edgar Elgar Publishing, 2017).

[2] C. Herrmann, 'Differentiated Integration in the Field of Monetary Policy and the Use of Semi-Extra Union Legal Instruments – The Case for Relative Treaty Amendments', in De Witte, Vos and Ott (eds.), *Between Flexibility and Disintegration.*

[3] F. Schimmelfennig and T. Winzen, 'Instrumental and Constitutional Differentiation in the European Union', *Journal of Common Market Studies*, 52(2), (2014), 354–70, at 365.

[4] Ibid., 355. [5] Ibid.

euro area immediately and why those that have not since joined the euro have a legal obligation to do so once they meet the relevant convergence criteria.

So not only is there differentiation between euro ins and euro outs, there has traditionally also been differentiation among the outs. It is clear that the non-euro area Member States have hardly ever been in the same position, either with regard to their legal obligations or with regard to their political intention to join the euro. Indeed, it seems that the group of outs is best defined in the negative: they are Member States who are not a member of the euro area. The Eurocrisis has even led to different obligations among euro ins: the conditionality imposed on Greece, Ireland, Portugal, Cyprus and Spain being a prominent example.[6] In fact, the Eurocrisis and euro-crisis law have made the differentiated status of European integration in the field of EMU substantially more complex, both among ins, between ins and outs, and among the outs.

The focus of this chapter is the legal position of non-euro area Member States and the various ways it has been affected by euro-crisis law. During the Eurocrisis, measures were adopted that affect euro area and non-euro area Member States differently. Although most measures were primarily directed at the stability of monetary union (at the ins), they confronted outs with challenges related to the potential effects on their legal position in terms of their future membership conditions, immediate new obligations and effects on their substantive interests. What new obligations to accept before joining the euro? How to avoid being excluded from decision-making determining both the (current) relationship between ins and outs, as well as rules of (future) euro area membership? How to make sure that substantive interests are safeguarded? Does euro-crisis law affect the obligation to join the euro? This chapter will discuss these and other legal issues, challenges and tensions specifically related to the outs and give insights into how individual Member States have dealt with them. We will see that the non-euro area Member States have not given the same answers to these and other questions.

[6] Another difference is the initial Slovakian opt-out from the Greek aid package. See the report on Slovakia prepared by T. Dumbrovsky for the 'Constitutional Change through Euro Crisis Law' project of the EUI Law Department, Section IV.1. All the country reports referred to in this paper are part of the same project and available on its website: www.eurocrisislaw.eui.eu.

Section 2.A will place this chapter in the context of existing literature on differentiation in EMU to illustrate its contribution to the ongoing academic debate. Section 2.B will then briefly provide a legal and historical overview of differentiation in the field of EMU before the crisis. Section 2.C will do the same for the Eurocrisis, with a focus on the legal position of non-euro area Member States, including the different rights and obligations following from euro-crisis law. In Section 3 a number of specific legal issues and political challenges – which relate to non-euro area Member States and have emerged, in particular, during or as a consequence of the Eurocrisis – will be discussed together with the individual Member State responses. A distinction will be made between issues that relate to the current opt-out and derogation situation of these outs (Section 3.A), to the possible moment of entry into the euro area (Section 3.B) and finally to the period after adoption of the euro (Section 3.C). Section 4 will conclude.

2 EMU and Differentiated Integration

A. Scholarly Debate

Differentiation has been present in all phases of European integration (not only in EMU) and its theory and practice have received plenty of scholarly attention.[7] Traditionally, an analytical distinction is made between differentiation on the basis of time (multi-speed), space (variable geometry) and policy area (à la carte).[8] Explanations of differentiation focus on the ability to break deadlock and to allow for further deepening and widening.[9] De Witte notes that next to this functional reason, differentiation is also 'normatively attractive since it allows for the diverse preferences of national governments and national public opinions to be accommodated'.[10] Interestingly, more recent calls for differentiated integration not only focus on breaking deadlock but are also motivated by

[7] A classic in legal scholarship is B. De Witte, D. Hanf and E. Vos (eds.), *The Many Faces of Differentiation in EU Law*, (Antwerp: Intersentia, 2001).

[8] See A. Stubb, 'A Categorization of Differentiated Integration', *Journal of Common Market Studies*, 34(2), (1996) 283–95.

[9] Schimmelfennig and Winzen, 'Instrumental and Constitutional Differentiation in the European Union', at 365.

[10] B. De Witte, 'Variable Geometry and Differentiation as Structural Features of the EU Legal Order', in De Witte, Vos and Ott (eds.), *Between Flexibility and Disintegration*.

making the current Union more sustainable, if necessary by reducing membership of differentiated integration initiatives.[11]

The most recent literature on EMU and differentiated integration tends to focus on the position of euro area Member States. Considering the remarkable development of EMU and, in particular, the euro area, it should not surprise that numerous examples of institutional analyses can be given. Piris explores the euro area as a potential basis for a federal core Europe, either within or outside the current Treaty framework.[12] Curtin and Fasone discuss the possibility and desirability of differentiated representation within the European Parliament.[13] Peers and Craig have studied the possibility of using EU institutions outside the treaties to the benefit of a limited number of Member States, notably the euro area Member States.[14] Beukers explores the challenges and opportunities of a euro area flexibility clause as a way for the euro area to respond to one of the institutional challenges exposed by the Eurocrisis, namely that Member States (permanently) outside the euro area can block change desired by the euro area Member States.[15] Herrmann argues for a differentiated treaty amendment procedure allowing for amendments to be made to the provisions listed in Article 139(2) Treaty on the Functioning of European Union (TFEU), which do not apply to the non-euro area Member States, by agreement and ratification by the euro area Member States only.[16]

By contrast, issues relating to the specific position of non-euro area Member States have received considerably less attention. A notable exception is Dashwood, who argues that non-euro area Member States

[11] Hirsch Ballin calls for realistic differentiation, proposing that Member States with sufficient social-economic cohesion form a new community with common legislation, combined with a flexible approach to membership. See E. Hirsch Ballin, 'Europese eenwording in verscheidenheid', *Nederlands Juristenblad*, 1 (2016), 7–15, at 14.

[12] J.-C. Piris, *The Future of Europe: Towards a Two-Speed EU?* (Cambridge University Press, 2012); See also M. Avbelj, 'Differentiated Integration – Farewell to the EU-27?', *German Law Journal*, 14(1), (2013), 191–211, at 205.

[13] D. Curtin and C. Fasone, 'Differentiated Representation: Is a Flexible European Parliament Desirable?', in De Witte, Vos and Ott (eds.), *Between Flexibility and Disintegration*.

[14] S. Peers, 'Towards a New Form of EU Law? The Use of EU Institutions outside the EU Legal Framework', *European Constitutional Law Review*, 9(1), (2013), 37–72; P. Craig, 'Pringle and Use of EU Institutions outside the EU Legal Framework: Foundations, Procedure and Substance', *European Constitutional Law Review*, 9(1), (2013), 263–84.

[15] T. Beukers, 'Flexibilisation of the Euro Area: Challenges and Opportunities', EUI Working Papers, MWP 2014/1 (2014).

[16] Herrmann, 'Differentiated Integration in the Field of Monetary Policy and the Use of Semi-Extra Union Legal Instruments – The Case for Relative Treaty Amendments'.

require constitutional recognition as a class and that concrete constitutional arrangements are needed for the appropriate ordering of the relationship between members and non-members of the euro area.[17] Craig and Markakis study the impact of euro area regulation on non-euro area member states, with a focus on the UK.[18] Ferran and Babis consider the implications of the European banking union for non-euro area Member States and conclude that it poses challenges to the ability of the EU's constitutional framework to cope with differentiated integration.[19] The present chapter adds to these exceptions by discussing legal issues, challenges and tensions specifically related to the outs, and offering insights into the different responses from *all* non-euro area Member States, including a comparative perspective.

B. *EMU before the Crisis: Main Legal and Political Events*

In the development of differentiation, the Treaty of Maastricht of 1992 takes a special position because it sowed the seeds for a deep and continued form of differentiation in the field of monetary policy and, related to that, in the area of economic policy. In 1997, the Stability and Growth Pact (SGP) was agreed, setting out in more detail the rules on fiscal discipline.[20] After the euro had been introduced as the common currency in 11 out of then-15 EU Member States in 1999 (all but the UK, Denmark, Sweden and Greece), it also entered into circulation through physical coins and banknotes in 2002. In the meantime, Greece became the 12th member in 2001.

The split between the ins and the outs in EMU occurred for two reasons, captured by the aforementioned distinction between instrumental and constitutional differentiation. First, it was recognised that the

[17] A. Dashwood, 'Guest Editorial. Living with the Eurozone', *Common Market Law Review*, 53(1), (2016), 3–10, at 3–4.

[18] P. Craig and M. Markakis, 'The Euro Area, Its Regulation and Impact on Non-Euro Member States', in P. Koutrakos and J. Snell (eds.), *Research Handbook on the Law of the EU's Internal Market* (Cheltenham: Edward Elgar Publishing, 2016).

[19] E. Ferran and V. Babis, 'The European Single Supervisory Mechanism', *Journal of Corporate Law Studies*, 13(2), (2013), 255–85.

[20] Resolution of the European Council on the Stability and Growth Pact of 17 June 1997 (OJ C 236, 2.8.97, p.1); Regulation (EC) No. 1466/97 of 7 July 1997 on the strengthening of the surveillance of budgetary positions and the surveillance and coordination of economic policies (OJ L 209, 2.8.1997, p. 1); Council Regulation (EC) No. 1467/97 of 7 July on speeding up and clarifying the implementation of the excessive deficit procedure (OJ L 209, 2.8.1997, p. 6).

(economic) benefits of membership of a single currency area rested on different dynamics than the benefits of membership of the economic area of the European Community. The former requires a higher level of convergence of some key economic indicators. Hence, it was decided that only Member States that met certain economic standards could adopt the euro. The other reason was the opposition of the UK towards the project of monetary integration. From the beginning of the negotiations it was clear that the UK would not want to join the single currency and even wanted to block its coming into existence. For monetary integration to progress, the UK had to be given an opt-out in a special protocol (No. 15 under the Lisbon Treaty). Denmark also received a special status in relation to EMU in a separate protocol (No. 16 under the Lisbon Treaty), albeit under different terms than the UK. The political agreement reached amongst the Member States in response to the negative referendum in Denmark on the ratification of the Maastricht Treaty confirmed the Danish opt-out.

So it was envisioned that not all Member States would make the jump to monetary union. For this group the term Member States with derogation was introduced in the Treaty of Maastricht. This derogation had different effects within the economic part of EMU and for the monetary side. Whereas most provisions on economic union are applicable to the Member States with a derogation, the important provisions on monetary union are not. With regard to the Multilateral Surveillance Procedure and the Excessive Deficit Procedure (EDP) described in Articles 121 and 126 TFEU respectively, only the sanctions mentioned in the EDP are not applicable to Member States with a derogation.[21] For example, this means that the no bailout clause (Article 125 TFEU) and the prohibition on monetary financing (Article 123 TFEU) are applicable to them (see Section 2.C for further discussion). For the monetary union, Member States with a derogation are not bound by the tasks and obligations of the European System of Central Banks (ESCB), acts of the ECB and the issuance of the euro.

From the Treaty the idea clearly arose that the split in integration would be temporary, save for the UK and later Denmark.[22] Early on, however, it became clear that that was not a realistic assumption. Sweden held a referendum in 2003 about whether the country should try to join

[21] Also excluded, by way of Art. 139 TFEU, are the broad economic policy guidelines that concern the euro area generally under Art. 121(2) TFEU.

[22] Art. 140 TFEU.

the euro; the proposal was rejected. Many European lawyers have argued that Sweden's refusal to join the Exchange Rate Mechanism (ERM II) – which is necessary before joining the euro – was a violation of EU law.[23] Whereas Denmark had required a protocol to specify its position before ratifying the Maastricht Treaty, Sweden used the convergence criteria to accomplish a similar feat. Dashwood rightfully argues that the Swedish case demonstrates that 'no Member State of the Union can be compelled to join the single currency if its people do not wish this'.[24]

There is therefore a wide gap between the political and legal realities when it comes to the obligation to join the euro. This gap can be partially explained by the fact that, for the new Member States, EMU came wrapped in a larger package of EU membership, without the possibility of an opt-out. Whereas the old Member States either willingly signed up for the euro in the Maastricht Treaty or received an opt-out, thereby endorsing the legal obligation to join the euro by an expression of political will, the new Member States did not express themselves in such a way in relation to EMU specifically, but to the EU generally.

Notwithstanding the gap between the political and legal realities when it comes to the obligation to join the euro, most of the Member States that joined the EU in the 2004 enlargement have since also joined the euro, including Slovenia (2007), Malta and Cyprus (2008) and Slovakia (2009). The composition of the group of non-euro area Member States has also changed during the Eurocrisis. Estonia (2011), Latvia (2014) and Lithuania (2015) have joined the euro area and thus left the group, while Croatia expanded the group when it joined the EU (2013).

During the negotiations for enlargement, EMU played only a minor role, except for the issue of central bank independence. For the Eastern European enlargement, the Commission stated that: 'Their central banks have to be independent and have price stability as their primary objective.'[25] As a result, central bank independence was established in the 10 new Member States before accession. For these outs, EMU has had constitutional implications for quite some time.

[23] Most prominently J.-V. Louis, 'The Economic and Monetary Union: Law and Institutions', 41(2) (2004), *Common Market Law Review*, 575–608, at 603–5.

[24] Dashwood, 'Guest Editorial. Living with the Eurozone', 5.

[25] Commission Opinion on Poland's Application for Membership of the European Union, 15 July 1997, DOC/97/16, p. 59. The soundness of the legal reasoning behind this requirement can be questioned, as under Art. 130 TFEU national central banks only have to be independent insofar as they are executing tasks conferred under the Treaties.

A relevant change in the framework of euro-differentiation was the introduction of a special Chapter IV in Title VIII to the Lisbon Treaty, titled 'Provisions Specific to Member States Whose Currency Is the Euro'. This treaty chapter includes Article 136 TFEU, which mandates secondary legislation to strengthen the coordination of budgetary surveillance of the Member States and to set economic policy guidelines for them.[26] The innovative element is that instead of the application of certain provisions being excluded for Member States with a derogation, these provisions are made only applicable to Member States whose currency is the euro. As we will see in the next section, this provision has been actively used during the Eurocrisis.

C. *Euro-Crisis Law and Non-Euro Area Member States: The Legal Framework*

This section briefly describes the main aspects of euro-crisis law and its pertinence for non-euro area Member States, distinguishing between financial assistance mechanisms, the economic governance framework, the banking union, and the relevance of the *Pringle* and *Gauweiler* judgments of the European Court of Justice (ECJ) for non-euro area Member States.[27]

Financial Assistance Mechanisms

Financial support to Member States in economic difficulties has taken many shapes during the crisis. In many of the instruments there was no participation or financial contribution by non-euro area Member States.[28] However, the financial assistance packages to Ireland and Latvia

[26] H. Bribosia, 'La Politique Économique et Monétaire' in G. Amato, H. Bribosia and B. De Witte (eds.), *Genesis and Destiny of the European Constitution* (Brussels: Bruylant, 2007); F. Amtenbrink and J. De Haan, 'Economic Governance in the European Union: Fiscal Policy Discipline versus Flexibility', *Common Market Law Review*, 40(5) (2003), 1075–106.

[27] For a detailed analysis of the way that non-euro area Member States have reformed their national fiscal policy framework in reaction to euro-crisis law, see Sections II and III of the country reports available at eurocrisislaw.eui.eu. See also T. Beukers and M. van der Sluis, 'The Variable Geometry of the Euro-crisis: A Look at the Non-Euro Area Member States', EUI Working Papers, LAW 2015/33 (2015), p. 5.

[28] For a discussion of legal issues involved, see A. De Gregorio Merino, 'Legal Developments in the Economic and Monetary Union During the Debt Crisis: The Mechanisms of Financial Assistance', *Common Market Law Review*, 49(5), (2012), 1613–45.

consisted partially of bilateral loans from the UK and Sweden in the case of Ireland in 2010, and Sweden, Denmark and Estonia in the case of balance of payments assistance for Latvia in 2008.[29] Moreover, EU support to non-euro area Member States on the basis of Article 143 TFEU (balance of payments assistance) to Hungary (2008), Latvia (2009) and Romania (2009) was indirectly supported by all Member States through the EU budget. Although for the contributing Member States the internal procedures for deciding on the assistance may have differed, no constitutional problems seem to have arisen. The European Financial Stabilisation Mechanism (EFSM) does concern non-euro area Member States, as it was created through a regulation binding all EU Member States, and the loans issued under it are guaranteed by the EU budget, for which all Member States are responsible. The European Financial Stability Facility (EFSF), which was created in the same weekend as the EFSM in May 2010, is a temporary special-purpose vehicle, created outside the framework of the EU treaties by the euro area Member States. When Estonia joined the euro in 2011 it also joined the EFSF. In 2012 the European Stability Mechanism (ESM) had come into force with the purpose of replacing the EFSF, so Latvia only joined the ESM upon entry into the euro area in 2014. Lithuania, in January 2015, similarly joined both the euro and the ESM.

In August 2015, there was great discontent amongst the non-euro area Member States after the difficult negotiations between Greece and the other euro area Member States on a third aid package led to the activation of the EFSM to provide for bridge financing to Greece. The EFSM regulation was subsequently amended to assuage their concerns.[30] The amendment requires that Union assistance to a euro area Member State be complemented with an arrangement 'guaranteeing that the Member States whose currency is not the euro are immediately and fully compensated for any liability they may incur as a result of any failure by the beneficiary Member State to repay the financial assistance'.[31]

[29] Whilst the euro-crisis is usually thought to have started in 2010, three non-euro area Member States already requested assistance during the financial crisis of 2008, when the EU provided balance-of-payments assistance to Latvia, Hungary and Romania.

[30] Council Regulation (EU) No. 407/2010 of 11 May 2010 establishing a European financial stabilisation mechanism (OJ L 118, 12.5.2010, p. 1).

[31] See Art. 1 of Council Regulation (EU) No. 2015/1360 of 4 August 2015 amending Regulation (EU) No. 407/2010 establishing a European financial stabilisation mechanism (OJ L 210, 7.8.2015, p. 1).

Although non-euro area Member States are not parties to the ESM Treaty, for several reasons its creation was nevertheless relevant for them. First of all, an amendment to Article 136 TFEU was supposed to precede its coming into force. Although the amendment addresses only euro area Member States, it required approval by all the Member States in accordance with the simplified revision procedure of Article 48(6) TEU. Second, the text of the amendment is interesting for non-euro area Member States, as it allows the euro area Member States to create a stability mechanism, prompting questions about possible obligatory accession to the ESM upon entry into the euro area (see Section 3.C). Third, under the ESM there is an active involvement of European institutions, in particular for the European Commission, European Central Bank (ECB) and ECJ. Representatives of the governments also of the non-euro area Member States expressed their support for this use on 20 June 2011, authorising the parties to the ESM Treaty to request the European Commission and the ECB to perform the tasks provided in the treaty.[32]

Fiscal and Economic Governance: Six Pack, Euro Plus Pact, Fiscal Compact and Two Pack

Whereas the first leg of euro-crisis law consists of a collection of mechanisms to provide financial stability, the second leg consists of measures to strengthen the fiscal and economic governance in EMU.[33] The 'Six Pack' is one of the most important parts of this leg and consists of one directive and five regulations that entered into force in 2011.[34] Articles 121, 126 and 136 TFEU have been used for the adoption of these acts.

[32] See para. 10 of the Preamble to the Treaty Establishing the European Stability Mechanism.

[33] For a broader overview and discussion, see A. De Streel, 'EU Fiscal Governance and the Effectiveness of Its Reform', in M. Adams, F. Fabbrini and P. Larouche (eds.), *The Constitutionalization of European Budgetary Constraints* (Oxford: Hart Publishing, 2014), pp. 85–104.

[34] 1) Regulation (EU) No. 1175/2011 of the European Parliament and of the Council of 16 November 2011 amending Council Regulation (EC) No. 1466/97 on strengthening the surveillance of budgetary positions and the surveillance and coordination of economic policies (OJ L 306, 23.11.2011, p. 12); 2) Council Regulation (EU) No. 1177/2011 of 8 November 2011 amending Regulation (EC) No. 1467/97 on speeding up and clarifying the implementation of the excessive deficit procedure (OJ L 306, 23.11.2011, p. 33); 3) Regulation (EU) No. 1173/2011 of the European Parliament and of the Council of 16 November 2011 on the effective enforcement of budgetary surveillance in the euro area (OJ L 306, 23.11.2011, p. 1); 4) Regulation (EU) No. 1176/2011 of the European Parliament and of the Council of 16 November 2011 on the prevention and correction of macroeconomic imbalances (OJ L 306, 23.11.2011, p. 25); 5) Regulation (EU) No. 1174/2011 of the

Two of the Six Pack regulations, the ones that set up the system of fines and interest-bearing deposits that accompany budgetary surveillance and the macro-economic imbalances procedure, are not applicable to non-euro area Member States.[35] These regulations are based also on Article 136 TFEU and therefore cannot be applicable to non-euro area Member States. Other regulations, which amend the preventive and corrective arms of the SGP, are only partially applicable to non-euro area Member States.[36] These regulations have many provisions that are applicable only to either 'participating' or 'non-participating' Member States, for example, in relation to the stability or convergence programmes that Member States have to submit and the procedural steps that are involved in sanctioning non-compliance.[37] Finally, Regulation (EU) No. 1176/2011 and Directive 2011/85/EU are fully applicable also to non-euro area Member States. Regulation (EU) No. 1176/2011 sets out the mechanism on the prevention and correction of macroeconomic imbalances and deepens the system of multilateral surveillance of Article 121 TFEU (which serves as its legal basis). Directive 2011/85/EU sets out the requirements of budgetary frameworks of the Member States and complements the EDP, with Article 126(14) TFEU as its legal basis. It includes obligations to maintain a system of reliable macroeconomic forecasts, the use of fiscal rules, a medium-term budgetary framework and an independent fiscal council.[38]

As a result of the protocol on its special position in EMU (No. 15), the UK is exempted from several obligations in the Six Pack, most notably those on fiscal rules and the fiscal council in Directive 2011/85/EU.

European Parliament and of the Council of 16 November 2011 on enforcement measures to correct excessive macroeconomic imbalances in the euro area (OJ L 306, 23.11.2011, p. 8); 6) Council Directive 2011/85/EU of 8 November 2011 on requirements for budgetary frameworks of the Member States (OJ L 306, 23.11.2011, p. 41).

35 Regulation (EU) No. 1173/2011 and Regulation (EU) No. 1174/2011.

36 Regulation (EU) No. 1175/2011 and Council Regulation (EU) No. 1177/2011.

37 Also see Regulation (EU) No. 1176/2011, Arts. 9(3) and 13(3). Further, it is noteworthy that Regulation (EU) No. 1175/2011 (in line with the reform of the SGP in 2005) differentiates with regard to the setting of the Medium Term Budgetary Objective (MTBO). Euro area Member States and Member States participating in ERM II, must set their MTBO at or below 1 per cent of government deficit to GDP, while for the other Member States there only has to be a safety margin before the infamous 3 per cent mark is hit. This has resulted in a differentiated application of the economic governance rules to non-euro area Member States: those who participate in the ERM II and those who do not.

38 See on Independent Fiscal Institutions in this book Chapter 4, 'Creation and Reform of Independent Fiscal Institutions in EU Member States: Incomplete and Insufficient Work in Progress?' by Diane Fromage.

The Euro Plus Pact was adopted in 2011 to foster competitiveness and employment and to improve the sustainability of public finances. It contains policy suggestions in fields that largely fall under the competence of the Member States. The committed Member States nevertheless promised to report on their implementation in their national reform programmes and stability programmes in the context of the European Semester. The pact was agreed in the context of a European Council meeting, during which the participants 'switched hats'. It is not an international treaty and lacks legally binding force. Hungary, the UK, the Czech Republic and Sweden did not join the pact.

The Treaty on Stability, Coordination and Governance in the Economic and Monetary Union (here, referred to in shorthand as the Fiscal Compact) builds upon the rules of the Six Pack. This international treaty, which entered into force on 1 January 2013, was created after it became clear that the UK would block an EU Treaty amendment that would oblige euro area Member States to adopt a constitutional 'golden rule'.[39] A weaker version of this obligation is now included in Title III of the Fiscal Compact. The UK, Croatia and the Czech Republic are the only Member States that are not parties to this Treaty, the latter having started but not yet successfully completed the ratification procedure. To non-euro area Member States which have joined, only Title V of the Treaty (on participation in Euro Summits) is applicable, unless a Member State submits that it intends to be bound by other parts as well (see on this in Section 3.A). Once a non-euro area Member State that is party to the Fiscal Compact joins the euro, the entire Treaty will automatically apply to it.

The EU economic governance framework, strengthened by the Six Pack, was further complemented by the 'Two Pack' in 2013, consisting of two regulations, neither of which is applicable to non-euro area Member States. One regulation deals with monitoring and assessing draft budgetary plans and ensuring the correction of excessive deficits[40] and the other deals with enhanced surveillance of euro area Member States experiencing or threatened with financial difficulties.[41]

[39] B. De Witte, 'Using International Law in the Euro Crisis: Causes and Consequences', ARENA Working Paper, 2013/4 (2013).

[40] Regulation (EU) No. 473/2013 of the European Parliament and of the Council of 21 May 2013 on common provisions for monitoring and assessing draft budgetary plans and ensuring the correction of excessive deficit of the Member States in the euro area (OJ L 140, 27.5.2013, p. 11).

[41] Regulation (EU) No. 472/2013 of the European Parliament and of the Council of 21 May 2013 on the strengthening of economic and budgetary surveillance of Member States in

Banking Union

The European banking union as envisaged contains three pillars:[42] supervision, resolution and deposit insurance.[43] The first two have so far been established. In the first pillar, established in 2013, the ECB has been conferred exclusive competence for specific prudential supervisory tasks of financial institutions in the euro area and in those non-euro area Member States which choose to join the Single Supervisory Mechanism (SSM).[44] In the second pillar, established in 2014, resolution of financial institutions subject to the SSM can take place through the Single Resolution Mechanism (SRM),[45] thus including financial institutions in the euro area and in those non-euro area Member States that have chosen to join the SSM. Participation in both SSM and SRM is obligatory for euro area Member States and free and optional for non-euro area Member States. So far, no non-euro area Member State has decided to participate.[46] For a non-euro area Member State that decides to participate in the SSM, a close cooperation is foreseen between the ECB and the national competent authority.[47]

the euro area experiencing or threatened with serious difficulties with respect to their financial stability (OJ L 140, 27.5.2013, p. 1).

42 For a broader overview and discussion of banking union, see N. Moloney, 'European Banking Union: Assessing Its Risks and Resilience', *Common Market Law Review*, 51(6), (2014), 1609–70.

43 In November 2015, the European Commission has proposed a euro area wide deposit insurance scheme (EDIS) for bank deposits.

44 Council Regulation (EU) No. 1024/213 of 15 October 2013 conferring specific tasks on the European Central Bank concerning policies relating to the prudential supervision of credit institutions (OJ L 287, 29.10.2013, p. 63).

45 Regulation (EU) No. 806/2014 establishing uniform rules and a uniform procedure for the resolution of credit institutions and certain investment firms in the framework of a Single Resolution Mechanism and a Single Resolution Fund and amending Regulation (EU) No. 1093/2010 (OJ L 225, 30.7.2014, p. 1).

46 A number of non-euro area Member States have expressed an intention to join the banking union. See, for example, 'Bulgaria Asks ECB to Supervise Banks as Crisis Festers', *Bloomberg* (15 July 2014), www.bloomberg.com/news/articles/2014-07-15/bulgaria-asks-ecb-to-supervise-banks-as-crisis-festers.

47 Article 7 of Council Regulation (EU) No. 1024/213. Belling, Mark and Vojta speak of 'secondary membership status' because the same duties of all SSM members are not accompanied by the same rights. See V. Belling, L. Marek and M. Vojta, *National Report: Czech Republic*, in FIDE Banking Union (2016), 97–136, at 110. Zagradišnik argues that, notwithstanding the safeguards that have been put in place, 'ultimately under the current institutional framework non-euro participating Member States are not equal to euro area

National supervisory authorities remain responsible for supervision of financial institutions in Member States not participating in banking union and, in general, for supervision of non-significant institutions in euro area Member States. This results in a complex institutional architecture of supervision in the EU, which is accompanied by substantive norms, known collectively as the 'Single Rulebook', which are applicable to both euro area and non-euro area Member States. This includes the Capital Requirements Regulation (CRR) and the Capital Requirements Directive IV (CRDIV), which harmonise capital requirements.[48] The European Banking Authority (EBA), established in 2010 as one of three new European Supervisory Authorities (the ESAs),[49] has a main task of contributing to the creation of the Single Rulebook through the adoption of Binding Technical Standards and Guidelines. In the EBA, all Member States are represented, but there is a risk of domination by euro area Member States. Therefore, a double majority rule was agreed in 2013 which requires that decisions by the Board of Supervisors are passed by a simple majority of Member States participating in the SSM and a simple majority of those not participating (until less than five non-participating Member States remain).[50]

An essential part of the SRM is the Single Resolution Fund (SRF), established by the same EU regulation. A substantive directive also exists for bank resolution, which provides for a common set of tools and

Member States', see R. Zagradišnik, *National Report: Slovenia*, in FIDE Banking Union (2016), 409–30, at 412–13.

[48] Regulation (EU) No. 575/2013 of the European Parliament and of the Council of 26 June 2013 on prudential requirements for credit institutions and investment firms and amending Regulation (EU) No. 648/2012 (OJ L 176, 27.6.2013, p. 1); Directive 2013/36/EU of the European Parliament and of the Council of 26 June 2013 on access to the activity of credit institutions and the prudential supervision of credit institutions and investment firms, amending Directive 2002/87/EC and repealing Directives 2006/48/EC and 2006/49/EC (OJ 176, 27.6.2013, p. 338).

[49] Regulation (EU) No. 1093/2010 of the European Parliament and of the Council 24 November 2010 establishing a European Supervisory Authority (European Banking Authority), amending Decision No. 716/2009/EC and repealing Commission Decision 2009/78/EC (OJ L 331, 15.12.2010, p. 12).

[50] See Art. 4 of Regulation (EU) No. 1093/2010, as amended by Regulation (EU) No. 1022/2013 of the European Parliament and of the Council of 22 October 2013 amending Regulation (EU) No. 1093/2010 establishing a European Supervisory Authority (European Banking Authority) as regards the conferral of specific tasks on the European Central Bank pursuant to Council Regulation (EU) No. 1024/2013 (OJ L 287, 29.10.2013, p. 5).

powers for dealing with failing banks.[51] However, the transfer of national funds, financed by the banking sector, to the SRF is governed by an 'Intergovernmental Agreement on the transfer and mutualisation of contributions to the Single Resolution Fund'. This treaty, concluded outside the framework of the Union, was signed on 21 May 2014 by 26 Member States. Apart from the UK and Sweden, this includes all non-euro area Member States, notwithstanding the fact that they have not yet decided to participate in the SSM or SRM.

The Relevance of the Pringle and OMT Judgments for the Outs

As noted previously, Articles 123 and 125 TFEU are applicable to the non-euro area Member States. These provisions were at the heart of two landmark cases before the ECJ during the Eurocrisis. The *Pringle* case concerned the interpretation of Article 125 (the 'no bailout-clause') and the creation of the ESM;[52] the *Gauweiler* case interpreted Article 123 TFEU (the prohibition on monetary financing) and the mandate of the ECB in relation to the decision of the ECB on Outright Monetary Transactions (OMT).[53] The legal position of the outs did not play any role in the reasoning of the Court in either of the cases. To the contrary, the ECJ interpreted these provisions in the context of regulating the institutions and Member States of the euro area. Given the questions before the Court, that approach is not surprising. This raises the question about the extent to which the interpretations given by the ECJ are relevant for, or have an impact on, the outs.

In the *Pringle* case the Court found that the objective of Article 125 TFEU is 'maintaining the financial stability of the monetary union'.[54] Accordingly, providing financial assistance 'by means of a stability mechanism such as the ESM is not compatible with Article 125 TFEU unless it is indispensable for the safeguarding of the financial

[51] The 'Bank Recovery and Resolution Directive' (BRRD): Directive 2014/59/EU of the European Parliament and of the Council establishing a framework for the recovery and resolution of credit institutions and investment firms and amending Council Directive 82/891/EEC, and Directives 2001/24/EC, 2002/47/EC, 2004/25/EC, 2005/56/EC, 2007/36/EC, 2011/35/EU, 2012/30/EU and 2013/36/EU, and Regulations (EU) No. 1093/2010 and (EU) No. 648/2012, of the European Parliament and of the Council (OJ L 173, 12.6.2014, p. 190).

[52] *Thomas Pringle* v. *Government of Ireland, Ireland and the Attorney General*, Case C-370/12.

[53] *Gauweiler and Others* v. *Deutscher Bundestag*, Case C-62/14.

[54] *Pringle*, para. 135.

stability of the euro area as a whole'.[55] Obviously this condition cannot be imposed on support to non-euro area member states. The two other conditions for financial assistance as formulated in Pringle are that a Member State remains responsible to its creditors for its commitments and that strict conditions must be attached to the granting of assistance. There is no reason not to apply these requirements to financial assistance provided to non-euro area Member States, especially if that assistance is provided outside balance of payments support based on Article 143 TFEU.

Also in the *Gauweiler* case, which interprets the prohibition on monetary financing, the conclusions of the Court are highly dependent on the specifics of the OMT decision by the ECB. Article 123 TFEU precludes the ECB and National Central Banks from directly buying the debt instruments of Member States. Purchases on the secondary market are also prohibited, according to the Court, 'under conditions which would, in practice, mean that its action has an effect equivalent to that of a direct purchase'.[56] Hence, such purchases on the secondary markets must contain 'sufficient safeguards' and must not 'lessen the impetus of the Member States concerned to follow a sound budgetary policy'.[57]

Which purchases on the secondary market would exactly violate the prohibition remains unclear, as the Court in its decision highlights several key characteristics of the OMT program but does not explicate which parts of these characteristics are necessary and which are supportive. This also leaves open the possibility that the prohibition of monetary financing will be applied differently in non-euro area Member States. Of particular interest in that regard are the purchases from 2009 by the Bank of England of UK debt instruments on the secondary markets in a monetary policy strategy called quantitative easing. This is not the place to investigate the extent to which these purchases conform to the general purposes of Article 123 TFEU or the interpretation of this provision by the ECJ in the *Gauweiler* case; it suffices to note that the legality of these purchases is not a foregone conclusion.[58] However, it should also be noted that any actual enforcement of the prohibition on monetary financing against non-

[55] B. Witte and T. Beukers, 'The Court of Justice Approves the Creation of the European Stability Mechanism Outside the EU Legal Order: *Pringle*', *Common Market Law Review*, 50(3), (2013), 805–48, at 838.

[56] *Gauweiler*, para. 97. [57] *Gauweiler*, paras. 102 and 109.

[58] D. Wilsher, 'Ready to Do Whatever It Takes? The Legal Mandate of the European Central Bank and the Economic Crisis', *Cambridge Yearbook of European Legal Studies*, 15, (2013), 503–36, at 529.

euro area Member States is not to be expected due to its extreme political sensitivity and a lack of clear beneficiaries of such enforcement.

3 Euro-Crisis Law and Non-Euro Area Member States: Challenges and Responses

In the following section a number of specific legal questions are discussed that relate to non-euro area Member States which have emerged during or as a consequence of the Eurocrisis. The discussion will illustrate how individual non-euro area Member States have approached different challenges, such as the tension between, on the one hand, an interest not to accept far-reaching obligations relating to the single currency before actually joining the euro and, on the other, an interest not to be excluded from important institutional settings and moments in which decisions are made on the current and future design of the euro area. The discussion will also include legal issues that have become topical because of the Eurocrisis, relating to non-euro area Member States and the Fiscal Compact, the ESM, or the question whether euro-crisis law affects the obligation to join the euro.

A distinction is now made between issues that relate to the current opt-out and derogation situation of the outs (Section 3.A), to the possible moment of entry into the euro area (Section 3.B) and, finally, to the period after adoption of the euro (Section 3.C).

A. Issues Relating to the Opt-Out and Derogation Period

Non-Euro Area Member States and the Decision to Be Bound by (Most of) the Fiscal Compact

In the Fiscal Compact, an interesting balance has been struck between the interest of euro area Member States to integrate further and the interest of non-euro area Member States not to be disadvantaged. This has resulted in Titles III and IV, which arguably include the most important and far-reaching provisions of the Treaty, binding only euro area Member States and those outs that opt-in to the provisions in question,[59] while the institutional Title V on Euro Summits ('Governance of the euro area') is binding on (read: provides entitlements for) all contracting parties, independent of whether they have adopted the euro (see below on this latter issue).

[59] On the basis of Art. 14(5) Fiscal Compact.

Most remarkable in this context is the choice of three non-euro area Member States to become bound by extra parts of the Fiscal Compact even before joining the euro. Romania and Denmark have decided to be bound by the entire Fiscal Compact, also meaning the optional Titles III (including the obligation to adopt a balanced budget rule) and Title IV (on economic policy coordination and convergence), whereas Bulgaria has decided to be bound by Title III. This creates an interesting case of differentiation among outs in terms of legal obligations. Why have three outs decided to be bound early by these optional titles? In particular, why have Bulgaria, Romania and Denmark decided to be bound by the important balanced budget rule, which touches upon fundamental national constitutional issues? If they felt pressure to do so, it is not the pressure put, for example, on Ireland[60] through making ESM support conditional on ratification of the Fiscal Compact and fulfilment of the requirements related to the balanced budget rule (fiscal responsibility in return for solidarity),[61] as Romania, Bulgaria and Denmark do not qualify for ESM support until they join the euro and the ESM.

In the case of Romania the political decision to be bound by the entire Fiscal Compact seems to have been taken solely by President Băsescu[62] and has been the subject of fierce criticism.[63] In the mandatory amendment of the constitution to implement the balanced budget rule, initially proposed in early drafts of the Fiscal Compact, he is said to have seen an opportunity to 'open' the Constitution for amendment. This would have created a possibility to operationalise the positive results of the November 2009 referendum. The proposals that were then put to a referendum (including a unicameral Parliament with 300 seats) had not yet been put in place because of lack of political support in the Parliament.[64] Băsescu's support for the Fiscal Compact was further bolstered by his conviction that it represented a necessary step towards European integration, rather than an intrusion into national sovereignty.[65]

In the end, however, Romania decided to implement the balanced budget rule through an ordinary law,[66] even though it can be argued to follow from the Romanian system of legal sources 'that, in order to comply with the provisions of Article 3(2) of the Fiscal Compact, in Romania the amendment of the Constitution would have been imminent' (sic).[67]

[60] See the report on Ireland prepared by S. Coutts. [61] ESM Treaty, Preamble, para. 5.
[62] See the report on Romania prepared by V. Vita, Section IX.1. [63] Ibid., Section IX.3.
[64] Ibid., Section IX.1. [65] Ibid., Section IX.5. [66] Ibid., Section IX.4. [67] Ibid.

In the case of Bulgaria, the national preoccupation was not with strong fiscal governance (Title III), but all the more present with regard to economic policy coordination (Title IV). There was a strong resistance to commitments for harmonisation of the Bulgarian tax policy and the concepts of coordination and convergence were considered too vague.[68] In fact, it has been a priority of the Bulgarian government during the negotiations of the Fiscal Compact to have the right of Member States to adopt their tax policies independently guaranteed. Although the provisions of Title IV seemed general and harmless, they could also be slippery and become burdensome in the future.[69] No such risk was perceived in relation to Title III: the Bulgarian government was convinced that the balanced budget rule is not going to negatively affect Bulgaria, that it would not require cardinal changes in its policy or additional sacrifice and that, by signing up to it, Bulgaria would be among the best performing Member States in the EU.[70]

Among the relevant factors determining the Danish decision to be bound by the entire Fiscal Compact may be the fact that an important part of the treaty negotiations took place under the 2012 Danish Presidency of the EU.[71] The treaty was also signed under its Presidency. Another element may be the traditional Danish approach to budgetary discipline. Certainly the successful attempt to downgrade the initial obligation to amend the constitution so as to adopt provisions with 'binding force and permanent character, preferably constitutional, or otherwise guaranteed to be fully respected and adhered to' (Article 3.2 Fiscal Compact) also made it easier to decide to be bound at an early stage. Amendment of the constitution to comply with the Fiscal Compact would have hardly been feasible in Denmark.

Still, even among the outs that decided to be bound early by optional Titles of the Fiscal Compact, Denmark remains an interesting case, because it has an opt-out from the euro itself. The Danish approach to the Fiscal Compact can be interpreted as an indication that Denmark's political elite is still much more favourable to the idea of adopting the euro than that of the other semi-permanent out, the UK.[72]

[68] 'Parliament Okays Bulgaria's Participation In EU Fiscal Compact, But without Harmonisation of Tax Policy', *Energy, Ecology, Economy* (28 January 2012), http://3e-news.net/en/economy/parliament-okays-bulgaria-s-participation-in-eu-fiscal-compact-but-without-harmonization-of-tax_13140.

[69] See the report on Bulgaria prepared by M. Vatsos, Section IX.1.

[70] Ibid., Section IX.5.

[71] See, for example, D. Beach, 'The Fiscal Compact, Euro-Reforms and the Challenge for the Euro-Outs', *Danish Foreign Policy Yearbook* (2013), 113–33.

[72] In fact, Danish Prime Minister Thorning-Schmidt has clearly advocated Danish membership of the euro area. See H. Jacobsen, 'Danish PM Says Country 'Should' Join the

How to Approach the Evolving Obligations under the Fiscal Compact

The Fiscal Compact provided all Contracting Parties with a choice: how to assess the obligations arising from the Treaty? And what conclusions to draw from this in terms of the ratification procedure? The nature of the obligations of a Treaty is often a determining factor for the procedure of ratification. Generally, treaties that transfer sovereign powers to an international organisation require larger majorities in parliament, or even a referendum. However, for the non-euro area Member States, there is an extra dimension to these choices, since the obligations under the Fiscal Compact will change depending on future events. This leads to the following question: has the treaty been ratified in light of the future obligations that can arise from it, or has it been ratified only in light of (the mandatory) Title V of the treaty? And especially in the latter case, what procedure should be followed in case a Member State decides to be bound by other parts of the Fiscal Compact?

These are relevant questions for a number of reasons. First, the Fiscal Compact obviously leaves the decision on how to ratify the treaty and whether to be bound by the entire treaty to the Contracting Parties. Second, an automatic transition of obligations occurs under the Fiscal Compact when a Member State joins the euro. Third, this is combined with a Treaty obligation for Member States with derogation to try to join the euro. Finally, the nature of the commitments under the Fiscal Compact is fundamentally different under optional Title III (Fiscal Compact) and mandatory Title V (Governance of the euro area).

So how did the outs approach these matters? It is interesting to note that Bulgaria, Denmark and Romania, which have already decided to be bound by optional titles of the Fiscal Compact, all ratified using only a simple majority procedure in Parliament.[73] This illustrates that several non-euro area Member States (like several euro area Member States)[74] have considered, in an overall assessment of the Fiscal Compact, that the

Euro', *Euractiv* (21 February 2014), www.euractiv.com/euro-finance/danish-pm-country-join-euro-news-533661.

[73] See the report on Romania prepared by V. Vita, Sections IX.2 and IX.8, and the Report on Bulgaria by M. Vatsos, Section IX.2. For Denmark, see the Table provided by the European Parliament, 'Table on the Ratification Process of Amendment of Art. 136 TFEU, ESM Treaty and Fiscal Compact', www.europarl.europa.eu/webnp/webdav/site/myjahiasite/shared/Publications/Fiscal%20Treaty%20ESM%20Overview%20table/art.%20136,%20ESM,%20Fiscal%20compact%20ratification.pdf.

[74] This was the case, for example, in Estonia, Italy, and the Netherlands.

obligations following from this treaty do not justify using a special majority for its ratification.

What about other outs? The Hungarian Government initially took the position that it was in the power of the government to ratify the Fiscal Compact, as there is no transfer of powers to the EU. The Hungarian Constitutional Court overruled this statement, on the grounds that the Fiscal Compact transfers powers in connection to the founding Treaties of the EU.[75] As a result, the treaty required a two-thirds majority in parliament.[76] It is unclear what (parliamentary) procedure would have to be followed before Hungary could declare itself bound by any other Title of the Fiscal Compact.

In Poland, opposition members from both chambers of parliament also argued that a two-thirds majority was required, as it had been for the Accession Treaty to the EU and the Lisbon Treaty.[77] The rapporteur in parliament stressed, however, that no competences are transferred and thus only a normal parliamentary majority was necessary.[78] The Government also stressed that it intended not to be bound by the rest of the Fiscal Compact. The treaty was ratified in accordance with the standard procedure. A case brought before the Constitutional Tribunal on this issue has been discontinued on formal grounds.[79] Interestingly, during the parliamentary debates, the Government took the position that a declaration to be bound by other parts of the treaty would require a new ratification procedure before parliament.[80]

Sweden ratified the Fiscal Compact under similar circumstances to Poland. The Government argued that no competences were transferred, that the treaty does not create any legal obligations for non-euro area Member States, and that a normal parliamentary majority was required for ratification.[81] Opposition members disagreed, but to no avail.[82] The Committee on Finance of the Swedish *Riksdag* held that before Sweden

[75] *Magyarország Alkotmánybírósága* (Constitutional Court of Hungary), Decision 22/2012. (V.11.) AB of 11 May 2012. See the report on Hungary prepared by D. Dojcsák, Section IX.4. For further discussion, see in this book Chapter 10, 'Legitimacy through Adjudication: The ESM Treaty and the Fiscal Compact before the National Courts' by Jan Herman Reestman.

[76] See the report on Hungary prepared by D. Dojcsák, Section IX.4.

[77] See the report on Poland prepared by K. Granat, Section V.2. [78] Ibid., Section IX.3.

[79] Ibid., Section IX.2 and IX.7. See also *Trybunale Konstytucyjnym*, Decision K11/13 of 21 May 2013.

[80] See the report on Poland prepared by K. Granat, Sections IX.3 and IX.8.

[81] See the report on Sweden prepared by A. Södersten, Section IX.3. [82] Ibid.

could declare itself bound by other parts of the Fiscal Compact, this would require further approval from parliament (supposedly with a three-quarters majority).[83] Some members of parliament argued that Sweden should receive an official opt-out from EMU before committing to the Fiscal Compact or Article 136(3) TFEU.[84]

The Risk of Being Marginalised from Important Euro Area Decisions

Two examples illustrate the risk for non-euro area Member States of being marginalised in fundamental decision-making relating directly or indirectly to the euro. The first example is exclusion from euro area meetings. The second example is caucusing. Marginalisation can have several negative consequences for outs: not being able to determine substantive rules of (future) euro area membership, negative spillover effects of euro area decisions, domination by euro area interests over non-euro area Member States' interests (see also the following section).

Non-euro area Member States are traditionally excluded from meetings of the Eurogroup and its preparatory bodies, such as the Eurogroup Working Group (EWG). Although the Eurogroup has no power to take legally binding decisions,[85] it is clear that it is a central body, politically preparing the legally binding EMU decisions relating to the euro (formally adopted by the ECOFIN Council with only euro area Member States voting), as well as those relating to the provision of financial assistance (formally adopted by the ESM Board of Governors). In fact, the Eurogroup was among the British concerns addressed in the New Settlement deal agreed at the European Council of 18–19 February 2016.[86] That deal is now off the table as a result of the negative outcome of the referendum of 23 June 2016 on UK membership in the EU.[87] Craig

[83] Ibid. [84] Ibid., Sections V.3 and IX.3.

[85] In the *Mallis* case, the General Court for this reason does not consider the Eurogroup to be a decision-making body. See *Mallis and Malli* v. *European Commission and European Central Bank*, Case T-327/13, para. 53.

[86] The Decision of the Heads of State or Government, meeting within the European Council, concerning a New Settlement for the United Kingdom within the European Union (2016/C 69 I/01) (OJ C 69 I, 23.2.2016, p. 1). Section A, para. 5 states: 'The informal meetings of the ministers of the Member States whose currency is the euro, as referred to in Protocol (No. 14) on the Euro Group, shall respect the powers of the Council as an institution upon which the Treaties confer legislative functions and within which Member States coordinate their economic policies'.

[87] European Council, Conclusions of 19 February 2016, EUCO 1/16, para I.4.

and Markakis note that the Eurogroup can be seen both positively as a natural institutional response to differentiated integration and negatively as a body leading to done deals that have a significant impact on non-euro area Member States.[88]

The Fiscal Compact entailed a further risk to non-euro area Member States of being excluded, now at the highest political level, namely that of heads of state and government, because of the creation – read: official recognition – of Euro Summits. In this euro area body, important political decisions are being taken relating to the euro area but which affect non-euro area Member States. One only needs to think of the Euro Summits of 22 June, 7 July and 12 July 2015 and their fundamental role in preventing a 'Grexit'.

In the first draft of the Fiscal Compact, non-euro area Member States were not foreseen to participate in Euro Summits, but were only kept closely informed. In the adopted text the President of the Euro Summit is tasked with keeping all the outs informed of both the preparations and outcome of Euro Summits,[89] thus including both the outs that ratified the Fiscal Compact and those that have not (i.e. the UK, Czech Republic and Croatia).[90] As a result of pressure from certain outs (including Poland, Denmark, Bulgaria, Sweden and Hungary) and helped by several ins that were wary of alienating certain natural allies (such as Germany and Finland), participation of non-euro area heads of state and government is provided for in Euro Summit discussions in certain specified circumstances.[91] In these instances, the British Prime Minister and his colleagues from the Czech Republic and Croatia are the only heads of government absent from the discussions.

[88] Craig and Markakis, 'The Euro Area, Its Regulation and Impact on Non-Euro Member States'.

[89] Compare to European Council, Conclusions of 23 October 2011, EUCO 52/1/11, para. 7: 'The President of the Euro Summit will keep the non-euro area Member States fully informed of the preparation and outcome of the Summits'.

[90] Art. 12(6), Fiscal Compact.

[91] Art. 12(3), Fiscal Compact: 'The Heads of State or Government of the Contracting Parties other than those whose currency is the euro, which have ratified this Treaty, shall participate in discussions of Euro Summit meetings concerning competitiveness for the Contracting Parties, the modification of the global architecture of the euro area and the fundamental rules that will apply to it in the future, as well as, when appropriate and at least once a year, in discussions on specific issues of implementation of this Treaty on Stability, Coordination and Governance in the Economic and Monetary Union.'

Most prominent in its insistence on participation in Euro Summits has been Poland.[92] Then Prime Minister Donald Tusk (now President of both the European Council and the Euro Summit!), threatened not to ratify the Fiscal Compact if non-euro area Member States could not participate in Euro Summits.[93] Several other non-euro area countries joined Poland in its calls to participate in Euro Summits.[94] The possibility of a Polish participation in Euro Summits was finally emphasised as one of the main added values of ratification of the Fiscal Compact.[95]

Another example related to possible exclusion is the fact that several non-euro area Member States have insisted on participation in the negotiations and decision-making on the main characteristics of the ESM Treaty. Thus, Latvia insisted on joining the extended meetings of euro area countries on the establishment and character of ESM; understandable considering its intention to join the euro soon after.[96] In the Polish national debate, it has been emphasised that it actively participated in the discussions on the amendment of not only Article 136 TFEU but also the related mechanism.[97]

The second example of possible marginalisation concerns the risk of caucusing, or the risk of euro area Member States forming a unified block in Council decision-making. Concerns have increased after new voting rules in the Treaty of Lisbon gave the euro area a qualified majority in the Council and are reinforced by the importance of the Eurogroup. We seem to be dealing with predominantly British concerns, which have been strongly voiced during the UK negotiations on a reformed Union and a New Settlement for the UK. These negotiations were mostly a result of its special relationship with the Union and of national Conservative party politics. At the same time, the British substantive reform wishes in the area of economic governance have to a significant extent been shaped by the British experience with the response to the Eurocrisis. So even though the New Settlement would

92 See the report on Poland prepared by K. Granat, Section IX.1.

93 'Euro Summit Tension Over Debt Crisis Plan', *BBC* (30 January 2012), www.bbc.co.uk/news/world-europe-16795673.

94 See the report on Hungary prepared by D. Dojcsák, Section IX.1; the Report on Bulgaria prepared by M. Vatsos, Section IX.1 and the Report on Sweden prepared by A. Södersten, Section IX.1.

95 See the report on Poland prepared by K. Granat, Section IX.3.

96 See the report on Latvia prepared by Z. Rasnača, Section VIII.1.

97 See the report on Poland prepared by K. Granat, Section V.1.

have impacted the position of all non-euro area Member States, its fate was dependent on the outcome of the UK referendum.

Although the lack of empirical evidence for caucusing is generally acknowledged,[98] there is nonetheless comprehension for the British concerns.[99] The Council decision of July 2015 to use the EFSM for emergency bridge financing for Greece (a decision prepared in the Eurogroup and taken with the support only of euro area members) was certainly perceived by the UK as a bad precedent. Under the now defunct New Settlement deal any Member State not participating in banking union would have been able to indicate its reasoned opposition to proposed legislation on banking union, obliging the Council to further discuss the issue.

The contrast between the broadly shared concern among the outs of being excluded from important euro area decision-making affecting the Union and what seem to have been predominantly British concerns over the risk of caucusing is striking. The latter cannot be understood in isolation from concerns of damaging effects of euro area decision-making on the substantive internal market interests of the outs. This again is a predominantly British concern, not surprising considering the importance of the City and impact of financial regulation on it.[100] To this we turn now.

Safeguarding the Substantive Interests of Non-Euro Area Member States

The development of the euro area affects the substantive interests of non-euro area Member States in various ways. The Eurocrisis provides an illustration of tension in several areas, most prominently in the single market in financial services and in banking union.[101] The issues are too

[98] See, for example, the Foreign Affairs Committee of the House of Commons, *The Future of the European Union: UK Government Policy*, Vol. 1 (2013), Chapter 3, paras. 76–7; Craig and Markakis, 'The Euro Area, Its Regulation and Impact on Non-Euro Member States'.

[99] A. Hinarejos, *The Euro Area Crisis in Constitutional Perspective* (Oxford University Press, 2015), p. 112; Dashwood, 'Guest Editorial. Living with the Eurozone', 7.

[100] Grant notes: 'Even a country such as Poland, which is many years away from joining the euro, is untroubled about the possibility of the eurozone acting in ways that harm the market'. See C. Grant, 'Could Eurozone Integration Damage the Internal Market?', *Centre for European Reform Bulletin*, No. 103 (August/September 2015), www.cer.org.uk/sites/default/files/publications/attachments/pdf/2015/bulletin_103_cg_article2-11728.pdf.

[101] Another example is the use of the EFSM in July 2015 to provide bridge financing for Greece. See Sections 2.C and 3.A of this chapter. As discussed, the EFSM regulation has been amended as a result of this event.

many and complex to give an extensive overview or detailed discussion here. Suffice it here to highlight two examples, the first one relating to the ECB relocation requirement for so-called clearinghouses.[102] The ECB's Eurosystem Oversight Policy Framework required clearinghouses involved in the clearing of securities to be located within the euro area. The UK challenged this policy before the EU's General Court, as it considered that the location requirement infringes the principle of non-discrimination. The General Court did not pronounce itself over the alleged discrimination, but nonetheless annulled the ECB Policy Framework insofar as it set the location requirement, deciding that the ECB did not have the necessary competence.[103]

The New Settlement deal stated that legal acts directly linked to the functioning of the euro area shall respect the internal market, and that discrimination between natural or legal persons based on the official currency of the Member State is prohibited.[104] Although the New Settlement is off the table, this statement could certainly be a guiding principle for the defence of the interests of other non-euro area Member States.

A second example relates to the effect of banking union on the substantive interests of non-participating Member States. As we saw in Section 2.C, the EBA, in which all EU Member States are represented, contributes to the creation of the Single Rulebook through the adoption of Binding Technical Standards and Guidelines. There is, however, a risk that the ECB, in providing a harmonised interpretation of the rules of banking union for the euro area and participating Member States, competes with the EBA in setting material rules. In fact, Belling, Marek and Vojta, writing on a personal title but working for the Czech National Bank, fear that the ECB could become the 'de facto' creator of standards, with the EBA reduced to a body for purely formal discussion and decision-making.[105] They expect that the role of non-SSM Member States in the EBA will be weakened and that they will be compelled to adopt the supervisory practices of the ECB.[106]

[102] Note that this ECB policy is not a consequence of caucusing in the Council.
[103] *United Kingdom* v. *European Central Bank*, Case T-496/11, para. 110.
[104] New Settlement for the United Kingdom (n. 86 above), Section A, para. 1.
[105] See Belling, Marek and Vojta, *National Report: Czech Republic*, p. 110.
[106] Ibid., p. 111.

B. *Issues Relating to the Decision to Join the Euro*

Does Euro-Crisis Law Affect the Obligation to Join the Euro?

As mentioned above, the Maastricht Treaty and the Accession Treaties included the obligation for non-euro area Member States to strive for admission to the euro area. It was also noted that this was a legal obligation, which did not correspond to political realities. In practice, Member States only join the euro if and when they want to (and when they fulfil the convergence criteria). Until the Eurocrisis, the situation was relatively clear: the law was clear; the political reality was equally uncomplicated. However, euro-crisis law may greatly complicate the matter. In fact, the impact of euro-crisis law on the obligation to join the euro has been subject to recent academic debate. Tuori and Tuori argue that now 'the legal obligation to join must be considered desuetude'.[107] According to Majone 'the view of monetary union as an obligation imposed by the dogma of the *acquis communautaire* seems increasingly outdated'.[108] Herrmann argues that there is only a theoretical obligation to join the euro area and that non-euro area Member States 'could still decide not to join the amended Euro area if they dislike what the older Euro area members have changed'.[109] What discussions have taken place in non-euro area Member States?

The Czech government has contended that the obligation that was agreed to in 2004 is not the same as today.[110] Euro-crisis law has transformed (the legal framework of) the euro area to such an extent that the obligation has become invalid, so the argument goes. Opponents to entry into the euro area could go a step further by arguing that no one would be obliged to board a sinking ship, if one were (still) inclined to see the current economic situation in the euro area as such. The opposite argument was voiced in Latvia, where the crisis was held up as one of the reasons – albeit not a legal one – for joining the euro area.[111]

In Sweden, some members of parliament asked the government to negotiate an official opt-out from EMU before ratifying the Fiscal

[107] K. Tuori and K. Tuori, *The Eurozone Crisis: A Constitutional Analysis* (Cambridge University Press, 2014), p. 193.

[108] G. Majone, *Rethinking the Union of Europe Post-Crisis. Has Integration Gone Too Far?* (Cambridge University Press, 2014), p. 47.

[109] Herrmann, 'Differentiated Integration in the Field of Monetary Policy and the Use of Semi-Extra Union Legal Instruments – The Case for Relative Treaty Amendments'.

[110] See the Report on the Czech Republic prepared by T. Dumbrovsky, Section VIII.1.

[111] See the Report on Latvia prepared by Z. Rasnača, Section III.9.

Compact and before approving Article 136(3) TFEU, thereby acknowledging the continuing existence of the obligation to join the euro.[112] However, the manner in which both Poland and Sweden have ratified the Fiscal Compact reinforces the emphasis on the political nature of the decision to join the euro in the future (see Section 3.A). In their assessment of the appropriate ratification procedure for the Fiscal Compact, both countries took only current obligations into account, not those that will arise automatically upon entry into the euro area. This means that the full contents of the Fiscal Compact will be considered during the decision-making process on entry into the euro area, or when an earlier decision is taken on being bound by the other parts of the treaty. In other words, if entry into the euro area would be a decision over which the Member State in question has no control, it would have been more difficult to argue for a ratification in which only part of the Fiscal Compact is considered.

C. *Issues Relating to the Period after Adoption of the Euro*

Does Joining the Euro Create an Obligation to Become a Member of the ESM?

There is no doubt that the Eurocrisis has led to a new set of rules that Member States are legally bound to accept once they join the euro, such as parts of the Six Pack, the Two Pack, the banking union (SSM and SRM) and those optional parts of the Fiscal Compact to which they are not yet bound (see Sections 2.C and 3.A). In short, euro-crisis law has changed the conditions of euro membership. What about the ESM? Is a Member State that joins the euro automatically obliged to become a member of the ESM? This interesting legal question has been the subject of debate in several non-euro area Member States.[113]

The EU Treaties do not explicitly provide for such an obligation. The ESM Treaty itself does state in a recital: 'All euro area Member States will become ESM Members. As a consequence of joining the euro area, a

[112] See the Report on Sweden prepared by A. Södersten, Sections V.3 and IX.3.

[113] A further legal question is whether amendment of the Treaty through Article 136(3) TFEU implies an automatic ratification of the ESM Treaty. The Polish Undersecretary of State in the Ministry of Foreign Affairs has explicitly denied this, as has the Senator rapporteur from the governing majority on the ratification act. See the Report of Poland prepared by K. Granat, Section V.3.

Member State of the European Union should become an ESM Member',[114] but it is obvious that this cannot create any legal obligation for the outs, who currently are not members of the ESM Treaty (nor can they be). It merely illustrates an opinion of the current ESM members. At the same time it should be mentioned that whether a member state will join the ESM is most likely to be determined more by political necessity than by a possible legal obligation to do so. Still, from a legal perspective it is relevant to see whether such a legal obligation can be – indirectly – constructed.

It seems that in no Member State such an obligation is being explicitly denied. On the contrary, in Latvia the annotation to the Draft Law on the ESM states that euro area Member States have to be members to the ESM.[115] The government of Hungary has argued that the approval of Article 136(3) TFEU imposes no legal commitments on Hungary until it joins the euro area in the future.[116] This reasoning must imply that a conviction that an obligation to join the ESM mechanism exists. Similarly, the Polish Undersecretary of State in the Ministry of Foreign Affairs has argued that the ESM Treaty will not bind Poland unless it joins the euro area.[117]

Still, it is argued here that only indirect arguments can be given for the existence of an obligation to join the ESM, none of which is convincing. In the following a number of options are explored. Does the obligation to join the ESM follow from Article 136(3) TFEU? That is clearly not the case, as this provision only confirms the competence of Member States (as opposed to the Union) to create a stability mechanism. It creates no legal obligation to do so – this is also the convincing position of the Polish Constitutional Tribunal[118] – making it difficult to base an obligation to join the ESM on this provision.

[114] ESM Treaty, Preamble, para. 7.

[115] See the Report on Latvia prepared by Z. Rasnača, Section VIII.2. Latvia did not 'join' the EFSF or the first Greek aid package after it joined the euro.

[116] See the Report on Hungary prepared by Dojcsák, Section V.3.

[117] See the Report on Poland prepared by K. Granat, Section V.3.

[118] Ibid., Section V.4. See *Trybunał Konstytucyjny*, Decision K 33/12 of 26 June 2013, para. 4.2 (English translation): 'no obligation arises from Article 136(3) of the TFEU or from the ESM Treaty for a euro area Member State to become an ESM Member'. For further discussion, see K. Granat, 'Approval of Article 136 TFEU Amendment in Poland: The Perspective of the Constitutional Court on Eurozone Crisis Law', *European Public Law*, 21(1), (2015), 33–46 and in this book Chapter 10, 'Legitimacy through Adjudication: The ESM Treaty and the Fiscal Compact before the National Courts' by Jan Herman Reestman.

Does the specific formulation of Article 136(3) TFEU, which confirms the power of the Member States whose currency is the euro to establish a stability mechanism, change anything?[119] Does this formulation mean that the mechanism can only be in conformity with the Treaty if all euro area Member States participate? And does this create an obligation for new members of the euro area to join the ESM, because, if not, the other members would not be in compliance with Article 136(3) TFEU? It is argued that constructing the obligation this way is too far-fetched.

Does an obligation to join the ESM fall under the conditions for the adoption of the euro under Article 139 TFEU and 140 TFEU, combined with the obligation to strive to join the euro? According to the Polish Constitutional Tribunal, the creation of the ESM did not change the conditions for accession to the euro area, as the provisions on the derogation did not change:[120] 'Apart from recognition that the euro area Member States have the competence to enter into an agreement to establish a stability mechanism, treaty rules for the accession to such an agreement have not changed (the criteria of convergence, Article 140 of the TFEU and Protocol No. 13 to the TEU); in particular, paragraph 3 added to Article 136 of the TFEU does not provide for the adoption of the euro to be dependent on (prior) ratification of the ESM Treaty.'[121]

Whereas it may not be entirely clear whether new euro area Member States should join the ESM, it is clear that the current members of the ESM cannot prevent them from acceding. Article 2 ESM Treaty states that membership shall be open to EU Member States as from the moment of the abrogation of the derogation from adopting the euro.[122] There is thus no legal ground to refuse membership of a new euro area Member States. As assistance from the ESM is dependent on the ratification and implementation of the Fiscal Compact, it must also be noted here that membership of the latter treaty is open to all EU Member States, without any legal possibility for current Member States to block new members.[123] There is, however, no legal obligation for the Czech

[119] 'The Member States whose currency is the euro may establish a stability mechanism to be activated if indispensable to safeguard the stability of the euro area as a whole. The granting of any required financial assistance under the mechanism will be made subject to strict conditionality.'

[120] See the report on Poland prepared by K. Granat, Section V.4.

[121] *Trybunał Konstytucyjny*, Decision K 33/12, para. 7.3.2 (English translation).

[122] See also ESM Treaty, Art. 44 on the procedure of application of membership and approval thereof.

[123] See the ESM Treaty, Preamble, para. 5 and Article 15 of the Fiscal Compact.

Republic or Croatia to ratify the Fiscal Compact should they become a member of the euro area.

Leaving the Euro Area?

As observed above, membership of the euro area grew during the crisis with the adoption of the euro by Estonia, Latvia and Lithuania. However, the crisis has also raised doubts in several euro area Member States about the desirability of continuing to be part of the euro area, most notably in Member States receiving financial assistance, such as Greece and Cyprus. But also in Finland a petition for a referendum on euro area membership garnered support.[124] Moreover, the crisis has raised serious doubts among certain Member States, most notably Germany, about the sustainability of a euro area with Greece as a member.[125] In fact, the possibility of a 'Grexit' was not at all unthinkable during the summer of 2015.

The legal framework of EMU does not foresee such an exit (at least not without withdrawal from the Union), with the Maastricht Treaty explicitly noting the irreversibility of participation in the third stage.[126] Any exit from the euro area will bring tough negotiations with the institutions and other Member States, possibly an amendment to the Treaties and most likely a comprehensive agreement outlining the stages and conditions under which that Member State can leave the euro (these challenges are partly analogous to the ones related to withdrawal from the Union for which an explicit procedure is foreseen in Article 50 TEU). Such an agreement would also have to take into consideration the new position of a Member State as an out. A Member State leaving the euro area might find that the legal obligations pertaining to the status of 'Member State with a derogation' are still too restrictive. For a Member State that has received financial assistance and wants to leave the euro area, the other Member States might demand that it remain bound to all

[124] 'Finnish Parliament Will Debate Next Year Leaving Euro Zone', *Reuters* (16 November 2015), www.reuters.com/article/us-eurozone-finland-exit-idUSKCN0T518O20151116.

[125] See the non-paper of the German government of 10 July 2015 suggesting the possibility of a Greek timeout from the euro area if debt sustainability and a credible implementation perspective cannot be ensured. Available at www.sven-giegold.de/wp-content/uploads/2015/07/grexit_bundesregierung_non_paper_10_juli_2015.pdf.

[126] Article 109L(4), Treaty Establishing the European Economic Community, as amended by the Maastricht Treaty of 1992.

rules on economic governance (including sanctions), so as to secure control and maintain the sustainability of the debt levels.

4 Conclusion

Non-euro area Member States have reacted differently to the challenges related to being either a semi-permanent out or a Member State with a derogation. Outs associated to the logic of constitutional differentiation, such as the UK, Denmark and Sweden, have not all reacted the same. Denmark and Sweden have signed up to the Fiscal Compact, while the UK has not. Denmark has even accepted far-reaching obligations under this Treaty, in contrast to Sweden, which had a clear motivation for ratification: the Treaty does not create any legal obligations for it, but by ratifying Sweden gave support to the work of the euro area, preserved its influence and prevented a further division between the ins and outs.[127] Denmark is also a party to the Intergovernmental Agreement on the transfer and mutualisation of contributions to the SRF, illustrating its different approach to banking union from the UK and Sweden, which are not a party. The UK, for domestic reasons, has increasingly put into question the relationship between ins and outs in a broad and fundamental way, including the effects of euro area legislation on the outs. More than any other out, the UK has been concerned with a decreasing membership of the group of outs,[128] and with the behaviour of other non-euro area Member States.[129] The Brexit result of the UK referendum

[127] See the report on Sweden prepared by A. Södersten, Section IX.3.

[128] See, for example, the Foreign Affairs Committee of the House of Commons, *The Future of the European Union: UK Government Policy*, Vol. 1, Chapter 3, para. 66: 'The assumption that they will one day be in the Eurozone does not at all rule such states out as allies for the UK in particular EU policy areas. However, it is likely to push their longer-term orientation in the EU away from the UK and towards the Eurozone "core"'. Volume 2 of this report collects oral and written evidence submitted to the Committee and quotes Foreign Secretary Hague, on 6 February 2013: 'So I think the assumption that those outside the eurozone are just reduced to a very small number may now be a rather out-of-date assumption, proceeding along the tramlines of the thinking of 10 years ago rather than now, in light of the financial and eurozone crises'. See Foreign Affairs Committee of the House of Commons, *The Future of the European Union: UK Government Policy*, Vol. 2 (2013), p. 46.

[129] See the Foreign Affairs Committee of the House of Commons, *The Future of the European Union: UK Government Policy*, Vol. 1, Chapter 3, para. 62: 'Charles Grant told us that UK officials were 'quite surprised' that more non-Eurozone states did not align themselves with the UK outside the TSCG'.

of 23 June 2016 can now remove the most influential member from the group of outs, profoundly changing the balance between euro ins and outs.

The derogation-outs traditionally associated to the logic of instrumental differentiation have also reacted in different ways, although all of them have signed the Intergovernmental Agreement on the transfer and mutualisation of contributions to the SRF. Apart from the Czech Republic (and later Croatia), all derogation-outs have signed the Fiscal Compact, with Romania and Bulgaria accepting further obligations under this treaty independently from future euro area membership. Estonia, Latvia and Lithuania have joined the euro area and ratified the ESM Treaty during the crisis, whereas the Czech government has argued that the obligation to join has become invalid as a result of euro-crisis law.[130]

These different responses to the Eurocrisis are due to different national constitutional and political contexts, and to diverging interests within the group of non-euro area Member States. They illustrate that the distinction between constitutional and instrumental differentiation is being blurred. The Czech Republic, for example, a Member State originally excluded from the euro for instrumental reasons, seems to be developing in the direction of the constitutional differentiation logic, partly due to the Eurocrisis, by not taking part in significant initiatives and putting into question its obligation to join the euro. At the same time the different responses show that the reality behind the distinction is more nuanced: a Member State like Denmark, associated to the constitutional differentiation logic has, notwithstanding the crisis, shown a remarkably strong commitment to the integration project, including the single currency.

Between the two extremes of disengagement (UK and the Czech Republic) and surprisingly strong commitment (Romania, Bulgaria and, surprisingly, Denmark), there is a group of non-euro area Member States that has found a middle ground in dealing with the tension between not accepting far-reaching obligations before euro area membership and an interest to preserve influence on euro area developments, well exemplified by Sweden and Poland. The Polish approach to the Fiscal Compact (but also the Swedish approach just mentioned) illustrates this middle ground very well. The Polish Secretary of State in the Ministry of Foreign Affairs in reply to concerns that the Fiscal Compact

[130] See the report on the Czech Republic prepared by T. Dumbrovsky, Section VIII.1.

limits the sovereignty of Poland stated that sovereignty for Poland means having an impact on the institutional, social and economic architecture of the EU.[131] Poland ratified the Fiscal Compact mainly because of the possibility to participate in Euro Summits, but at the same time decided not to be bound by those parts that are optional before adoption of the euro.

Future measures in EMU would do well to take the diversity amongst the outs into account.

[131] See the report on Poland prepared by K. Granat, Section IX.3.

PART II

National Constitutional Manifestations of Economic Emergency

6

Greece: Constitutional Deconstruction and the Loss of National Sovereignty

AFRODITI MARKETOU

During the last six years Greece has experienced socio-political developments that are unique for a Western state: five national elections, at least ten governments, a referendum, three economic adjustment programmes and unprecedented austerity policies with socio-economic consequences resembling those of a war. These developments, causing a total transformation of Greek constitutional politics, were not accompanied by formal constitutional change. Instead, they have been made possible through an extended deconstruction of constitutional forms, justified through the use of emergency discourse. Is there any place for the Constitution as a valid point of reference in domestic constitutional politics?

1 Deconstructing Constitutional Forms: The Economic Adjustment Programmes in the Domestic Sphere

The Greek constitutional story of the Eurocrisis starts with Law 3845/2010.[1] Under the title 'Measures for the implementation of the support mechanism for the Greek economy by the euro area Member States and the International Monetary Fund', the statute included, as an annex, a draft of the first Memorandum of Understanding (MoU) between Greece and its creditors, as well as relevant statements by the Heads of State and Government of euro area Member States. The policies announced in these texts were partly implemented in the main provisions of Law 3845/2010. Article 3 imposed severe cuts on the revenues of public employees and pensioners. This article also affected employees with a private law contract and declared that it prevailed over any contrary provision, be it

[1] Law 3845/2010, OJ A' 65/11.05.2010.

part of a collective agreement, arbitral award or individual contract. The rest of the articles imposed tax increases and exceptional levies. Due to these substantive changes in socio-economic policy, the discussion of Law 3845/2010 in Parliament was perceived by all parties as an 'historical moment' which would determine the future of the country.[2]

It is no exaggeration to say that Law 3845/2010 was the legal event that divided the Greek political world and society into pro-MoU and anti-MoU forces. Despite its historical importance, however, emergency left no place for parliamentary discussion on the policies or the specific measures enacted by the statute. The bill was brought to Parliament under the emergency procedure, instituted by Article 76, paragraph 4 of the Constitution: 'A Bill or law proposal designated by the Government as very urgent shall be introduced for voting after a limited debate in one sitting'.[3] The Government stated that the voting of the bill was urgent, in order for the relevant Loan Agreement to be concluded before 19 May 2010. On this date, a €10 billion bond loan matured and, if the country was unable to repay its creditors, it would face bankruptcy and isolation from its euro area partners.[4] Deputies had less than three days to read the statute and its annexes and only one day to discuss it in Parliament. Even members of the Government later admitted that they had not had time to read the MoU. The support mechanism and the measures it implied were approved as a whole in one single article, rendering any amendments to specific austerity provisions impossible. Strict party discipline was imposed on the members of the two major parties in Parliament. Errors in the Greek translation of the MoU further poisoned the national debate.

However, from a legal scholar's point of view, Law 3845/2010 was even more intriguing in formal terms, that is, as far as legal norm production is concerned. What was Parliament actually doing when voting on the statute? Was it adopting a piece of internal legislation or was it, at the same time, approving an international agreement, namely the MoU? Article 36 of the Constitution regulates the conclusion of international treaties and attributes the relevant constitutional competence to the President of the Republic. Paragraph 2 of the same article declares that

[2] See 'ιστορική στιγμή' ('historical moment') in Minutes of the Greek Parliament, 6 May 2010, www.hellenicparliament.gr/UserFiles/a08fc2dd-61a9-4a83-b09a-09f4c564609d/es20100506_1.pdf, pp 6715 and 6742.

[3] An official parliamentary translation of the Constitution of Greece (last revised 27 May 2008) is available at www.hellenicparliament.gr/UserFiles/f3c70a23-7696-49db-9148-f24dce6a27c8/001-156%20aggliko.pdf.

[4] See, for example, Minutes of the Greek Parliament, 6 May 2010, p. 6728.

conventions on trade, taxation, economic cooperation, participation in international organisations or unions, as well as all other conventions containing concessions for which a statute is required by the Constitution, or which may burden the Greeks individually, 'shall not be operative without ratification by a statute voted by the Parliament'.

Once operative according to Article 36, Article 28 of the Constitution defines the status of international law in the domestic legal order. Paragraph 1 states that ratified international conventions 'shall be an integral part of domestic Greek law and shall prevail over any contrary provision of the law'. Paragraphs 2 and 3 set particular procedural and substantive conditions for the ratification of certain conventions. They declare:

> 2. Authorities provided by the Constitution may by treaty or agreement be vested in agencies of international organizations, when this serves an important national interest and promotes cooperation with other States. A majority of three-fifths of the total number of Members of Parliament shall be necessary to vote the law ratifying the treaty or agreement.
>
> 3. Greece shall freely proceed by law passed by an absolute majority of the total number of Members of Parliament to limit the exercise of national sovereignty, insofar as this is dictated by an important national interest, does not infringe upon the rights of man and the foundations of democratic government and is effected on the basis of the principles of equality and under the condition of reciprocity.

Article 28 of the Constitution is followed by an interpretative clause stating that it 'constitutes the foundation for the participation of the Country in the European integration process'.

Was the MoU an international agreement requiring ratification? Should it then be voted by a qualified majority, as Article 28 imposes? Or was it simply the political programme of the Government, attached to the statute as part of its explanatory report? These questions raised important academic, political and judicial debates.[5] In its first article, Law 3845/2010 contained a description of the steps taken for the activation of the support mechanism. In the introductory report to the draft law it was stated that the annexed MoU was an 'integral part of the draft bill'.[6] Nonetheless, the Council of State, the Supreme Administrative

[5] See Section X.3 of the 'Report on Greece' prepared by A. Marketou and M. Dekastros (last revised 9 June 2015) for the 'Constitutional Change through Euro Crisis Law' project of the EUI Law Department, available on its website: http://eurocrisislaw.eui.eu.

[6] See 'αναπόσπαστο μέρος του σχεδίου νόμου' ('integral part of the draft bill) in the introductory report to the bill, www.hellenicparliament.gr/UserFiles/c8827c35-4399-4fbb-8ea6-aebdc768f4f7/AOIKONOMIKVN.pdf, p. 3.

Court of the country, in its relevant decision denied legal force to the MoU and found it to be the political programme of the Government, which could not be submitted to judicial scrutiny.[7] The court decided so, despite the Prime Minister having repeatedly stated in the relevant parliamentary debates that the MoU and the statute were not the Government's political choice but had been imposed by the creditors.[8] In the public discourse of the Government, the fulfilment of the Loan Agreement conditions was presented as a binding obligation imposed on the country. Was governmental policy in Greece defined according to a non-ratified international agreement? And what did this mean for national sovereignty?

The ambiguity of the status of the MoU and the Loan Agreement was deliberately preserved in the second economic adjustment programme. Drafts of the relevant texts were annexed to Law 4046/2012, before their signature.[9] The Government was asking for the *approval* of the annexed drafts, together with the adoption of the statute. It was also requesting an authorisation for the Minister of Finance and the President of the Bank of Greece to represent the country in the negotiations and to sign the agreements, which would then become immediately operative.[10] However, prospective approval is not foreseen by the Constitution, which only provides for *ratification* of international agreements. In the competent Parliamentary Committee, the Minister of Finance at the time argued that the MoUs were staff-level agreements, not necessitating such ratification.[11] However, Article 1, paragraph 6 of Law 4046/2012 declared that certain provisions of the MoU on the Specific Conditions of Economic Policy were 'perfect legal rules of direct application' and thus, in a sense, ratified them.[12]

For subsequent versions of the second economic adjustment programme documents, the Government chose another road: the use, or rather abuse, of constitutional emergency procedures. Indeed, the

[7] See CoS Pl., Decision 668/2012, 20 February 2012, www.dsanet.gr/Epikairothta/Nomologia/668.htm, para. 28.

[8] See Minutes of the Greek Parliament, 6 May 2010, p. 6766.

[9] Law 4046/2012, OJ A' 28/14.02.2012.

[10] Ibid., Art. 1 Para. 3 and f. The statute in its title itself explicitly stated that the Government was asking for the approval of the annexed texts.

[11] See the speech by Evangelos Venizelos in the permanent committee of financial affairs, 11 February 2012. Indeed, the video is not uploaded anymore and, unfortunately, I cannot find any other reference to this speech.

[12] In the words of the statute, 'συνιστούν πλήρεις κανόνες δικαίου άμεσης εφαρμογής'.

practice used to circumvent the ratification requirement would confuse even the most cunning constitutional lawyers. The Government issued an emergency decree-law, approving the draft of the relevant Loan Agreement and authorising the competent authorities to sign it. Subsequently, when agreements were already valid and operative in the international economic sphere, the relevant decree-laws were introduced into Parliament for ratification, which validated the approval of the draft Loan Agreements retroactively in the domestic legal order.[13]

This is not the only example of Parliament having been called upon to ratify *de facto* established situations. Indeed, during the crisis governments have made extensive use of the emergency decree-laws, in Greek called 'acts of legislative content' (*πράξεις νομοθετικού περιεχομένου*). According to Article 44, paragraph 1 of the Constitution,

> Under extraordinary circumstances of an urgent and unforeseeable need, the President of the Republic may, upon the proposal of the Cabinet, issue acts of legislative content. Such acts shall be submitted to Parliament for ratification, as specified in the provisions of Article 72 paragraph 1, within forty days of their issuance or within forty days from the convocation of a parliamentary session. Should such acts not be submitted to Parliament within the above time-limits or if they should not be ratified by Parliament within three months of their submission, they will henceforth cease to be in force.

Usually putting forward a formal, self-serving justification,[14] crisis governments have used this *sui generis* instrument to enact complex and contentious provisions, either directly connected to the crisis or not. This practice is even more degrading for the role of Parliament, if one considers that often many such administrative acts have been subsequently ratified en masse, annexed to legal statutes that were brought for voting under the emergency procedure.[15] What is more, the relevant acts have been usually ratified in one single article, thus limiting any

[13] See 'Report on Greece' prepared by Marketou and Dekastros (n.5). See Act of Legislative Content, OJ A' 55/14.03.2012, Art. 1 and 2 and Law 4060/2012, OJ A' 65/22.03.2012, retroactively validating it.

[14] Typically, these acts start with a statement that the Government took into account the 'extraordinary circumstances of an urgent and unforeseeable need to . . .' take the measures each time contained in the act. See, for example, the acts ratified by Law 4111/2013 (OJ 98 A'/25-01-2013).

[15] See, for example, Law 4111/2013. This statute ratified, under the emergency procedure, six decree-laws containing various complex and totally irrelevant provisions. Among them, there were certain austerity measures, as well as an amendment of the Second Loan Agreement.

possibility of amendment of particular provisions included therein. It is not difficult to see that this practice effectively deprives parliamentary discussion from its content.

The excessive use of emergency procedures and instruments bears a strong symbolic meaning as well: a similar practice by Ioannis Metaxas in the 1930s completely degraded the role of Parliament and led to the dictatorship of August 1936. Symbolism is important, especially when it concerns what is generally accepted as fundamental in a constitutional democracy. The public television and radio have long functioned as national symbols of freedom of speech and have always been attacked by oppressive regimes. The public media were abruptly shut down on 11 June 2013 through a joint ministerial decision.[16] Having in mind that the closure of the public broadcaster did not enter within the powers of the Ministers who signed the relevant decision, the Government issued an act of legislative content that extended these Ministers' powers.[17] The urgent closure of the public media was presented by the Government as satisfying a requirement set by the creditors for reducing the number of public employees.[18] This allegation was denied by the creditors.[19] Whatever its source and the reasons for the emergency, the relevant act of legislative content was never ratified by Parliament and therefore ceased to be valid. However, it succeeded in fully producing its de facto consequences: effectively, the public broadcaster was closed down for a period of two years. This left Greece without state-owned public television for a month and without state-owned public radio for more than two months.

It seems thus that under the force of economic adjustment the Greek political regime has deviated into a system whereby Parliament is impotent and faced with an 'executive unbound'.[20] Yet, Government has not been alone in this reign of the executive. Policy has in fact been defined in meetings with the Troika, a technocrat tripartite body composed of the

[16] Joint Ministerial Decision OIK 02/11.6.2013, 'Suppression of the public enterprise Greek Radio-Television, A.E. (ERT-A.E.)', OJ B' 1414/11.6.2013.

[17] See Act of Legislative Content, OJ A' 139/11.6.2013. This act was the legal basis of the administrative decision that closed the public broadcaster.

[18] Ibid., Introduction.

[19] See the 'Joint answer given by Mr. Rehn on behalf of the Commission' to the questions raised in the European Parliament on the closure of ERT www.europarl.europa.eu/RegData/questions/reponses_qe/2013/006815/P7_RE(2013)006815_EN.pdf, p. 5.

[20] L. Papadopoulou, 'Can Constitutional Rules, Even if 'Golden', Tame Greek Public Debt?', in M. Adams, F. Fabbrini and P. Larouche (eds.), *The Constitutionalization of European Budgetary Constraints*, (Oxford: Hart Publishing, 2014), p. 236.

representatives of the European Central Bank (ECB), the International Monetary Fund (IMF) and the European Commission.[21] The broad powers acquired by the Troika in the determination of governmental policy have not been mirrored in legislation. They have operated de facto instead, 'coated' with a domestic political garb by the Constitution. In other words, whenever the international or constitutional legality of the Troika's requirements was contested, the creditors have claimed that the particular measures were the Greek Government's political choice under its exclusive competence for the implementation of obligations resulting from the economic adjustment programmes.[22] However, in public debates the recommendations of the Troika have been claimed to determine every aspect of governmental policy. They have been repeatedly invoked by the Government as the justification of the use of emergency procedures and instruments. Yannis Drossos described this situation as the Polity's new way of functioning.[23]

The loss of national sovereignty and legislative autonomy caused by the Troika review missions, combined with the lack of political accountability of the Troika members, provoked constant contention in public and parliamentary debates. Still, under the second 'rescue package', not only did the Troika preserve its broad powers, but it also became subtly institutionalised. Indeed, it was mentioned with its own name in official documents of the second economic adjustment programme.[24]

It was only in 2015 that the SYRIZA-ANEL government officially rejected the de facto powers that the tripartite body of technocrats had

[21] Paragraph 8 of the Preamble of the First Loan Facility Agreement defines that: 'The release of Loans subsequent to the first one shall be conditional upon the Euro Area Member States (except Greece) deciding favourably after consultation with the European Central Bank (hereinafter the "ECB") on the basis of the findings of verification by the Commission that the implementation of the economic policy of the Borrower accords with the adjustment programme or any other conditions laid down in the Council decision on the basis of Art. 126(9) and 136 TFEU and the MoU.' This provision constituted the basis for the Troika's intervention in domestic policy-making. The Agreement is available at www.irishstatutebook.ie/eli/2010/act/7/schedule/2/enacted/en/html.

[22] See the 'Joint Answer given by Mr. Rehn on behalf of the Commission'.

[23] G. Drossos, 'Το 'Μνημόνιο' ως σημείο στροφής του πολιτεύματος' ('The 'Memorandum' as a Turning Point of the Polity'), www.constitutionalism.gr. Also published in *The Book's Journal*, 6, April 2011, p. 42

[24] See, for example, European Commission, *The Second Economic Adjustment Programme for Greece – Second Review* (Occasional Paper on the European Economy No. 148, May 2013), ec.europa.eu/economy_finance/publications/occasional_paper/2013/pdf/ocp148_en.pdf.

acquired to the detriment of constitutional democracy and national sovereignty. This changed the situation for some months. The Troika missions to Athens were suspended and the Greek government, after five years, was able again to implement governmental policy without consulting the creditors and sometimes even against their explicit disagreement.[25]

However, the situation could not last long. In the end, the Government had to pay a high price for its defiance of the Troika's technocratic 'advice'. Following the striking results of the July referendum and two weeks of capital controls and bank holidays in Greece, a Euro Summit took place on 12 and 13 July 2015. The result of what has been described by all witnesses as a very hard meeting was a common Statement, according to which the Greek Government agreed to implement 'without delay' a set of priority actions, in order for the negotiations with its European partners to restart.[26] For some major reforms, the words 'without delay' meant in three days' time.[27] Determination of governmental policy went so far as to require changes in the core of the Greek legal system such as, most notably, an extensive reform of the code of civil procedure.[28] What is more, the Greek authorities committed to 'reexamine with a view to amending legislations that were introduced counter to the February 20 agreement by backtracking on previous programme commitments or identify clear compensatory equivalents for the vested rights that were subsequently created'.[29] The prior actions required by the creditors were included in an emergency omnibus bill and were voted in one article. To justify the circumvention of constitutional procedures the Government invoked the Euro Summit Statement and the 'particularly exceptional circumstances' triggered by it.[30]

[25] See, for example, Law 4320/2015, 'Provisions for adopting immediate measures to face the humanitarian crisis, for the organisation of Government and of Government organs and other provisions', OJ A' 29/19.03.2015.

[26] See the Euro Summit Statement 12 July 2015 (SN 4070/15), www.consilium.europa.eu/en/press/press-releases/2015/07/pdf/20150712-eurosummit-statement-greece/, p. 1.

[27] Ibid., pp. 1ff.

[28] Ibid., p. 2. Note that the deadline for the implementation of this reform was 11 days.

[29] Ibid., p. 5.

[30] See Law 4334/2015, OJ A' 80/16.07.2015 and the relevant explanatory report at www.hellenicparliament.gr/UserFiles/2f026f42-950c-4efc-b950-340c4fb76a24/e-ems-eis.pdf, p. 1.

Under the subsequent European Stability Mechanism (ESM) programme,[31] which is still operative, contempt of the Constitution and national sovereignty persists, with the exception of some purely aesthetic changes. For the application of the economic adjustment programme, the Troika, now elegantly renamed as the 'Institutions', continues its review missions to Athens.[32] The Greek government has committed 'to consult and agree with the Institutions on all draft legislation in relevant areas with adequate time before submitting it for public consultation or to Parliament'.[33]

The economic adjustment programmes have thus operated in the domestic legal order with no respect for constitutional procedures and forms. Incoherent justifications of the measures, opportunistically advanced by Government according to the forum to which they were submitted, have excluded any kind of accountability. Legal accountability has been excluded, as the MoU has been argued to be a political programme. Political accountability has also been considerably limited, since the programmes have been argued to result from binding supranational or international obligations and their specific provisions have been hardly discussed in parliamentary debates. Economic emergency has left no place for democracy and has progressively led to a major limitation of national sovereignty. As their lengthy duration indicates, these features have acquired a permanent character and have now become a typical trait of everyday constitutional politics in Greece.

2 Economic 'Emergency'?

The constant use of abbreviated procedures and the de facto operation of euro-crisis instruments in the domestic sphere seem to indicate the existence of an economic emergency. Though Article 48 of the Constitution, which provides for a constitutional state of siege, was never invoked,[34] governments have often used a rhetoric reminiscent of a state

[31] See the Financial Assistance Facility Agreement, 19 August 2015, www.esm.europa.eu/pdf/2015-08-19%20GR%20-%20ESM%20-%20FFA%20publication%20version.pdf and the relevant MoU, 19 August 2015, http://ec.europa.eu/economy_finance/assistance_eu_ms/greek_loan_facility/pdf/01_mou_20150811_en.pdf.

[32] See Euro Summit Statement (SN 4070/15), p. 5.

[33] Ibid.

[34] Besides, the very strict conditions of this article would not be met. It can only be invoked 'in case of war or mobilization owing to external dangers or an imminent threat against

of war or exception.[35] In the explanatory report accompanying Law 3845/2010, the Government argued that the activation of the support mechanism and the onerous measures agreed in the MoU were an 'action of responsibility and an historical obligation to face the danger of collapse of the Greek economy'.[36] Moreover, in the introductory report annexed to the statute, it was mentioned that the only alternative to these measures would be 'collapse and destruction'.[37] This perception of an imminent emergency persisted under the second economic adjustment programme, as well as during the 12 months of the SYRIZA-ANEL government.[38]

In its decision on the constitutionality of Law 3845/2010 the Council of State translated the emergency rhetoric used by the Government into legal terms. To this purpose, the Court invoked a situation of 'fiscal emergency'. This situation was to be identified exclusively by the legislator; the judiciary would have no say in legislative evaluations in this respect.[39] Further, in the decision, the Court referred very extensively to the economic and political situation that the country was facing, before concluding that the impugned measures were justified by the 'compelling public interest' of the consolidation of public finances. Until recently, the Supreme Administrative Court had constantly rejected the nature of a 'fiscal interest of the State' as a legitimate reason justifying fundamental rights' restrictions. However, since the beginning of the crisis, the path to Decision 668/2012 had been paved in previous cases: the financial public interest had been progressively qualified as a 'compelling national interest'.[40] Thus, in Decision 668/2012, deferring to governmental policy choices, the administrative judges stated that no examination of less-

national security, as well as in case of an armed coup aiming to overthrow the democratic regime'.

35 See Minutes of the Greek Parliament, 6 May 2010, p. 6714.

36 See 'πράξη ευθύνης και ιστορική υποχρέωση απέναντι στον κίνδυνο κατάρρευσης της οικονομίας' in the explanatory report, www.hellenicparliament.gr/UserFiles/2f026f42-950c-4efc-b950-340c4fb76a24/M-DNTAMEIO-eis1.qxp.pdf, p. 1.

37 See 'η εναλλακτική πορεία θα ήταν η κατάρρευση και η καταστροφή' in the introductory report, www.hellenicparliament.gr/UserFiles/c8827c35-4399-4fbb-8ea6-aebdc768f4f7/AOIKONOMIKVN.pdf, p. 2.

38 'Acts of legislative content' and emergency procedures were used to transfer public sector funds to a special Bank of Greece account, to amend pre-existing legislation on the referendum procedure and on other matters.

39 See CoS Pl. Decision 668/2012, para. 35. The Court did not explicitly refer to the concept of exceptional circumstances. See, on the contrary, the concurring opinion, para. 38.

40 Decision 1620/2011, para. 8; see I. Mathioudakis, 'Μετασχηματισμοί του ταμειακού συμφέροντος του Δημοσίου σε περίοδο έντονης οικονομικής κρίσης'

restrictive alternatives was required, since the impugned measures were part of a general programme for facing the economic crisis.

Emergency, in turn, indicates that the situation of constitutional deconstruction should be exceptional or temporary. The Socialist government itself had promised in 2010 that 'the national effort [would have] a beginning, a middle and an end'.[41] However, this has not been the case; in fact, constitutional deconstruction has become a permanent feature of Greek constitutional politics. This is due both to the practice of domestic actors and to that of the creditors.

Let's start again with Law 3845/2010. In its main body, the government exploited the ambiguity as to the nature of euro-crisis instruments and limited the role of parliament in their implementation. Article 1, paragraph 4 delegated to the Minister of Finance the signature of future agreements for the application of the economic adjustment programme. The original version of the provision required that relevant agreements be brought to parliament for ratification. However, it was amended two days later, by a last minute 'legal-technical' correction, voted again through the emergency procedure of Article 76, paragraph 4 of the Constitution: the term 'ratification' was replaced by the terms 'discussion and briefing', rendering agreements operative from their signature. According to the representative of the government, the amendment was necessary for the First Loan Agreement, signed some days later, to come into immediate effect, and thus before 19 May 2010, the date that the bond loans matured.[42] Less than a month later Article 93 of Law 3862/2010 repeated that agreements and MoUs relevant to the participation of the country in the European Financial Stability Facility (EFSF), as well as to loans agreed with this organisation, should be brought before parliament only for discussion and briefing.[43] Circumvention of constitutional procedures for the ratification of international agreements became thus a permanent possibility, at least as far as participation to the EFSF is concerned.[44]

('Transformations of the cash interest of the State in a period of intense economic crisis'), www.constitutionalism.gr.

41 See the introductory report to the bill, cited above (n. 37) p. 2: 'Ολη αυτή η εθνική προσπάθεια έχει αρχή, μέση και τέλος'.

42 See Minutes of the Greek Parliament, 6 May 2010, p. 6742.

43 See Law 3862/2010, OJ A' 113/13.07.2010.

44 Indeed, such instruments, creating economic burdens for the Greek people and imposing austerity policies, are arguably subject ratification according to Art. 36, para. 2 of the Constitution.

Constitutional deconstruction did not only concern the openness of the domestic system to international or supranational legal agreements; it also concerned the internal distribution of constitutional competences between the legislature and the executive. Article 2 of Law 3845/2010 conferred a broad range of powers on the executive to take the necessary measures for the application of the economic adjustment programme. This broad delegation met objections even by parties that voted in favour of the MoU.[45] Article 43 of the Constitution concerns the delegation of powers to the executive. It declares:

> 2. The issuance of general regulatory decrees, by virtue of special delegation granted by statute and within the limits of such delegation, shall be permitted on the proposal of the competent Minister. Delegation for the purpose of issuing regulatory acts by other administrative organs shall be permitted in cases concerning the regulation of more specific matters or matters of local interest or of a technical and detailed nature.
>
> ...
>
> 4. By virtue of statutes passed by the Plenum of the Parliament, delegation may be given for the issuance of general regulatory decrees for the regulation of matters specified by such statutes in a broad framework. These statutes shall set out the general principles and directives of the regulation to be followed and shall set time-limits within which the delegation must be used.

The MoU, affecting virtually all domains of governmental policy, could not be considered 'more specific matters or matters of local interest or of a technical and detailed nature' as Article 44, paragraph 2 stipulates. Nor was Law 3845/2010 valid as a framework statute, according to paragraph 4 of the same article: constitutional law scholars agree that the formal conditions for such a statute were not fulfilled.[46] Therefore, the relevant statutory provisions, far too broad to meet the commonly accepted constitutional limits to the delegation of legislative power, made emergency norm production a possibility which became permanent and normal, like economic adjustment itself.

Indeed, while constitutional forms were deconstructed, a web of international legality was being fashioned around the Loan Facility and the programmes agreed between Greece and its creditors. As we saw, Article 93 of Law 3862/2010, voted on 5 July 2010, declared that agreements and

[45] See Minutes of the Greek Parliament, 6 May 2010, p. 6788.

[46] It is generally accepted that a framework-statute must concern a homogeneous subject matter and must determine the general legislative guidelines for the regulation of the matter. See the Report on Greece prepared by Marketou and Dekastros (n. 5).

MoUs relevant to the participation of the country in the EFSF are brought before Parliament only for discussion and briefing. However, the same article explicitly provided for the legal status of loan agreements as *international conventions* which, contrary to other agreements, are brought to Parliament for *ratification* and are valid only after the publication of the relevant statute in the Official Gazette.[47] Following this provision, the EFSF Framework Agreement together with its amendments was brought to Parliament for ratification, more than a year after its initial signature.[48] If we take into account that such ratification did not take place in other EFSF countries, why was it needed in Greece?

The answer is that the legalisation of international agreements in the domestic sphere was deemed to protect creditors from the consequences of an abrupt political change, already predictable at the time.[49] Indeed, Article 28, paragraph 1 of the Constitution confers supra-legislative status to ratified international agreements. Therefore, promoters of austerity have always, in public debates, presented the measures as resulting from a *legal* obligation of the government. Possessing an ambiguous status (European norms, international norms or economic agreements concluded by the State as a private person), euro-crisis legal instruments have acquired a de facto validity and binding character in the domestic sphere.

Sometimes this was obtained by invoking the European commitments of the country. Austerity measures included in Law 3845/2010 did not have a temporary character. Since economic emergency was invoked for their justification, the measures were contested before the Council of State as disproportionate to their aim. However, the Court specified that the legislative purpose was 'not only to face, according to the assessments of the legislature, the sharp fiscal crisis but also [to consolidate] public finances in a way that will be sustainable in the future'.[50] This purpose was characterised as a 'compelling public interest' and 'a common

47 Yet according to Art. 94 of the same law, this provision is retroactively valid only from 1 June 2010; it thus does not concern the First Loan Agreement. See ibid. It is interesting to note that the same provisions had been included in the draft law ratifying the First Loan Agreement, which was never discussed or voted in Parliament.

48 Art. 48, Law 4021/2011, OJ A' 218/03.10.2011.

49 The representatives of the socialist government actually admitted that ratification was required by creditors in some cases. See Minutes of the Greek Parliament, 5 July 2010, www.hellenicparliament.gr/UserFiles/a08fc2dd-61a9-4a83-b09a-09f4c564609d/es20100705.pdf, p. 9581.

50 See CoS Pl. Decision 668/2012, para. 35.

interest for Eurozone Member States, in view of the obligation of fiscal discipline and of ensuring the stability of the Eurozone as a whole, established by EU legislation'. Was it thus an economic *emergency* that the country was facing or was it rather an *EU legal requirement* to follow a certain economic policy?

As far as the second economic adjustment programme is concerned, ambiguity as to its nature was preserved at a supranational level as well. The First Review of the second economic adjustment programme declared that 'The EU Council decision . . . adopted upon a recommendation of the European Commission, sets the steps and deadlines to be respected to correct the situation of excessive deficit.'[51] In other words, it seems that the programme acquired an official European legal mantle. However, the Fourth Review went on to state that the MoU documents were drafted jointly by the Troika and the competent Greek authorities and were implemented according to a pre-agreed timetable.[52] In other words, though the 'steps and deadlines' were defined as European legal obligations, the specific provisions in the MoU – 'comprehensively identif[ying] the specific measures to be taken, going into a high degree of detail' – were not.[53]

The ambiguous nature of the MoU commitments did not reassure the country's creditors, who sometimes required *personal written confirmations* by Greek political leaders that they would follow the policies defined in them.[54] Even though such confirmations would only have a political nature, their international and constitutional legality is doubtful, especially insofar as they were required as a condition for the creditors to abide by the Loan Agreement. Even more, in the First Review of the second economic adjustment programmes it was stated that the MoU documents would be 'subsequently transformed into a *cogent* law through a vote in Parliament.'[55] Still, when a normal voting procedure

[51] European Commission, *The Second Economic Adjustment Programme for Greece – First Review* (Occasional Paper on the European Economy No. 123, December 2012), ec.europa.eu/economy_finance/publications/occasional_paper/2012/pdf/ocp123_en.pdf, p. 7.

[52] See European Commission, *The Second Economic Adjustment Programme for Greece – Fourth Review* (Occasional Paper on the European Economy No. 192, April 2014), ec.europa.eu/economy_finance/publications/occasional_paper/2014/pdf/ocp192_en.pdf, p. 9.

[53] See the First Review of the Second economic adjustment programme, p. 7.

[54] See J. Strupczewski, 'Eurogroup Set to Release Greek Tranche, Fix EFSF Leveraging Rules', in *Reuters US*, 25 November 2011, www.reuters.com/article/2011/11/25/eurogroup-idUSL5E7MO3NZ20111125.

[55] See the Fourth Review of the Second AEP, p. 7 (emphasis added).

is employed, a law can be 'cogent' (i.e. it will prevail over contrary legislation) in Greece only if it is ratifying international legal agreements. In other words, it seems that, although a web of international legality was being constructed, it was only operating in the domestic legal sphere, binding Parliament and future Governments. On the contrary, the Troika's missions and the MoUs did not need to be founded on any international or European legal text and did not engage the accountability of European institutions involved before the ECJ.

What is more, progressively the MoUs ceased to be perceived as exceptional instruments to face the economic emergency; in a way, they were normalised and institutionalised. For the first time, the First Review of the second economic adjustment programme stated that the MoU texts:

> are living documents and are modified at every quarterly review mission, based on implementation of previous commitments and identification of new ones. The first programme documents were established in May 2010. The set of documents included in this publication constitutes the seventh version since then.[56]

This declaration, repeated in following reviews, established continuity and coherence between the first and the second economic adjustment programme. Most importantly, omitting any reference to exceptional circumstances and establishing a procedure and timeline, albeit in an embryonic form, for the modification of the MoUs, the declaration undermined their exceptional nature.

Ironically, the calls of the SYRIZA-ANEL government for a political solution to the situation only led to more institutionalisation and normalisation of the economic adjustment programmes. The third programme and its technocratic rationale were not anymore dictated by the Troika specialists, but were explicitly endorsed by the euro area heads of state and government.[57] Subsequently their concrete terms were politically approved by the Eurogroup Ministers[58] and were even voted upon by the parliaments of the euro area Member States.[59] The Loan Agreement now operates under the ESM framework, which was accommodated by the EU treaties through an amendment of Article 136 and thus

[56] Ibid. [57] See Euro Summit Statement (SN 4070/15).

[58] See 'Eurogroup statement on the ESM programme for Greece', 14 August 2015, www.consilium.europa.eu/en/press/press-releases/2015/08/14-eurogroup-statement/.

[59] B. Sills, 'Greece Countdown: How Europe Votes on the New Bailout' in *Bloomberg*, 18 August 2015, www.bloomberg.com/news/articles/2015-08-18/greece-bailout-european-lawmakers-vote-on-new-deal.

does not have an ad hoc or exceptional nature. The MoUs are also no longer ad hoc exceptional instruments, but enjoy the legitimacy of an international treaty. The euro-crisis agreements are perceived as binding international obligations by the Greek government and are ratified as such (though without application of Article 28 of the Constitution).[60] Besides, refusal to reconsider the Greek debt leads to an indefinite prolongation of the loss of national sovereignty. In the last elections that took place in Greece in September 2015, the political programme that the new Government would apply was pre-defined. The only stake of the elections was *who* would apply it.[61]

3 Afterword: The Judiciary as the Last Hope for the Constitution

More than six years of prolonged economic crisis have thus produced in Greece an unusual constitutional-political situation for a Western democracy. Constitutional politics and norm production are no longer based on democratic deliberation, as the Constitution imposes, but on international agreements, of ambiguous nature and changing content, concluded by the executive. Constitutional rules are constantly circumvented or abused. Constitutional deconstruction even seems to have acquired a permanent nature independent of any state of exception or emergency. Besides, the economic adjustment programme instruments and procedures are institutionalised and normalised both in the domestic and the supranational sphere. Still, the Constitution is broadly recognised as a valid legal text. Though emergency has sometimes corroded its forms, the institutions that it provides for are operating according to its procedures and in its name. Is there any hope for constitutional democracy in Greece? Is there any place for the Constitution as a valid point of reference in constitutional-political decision-making?

In this context of constitutional chaos, the last hope for the Constitution is the judiciary. Due to its position and function, the judiciary is

[60] See Law 4336/2015, OJ A' 94/14.08.2015. Note that this statute ratified the *draft* agreement and MoU (the creditors would not sign it before it was approved by all European parliaments). Interestingly, the Euro Summit statement (SN 4010/15) of 12 July 2015 was also ratified by Law 4334/2015.

[61] See the announcement of the early elections of September 2015 by Alexis Tsipras, www.youtube.com/watch?v=OGVoWlhVBJE.

among the last institutions expressing a faith in the formal Constitution.[62] Judicial activism has been quite rare in Greek constitutional politics. Besides, possibilities for such activism during the crisis are limited to the scrutiny of the substantive evaluations of public authorities. Indeed, Greek courts traditionally do not check for eventual violation or abuse of the procedures set by the Constitution for legal norm production; this is because, according to the Greek conception of the separation of powers, the *interna corporis* of Parliament are not subject to judicial review. Further, the Council of State usually refrains from contesting public authorities' determinations as to the existence of emergency situations. This considerably limits the possibility for the Supreme Administrative Court to sanction the abusive use of emergency decree-laws.

Still, after a period of inaction, the Greek supreme courts finally assumed a more active role.[63] In the beginning they mobilised clear constitutional provisions such as those ensuring collective labour rights, to disapply legislation that implemented MoU requirements.[64] Subsequently, the Supreme Administrative Court and the Court of Audit required the preserving of a minimum normative content to other constitutional rights as well, through the principle of proportionality. Thus, in recent decisions, the courts have assessed in detail the cumulative effect of austerity policies on certain groups of individuals.[65] Further, they have sometimes set important justification requirements on austerity legislation. In this way, they have thoroughly scrutinised the substantive evaluations of the legislature when imposing onerous measures, requiring the examination of less restrictive alternatives and the respect of the principles of equality, solidarity and human dignity.[66]

What is more, the Supreme Administrative Court and the Court of Audit have started abandoning their deferent stance concerning

[62] On the loss of faith in the Constitution as a way to approach constitutional-political change in Greece during the crisis, see A. Marketou, 'Economic Emergency and the Loss of Faith in the Greek Constitution, How Does a Constitution Function when It Is Dying?', in *Cambridge Journal of International and Comparative Law* 4(2), pp. 289–318.

[63] See CoS Pl. Decision 668/2012; Decisions 1283, 1284 and 1285/2012, 2 April 2012.

[64] See CoS Pl. Decision 2307/2014, 27 June 2014.

[65] See Court of Audit, Fourth Special Sitting of the Plenum, 31 October 2012; Second Special Sitting of the Plenum, 27 February 2013; Court of Audit, Decision 4327/2014, 23 June 2014; CoS Pl., Decision 2192-2196/2014, 13 June 2014.

[66] See CoS Pl. Decision 2192-2196/2014, paras. 19ff.

legislative determinations as to the existence of an economic emergency. Interestingly, the courts have sometimes disapplied austerity legislation, as they found that 'the financial interest of the State [that justified it] was no longer peremptory'.[67] Having by now clearly identified the connection between the measures and the EU obligations of the country, the Greek supreme courts insist that domestic constitutional values should be preserved as well.[68] Therefore, they impugn onerous measures imposed upon certain groups of citizens according to 'a purely mathematical' and thus 'profoundly inappropriate' criterion.[69]

However, the substantive human rights values that the Greek courts invoke have a content that is not easily observable and agreed upon. Despite their entrenchment in the EU Charter of Fundamental Rights and in other international conventions, court decisions declaring a violation of social rights are translated only into fiscal numbers in the technocratic discourses of the 'Institutions', the media and even the other euro area leaders. For example, the Euro Summit stated that the Greek Government must 'carry out ambitious pension reforms and specify policies to fully compensate for the fiscal impact of the Constitutional Court ruling on the 2012 pension reform'.[70] No matter that the purely mathematical rationale of austerity was generally criticised in the decision. No matter that Greece does not have a constitutional court at all. All that matters is what the creditors perceive as the ruling's *fiscal impact*.

Will the Council of State and the Court of Audit continue to resist the quantification of politics and of the Constitution on which technocrats and the media insist? Will the European institutions continue to neglect the constitutions and democratic procedures of (certain of) its member states? And, if Weiler is right in saying that the EU has to turn to its Member States in order to compensate for its legitimacy deficit,[71] what does the shift in Greek constitutional politics mean for the process of European integration?

67 See CoS Pl. Decision 2192-2196/2014. Similarly, Court of Audit, Decision 4327/2014.

68 See Decision 2192-2196/2014, para. 21.

69 See CoS Pl. Decision 4741/2014, 29 December 2014. The official summary of the judgement is available in English at www.ste.gr/images/StE/content/deltia/Judgment%20Summaries.pdf.

70 See Euro Summit Statement (SN 4070/15), p. 3.

71 J. Weiler, 'Europe in Crisis – On 'Political Messianism', 'Legitimacy' and the 'Rule of Law'', in *Singapore Journal of Legal Studies*, 2, 2012, 248–69, at 249.

4 Conclusion

This paper has examined the changes brought about by euro-crisis instruments in the domestic sphere from the point of view of constitutional forms and procedures. Focusing on these technical features is a way to escape the criticism of ideological bias that an analysis from the point of view of social rights or other constitutional values would necessarily entail. Indeed, constitutional values have a vague and relative content in situations like the current one, which is perceived as an economic crisis that has often acquired 'existential dimensions' for the Greek state.[72]

I have shown how the economic adjustment programme instruments, MoUs and Loan Agreements operate in the domestic sphere in the margins of constitutional forms and procedures and bind governmental policy and the exercise of national sovereignty. Having an ambiguous nature, they exclude the Government's accountability as regards their implementation, both before the parliament and the courts. De facto situations resulting from the violation or abuse of constitutional procedures – most prominently, the Troika review missions – are perceived as normative due to their alleged efficiency in the implementation of the transnational technocratic precepts of the economic adjustment programmes. The prevalence of economic rationality, which is claimed to be dictated by the creditors, even on the most valuable constitutional freedoms, like the freedom of speech and information, shows that the current situation has left no leeway to democratic politics. Even though the flagrant disregard for constitutional procedures would indicate the existence of a state of emergency, the fundamental constitutional-political changes brought about by the Eurocrisis do not seem to have a temporary character. On the contrary, the practice of the crisis-stricken governments and their creditors has normalised and institutionalised the circumvention of constitutional forms and procedures, in order to ensure domestic politics' compliance with a transnational technocratic rationale. In this way, the economic adjustment programmes have considerably undermined the fundamental grounds of Greek constitutional democracy, namely the rule of law and parliamentary deliberation.

72 A. Manitakis, 'Τα συνταγματικά ζητήματα του Μνημονίου ενόψει κρατικής κυριαρχίας και επιτηρούμενης δημοσιονομικής πολιτικής' ('The Constitutional Issues of the Memorandum in View of the Divided National Sovereignty and the Monitored Fiscal Policy') (2011) 51 DtA 689, 707.

To describe this evolution, I have used the metaphor of constitutional deconstruction. Indeed, the formal Constitution, until recently a coherent whole of forms and procedures ensuring popular sovereignty, now seems void and misplaced compared to the modern, rational and efficient instruments decided in the opaque meetings of technocratic institutions. Because the perception of an economic emergency has left no place for politics and since the will of the creditors has replaced the will of the people, the formal Constitution has lost its fundamental reason for existence. It is valid only when the economic situation allows it; constitutional authorities, procedures and norms are used only when no more efficient option exists. In this way, the Constitution is deprived of its internal coherence and the 'purely mathematical' rationale of the economic adjustment programmes has replaced the polity's democratic foundation.

7

Spain: Dealing with the Economic Emergency through Constitutional Reform and Limited Parliamentary Intervention

LETICIA DÍEZ SANCHEZ

The Spanish economic emergency has been translated into unprecedented austerity measures, a constant reform of the labour regime, an accelerated constitutional amendment and an opaque bailout for re-capitalising the banking sector. Parallel to the measures has been a re-centralisation of economic governance to the detriment of autonomous communities and municipalities. The sense of emergency impregnates not only the substance but also the legislative forms chosen: royal decree-laws as a substitute of ordinary laws and abbreviated parliamentary procedures instead of regular processes of contestation and approval.

Spain has experienced constitutional reform in a wide sense: formally, through the amendment of Article 135 of the constitution, as well as informally, through a significant change away from the manner in which the constitution had been interpreted up to the Eurocrisis. The greatest ally of such reform has been the Spanish Constitutional Court and its reluctance to interfere with the economic policies of the executive.

This chapter is structured as follows. The following section will introduce the various reforms instigated in reaction to the Spanish economic emergency, including economic and social measures, the amendment of Article 135 of the Spanish Constitution and the bailout of the banking sector. The remarkable use of emergency legislation during the crisis will then be analysed. The chapter progresses to an account of the judiciary's reaction to euro-crisis measures and the contagion of the language of pressing economic circumstances from the political to the judicial spheres. The result is a transformation of the Spanish constitutional regime, whose consequences will remain after an eventual economic recovery.

1 Economic and Social Measures, Constitutional Amendment and (Banking) Bailout

The report of the Bank of Spain in 2009 acknowledged that the country was in recession and marked the beginning of the Eurocrisis in Spain.[1] The socialist José Luis Rodríguez Zapatero, then–Prime Minister, faced an escalating risk premium on sovereign bonds and soaring unemployment figures.[2] Foreign investors were dissuaded by the downgrading of Spanish sovereign bonds,[3] while low employment levels meant a decrease of governmental revenues via taxes and an increase of expenditure in social benefits. The state finances were, as a result, in a compromised position.

The first set of austerity measures was introduced in 2010, still under Zapatero's office. VAT rates were raised from 16 to 18 per cent[4] and, most importantly, the labour regime commenced an endless process of reform. Royal Decree-Law 8/2010 made significant reductions in the salaries of civil servants, among other deficit-correcting measures.[5] The cuts, which breached the collective agreements in force at the time, were followed by further amendments of the general labour market. Royal Decree-Law 7/2011 modified the regime of collective bargaining to make collective negotiation more 'flexible'.[6] Lastly, the pensions system also experienced an important transformation when the age for retirement rose from 65 to 67 years old.[7]

Zapatero decided to end his term in November 2011, four months before the ordinary end of the legislative period. His decision to leave office early was motivated by the need to have a new government that

[1] Bank of Spain, 'Annual Report 2008', www.bde.es/f/webbde/Secciones/Publicaciones/PublicacionesAnuales/inf2008e.pdf, p. 15.

[2] The unemployment rate was 17.4 per cent at the beginning of 2009, reaching 24.4 per cent by 2012. See ibid., p. 156 and Bank of Spain, 'Annual Report 2011', www.bde.es/f/webbde/SES/Secciones/Publicaciones/PublicacionesAnuales/InformesAnuales/11/Fich/inf2011e.pdf, p. 16, respectively.

[3] See N. Gaillard, 'What Is the Value of Sovereign Ratings?', *German Economic Review*, 15(1), 2014, 208–24, at 220f.

[4] Law 26/2009 on the General State Budget for the year 2010, Boletín Oficial del Estado, No. 309, 24 December 2009.

[5] Royal Decree-Law 8/2010 of 20 May adopting extraordinary measures for the reduction of the public deficit, Boletín Oficial del Estado, No. 126, 24 May 2010.

[6] Royal Decree-Law 7/2011 of 10 June on urgent measures for the reform of collective bargaining, Boletín Oficial del Estado, No. 139, 11 June 2011.

[7] Law 27/2011 on the updating, adjusting and modernisation of the system of Social Security, Boletín Oficial del Estado, No. 184, 2 August 2011.

could bring the stability needed for an economic recovery.[8] Just before leaving office, however, the Socialist party orchestrated a reform of Article 135 of the Spanish Constitution so as to give constitutional status to the principle of budgetary stability. This amendment was initiated a few days after Zapatero received a letter from the European Central Bank in August 2011 urging him to 'take bold measures to ensuring the sustainability of public finances'.[9] Besides, the Euro Plus Pact prescribed that the balanced budget rule shall take effect in national law through binding provisions.[10] While the former Article 135 briefly regulated the issuing of sovereign bonds, the new Article 135 gave constitutional status to the maximum structural deficit margins established by the European Union and compelled all levels of government to respect these budgetary limits.[11]

The unexpected and quick reform of the Spanish Constitution generated a strong controversy.[12] Article 135 was among the sections of the Constitution that could be modified through a simplified procedure (with a three-fifth majority in both the Congress and the Senate and without referendum). The government further shortened the parliamentary formalities by processing the initiative of amendment through the 'single reading procedure' and passing the amendment itself through the 'urgency procedure'. The two largest parties (the governing Socialist Party and the opposing Popular Party) had previously agreed on the content of the constitutional amendment. In contrast, the other parliamentary groups complained that they had not had time to react to an

[8] 'Zapatero convoca el 20-N para que otro gobierno dé certidumbre', *El País* (29 July 2011), http://politica.elpais.com/politica/2011/07/29/actualidad/1311929850_613039.html.

[9] The letter was reclassified by the European Central Bank on 19 December 2014. See www.ecb.europa.eu/pub/pdf/other/2011-08-05-letter-from-trichet-and-fernandez-ordonez-to-zapateroen.pdf?e5c1a67f9627c5f087d5c7f02168e0da.

[10] European Council, 'Conclusions', EUCO 10/1/11, REV 1 (25 March 2011), www.consilium.europa.eu/uedocs/cms_data/docs/pressdata/en/ec/120296.pdf.

[11] A reference to the deficit levels fixed in the Stability and Growth Pact was made through Article 135(2) ('Neither the State nor the Autonomous Communities shall enter into a structural deficit beyond the limits stipulated, if applicable, by the European Union for its Member States'). In the same vein, Article 135(3) enshrined the limits to public debt set forth in Protocol No 12 of the TFEU ('The volume of public debt for all the Public Administrations as a whole as a ratio of the State's Gross Domestic Product shall not surpass the benchmark figure set forth in the Treaty on the Functioning of the European Union.'). An Agencia Estatal Boletín Oficial del Estado translation of the Constitution of Spain is available at https://boe.es/legislacion/documentos/ConstitucionINGLES.pdf.

[12] E. Álvarez Conde et al., 'La reforma del artículo 135 CE', *Revista Española de Derecho Constitucional*, 93, 2011, 159–210, esp. 175 and 181.

amendment they hardly expected.[13] Only 32 days passed from the announcement of the amendment to its promulgation on 27 September 2011;[14] it has since been mocked as the 'express reform'.

In this climate of general discontent with the socialist government, the general elections of November 2011 took place.[15] The conservative Mariano Rajoy achieved an absolute majority, while a significant portion of former votes for the Socialist party shifted towards United Left. The new conservative government installed by Rajoy continued the labour market reforms initiated by Zapatero. Royal Decree-Law 3/2012 reduced the severance payments of permanent job contracts and created a one-year probation contract with no severance payment at all.[16] The same decree-law specified economic circumstances under which the employer can reduce the wages or the working time of employees. Lastly, Royal Decree-Law 20/2012 included among others a provision allowing for the suspension of collective agreements of public employees when the government considers a severe economic situation to exist.[17]

Austerity also accentuated under the conservative mandate. In April 2012, the government cut €10,000 million in the education and the healthcare sectors. Royal Decree-Law 14/2012 increased the working time of school teachers and made the maximum number of students per class more flexible, as well as setting stringent rules for managing the budget of public universities.[18] Royal Decree-Law 16/2012, on the other hand, introduced the co-pay of medicines that used to be fully funded through social security.

[13] Congreso de los Dipudatos, 'Diario de Sesiones del Congreso de los Diputados', No. 269, 30 August 2011, www.congreso.es/public_oficiales/L9/CONG/DS/PL/PL_269.PDF, p. 11 and No. 270, 2 September 2011, www.congreso.es/public_oficiales/L9/CONG/DS/PL/PL_270.PDF, p.4.

[14] Reforma del Artículo 135 de la Constitución Española, Boletín Oficial del Estado, No. 233, 27 September 2011. See P. García-Escudero Márquez, 'La Acelerada Tramitación Parlamentaria de la Reforma del Artículo 135 de la Constitución', *Teoría y Realidad Constitucional*, 29, 2012, 165–98.

[15] The famous '15M' movement, which began as a series of peaceful demonstrations on 15 May 2011, had achieved international echoes by this point and set the foundations for more stable political projects and associations. It is said that these social movements were the origin of Podemos, the left-wing party that achieved third place in the most recent general elections of 20 December 2015.

[16] Royal Decree-Law 3/2012 of 10 February on urgent measures for the reform of the labour market, Boletín Oficial del Estado, No. 36, 11 February 2012.

[17] Royal Decree-Law 20/2012 of 13 July on measures for guaranteeing budgetary stability and the promotion of competitiveness, Boletín Oficial del Estado, No. 168, 14 July 2012.

[18] Royal Decree-Law 14/2012 of 20 April on urgent measures for the streamlining of public expenditures in the education sector, Boletín Oficial del Estado, No. 96, 21 April 2012.

Parallel to the reshuffle of economic and social rights was the implementation of the balanced budget rule in the public sector, which ultimately meant a deep transformation of the Spanish public administration. Organic Law 2/2012 on budgetary stability[19] reformed the previous Law 18/2001 so as to guarantee compliance with the EU guidelines.[20] This organic law developed the objective of budgetary stability, as enshrined in the new Article 135 of the Spanish Constitution, while also serving as partial implementation of the Fiscal Compact.[21] Among the main innovations of Organic Law 2/2012 were the creation of an Independent Authority for Fiscal Responsibility for stronger fiscal surveillance,[22] the introduction of strict sanctions in case of non-compliance by the regional authorities (including the suspension of their taxation competences) and the establishment of a bailout mechanism for regions in financial difficulties. Other legal instruments enhancing the impact of Organic Law 2/2012 (and, ultimately, of the constitutional principle of budgetary stability) were Royal Decree-Law 21/2012 on measures of liquidity of the public administrations and on the financial sector,[23] Royal Decree-Law 515/2013 regulating the criteria and the procedure to determine and demand the responsibilities for breach of EU Law[24] and Law 19/2013 on transparency, access to public information and good governance.[25] These instruments made explicit mention of the 'extraordinary situation of [the] pressing need for financing of the Autonomous Communities',[26]

[19] Organic Law 2/2012 of 27 April on Budgetary Stability and Financial Sustainability, Boletín Oficial del Estado, No. 103, 30 April 2012.

[20] Ibid., Preamble.

[21] The 'Fiscal Compact' signifies the obligations set out in Title III of the Treaty on Stability, Coordination and Governance in the European Monetary Union (TSCG). The TSCG is an international treaty and was signed on 2 March 2012 by all Member States of the EU, bar the UK and the Czech Republic.

[22] For further discussion on the establishment of Independent Financial Institutions through euro-crisis law, see in this book Chapter 4, 'Creation and Reform of Independent Fiscal Institutions in EU Member States: Incomplete and Insufficient Work in Progress?' by Diane Fromage.

[23] Royal Decree-Law 21/2012 of 13 July 2012 on measures of liquidity of the public administrations and on the financial sector, Boletín Oficial del Estado, No. 168, of 14 July 2012.

[24] Royal Decree-Law 515/2013 of July 5 2013 regulating the criteria and the procedure to determine and demand the responsibilities for breach of EU Law, Boletín Oficial del Estado, No. 161, 6 July 2013. The purpose of this measure was to detail the mechanisms by which a public administration of any level can be compelled to pay damages if it causes Spain to be found in breach of EU law.

[25] Law 19/2013 of December 9 2013 on transparency, access to public information and good governance, Boletín Oficial del Estado No. 295, 10 December 2013.

[26] Preamble of Royal Decree-Law 21/2012, above n. 23 (own translation).

the need for every Administration 'to internally comply with the European obligations'[27] as well as of the 'promotion of the efficiency and efficacy of the State and of economic growth'.[28]

The last package of reforms worth mentioning is that affecting the banking sector. Spanish banks faced a severe lack of liquidity following the burst of the housing bubble in 2008. The credit squeeze was initially tackled through the creation of a Fund for Orderly Bank Restructuring (*Fondo de Reestructuración Ordenada Bancaria*, FROB).[29] The fund was allocated €9,000 million and provided banks with liquidity through a variety of instruments, proceeding in some cases to nationalise those with acute problems, such as CAM (Caja Mediterráneo) and Bankia.[30] When the nationalisation of Bankia took place, it became apparent that the assistance provided by FROB was insufficient for the magnitude of the banking problem. As a result, on 9 June 2012, the government announced its request for a bailout from the European institutions with the purpose of re-capitalising the banking sector. The announcement was heavily criticised by the opposition parties as the conditions of the bailout had not been made transparent. Although Rajoy's government insisted that the funds were not a state bailout but a loan to the banking sector, the Memorandum of Understanding (MoU) concluded between the European Commission and Spain later revealed that general macroeconomic conditionality had been enclosed.[31] Among these conditions were further labour market reforms, the completion of electricity and gas connections with neighbourhood countries and the adjustment of the taxation system.

2 Prevalence of Emergency Legislation: Royal Decree-Law and Abbreviated Parliamentary Procedures

An aspect that seems particularly remarkable in the Spanish case is the fact that most of the euro-crisis measures have been introduced through

[27] Preamble of Royal Decree-Law 515/2013, above n. 24 (own translation). [28] Ibid.

[29] Royal Decree-Law 9/2009 of 26 June on bank restructuring and reinforcement of the own resources of the credit entities, Boletín Oficial del Estado, No. 155, 27 June 2009.

[30] F. Villar, 'Crisis Económico-financiera: Crisis de la Administración Pública', in A. González Sanfiel (ed.), *El Derecho Ante la Crisis: Nuevas Reglas de Juego* (Barcelona: Atelier, 2013), pp. 43–83, at 56ff.

[31] European Commission, 'Memorandum of Understanding between the European Commission and Spain', SEC (2012) final (20 July 2012), http://ec.europa.eu/economy_finance/eu_borrower/mou/spain-mou_en.pdf.

emergency legislation; that is, legislation that effectively bypasses parliamentary debate or strongly limits it. Such emergency instruments are royal decree-laws, which have been used to effect most of the structural changes needed in the aftermath of the crisis, and the abbreviated parliamentary procedures, which were used to reform the Spanish Constitution.

A. *The Decree-Law as the Main Instrument of Euro-Crisis Legislation*

The royal decree-law is a norm with the status of a law that can be passed by the Government in case of 'extreme and urgent necessity' pursuant to Article 86 of the Constitution.[32] The decree-law becomes binding from the date of publication – often a few days after its approval. For its content to become permanent, it requires the approval of the Congress of Deputies (the lower chamber of the Spanish Parliament) within 30 days from the date of promulgation. This approval consists of a vote over the decree-law as a whole, after which it becomes an ordinary law. It is often said that the decree-law represents an ideal instrument for the executive to legislate on its own: first, because the decree-law has immediate effects without the need for parliamentary involvement and, second, because when parliamentary validation takes place, the decree-law is voted as a whole without any room for individual amendments.

Given the risk that the executive could abuse the decree-law, the Spanish Constitution limits the fields that can be regulated with this instrument. The basic institutions of the state, the rights, duties and freedoms of the citizens, the regime of the regions and the electoral regime can only be altered by an organic law.[33] In addition, the very description of the decree-law circumscribes it to situations of 'extreme and urgent necessity'. Defining what can be understood by 'extreme and urgent necessity' is the most problematic issue of the royal decree-law. In this regard, the Spanish Constitutional Court has stated that, whereas the

[32] Spanish Constitution, Art. 86(1): 'In cases of extraordinary and urgent need, the Government may issue temporary legislative provisions which shall take the form of decree-laws and which may not affect the regulation of the basic State institutions, the rights, duties and liberties contained in Title 1, the system of the Autonomous Communities, or the General Electoral Law'.

[33] Ibid.

existence of an urgent necessity is a political judgment of a discretionary nature,[34] the government cannot use the decree-law for tackling issues that are structural rather than unexpected.[35]

Matters regulated by decree-law have often consisted of natural disasters, weather-related setbacks and terrorist events. From 2009 onwards, however, most decree-laws focused on economic matters. The number of decree-laws has increased progressively since 2008 and, by 2012, when the lion's share of anti-crisis measures were approved, the decree-law had completely dominated the legislative activity. This phenomenon has been referred to as the 'use and abuse of the Decree-Law'[36] (note how the decree-law was indeed the instrument by which most measures described in the previous section were introduced).[37]

Respect for the constitutional limits imposed on the content of decree-laws is far from clear in the euro-crisis measures. Royal Decree-Law 3/2012 has introduced a one-year probationary contract without severance payment, despite the constitutional jurisprudence enshrining severance payments as an essential part of labour rights.[38] In the same vein, the reform of the Statute for Civil Servants suspended the collective agreements then in force,[39] despite the jurisprudence of the Constitutional Court recognising the transcending value of social dialogue in the Spanish system.[40]

Amidst these controversies (to which the Constitutional Court has not been very responsive)[41] the government has continued using and abusing decree-laws as an alternative mechanism for regulation. A recent illustration is the Royal Decree-Law 08/2014, which reformed 25 ordinary

[34] Sentencia del Tribunal Constitucional 29/1982, Boletín Oficial del Estado, No. 153, 28 June 1982.

[35] Sentencia del Tribunal Constitucional 68/2007, Boletín Oficial del Estado, No. 100, 26 April 2007.

[36] A. Díaz de Mera Rodríguez, 'Gobierno de Crisis. Uso y Abuso del Decreto-ley', *Revista Parlamentaria de la Asamblea de Madrid*, 24, 2011, 137–78.

[37] A. Ruiz Robledo, 'The Spanish Constitution in the Turmoil of the Global Financial Crisis', in X. Contiades (ed.), *Constitutions in the Global Financial Crisis: A Comparative Analysis* (Farnham: Ashgate, 2013), pp. 141–67, p. 145.

[38] Sentencia del Tribunal Constitucional 20/1994, Boletín Oficial del Estado, No. 52, 2 March 1994.

[39] Royal Decree-Law 8/2010 of 20 May 2010 adopting extraordinary measures for the reduction of the public deficit, Boletín Oficial del Estado, No. 126, 24 May 2010.

[40] Sentencia del Tribunal Constitucional 68/2007, Boletín Oficial del Estado, No. 100, 27 April 2007.

[41] See the final section of this chapter for a discussion of the euro-crisis jurisprudence of the Constitutional Court.

laws with a single mechanism.[42] Among the issues affected are not only labour-related provisions, such as measures to promote youth employment, but other topics whose need for urgent legislation is doubtful, such as the management of the Civil Register and the regulation of unmanned drones.

B. *The 'Urgency Procedure' and the Reform of Article 135 of the Spanish Constitution*

In 2011, the Spanish government was prompted to give constitutional status to the principle of budgetary stability.[43] The Constitution foresees different amendment procedures depending on the area to be reformed.[44] The Preliminary Title, the regime of Fundamental Rights and Freedoms and the section dedicated to the Crown are subject to an 'aggravated procedure' that requires a majority of two-thirds in both the Congress and the Senate as well as a referendum. In contrast, the remaining parts of the Constitution can be amended by a three-fifths majority and without a referendum.

Article 135 was among the sections of the Constitution that could be subject to a simple constitutional reform. What the Constitution did not specify, however, was the *parliamentary procedures* through which a simplified reform of the Constitution could be carried out. The legislation regulating the functioning of the Congress and the Senate foresees 'abbreviated legislative procedures' that simplify the procedural phases of the adoption of ordinary laws.[45] To the surprise of many, not only did the Socialist government propose an unexpected constitutional reform two months before the elections, but it also used two of these abbreviated legislative procedures: the 'single reading procedure' and the 'urgency procedure'.

By virtue of the single reading procedure, the proposal for constitutional reform was presented before the Congress and the Senate in the absence of

[42] Royal Decree-Law 8/2014 of 4 July passing urgent measures for growth, competitiveness and efficiency, Boletín Oficial del Estado, No. 163, 5 July 2014.

[43] As noted above, this was done through the Euro Plus Pact and a letter from the European Central Bank addressed to José Luis Rodríguez Zapatero.

[44] Spanish Constitution, Arts. 167–8.

[45] These procedures are different from those for royal decree-law, described above, which do not constitute an ordinary law but a different legal instrument introduced by the executive and which requires later parliamentary ratification.

the usual report from a Parliamentary Commission.[46] The single reading also entailed that such proposal could only be debated and voted as a whole – hence precluding the presentation of amendments. By means of the 'urgency procedure', on the other hand, the timing for parliamentary approval was halved in the case of the Congress and reduced to 20 days in the case of the Senate. As a result, the reform was duly approved both at the Congress and at the Senate only within two weeks after the initial announcement on 23 August.[47] A number of parties walked out of the voting session.[48] While the Socialist Party and the Popular Party had previously agreed on the drafting of the reform, the other parties had not had time to react to an amendment they hardly expected.[49]

The extent to which the constitutional reform required urgency mechanisms for its approval is controversial.[50] Article 150 of the Regulation of the Congress reserves the single reading procedure for cases in which the nature of the legislation makes it desirable.[51] This has been related to legislation enjoying a broad parliamentary consensus, dealing with extremely simple issues or requiring a prompt solution.[52] In contrast, all the parliamentary groups but the Socialists and the Conservatives viewed the reform with scepticism or open disapproval and the provisions of Article 135 will only enter into force in 2020.[53]

As Ridaura Martínez observes, it seems likely that the reform and its short timing was caused by a desire to calm the markets before the imminent general elections of 2011.[54] Only 32 days passed from the

[46] Parliamentary commissions are working groups formed in specific fields that discuss and write reports on the legislative proposals presented before the Spanish Parliament.

[47] This informal announcement on the forthcoming constitutional reform was made during the extraordinary plenary session of the Congress. Three days later, on 26 August 2011, the Socialist and the Popular parliamentary groups lodged the formal proposal for reform of Article 135 before the Congress. See Congreso de los Diputados, Boletín Oficial de las Cortes Generales – Congreso de los Diputados (Serie B: Proposiciones de Ley), No. 329-1, 26 August 2011, www.congreso.es/public_oficiales/L9/CONG/BOCG/B/B_329-01.PDF, pp. 1–2.

[48] These were Esquerra Republicana de Catalunya, Nafarroa Vai, Initiativa per Catalunya Verts and Bloque Nacionalista Galego.

[49] See above n. 13 for the parliamentary debate.

[50] Álvarez Conde et al., 'La reforma del artículo 135 CE'.

[51] Regulation of the Congress, Boletín Oficial del Estado, No. 55, 5 March 1982.

[52] M. Ridaura Martínez, 'La Reforma del Artículo 135 de la Constitutión: Pueden los Mercados Quebrar el Consenso Constitucional?', *Teoría y Realidad Constitucional*, 29, 2012, 237–60, at 254.

[53] Ibid., 254. [54] Ibid., 250.

proposal of the amendment to its approval; hence some mockery in its name the 'express reform'.[55]

3 The Crisis as a Mechanism of Re-Centralisation

One of the most problematic aspects of the Eurocrisis in Spain has been the difficult equilibrium between efficient implementation of anti-crisis measures and respect for regional and local spheres of government. So far, the Spanish legislation has favoured the former over the latter through a marked re-centralisation of economic governance.[56]

The Spanish constitutional system is based on the allocation of competences between the central government, the regions (the autonomous communities) and, to a lesser extent, the local entities. Although each region enjoys different competences depending on their own statute of autonomy, most of them have taken over social assistance, healthcare, education and certain taxation measures. At the same time, local entities bear responsibility over matters such as the provision of public services and local policing. The corollary of the recognition of regional and local particularities is a complex (often inefficient) system of public administration and the risk of the state finances being affected by the bad economic performance of a particular entity. Unsurprisingly, Directive 2011/85/EU gave a clear mandate to improve the accountability and fiscal performance of sub-national government sectors.[57]

The first tangible impact of the Eurocrisis over the Spanish territorial balance of powers was the constraint of regional fiscal powers through

[55] 'Reforma exprés y sin referéndum', *El País* (23 August 2011), http://politica.elpais.com/politica/2011/08/23/actualidad/1314128715_080054.html.

[56] See M. Medina Guerrero, 'El Estado Autonómico en Tiempos de Disciplina Fiscal', *Revista Española de Derecho Constitucional*, 98, 2013, 109–47. See also E. Albertí Rovira, 'El Impacto de la Crisis Financiera en el Estado Autonómico Español', *Revista Española de Derecho Constitucional*, 98, 2013, 63–89, at 69.

[57] Council Directive 2011/85/EU of 8 November 2011 on requirements for budgetary frameworks of the Member States (OJ L 306, 23.11.2011, p.41), Arts. 3, 12, 13, 14 and 16, in the light of the Preamble, para. 24: 'A significant number of Member States have experienced a sizeable fiscal decentralisation with the devolution of budgetary powers to sub-national governments. The role of such sub-national governments in ensuring that the SGP is complied with has thereby increased considerably, and particular attention should be paid to ensuring that all general government sub-sectors are duly covered by the scope of the obligations and procedures laid down in domestic budgetary frameworks, in particular, but not exclusively, in those Member States'.

Organic Law 2/2012 on Budgetary Stability. Such constraint of regional expenses in the name of budgetary stability was not new and the previous Law on Budgetary Stability of 2001 had already prompted litigation between the autonomous communities and the central government.[58] The real novelty of 2012 was the introduction of a bailout system for regions in financial need, subject to conditionality from the central government,[59] and the establishment of stringent sanctions for regions that breach their financial commitments, including the suspension of their taxation competences.[60] The bailout scheme had great political dimensions. Nine autonomous communities requested financial assistance[61] and Catalonia received the biggest amount by far, amidst claims that the central government would seize the opportunity to re-centralise the Catalan finances.[62]

The second manifestation of the territorial reshuffle in the aftermath of the Eurocrisis has been the ambitious reform of the Public Administration and the consequent modification of the local regime. In 2012, the Conservative government formed the Commission for the Reform of the Public Administration (CORA) to supersede an administrative regime that dated back to 1992[63] and 1985.[64] Whereas the reform of the public administration was a pending subject for a long time, it was finally compelled by the pressing economic situation. In the words of CORA, the reform was part of the measures designed 'to overcome the worst economic crisis in the last decades, to correct the imbalances that slow down our growth and to set the appropriate basis over which to build a new cycle of economic prosperity and employment for the Spanish'.[65]

[58] This law (see above n. 19) implemented the former Stability and Growth Pact. The judicial controversies that emanated from it were recently settled by the Spanish Constitutional Court (see next section).

[59] Organic Law 2/2012, Additional Disposition No. 1.

[60] Ibid., Article 25.

[61] Andalusia, Castile-La Mancha, Catalonia, Canary Islands, Valencia, Asturias, Balearic Islands, Cantabria and Murcia.

[62] 'Cataluña pide el rescate con urgencia', *El País* (28 August 2012).

[63] Law 30/92 of 26 November of the legal regime of the public administration and of the common administrative procedure, Boletín Oficial del Estado, No. 285, 27 November 1992.

[64] Law 7/1985 of 2 April regulating the bases of the local regime, Boletín Oficial del Estado, No. 80, 3 April 1985.

[65] Comisión para la Reforma de las Administraciones Públicas, Ministry of Finance and Public Administrations, 'Reforma de las Administraciones Públicas', NIPO: 630-13-106-7 (own translation). available at www.seap.minhap.gob.es/dms/es/web/areas/reforma_aapp/INFORME-LIBRO/INFORME%20LIBRO.PDF.

Some of these measures have been relatively uncontroversial, such as Law 20/2013 on the Unity of the Market[66] (aimed at removing barriers on trade between autonomous communities) and Organic Law 9/2013 for the control of the commercial debt in the public administration.[67] Others, however, have been perceived as a hindrance to the autonomy of local entities and to the regional competences to shape their local regime. Law 27/2013 for the Streamlining and Sustainability of the Local Administration makes the autonomy of the local government conditional on the respect of budgetary stability and financial sustainability. The specific measures contained in the law include limitations to the provision of public services for municipalities with fewer than 20,000 inhabitants and restrictions to the transfer of competences from autonomous communities to local entities. This has resulted in several actions of unconstitutionality by autonomous communities,[68] members of the Spanish Parliament[69] as well as municipalities. Note that an action of unconstitutionality for breach of local autonomy (*conflicto en defensa de la autonomía local*) can only be brought about by a minimum of 1,160 municipalities, representing at least one-sixth of the Spanish population. For the first time in the history of the Spanish democracy, a total of 3,000 municipalities (about 850 of them from Catalonia) achieved this threshold and the action is now pending before the Spanish Constitutional Court.

A third and last reflection must be made on the reform of Article 135 of the Spanish Constitution mentioned above. Despite the content of the reform not entering into force until 2020, the article has already been interpreted by the Spanish Constitutional Court as a reinforcement of the prerogatives of the central government to impose limits over the regional finances.[70] The constitutional principle of budgetary stability has therefore become part of the strategy for the centralisation of fiscal matters. As the next section explores, the Court's unconditional support for the

[66] Law 20/2013 of 9 December 2013 on the unity of the market, Boletín Oficial del Estado, No. 295, 10 December 2013.

[67] Organic Law 9/2013 of 20 December 2013 for the control of the commercial debt in the public administration, Boletín Oficial del Estado, No. 305, 21 December 2013. Some aspects of this legislation are also prone to hinder the spheres of power of the autonomous communities. See 'Crisis y Centralización de Estado', *El País,* 11 March 2014.

[68] Andalusia, Canarias, Catalonia, Extremadura and Navarra.

[69] This action was presented by 50 members of the Spanish Parliament, mainly from the Socialist Party, United Left and Unión Progreso y Democracia.

[70] See next section.

euro-crisis measures has been much influenced by its fear of hindering the economic recovery of Spain.

4 The Emergency before the Constitutional Court

Pending some of the actions of unconstitutionality against euro-crisis legislation, the Constitutional Court has already issued decisions on some of the most controversial measures: the labour reform of both the public and private sectors, the Constitutional amendment and Law 2/2012 on Budgetary Stability. In all these decisions the Court has been remarkably lenient.

On 19 November 2011, the *Sala de lo Social de la Audiencia Nacional* (Labour Chamber of the National High Court) requested from the Spanish Constitutional Court an assessment on the constitutionality of Royal Decree-Law 8/2010 adopting extraordinary measures for the reduction of the public deficit. The request originated in an action lodged by the trade unions *Comisiones Obreras, Unión General de Trabajadores* and *Nueva Plataforma* against the 5 per cent wage reduction for public workers. Such reduction seemed to transgress the prohibition against affecting fundamental rights through a decree-law, given that the measure implied a suspension of the collective agreement of the public sector. Yet the Constitutional Court considered that the decree-law did not attack the content or the essential elements of the right to collective bargaining. This was so because what was affected was the *specific content* of a collective agreement and not the *general regime* of collective bargaining. The Court additionally remarked that, within the legal hierarchy, agreements are always subject to legislation of legal status.[71]

In similar terms, the Constitutional Court has dismissed the actions of unconstitutionality lodged by the Parliament of Navarra against the labour law reforms of 2012.[72] First, the Court upheld the suspension of collective agreements at the initiative of the employer and the resolution of such 'conflict' by a tripartite committee of trade union, business and

[71] Auto del Tribunal Constitucional 85/2011, Boletín Oficial del Estado, No. 158, 7 June 2011. The Spanish Constitutional Court had previously declared social dialogue to bear a transcending value in the social and democratic rule of law. See Sentencia del Tribunal Constitucional 68/2007, Boletín Oficial del Estado, No. 100, 26 April 2007.

[72] Sentencia del Tribunal Constitucional 119/2014, Boletín Oficial del Estado, No. 198, 15 August 2014, on Royal Decree-Law 3/2012 (see n. 16), which became Law 3/2012 following parliamentary ratification.

public administration representatives.[73] Despite the fact that a similar measure was declared unconstitutional in 1981,[74] the Court was more permissive this time due to the 'legitimate constitutional aim' of defending productivity in the context of serious levels of unemployment in Spain.[75] Equally optimistic was the assessment on the primacy of company agreements over provincial collective agreements, a measure considered appropriate for guaranteeing the productivity and viability of the company.[76] Finally, the one-year contract of probation without severance payment was also upheld for supporting the creation of employment.[77]

Another controversy unsuccessfully brought before the Court was the reform of the Spanish Constitution through simplified parliamentary procedures. The promoters of the action of unconstitutionality were members of the Spanish Parliament from the left-wing *Esquerra Republicana-Izquierda Unida-Iniciativa per Catalunya* parliamentary group that, as mentioned above, were caught by surprise when the

[73] Note how problematic this can be, given that the administration and the business representative will most likely agree on a more business-friendly solution than the representative from the trade union.

[74] Sentencia del Tribunal Constitutional 11/1981, Boletín Oficial del Estado, No. 99, 25 April 1981.

[75] Legal basis no. 5. Spanish judicial decisions are structured over a number of 'factual basis' (the facts, *fundamento de hecho*) as well as 'legal basis' (*fundamento jurídico*). Legal bases are different to the traditional 'paragraphs' since each legal basis is comprised by an (usually high) number of paragraphs.

[76] Legal basis no. 6.

[77] Legal basis no. 3. The dissenting opinion written by Fernando Valdés Dal-Ré and subscribed by Adela Asua Batarrita. Luis Ignacio Ortega Álvarez disagreed with the majority decision. The arbitral entity that was declared unconstitutional in STC 11/1981 (see above n. 74) had been set up by the public administration, whereas, in Law 3/2012, the Committee also comprised business and trade union representatives. Such distinction was, according to these judges, irrelevant, given that the very configuration of the Committee (and the limited cases in which its decisions could be appealed before a judge) was set up to conform with the interests of the public administration – namely, weakening the interests of trade unions while giving wider room to manoeuvre to the employer. The dissenting opinion also denounced the possibility of substituting provincial collective agreements with those reached within SMEs. In a country where more than 99 per cent of companies are of a small size, this meant replacing the power of collective bargaining between trade unions and business organisations with settings where conditions are negotiated between the business owner and a single union representative. Lastly, the opinion recalled the long constitutional jurisprudence enshrining severance payment as an essential part of labour rights. Under this light, the aim of the probation contract should be constrained to testing the performance of the worker and not to verifying the economic viability of the job position.

constitutional amendment took place. The MPs argued that the *Mesa del Congreso* was not prevented from using the single reading procedure, but that it needed a solid justification. Given the importance of a constitutional reform and the fact that the new Article 135 would only enter into force in 2020, the MPs considered that the proper exercise of the parliamentary functions had been unnecessarily impaired. The Court disagreed and found that the *Mesa* did not need to motivate its decision, which was justified in any case by the general elections taking place three months later.[78]

Finally, the Court's decisions tackling the territorial implications of budgetary stability must be mentioned. The tension between the fiscal competences of the central government and those of the regions was partly addressed in the judicial decisions (issued in 2011) on the General Law of Budgetary Stability of 2001.[79] These decisions used the new Article 135 of the Spanish Constitution to legitimise the regional financial constraints: according to the Court, the requirement of budgetary stability is now placed beyond the powers of both the central government and those of the Regions, hence a tight control of the regional finances should not be understood as a usurpation of regional competences but as a constitutional imperative in itself.

Three years later, the Court issued another judgment on the novelties introduced by the Law on Budgetary Stability of 2012[80] and contested by

[78] Auto del Tribunal Constitucional 9/2012, Boletín Oficial del Estado, No. 36, 11 February 2012.

[79] Sentencia del Tribunal Constitucional 134/2011 (action of unconstitutionality lodged by the Parliament of Catalonia), Boletín Oficial del Estado, No. 197, 17 August 2011; Sentencia del Tribunal Constitucional 157/2011 (action of unconstitutionality lodged by the government of Asturias), Boletín Oficial del Estado, No. 275, 15 of November 2011; Sentencia del Tribunal Constitucional 195/2011 (action of unconstitutionality lodged by the Government of Catalonia), Sentencia del Tribunal Constitucional 196/2011 (action of unconstitutionality lodged by the Government of Aragon), Sentencia del Tribunal Constitutional 197/2011 (action of unconstitutionality lodged by the Parliament of Aragon), Sentencia del Tribunal Constitucional 198/2011 (action of unconstitutionality lodged by the Government of Extremadura), Sentencia del Tribunal Constitutional 199/2011 (action of unconstitutionality lodged by 72 Socialist MPs), Sentencia del Tribunal Constitucional 203/2011 (action of unconstitutionality lodged by the Parliament of Castile-La Mancha), Boletín Oficial del Estado, No. 9, 11 January 2012.

[80] Organic Law 2/2012 on Budgetary Stability (see n. 19) was passed to implement, among others, the provisions of the Six Pack (especially Council Directive 2011/85/EU). It featured a much more complete (and strict) content than its predecessor, the General Law 18/2001 of 12 December 2001 on Budgetary Stability, Boletín Oficial del Estado, No. 298, 13 December 2001, which was approved in the aftermath of the Stability and Growth Pact.

the Government of the Canary Islands.[81] First, the new Article 135 of the Constitution states that an organic law should fix the methods adopted for the calculation of the structural deficit, yet the Law on Budgetary Stability vaguely refers to the methods and outcomes reached by the European Union. Second, the same law exceeds the previous financial constraints imposed on the autonomous communities, inasmuch as it allows the central government to detail compulsory measures and to force their execution. The Constitutional Court upheld all the measures, given the need to comply with the obligations derived from the EU[82] as well as to ensure fiscal consolidation after the severe economic crisis.[83] Strong disagreement was evidenced in the dissenting opinion signed by five of the judges.[84] The opinion bluntly argued that, regardless of the economic reasons behind it, the Law on Budgetary Stability had breached the constitutional mandate to regulate the structural deficit through an organic law as well as the constitutional power balance between central and regional governments.

5 Conclusion

The economic emergency has had a deep impact on the Spanish constitutional and legal settings. The consequences of the Eurocrisis are a constitutional amendment, a bailout with a current outstanding debt of €35.5 billion,[85] a reconfiguration of the labour and social regimes and a re-structuring of the public administration. In an attempt to strengthen the streamlining of public finances, the competences of sub-national entities have been curtailed.

It is remarkable that the policy of economic survival has met such strong judicial permissiveness from the Constitutional Court. The previous line of jurisprudence has been of little importance when judging euro-crisis instruments. This has been particularly acute with labour rights, to the extent that the latest reforms and their subsequent judicial approval have been termed as a 'de-constitutionalisation' of the Spanish

[81] Sentencia del Tribunal Constitucional 215/2014, Boletín Oficial del Estado, No. 29, 3 February 2015.

[82] Legal basis no. 3. [83] Legal bases nos. 4 and 7.

[84] Adela Asua Batarrita, Luis Ignacio Ortega Álvarez, Encarnación Roca Trías, Fernando Valdés Dal-Ré and Juan Antonio Xiol Ríos.

[85] As of end October 2015. See European Commission, 'Post-Programme Surveillance Report: Spain, Autumn 2015', European Economy, Institutional Paper 13, http://ec.europa.eu/economy_finance/publications/eeip/pdf/ip013_en.pdf, p. 8.

labour law.[86] By allowing legislation that contradicts a long-settled interpretation of constitutional provisions (and that would not have been permitted under normal circumstances), the Court has engaged in a constitutional change without formal amendment. Its decisions on the allocation of competences between territorial entities under the principle of budgetary stability have been equally controversial. Constitutional jurisprudence in this field is more limited and, one could say, it has generally favoured the interests of the central government.[87] Yet, as the dissenting opinion subscribed by five judges and the general academic reactions manifest, there is a difficult fit between the territorial architecture envisaged by the Spanish Constitution and the one imposed by euro-crisis legislation.

The treatment of the economic emergency is coming at a price. There has been a retrenchment of labour and social rights, which has been accentuated by financial pressures on sub-national entities, as these play an essential role in the configuration and provision of social and public services. The political panorama has also experienced a transformation. New parties have broken into the political scene and forced a more critical appraisal of the management of the crisis.[88] Besides, discontent over the re-centralisation of economic governance has caused strong reactions from the autonomous communities and fed the independence aspirations of Catalonia.

This emergency has thus been an event with permanent repercussions. The use and abuse of emergency legislation has been normalised and most euro-crisis instruments (especially those of constitutional status) will remain in force long after a hypothetical economic recovery. The latest political events and the judicial reactions to the euro-crisis measures portend that the deep legal changes performed go hand in hand with a shift of political and legal cultures.

[86] A. Baylos, 'La Deconstitucionalización del Trabajo en la Reforma Laboral del 2012', *Revista de Derecho Social*, 61, 2013, 19–41, at 29.

[87] A. Pereira-Menaut and F. Martínez Arribas, 'Acerca del Fracaso del Modelo Territorial Español', in G. Mendoza et al. (eds.), *Una Mirada a las Regiones Desde la Justicia Constitucional* (Bogotá: Editorial Universidad del Rosario), pp. 37–92, at 68–9.

[88] The left-wing Podemos obtained 21 per cent of the vote while the liberal Ciudadanos obtained 13.1 per cent at the General Elections of 20 December 2015, challenging for the first time the traditional Spanish bi-partidism.

8

Constitutional Change through Emergency Decrees: The Abolition of Provinces in Italy

LEONARDO PIERDOMINICI*

In the social sciences the term 'emergency' (*emergenza, emergencia, urgence*, etc.) is used, not necessarily in a technical sense, to indicate sudden situations of difficulty or danger which tend to be transient in nature (although not necessarily brief) and which involve a crisis of the institutions operating within a given social structure.[1] In the same vein, in legal terms, the idea of a 'state of emergency' generally suggests: a) the existence of factual circumstances of special gravity for a certain community producing such crisis and b) consequent legal manifestations in the behaviour of institutions; sometimes as mere distorting *epiphenomena* of the impact of the crisis, sometimes as formalised *recognition* of the *phenomenon* and provision of specific correctional effects to guarantee the survival of a given legal system.[2]

The two mentioned forms of legal manifestations are surely different. Nonetheless, they have some aspects in common. They tend to create *derogations* (more or less extensive and more or less incisive) to the ordinary allocation of responsibilities, competences and powers between public authorities. Moreover, they tend to be explicated, in particular, in a varied/altered use of the relevant *sources* of law.

* The paper draws on my report on Italy for the 'Constitutional Change through Euro Crisis Law. Country Reports on the impact of crisis Instruments on the legal structures of the EU Member States' project of the EUI Law Department, available on its website: http://eurocrisislaw.eui.eu. Thanks are due to Prof. Giuseppe Martinico and Dr Francesco Paniccià for their precious comments on an early version.

1 According to the definition by A. Pizzorusso, 'Emergenza (Stato di)', in *Enciclopedia delle Scienze sociali* (Roma: Istituto dell'Enciclopedia italiana, 1993), Vol. III, *ad vocem*, pp. 551–9.

2 See in this sense the difference between a 'normalised' and an always present 'innovative' dimension of emergency suggested by G. de Vergottini, 'Necessità, costituzione materiale e disciplina dell'emergenza. In margine al pensiero di Costantino Mortati', in M. Galizia (ed.), *Forme di stato e forme di governo: nuovi studi sul pensiero di Costantino Mortati* (Milano: Giuffrè, 2007), pp. 475–526, at 476ff.

In the context of general reflections on the concept of 'emergency', the difficulty of formulating or prescribing a substantial response to economic crises, given their variety and complexity, has already been indicated (as well as their distinction from political or social ones).[3] The current multifaceted European crisis is no different.[4] Given its magnitude, the observer is faced by a vast congeries of interventions – of various natures.

Instead, the clearest developments are (for now) at the formal level, in terms of the sources of law employed. The recognition of a 'state of emergency' and the sanction of certain legal effects (optimal or not, efficient or not) were, in large part, centralised at the supranational level.[5] The legal response can be studied through the lenses of the *extra-ordinem* nature of the measures, their provided derogations and the varied use of sources.[6] At the national level, in my view, we can primarily find relevant legal *epiphenomena* of emergency: the first impression is of the struggle of Member States to comply, in critical situations, with what we generally

[3] See again Pizzorusso, 'Emergenza (Stato di)', 559.

[4] See A. Menéndez, 'The Existential Crisis of the European Union', *German Law Journal*, 14, 2013, 453–526, in particular at 453: 'the European Union is not undergoing one crisis, but is instead suffering several simultaneous, interrelated, and intertwined crises – crises, which are global, not exclusively European. Put differently, the subprime crisis turned the economic, financial, fiscal, macroeconomic, and political structure weaknesses of the Western socio-economic order into at least five major crises'.

[5] See for instance the jargon of Recitals no. 1 and 2 of the EFSF (European Financial Stability Facility) Framework Agreement, of Recitals no. 3 and 4 of the European Council Decision amending Article 136 of the Treaty on the Functioning of the European Union (2011), of Recitals no. 4, 5 and 6 of the Treaty Establishing the European Stability Mechanism (2012); see also, for a similar reflection, U. Beck, *German Europe* (Cambridge: Polity Press, 2013), especially p. 27: 'In dealing with the threat to the euro and the European Union, the relevant players are effectively *negotiating about an exceptional situation whose ramifications are no longer confined to individual nation-states. Instead we are facing a 'transnational emergency'*, which can be exploited in various ways [legitimated by either democratic or technocratic means] by a variety of players, including national politicians, the unelected representatives of European institutions such as the ECB, social movements, or even the managers of powerful financial organizations' (emphasis added).

[6] See, for example, the interesting analysis by E. Chiti and P.G. Teixeira, 'The Constitutional Implications of the European Responses to the Financial and Public Debt Crisis', *Common Market Law Review*, 50, 2013, 683–708, and G. Martinico, 'EU Crisis and Constitutional Mutations: A Review Article', *Sant'Anna Legal Studies Research Paper* n. 3/2014, available at the website stals.sssup.it/files/martinico%20crisis.pdf; and on the formal point in particular, by C. Kilpatrick, 'Abnormal Legal Sources in the EU Sovereign Debt Crisis', paper presented at the Academy of European Law specialised course, 30 June–11 July 2014, European University Institute, Florence.

intend here as euro-crisis law measures, namely the legal instruments adopted at the European and international level in response to the Eurocrisis.[7] There is no formal recognition of a 'state of emergency' at this level, but there are, as will be explored through the Italian case, evident traces of the same idea of exceptionality and derogatory nature, and the same distorted use of sources.

To substantiate such a claim, I selected one of the most relevant examples for the Italian case in the last years: the much discussed, still ongoing process of reform of the constitutional system of territorial decentralisation of the Republic. I focus, in particular, on its first steps, discussed in this context as a specific paradigmatic example.

1 Constitutional Decentralisation in the Italian Peninsula: How It Was – and How It Suddenly Changed

As is well known, the historical heritage of the pre-unified Italian peninsula is one of profound fragmentation. This, and the influence of the French-Napoleonic model of decentralised local administration, shaped the strong role of the Italian municipalities (*Comuni*) and of the Provinces as superordinate territorial authorities.[8] Provinces already existed in some pre-unitary states, for example, being adopted directly from the French system by the Kingdom of Sardinia in 1859.[9] They subsequently emerged also in the Lombardo-Venetian Kingdom and in other southern and central territories during the unification process, led by the interim dictators.[10] This is not the place for a comprehensive history of decentralisation in Italy.[11] For present purposes, however, it is relevant to note that the co-existence of *Comuni* and Provinces was restated by the

[7] See also the introduction of this book, as well as Chapter 11, 'Constitutions, Social Rights and Sovereign Debt States in Europe: A Challenging New Area of Constitutional Inquiry' by Claire Kilpatrick for a definition of 'euro-crisis law', as opposed to the Eurocrisis.

[8] See the comparative analysis by L. Vandelli, *Poteri locali: le origini nella Francia rivoluzionaria, le prospettive nell'Europa delle regioni* (Bologna: Il Mulino, 1990), and recently M. Mazza, 'Federalismo, regionalismo e decentramento nella prospettiva della comparazione tra i sistemi di amministrazione (o governo) locale', *Istituzioni del federalismo*, 4, 2012, 829–56.

[9] With the so-called Decreto Rattazzi, legge 23 ottobre 1859 n. 3702 del Regno di Sardegna.

[10] See for details A. Sandulli and G. Vesperini, 'L'organizzazione dello Stato unitario', *Rivista trimestrale di diritto pubblico*, 1, 2011, 47–95, in particular at 58.

[11] See for a comprehensive study F. Fabrizzi, *La Provincia. Analisi dell'ente locale più discusso* (Napoli: Jovene, 2012).

unitary Italian *Legge sull'amministrazione comunale e provinciale* of 20 March 1865 and confirmed, decades later, by the Republican Constitution of 1947. The 1947 Constitution not only included Article 5, on the principles of autonomy and decentralisation,[12] but, in the Fifth Title (dedicated to the territorial organisation of the State), added new entities with legislative and administrative powers, the Regions, modelled on the old compartments used for statistical purposes in the (unified) Kingdom.[13]

In the preliminary debates and the preparatory works of the Constituent Assembly, the introduction of Regions was intended to replace the Provinces.[14] However, inertia prevailed in the actual drafting of the Constitution and persisted in 1970, when the ordinary Regions came into existence.[15] Various rounds of tentative constitutional reform[16] kept the Provinces alive, together with the *Comuni* and the Regions, despite

[12] Article 5 of the Italian Constitution: 'The Republic is one and indivisible. It recognises and promotes local autonomies, and implements the fullest measure of administrative decentralisation in those services which depend on the State. The Republic adapts the principles and methods of its legislation to the requirements of autonomy and decentralisation'. (An official parliamentary translation of the Constitution of Italy is available at www.senato.it/documenti/repository/istituzione/costituzione_inglese.pdf.)

[13] For several reasons, both theoretical and contingent. See, for comprehensive accounts, *ex multis*, the pioneering studies of A. Amorth, *Il problema della struttura dello Stato in Italia. Federalismo, regionalismo, autonomismo* (Como-Milano: Marzoranti, 1945), and G. Ambrosini, *L'ordinamento regionale. La riforma regionale nella Costituzione italiana* (Bologna: Zanichelli, 1957), and the recent summary by A. D'Atena, *Diritto regionale* (Torino: Giappichelli, 2013), pp. 9ff. In the literature in English, see now S. Mangiameli (ed.), *Italian Regionalism: Between Unitary Traditions and Federal Processes. Investigating Italy's Form of State* (Berlin-Heidelberg: Springer, 2014).

[14] Both the discussions in the context of the *Ministero per la Costituente*, established with decreto luogotenenziale 31 luglio 1945, n. 435, and in the *Commissione dei settantacinque* within the Constituent Assembly were in this sense: see F. Fabrizzi, 'La Provincia: storia istituzionale dell'ente locale più discusso. Dalla riforma Crispi all'Assemblea Costituente', *Federalismi.it. Rivista di diritto pubblico italiano, comunitario e comparato*, 12, 2008.

[15] See, for example, the rejected proposal of the Partito Repubblicano Italiano in 1977 'Soppressione dell'ente autonomo territoriale provincia: modifica degli articoli 114, 118, 119, 128, 132, 133 e della VIII disposizione di attuazione della Costituzione; abrogazione dell'articolo 129 della Costituzione', based explicitly on 'a chain of negative findings on the institutional and administrative role of the province'.

[16] For instance, all the bicameral committees convened to draft organic reforms of the Italian Constitution (the Commissione Bozzi of 1983, the Commissione De Mita/Iotti of 1992, the Commissione D'Alema of 1997) critically discussed the actual role and the very existence of the Provinces, but with no results: see F. Fabrizzi, 'La Provincia: storia istituzionale dell'ente locale più discusso. Dall'Assemblea costituente ad oggi', *Federalismi.it. Rivista di diritto pubblico italiano, comunitario e comparato*, 23, 2008.

being accompanied by a repeated debate at the political level on the futility of a middle layer of local government.[17]

It is interesting to evaluate the impact of euro crisis law in Italy against this static background. A famous letter was addressed by the then-President of the European Central Bank (ECB), Jean-Claude Trichet, and his designated successor, Mario Draghi (then-President of the Italian Central Bank and a member of the Governing Council of the ECB), to the President of the Italian Council of Ministers on 5 August 2011, setting various 'conditions' for the application of the Securities Markets Programme (SMP) to Italy,[18] a bond-buying programme of the ECB capable of calming the sovereign bond market for certain Member States. The letter explicitly emphasised the 'need for a strong commitment to abolish or merge some intermediate levels of administration (such as provinces)'.[19]

The inertia of decades was broken by this supranational (co)action. Only a few months after the letter, a 'technical' Government of so-called national commitment, led by Professor Mario Monti and with a mandate to manage the critical Italian situation,[20] replaced the fourth government of the resigned Silvio Berlusconi in late 2011. In one of its first interventions, Decree-law n. 201/2011, containing various 'urgent measures for growth, fairness and consolidation of public accounts' (the so-called Salva-Italia),[21] the new government tried to comply with the recommendations of the ECB letter. It dictated inter alia the immediate

[17] Again, at the end of June 2010, a proposal to abolish the Provinces with less than 220,000 inhabitants made its way in a draft of the Decree-Law n. 78/2010, but then disappeared from the official text; in July 2011, a new constitutional bill for their suppression (XVI Legislatura, AC n. 1990-1836-1989–2264-2579-A/R) was rejected.

[18] The SMP was activated in 2011 and 2012 in Italy, resulting in the purchase of €102.8bn of Italian bonds, the largest quota among all the Eurozone members. See European Central Bank, 'Details on Securities Holdings Acquired under the Securities Markets Programme' (21 February 2013), www.ecb.europa.eu/press/pr/date/2013/html/pr130221_1.en.html.

[19] See the full text, as revealed at the time by the Italian main newspaper, the *Corriere della Sera*, at the web page www.corriere.it/economia/11_settembre_29/trichet_draghi_italiano_405e2be2-ea59-11e0-ae06-4da866778017.shtml.

[20] In itself seen by some observers as evidence of a state of exception, given the particularly active role of the President of the Republic in this appointment. See, for an early reflection on the point, A. Ruggeri, 'Art. 94 della Costituzione vivente: "Il Governo deve avere la fiducia dei mercati" (nota minima a commento della nascita del Governo Monti)', *Federalismi.it. Rivista di diritto pubblico italiano, comunitario e comparato*, 23, 2011.

[21] Decreto-legge 6 dicembre 2011, n. 201 – Disposizioni urgenti per la crescita, l'equita' e il consolidamento dei conti pubblici. (11G0247) (GU n.284 del 6-12-2011 – Suppl. Ordinario n. 251).

transformation of Provinces into institutions with mere functions of direction and coordination of the municipalities, governed by a council and a president expressed by the municipalities themselves, and devoid of a collegiate executive and, ultimately, of autonomy.

2 The Form of the Reform – and Its Judicial Sanction

From the perspective of this chapter, the most relevant aspect was not the sudden political change (the technical and pro-EU nature of the new government could be taken for granted). Instead, attention turns to the choice of the formal measure used, at least originally, to implement the reform: decree-laws (specifically, Decree-laws n. 201/2011 and n. 95/2012).

In the Italian legal system, decree-laws are legislative acts of a temporary nature but with the force of law. They are adopted directly by the government in 'extraordinary cases of necessity and urgency', pursuant to Article 77 of the Constitution of the Italian Republic.[22] To convert decree-laws into formal law, Parliament must vote to do so within 60 days of their publication. They are, therefore, sources of law specifically designed for extraordinary cases which facilitate immediate normative interventions, but which require subsequent ratification by the legislature.

Nonetheless, the practical use of decree-laws has over time been trivialised by their frequent employment by the government to circumvent the ordinary legislative procedure, their inhomogeneous content and their reiteration.[23] Still, for all these cases, the Italian Constitutional

[22] Article 77 of the Italian Constitution: 'The Government may not, without an enabling act from the Houses, issue a decree having force of law. When the Government, in extraordinary cases of necessity and urgency, adopts under its own responsibility a temporary measure, it shall introduce such measure to Parliament for transposition into law. During dissolution, Parliament shall be convened within five days of such introduction. Such a measure shall lose effect from the beginning if it is not transposed into law by Parliament within sixty days of its publication. Parliament may regulate the legal relations arisen from the rejected measure'.

[23] For recent general reconstructions see, *ex multis*, A. Celotto, *L''abuso' del decreto-legge* (Padova: CEDAM, 1997); A. Simoncini (ed.), *L'emergenza infinita. La decretazione d'urgenza in Italia* (Macerata: EUM, 2006); on the most recent trends R. Calvano, 'La decretazione d'urgenza nella stagione delle larghe intese', *Rivista AIC – Associazione Italiana dei Costituzionalisti*, 3, 2014; A. Simoncini and E. Longo, 'Dal decreto-legge alla

Court has often underlined the political discretion inherent in their use[24] and has rarely struck down decree-laws or subsequent formal laws for reasons relating to their selection, misuse of the procedure or failure to fulfil the relevant criteria.[25]

Decree-law n. 201/2011 had a different fate. It came into being as a first organic measure of the new government tackling the urgent need to give a strong signal to the markets on the rationalisation of public finances. In fact, it contained several spurious measures, ranging from tax adjustments to new State guarantees for bank debts, from the suppression of public entities to a new reform of the pension system. As said, it also significantly affected the territorial decentralisation of the Italian Republic. Decree-law n. 95/2012 followed some months later, as an organic spending review measure which also impacted again on territorial decentralisation, by setting the basis for the reorganisation of the provinces' territorial constituencies.

Given their clear constitutional significance in this respect, Decree-laws n. 201/2011 and n. 95/2012 were challenged by a series of Regions before the Constitutional Court. The two decree-laws had already been ratified by the legislature. However, the appellants argued that the laws' norms should be considered as running counter to the concept of autonomy of territorial entities, ranging from respect for their core competences to the principle of loyal cooperation, particularly in the context of a radical reform. The appellants also challenged the norms for

legge di conversione: dal controllo potenziale al sindacato effettivo di costituzionalità', *Rivista AIC - Associazione Italiana dei Costituzionalisti*, 3, 2014.

24 See, for example, Corte costituzionale 23 maggio 2007, n. 171, at par. 4 of the *Considerato in diritto*: 'E' sulla base di siffatti presupposti che questa Corte, con giurisprudenza costante dal 1995 (sentenza n. 29 del 1995), ha affermato che l'esistenza dei requisiti della straordinarietà del caso di necessità e d'urgenza può essere oggetto di scrutinio di costituzionalità. *Tuttavia, nell'affermare l'esistenza del suindicato proprio compito, è stata ed è consapevole che il suo esercizio non sostituisce e non si sovrappone a quello iniziale del Governo e a quello successivo del Parlamento in sede di conversione – in cui le valutazioni politiche potrebbero essere prevalenti – ma deve svolgersi su un piano diverso*, con la funzione di preservare l'assetto delle fonti normative e, con esso, il rispetto dei valori a tutela dei quali detto compito è predisposto' (emphasis added).

25 This created a paradoxical convergence with the practice of the Fascist period, when a formal law, the Legge 31 gennaio 1926, n. 100, explicitly provided for the exclusion of judicial review on the criteria of necessity and urgency, as 'political questions': see M. Benvenuti, 'Alle origini dei decreti-legge. Saggio sulla decretazione governativa di urgenza e sulla sua genealogia nell'ordinamento giuridico dell'Italia prefascista', in *Scritti in onore di Claudio Rossano* (Napoli: Jovene, 2013), Vol. I, pp. 21–79.

violation of Article 77 of the Constitution, and therefore with specific regard to the formal aspect of the use of decree-laws for giving birth to such a radical reform.

The Court's intervention (Judgment n. 220/2013) explicitly left untouched the 'merits of the choices made by the legislature'.[26] It pointed solely to the abnormality of the source of law employed.[27] The urgency invoked by the government to justify its use of a decree-law was judged in light of the explicit aim of organic constitutional reform of the territorial organisation of the Republic. The reform could, on the one hand, be linked to the short-term necessity of immediate revenue savings.[28] However, on the other hand, as an organic reform, it necessarily required a long-term process of implementation premised on possible 'suspensions of effectiveness, referrals, and progressive systematisations, which do not accord with the immediacy of effects inherent to the decree-law, according to the constitutional design'.[29]

Moreover, the use of a decree-law to modify the Provinces' territorial constituencies was found by the Constitutional Court to constitute a

[26] See Corte costituzionale 19 luglio 2013, n. 220, at para. 12.1 of the *Considerato in diritto.*

[27] Ibid.: 'Dalla disposizione sopra riportata non risulta chiaro se l'urgenza del provvedere – anche e soprattutto in relazione alla finalità di risparmio, esplicitamente posta a base del decreto-legge, come pure del rinvio – sia meglio soddisfatta dall'immediata applicazione delle norme dello stesso decreto oppure, al contrario, dal differimento nel tempo della loro efficacia operativa. Tale ambiguità conferma la *palese inadeguatezza dello strumento del decreto-legge a realizzare una riforma organica e di sistema*, che non solo trova le sue motivazioni in esigenze manifestatesi da non breve periodo, ma *richiede processi attuativi necessariamente protratti nel tempo, tali da poter rendere indispensabili sospensioni di efficacia, rinvii e sistematizzazioni progressive, che mal si conciliano con l'immediatezza di effetti connaturata al decreto-legge*, secondo il disegno costituzionale. *Le considerazioni che precedono non entrano nel merito delle scelte compiute dal legislatore* e non portano alla conclusione che sull'ordinamento degli enti locali si possa intervenire solo con legge costituzionale – indispensabile solo se si intenda sopprimere uno degli enti previsti dall'art. 114 Cost., o comunque si voglia togliere allo stesso la garanzia costituzionale – ma, più limitatamente, che non sia utilizzabile un atto normativo, come il decreto-legge, per introdurre nuovi assetti ordinamentali che superino i limiti di misure meramente organizzative' (emphasis added).

[28] Doubts were in any case raised by local scholars, like M. Massa, 'Come non si devono riformare le province', *Le Regioni*, 5–6, 2013, 1168–84, and S. Staiano, 'Il DDL Delrio: considerazioni sul merito e sul metodo', *Federalismi.it. Rivista di diritto pubblico italiano, comunitario e comparato*, 1, 2014, and by the national Court of Auditors: see Corte dei Conti – Sezione delle autonomie, Audizione sul d.d.l. Città metropolitane, Province, Unioni e fusioni di Comuni A.C. 1542, Commissione Affari costituzionali, 6 novembre 2013.

[29] See Corte costituzionale 19 luglio 2013, n. 220, at par. 12.1 of the *Considerato in diritto, supra.*

radical breach (a 'logical and legal incompatibility') of the requirement contained in Article 133 of the Constitution:[30] that 'changes in provincial boundaries and the institution of new Provinces within a Region are regulated by the laws of the Republic, on the initiative of the [*Comuni*], after consultation with the Region'. The *Comuni*'s right to initiative was not respected in this case.

The distorted use of Article 77 of the Constitution was therefore subject to a declaration of unconstitutionality. The Constitutional Court highlighted the discrepancy between the transient nature of decree-laws and the importance of organic constitutional reform. Implicitly, the Court signalled the difference between the *urgency* inherent in the employment of decree-laws and the extraordinary situation of *emergency* that the reform tried to combat.[31]

The story did not end there. In the meantime, Decree-Law n. 188/2012[32] was issued to identify the new territorial constituencies of the Provinces. However, this time around, the decree-law was never converted into law by the Parliament, and its effects expired. A legislative bill to regulate the 'second-order' elections of the Provinces' organs was also presented by the Government in May 2012.[33] Once again, parliamentary approval was not forthcoming.

The annulment of the relevant parts of Decree-laws n. 201/2011 and n. 95/2012 by the Constitutional Court led to a further stratification and complication of measures on the same matters. In the same week as the hearing of the Court, whose results were anticipated by a press release, the Council of Ministers deliberated the approval of a constitutional bill,

[30] *Ibidem*, at par. 12.2: 'Emerge dalle precedenti considerazioni che *esiste una incompatibilità logica e giuridica – che va al di là dello specifico oggetto dell'odierno scrutinio di costituzionalità – tra il decreto-legge, che presuppone che si verifichino casi straordinari di necessità e urgenza, e la necessaria iniziativa dei Comuni,* che certamente non può identificarsi con le suddette situazioni di fatto, se non altro perché l'iniziativa non può che essere frutto di una maturazione e di una concertazione tra enti non suscettibile di assumere la veste della straordinarietà, ma piuttosto quella dell'esercizio ordinario di una facoltà prevista dalla Costituzione, in relazione a bisogni e interessi già manifestatisi nelle popolazioni locali' (emphasis added).

[31] See, for an analysis of the two dimensions, R. Bin, 'Il nodo delle province', and G. Di Cosimo, 'Come non si deve usare il decreto legge', *Le Regioni*, 5–6, 2013, 899–912 and 1163–7 respectively.

[32] Decreto-legge 5 novembre 2012, n. 188. Disposizioni urgenti in materia di Province e Citta' metropolitane (12G0210) (GU n. 259 del 6-11-2012).

[33] Disegno di legge 'Modalità di elezione del Consiglio provinciale e del Presidente della Provincia, a norma dell'articolo 23, commi 16 e 17, del decreto-legge 6 dicembre 2011, n. 201, convertito, con modificazioni, dalla legge 22 dicembre 2011, n. 214' (5210).

consisting of only three articles, intended to radically eliminate the Provinces from the Italian constitutional architecture.[34] This was then absorbed in the organic project of constitutional reform finally approved by the Parliament in 2016, and which, at the time of writing, must be confirmed by a popular referendum in autumn 2016.

Moreover, new *interim* measures were considered necessary, following the Constitutional Court's intervention, to consolidate the effects of other, non-annulled parts of Decree-laws n. 201/2011 and n. 95/2012. Thus, Decree-law n. 93/2013, devoted to 'Urgent provisions for civil security and to combat gender-based violence, as well as on the subject of civil protection and commissioned administration of the Provinces'[35] (a case study in inhomogeneous content), confirmed the dissolution of the political organs of the (still existing) Provinces, the nomination of Government Commissioners and the efficacy of their acts. A new Law n. 147/2013 provided the same effects for those other Provinces whose organs had natural expiration or early termination between 1 January and 30 June 2014.

A new Law n. 56/2014 was then approved, establishing the *Città metropolitane* already envisioned in the constitutional reform of 2001 and regulating the new *Unioni di Comuni* ('Unions of Municipalities'). There is a clear overlap of competences between these new layers of territorial government and the Provinces. In fact, the Law n. 56/2014 also aimed to adjust the legal framework of the remaining Provinces, by transforming them into second-level authorities with no directly elected organs but composed of representatives of the relevant municipalities.

In Law n. 56/2014 there is a clear, and commendable, tendency towards optimisation and reduction of expenditure; for instance, with regard of the eradication of a whole layer of local representatives and their emoluments (Article 1, paragraph 84 of Law n. 56/2014 explicitly provides for the non-remunerated nature of political appointments at the level of the Province). Nevertheless, again, problematic issues of form and substance arise. With regard to substance, doubts concerned the constitutionality of the reform, which possibly undermined the

[34] Disegno di legge costituzionale: 'Abolizione delle province' (1543), presented on the 20 August 2013 at the Camera dei Deputati: see the text at the web page of the lower house of the Parliament www.camera.it/_dati/leg17/lavori/stampati/pdf/17PDL0009060.pdf.

[35] Decreto-legge 14 agosto 2013, n. 93 Disposizioni urgenti in materia di sicurezza e per il contrasto della violenza di genere, nonche' in tema di protezione civile e di commissariamento delle province (13G00141) (Gazzetta Ufficiale n.191 del 16-8-2013), convertito con modificazioni dalla L. 15 ottobre 2013, n. 119 (in G.U. 15/10/2013, n. 242).

autonomy of local authorities. Such questions of substance were explicitly left untouched by the Constitutional Courts in its decision of Decree-Laws n. 201/2011 and n. 95/2012 (see earlier discussion of Judgment n. 220/2013).

As to problematic issues of form, the first tangible concern is the structure of Law n. 56/2014, which is composed of a single article of 151 (!) internal paragraphs and an attachment. In this sense, emergency is here again visible – *epiphenomenally* – in the extreme use of an already infamous Italian drafting technique, aimed at reducing the time needed to gain the approval of Parliament,[36] given the perceived need for quick action, but certainly detrimental to legislative quality.[37] The strategy becomes even more suspect given the constitutional significance of the issue at hand.

A second concern is that the technique used in drafting the contents of Law n. 56/2014 is somewhat perplexing. It made continuous reference to the 'reform of Title V of Part II of the Constitution and of its implementing rules (. . .)' being 'pending' (Article 1, para. 5 and 51), and therefore also to the aforementioned constitutional bill of radical suppression of the Provinces (deliberated by the Council of Ministers following Judgment n. 220/2013) but later absorbed into an organic one. Not only has the approval of such reform been pending for months (and will be until a referendum in autumn 2016) and was for a long time uncertain on both legal and political levels, but it has been argued that the entire Law, as a general reform with no contextually clear

[36] The technique is the result of combined parliamentary tactics: basically, a so-called maxi-amendment to a single article (containing, in its sub-paragraphs, all the text of the original legislative bill) takes the place of possible various amendments to various articles. If a vote of confidence is asked on such maxi-amendment, it has temporal and logical precedence, and precludes the vote on other proposed amendments. It must be noted that Article 72 of the Italian Constitution states that 'Every bill submitted to one of the Houses is, in accordance with its Rules, considered by a Committee and then by the House itself, which approves it article by article and with a final vote'.

[37] And therefore for the prerogatives of the Parliament and for the certainty of the law: see, on these points, *ex multis*, A. Pisaneschi, 'Fondamento costituzionale del potere di emendamento, limiti di coerenza e questione di fiducia', *Diritto e società*, 2, 1988, 203–58; M. Ainis, *La legge oscura. Come e perchè non funziona* (Roma-Bari, Laterza, 1997), at pp. 4ff in particular; G.U. Rescigno, *L'atto normativo* (Bologna: Zanichelli, 1998), at pp. 139ff; N. Lupo, 'Emendamenti, maxi-emendamenti e questione di fiducia nelle legislature del maggioritario', in E. Gianfrancesco and N. Lupo, (eds.), *Le regole del diritto parlamentare nella dialettica tra maggioranza e opposizione* (Roma: LUISS University Press, 2007), at pp. 41ff; G. Piccirilli, *L'emendamento nel processo di decisione parlamentare* (Padova: CEDAM, 2009), especially pp. 223ff.

fundamental choices about the overall structure of local government, was disproportionate as a means to make a new round of elections of Provinces' representatives impossible.[38]

3 Conclusions

Territorial decentralisation has always been an open question in Italy. The peninsula has a history of great differentiation. The 1947 Republican Constitution provided for the establishment of a complex system of decentralisation, which preserved previously settled local autonomies such as *Comuni* and *Provinces* and added *Regions*. Ordinary Regions came into being only in 1970. Important rounds of constitutional reform followed throughout the years, coupled with regular debates on the preservation of such a stratified architecture. The issue was rekindled by the crisis of recent years; as said, an organic constitutional reform is still pending at the time of writing, providing, among other things, for a reallocation of powers between the national government and the Regions (to address the fragmentation, overlap and conflicts in the vertical division of mandates) and for a transformation of the parliamentary system, with a Senate envisaged as a chamber to represent regional and local authorities.

This chapter therefore described just a segment of a long evolutionary line. Still, a reform of clear constitutional significance for the Italian Republic (with its origins located, at least in part, in euro crisis law measures) has recently been undertaken. 'Emergency' has dominated its first steps, with clear distortions of the relevant sources of law. A whole range of pathologies were detectable in the employment of sources deployed to intervene, abruptly, in matters historically difficult to amend:[39] patent misuse of decree-laws which remained unconverted or were of inhomogeneous/compendious quality, withdrawn governmental bills, repeated *interim* measures to block elections and the unconstitutional drafting style of general reforms, with dubious formal reference to uncertain constitutional amendments still to be approved.

[38] See, in this sense, F. Giglioni, 'La riforma del governo di area vasta tra eterogenesi dei fini e aspettative autonomistiche', *Federalismi.it. Rivista di diritto pubblico italiano, comunitario e comparato*, 1, 2014.

[39] See also F. Fabrizzi, 'Il caos normativo in materia di province', *Federalismi.it. Rivista di diritto pubblico italiano, comunitario e comparato*, 1, 2014.

Unusually, such measures were sanctioned by the (traditionally deferential) Constitutional Court for violation of Article 77 of the Italian Constitution. The origin of reform was a letter by central bankers to the head of a national executive. One might wonder if this was just an unconventional soft law measure[40] or the prodrome of the future 'Partnerships for Growth, Jobs and Competitiveness', in the form of contractual arrangements, as discussed at the European Council of 19–20 December 2013 in Brussels.[41] Regardless, it is a development that allows us to further consider the multilevel phenomenology of emergency measures.

[40] As always existed in European integration history, also in rather relevant sectors. See, for theoretical reconstructions on the concept and reflections on the transformation of soft into hard law, the classic studies of K. C. Wellens and G. M. Borchart, 'Soft Law in European Community Law', *European Law Review*, 14, 1989, 267–321; F. Snyder, 'Soft Law and Institutional Practice in the European Community', in S. Martin (ed.), *The Construction of Europe: Essays in Honour of Emile Noël* (Dordrecht: Kluwer Academic Publishers, 1994), pp. 197–225; D. M. Trubek, P. Cottrell, and M. Nance, '"Soft Law", "Hard Law", and European Integration: Toward a Theory of Hybridity', in J. Scott and G. de Bùrca (eds.), *New Governance and Constitutionalism in Europe and the US* (Oxford: Hart, 2006) pp. 65–94.

[41] See European Council, 'Conclusions', EUCO 217/13 (20 December 2013), www.consilium.europa.eu/uedocs/cms_Data/docs/pressdata/en/ec/140245.pdf, para. 30–7.

9

Ireland: Traditional Procedures Adapted for Economic Emergency

STEPHEN COUTTS

Article 28.3.3° *Bunreacht na hÉireann* (the Constitution of Ireland) provides that 'nothing in this Constitution . . . shall be invoked to invalidate any law enacted by the Oireachtas, which is expressed to be for the purpose of securing the public safety and the preservation of the State in time of war or armed rebellion'.[1] While the economic and financial crisis that engulfed the state in 2008 and subsequent years has frequently been described as a period of general crisis, an attempt to draw an analogy to Article 28.3.3° by invoking a legal emergency arising from the economic crisis has not been a feature of the Irish implementation of euro-crisis law. Unlike some other Member States implementing structural reforms as a result of European Union and International Monetary Fund programmes,[2] Ireland has not made use of an expressly exceptional legislative procedure.[3] Nonetheless, certain features of the law-making process have been reminiscent of a state of emergency, including accelerated legislative procedures and delegation of substantial and, at times, ill-defined powers to the executive. Furthermore, an awareness on the part of the courts to the general political and, above all, financial context of some of the measures adopted to combat the economic crisis has

[1] Bunreacht na hÉireann, Art. 28.3.3°.

[2] See, for example, the use of decree laws in Italy and Spain and the Art. 44 procedure in Greece. For a discussion see the other chapters in this part of the book: Chapter 6, 'Greece: Constitutional Deconstruction and the Loss of National Sovereignty' by Afroditi Marketou; Chapter 7, 'Spain: Dealing with the Economic Emergency through Constitutional Reform and Limited Parliamentary Intervention' by Leticia Díez Sanchez; and Chapter 8, 'Constitutional Change through Emergency Decrees: The Abolition of the Provinces in Italy' by Leonardo Pierdominici.

[3] Nonetheless, although the Irish government has not relied on a distinct law-making procedure provided for in the Constitution (indeed Bunreacht na hÉireann does not provide for such 'decree laws'), it has relied on its in-built majority in Parliament to 'guillotine', or radically cut short, the period allocated for debate, albeit formally remaining within the 'ordinary' procedure for adopting legislation.

emerged in certain discrete areas; in particular, in relation to measures adopted in the immediate aftermath of the financial crisis to deal with the state's deteriorating financial position and its insolvent banking system. Irish crisis-era law-making and judging has therefore been characterised by the adaptation of traditional methods to meet the requirements of urgency and flexibility deemed necessary in a state of emergency. A possible explanation for this may lie in certain features of the Irish Constitution and legal-political culture, in particular, an already especially strong executive and a relative absence of an economic and social rights culture in Ireland.

The analysis focuses on the period immediately following the global financial crisis and prior to Ireland's formal entry into a programme of financial assistance. This is due to the historical evolution of the Irish crisis and the steps taken to deal with it. The most intense period of crisis took place immediately prior to entry into the programme of financial assistance and the most dramatic measures were adopted during this period. A blanket guarantee of banking debts (the Credit Institutions [Financial Support] Act 2008, hereinafter CIFSA 2008), major efforts to curtail expenditure through sweeping cuts to public-sector pay (Financial Emergency Measures in the Public Interest Act 2009, hereinafter FEMPI Act 2009) and, finally, the setting up of a 'bad bank' agency with wide powers to acquire certain private assets (the National Asset Management Agency Act 2009, hereinafter NAMA Act 2009) all occurred during this period. Indeed, it is precisely the government's dramatic efforts to deal with the deteriorating situation of the financial sector (and the consequential budgetary difficulties) that led to the formal application to request a bailout.[4] The programme of financial assistance therefore had a considerable degree of continuity with policies pursued immediately prior to the signing of the Memorandum of Understanding (MoU), especially as regards repairing the financial sector and the budgetary position of the state. Much of the programme of financial assistance was focused on completing processes and measures already commenced prior to the bailout[5] and many of the more dramatic measures were

[4] For an analysis of the troubles of the Irish banking sector and the ill-fated efforts of the Irish government to deal with them, see European Commission, *Ex post Evaluation of the Economic Adjustment Programme, Ireland 2010–2013* (Institutional Paper on the European Economy No. 4, July 2015), http://ec.europa.eu/economy_finance/publications/eeip/pdf/ip004_en.pdf, pp. 43ff.

[5] Ibid., pp. 28ff.

begun prior to the actual programme.[6] In short, an analysis based on the period of the bailout would neglect the historical continuity between the pre-bailout and bailout periods and, in fact, would fail to take account of the period most characterised by emergency and the legal response to that emergency. Nonetheless, the limited temporal scope of the following analysis should be acknowledged as well as the possibility of law-making during the bailout period, implementing the MoU *stricto senso*, also displaying emergency-type characteristics.[7]

1 Emergency in Legislative Procedures

Bunreacht na hÉireann does not provide for any form of emergency rule-making by the executive by decree or otherwise, nor has Article 28.3.3° been invoked to derogate from the Constitution to grant any exceptional law-making powers to the government.[8] Nonetheless, as pointed out by Greene,[9] a number of features of law-making during the crisis period presented certain emergency-type features, in particular, truncated legislative procedures in Parliament and the delegation of substantial and at times ill-defined law-making powers to the executive, be it to the Minister himself or to a statutory agency. Both features are characteristic of economic emergency-type legislation: the first facilitates quick reactions to rapidly evolving economic and financial circumstances, while the second delegates rule-making to technical agencies enjoying expertise and an ability to act quickly.[10]

Ireland's crisis was closely linked with a massive property bubble and burst and the subsequent quasi-collapse of the banking system.

[6] Ibid., p. 30.

[7] One fruitful area of analysis in this regard may be the major restructuring of the financial sector from 2011 onwards.

[8] The terms of Article 28.3.3°, to be used only in times of 'war or armed rebellion' (albeit either domestically or abroad), would appear to preclude it, a point made in an obiter statement by Hardiman J in *Dellway Investments Ltd et al.* v. *National Asset Management Agency et al.* (2011) 4 IR 1 (High Court, Supreme Court), 289.

[9] A. Greene, 'Questioning Executive Supremacy in an Economic State of Emergency', *Legal Studies*, 35(4), (2015), pp. 594–620.

[10] W. Scheuerman, 'The Economic State of Emergency', *Cardozo Law Review*, 21 (1999–2000), 1869–94, 1891ff. See also Greene, 'Questioning Executive Supremacy', 619: 'Of all the various different types of phenomena that can trigger an emergency response in a state, crises that are economic in nature are those that are most affected by the compression of time and space'.

A number of legislative acts, especially those linked with the stability of the financial system, were passed in remarkably short time frames. The CIFSA 2008, introduced to give effect to a state guarantee of all banking debts announced in September 2008, was adopted in less than two days and was justified as being 'necessary to address a unique and unprecedented economic crisis'.[11] Introduced on the morning of 30 September 2008 it passed all legislative stages, including a first and second reading and committee stage in both the *Dáil* and *Seanad* by the evening of 1 October 2008, with the *Seanad* sitting until 05:40 in the morning on 1 October 2008. An early signature motion was subsequently passed on 2 October 2008 allowing the President to sign the act and for its entry into force on the same day.[12] Similarly the Credit Institutions (Stabilisation) Act 2010 (CISA 2010), allowing the Minister to make far-reaching directions to financial institutions, was presented to the *Dáil* on 14 December 2010 and had passed all legislative stages by 15 December 2010, including a motion for early signature.[13]

At the same time some crisis-era legislation has granted relatively wide-ranging powers to both government ministers and other bodies. Thus, under the CISA Act 2010, the Minister is entitled to issue instructions to financial institutions directing the institution 'to take (within a specified period) or refrain from taking (during a specified period) any action'.[14] A subsequent non-exhaustive list suggests alterations of the founding company documents, de-listing of shares or the issuing of shares to any person, including the Minister himself. The other main substantial part of the act allows the minister to make 'special management' orders appointing an individual or firm to effectively take over the management of any institution if necessary for the goals of the act.[15] It should be noted that certain controls are nonetheless introduced, principally, the need to have any ministerial direction confirmed by a court

[11] Credit Institutions (Stabilisation) Act 2010, Preamble.

[12] See Houses of the Oireachtas, 'Credit Institutions (Financial Support) Bill 2008 Legislative History', www.oireachtas.ie/viewdoc.asp?DocID=10023&&CatID=59&StartDate=01%20January%202008&OrderAscending=0.

[13] The entry into force of the act was ultimately delayed until 21 December 2010 following consultation by the President with the Council of State for constitutional compatibility. See Houses of the Oireachtas, 'Credit Institutions (Stabilisation) Bill 2010 Legislative History', www.oireachtas.ie/viewdoc.asp?DocID=17046&&CatID=59&StartDate=01%20January%202010&OrderAscending=0.

[14] Credit Institutions (Stabilisation) Act 2010, s. 7.

[15] Primarily, financial stability and the stability of particular institutions. See ibid., Preamble.

order.[16] Similarly, under NAMA Act 2009, the Minister is able to make orders designating what types of assets are to be deemed bank assets for the purpose of the act.[17] Those same assets can then be subject to acquisition by the National Asset Management Agency (hereinafter NAMA), exercising a relatively broad degree of discretion.[18]

2 Emergency in Judicial Decision-Making

The language of emergency has emerged not only in the legislative arena but has also appeared in certain areas of judicial decision-making. The area where the state's economic circumstances have played the greatest role in the reasoning of the courts is that of public-sector employment and, in particular, efforts to reduce public-sector pay and pensions. The FEMPI Act 2009,[19] granting the government the power to impose a levy on public servants to fund their pensions and to reduce payments to service providers has been challenged, unsuccessfully, before the courts on the grounds of property rights. In all cases the High Court has noted the special circumstances and purposes of the FEMPI Act 2009 in contributing to the stabilisation of the State's finances and in ensuring that the public sector makes a 'fair contribution' to such a stabilisation. In *Haire*[20] and *UNITE*,[21] the High Court found that the economic context in which the FEMPI Act 2009 was adopted and its stated public-interest purposes supported the conclusion that any purported attack on property rights would not be 'unjust' within the meaning of Article 40.3.2° of the Constitution.[22] In *Garda Representative Association*, the High Court, while discussing the provisions of the FEMPI Act 2009 itself, rather than the constitutional context, found that, when deciding whether to exclude a particular group (in this case the police) from the pension levy, the

[16] Ibid., ss. 9 and 14. [17] National Asset Management Agency Act 2009, s. 69.

[18] Ibid., s. 84. This aspect of the act was contested on constitutional grounds for infringing the right to property in *Dellway*, 183ff.

[19] Financial Emergency Provisions in the Public Interest Act 2009. Since supplemented by further acts in 2009, 2010, 2013 and 2015. Perhaps demonstrating its emergency quality (and in time for an upcoming general election), the government has started to undo the cuts carried out under the FEMPI legislation in the latest act.

[20] *J & J Haire & Company Ltd & Ors* v. *Minister for Health and Children & Ors* (2009), IEHC 562.

[21] *UNITE & Anor* v. *Minister for Finance* (2010), IEHC 354.

[22] It should be noted that in *Haire* the Court found that, in any event, the alleged property right did not exist and it was on this basis the decision was decided.

Minister for Finance had a significant degree of discretion due to the fact that the FEMPI Act 2009 was a question of political choice and was 'both policy-based and fiscal'.[23] Finally, in the perhaps closest example of an explicit reliance on the concept of an economic emergency, in *McKenzie*, the High Court found that the Minister for Defence was entitled to bypass a Conciliation and Arbitration Scheme (the CA Scheme) when imposing a general government-wide reduction in allowances for travel.[24] In finding in favour of the Minister, the Court found that the government was acting 'in the urgent national interest' when adopting measures in response to the 'most serious economic crisis in [the state's] history that has been deepening by the week', allowing it to bypass the CA Scheme under Article 3 of that scheme.

Second, the High Court has also highlighted the economic considerations in the context of the issuance of promissory notes to recapitalise the banking sector. In *Collins* the High Court found that once the *Oireachtas* has authorised the government to make payments for a specific purpose (here, in extending financial aid to credit institutions) there is no limit on the amount the government may spend, and there is no corresponding need to return to Parliament to obtain further authorisation. It should be noted that the Court mentions the economic crisis as a mere context for the discussion and the judgment is a general discussion of the constitutional framework of the budget. However, while the Court expressly excludes the economic context as a relevant consideration in its legal analysis, an emphasis is placed on a need to secure freedom of action for the government in its executive role, with the Court noting that 'as recent experience has all too painfully demonstrated, the welfare of the entire citizenry is hugely dependent on the capacity of the State to be able to raise money without hindrance on international markets.'[25]

Finally, in the outlier case of *Dellway*, the Supreme Court upheld an individual's constitutional rights to fair procedures in the context of acquisition of loan books by a 'bad bank', designed to remove toxic assets from the Irish banking system after the property market collapse. In doing so, it explicitly rejected the contention that the national economic

[23] *Garda Representative Association* v. *Minister for Finance* (2010), IEHC 78, para. 23. This analysis would seem to flow both from the nature of the act as one regulating public-sector pay but more importantly from its purpose and general place in the response of the government to the economic crisis and the policy decision to ensure that the public sector make a proper contribution to its resolution.

[24] *McKenzie & Anor* v. *Minister for Finance & Ors* (2010), IEHC 461.

[25] Ibid., para. 124. The case is currently on appeal before the Supreme Court.

emergency might justify an infringement on constitutional rights. In *Dellway*, an individual challenged the decision of NAMA under the NAMA Act 2009 to acquire his loans from his bank without any hearing.[26] While a relatively minor part of the decision, a number of individual judgments indicated a hostility to an attempt by the government to raise the possibility of an economic state of emergency analogous to the state of war or rebellion found in Article 28.3.3° *Bunreacht na hÉireann*, with Hardiman J noting that '[o]ur Constitution makes specific provision for "war or armed rebellion". It is not for the courts to extend those provisions to a situation which is not one of war or armed rebellion. That would require a decision of the people in a referendum, if they thought it necessary or prudent to confer such unreviewable powers on the State. The cry of "emergency" is an intoxicating one, producing an exhilarating freedom from the need to consider the rights of others and productive of a desire to repeat it again and again.'[27]

3 Traditional Procedures Adapted for Economic Emergency

In both legislation and in court decisions, the economic crisis has been invoked as a justification for a transfer of power from Parliament to the government. In legislation this has taken the shape of truncated legislative procedures as in the case of the CIFSA 2008 and the CISA 2010 or delegation of rule-making powers, such as in the case of the NAMA Act 2009. Similarly, in both the case of the FEMPI Act 2009 litigation and the *Collins* judgment, the economic crisis has been invoked directly or served as the context for a facilitation of governmental discretion. In *Garda Representative Association* the description of the FEMPI Act 2009 as a reaction to the economic crisis and its stated goal to 'share the burden' ensured that the decisions of the Minister were of a political and policy-based nature, thereby securing a minimal level of judicial scrutiny. Similarly, in *Haire* and *UNITE*, the economic crisis served as the context in which any attack on property rights were to be considered proportionate and therefore not unjust within the meaning of the constitution.

Nonetheless, in all cases, considerations relating to the financial crisis and the 'economic emergency' have been located and accommodated within the existing legal framework and practices. In legislative terms, the

[26] See *Dellway*. [27] Ibid., 289.

government, through its tightly controlled majority in both houses of Parliament, is empowered to place time limits on parliamentary debates and frequently makes use of this power to swiftly adopt legislation.[28] However, the crisis-era legislation analysed in this chapter was adopted in an exceptionally short period of time, even by Irish standards. Moreover, the shortening of the legislative procedure was justified by the perceived emergency nature of the situation rather than mere administrative convenience, as is commonly the case. Thus, if the legislative form or technique is not particularly novel, the concept of emergency was clearly at play both in terms of the extent and the justification for accelerated legislative procedures. Similarly, the use of delegated legislation is provided for by the Constitution and, until recently, Courts rarely struck down regulations as being an unconstitutional delegation of law-making power.[29]

At the same time, the Courts have fitted the language and justification of emergency into existing legal tests, be it the test for an 'unjust' attack on property rights in the cases of *Haire* and *UNITE* or the constitutional framework for the budget in *Collins*. Even *McKenzie*, perhaps the clearest assertion of a national economic emergency, is fitted within Article 3 of the CA Scheme, allowing the scheme to be bypassed if its application would hinder the government in the discharge of its responsibilities in the public interest. While, particularly in the case of the FEMPI Act 2009 litigation, the economic circumstances of the state have had an influence on the legal analysis, in no case has an explicit stand-alone doctrine of a national economic emergency been developed or applied to justify governmental action that would otherwise be illegal. It would seem the existing judicial review framework is sufficiently flexible to accommodate considerations of a general economic nature. Indeed, in *Dellway*, the Supreme Court endorsed this approach of allowing economic circumstances to play a role in legal analysis, such as in a proportionality analysis, while arguing strongly that this is done within the existing legal framework and the Constitution itself.[30]

[28] A practice continued by the 2011–16 government, despite promises to end the wholesale use of the practice. See Labour Party, 'Towards Recovery – Programme for a National Government' (2011), www.labour.ie/download/pdf/labour_towards_recovery_report.pdf. It remains an unfulfilled promise of its Programme for Government.

[29] See O. Doyle, *Constitutional Law: Text, Cases and Materials* (Dublin: Clarus Press, 2008), ch. 11. Recently, this position has begun to change. See, for example, *Bederev v. Ireland* (2015), IECA 38 (2015), 3 JIC 1001.

[30] With one Justice noting that 'the Act of 2009 requires to be construed in accordance with the Constitution. Clearly the Act of 2009 was part of governmental policy introduced to

4 Conclusion

Two instances where a state of legal emergency may justify derogation from the ordinary constitutional order are, first, to allow governments to bypass ordinary legislative procedures and pass forms of decree or emergency laws[31] and, second, as a justification for limiting fundamental social rights.[32] Ireland has not made use of exceptional or emergency law-making procedures to bypass the usual legislative process. Nor has the economic context, although a relevant consideration in certain cases dealing with individual rights, led to an explicit application of an emergency powers doctrine overriding individual rights. Rather, this has been accommodated within the existing legislative procedures and legal concepts available in the Irish legal order.

While space precludes an in-depth analysis, two features of the Irish constitutional order might explain these developments: a strong executive and a weak economic and social rights culture. Ireland's constitutional architecture and political culture has resulted in an exceptionally strong executive vis-à-vis the legislature. A fused executive-legislative in the lower house, an in-built government majority in the upper house, a budgetary process dominated by government, an especially strong whip system and a weak independent parliamentary culture has resulted in an exceptional executive dominance.[33] A special parliamentary procedure allowing the government to 'guillotine' legislative debate allows the swift passage of legislation by government, which automatically holds a majority, and removes, to some extent, the need for emergency decree–type legislation. The government already has a large scope for manoeuvre within the legislative process and is relatively free from political constraints. There is, therefore, little need for the

meet the very serious banking crisis within the State. However, this does not exempt it from the principles of the Constitution.' *Dellway*, 230.

31 See, for example, the use of decree laws in Spain and Italy and the Art. 44 procedure in Greece, as discussed in the other chapters in Part II: National Constitutional Manifestations of Economic Emergency.

32 See, for example, limitations on social and labour rights, as discussed in this book in Chapter 7, 'Spain: Dealing with the Economic Emergency through Constitutional Reform and Limited Parliamentary Intervention' by Leticia Díez Sanchez.

33 M. MacCarthaigh, 'The Role of the Oireachtas: Theory and Practice' in M. MacCarthaigh and M. Manning (eds.), *The Houses of the Oireachtas: Parliament in Ireland* (Dublin: Institute of Public Administration, 2010), pp. 35–53, pp. 46ff. This paradigm may be dramatically upset following a general election in February 2016 in which no party, or group of parties, won a clear majority; leaving a fragmented party system and the possibility of a much weaker government vis-à-vis the Parliament.

government to bypass ordinary legislative procedures.[34] The judgment in *Collins*, while careful to identify a role for Parliament, additionally illustrates the importance of the executive in budgetary matters and the discretion afforded it by the Constitution.

In relation to the use of an emergency doctrine to justify infringements of fundamental rights, it should be noted that Ireland's fundamental rights tradition is liberal in nature, with strong protection of classic rights of personal autonomy and property but a weakly developed economic and social rights culture.[35] While there have been some judicial pronouncements on the need to judicially enforce social rights,[36] the Courts have been reluctant to endorse a set of judiciable socio-economic rights[37] and social rights.[38] This dichotomy is mirrored in the euro-crisis case law, with the Courts unwilling to intervene in challenges to the FEMPI Act 2009, while individual property rights and especially the fair procedures associated with them are protected in *Dellway*. This is overlain by a policy-making/individual decision distinction, thus justifying the differing standards of review and protection.[39] Instances of cuts to public-sector pay and benefits have been characterised as policy-making, thus justifying the reluctance of the Courts to intervene and carving out a protected space of government discretion. At the same time, the one case where the Courts have been willing to intervene, *Dellway*, is seen as an administrative decision compromising an individual right to property – and therefore triggering the robust fair procedures protections offered by the Irish Constitution.

34 Nor, indeed, beyond invoking the emergency powers found in Art. 28 of *Bunreacht na hÉireann*, is there a possibility to do so.

35 See A. Nolan, 'Welfare Rights in Crisis in the Eurozone: Ireland' in C. Kilpatrick and B. de Witte (eds.), *Social Rights in Times of Crisis in the Eurozone: The Role of Fundamental Rights* (EUI Working Papers, LAW 2014/05, Department of Law, 2014), 30–41.

36 See *TD* v. *Minister for Education* (2000), 3 IR 62 (High Court), later overturned in *TD* v. *Minister for Education* (2001), 4 IR 259 (Supreme Court).

37 *Sinnott* v. *Minister for Education et al.* (2001), 2 IR 545.

38 See A. Nolan, 'Welfare Rights in Crisis'.

39 See, for a comparative analysis of the basis and standard of review in constitutional court challenges in the various sovereign debt states, in this book Chapter 11, 'Constitutions, Social Rights and Sovereign Debt States in Europe: A Challenging New Area of Constitutional Inquiry' by Claire Kilpatrick.

PART III

Constitutional Judicial Challenges to Euro-Crisis Law

10

Legitimacy through Adjudication: The ESM Treaty and the Fiscal Compact before the National Courts

JAN-HERMAN REESTMAN*

1 Introduction

National constitutional courts are often seen as stumbling blocks to further European integration. Indeed, they often pose limits as to how far European integration may proceed under their respective constitutions. Nevertheless, these limits may be exceeded or even set aside by the respective constituent powers. Moreover, the constitutional courts also play another role in the integration process. They facilitate the current functioning of the EU in several respects and may help to legitimise new steps in European integration. We encounter all these different roles in the judgments of the national (constitutional) courts on the Treaty Establishing the European Stability Mechanism (ESM Treaty) and the Treaty on Stability, Coordination and Governance in the Economic and Monetary Union (Fiscal Compact),[1] as will be argued in this contribution.

The ESM Treaty and the Fiscal Compact are two of the main integration instruments developed during the Eurocrisis. They are in several respects related. As to their form, both treaties fall outside the EU structure and are 'ordinary' international treaties, but substantively they concern EU issues and pursue EU objectives. Also, various EU institutions (Council, Commission, European Central Bank [ECB], Court of Justice [ECJ]) participate in their execution. In addition, both were

* This contribution is an expanded and revised version of the author's previous article 'Het ESM – en het Stabiliteitsverdrag voor de constitutionele rechters in Estland, Frankrijk en Duitsland', *Sociaal Economische Wetgeving*, 61, 2013, 103–13.

[1] The Fiscal Compact is typically used to refer to Title III of the Treaty on Stability, Coordination and Governance in the Economic and Monetary Union. Here, it is used to signify the whole treaty, for reasons of clarity when referring to Articles from outside of Title III.

introduced to combat the Eurocrisis: the ESM Treaty by establishing a permanent fund for euro area states whose financial distress threatens the stability of the euro area, the Fiscal Compact by (slightly) accentuating the required budgetary discipline of the euro area Member States and by requiring those states to guarantee compliance with a balanced budget rule in national legislation. Therefore, both innovate: the ESM Treaty by establishing a form of permanent financial solidarity which, until recently, was anathema in the Economic and Monetary Union (EMU), the Fiscal Compact by outsourcing and nationalising the supervision of compliance with the treaty's budget rule (and indirectly also with an EU budget rule). All in all, the treaties thus 'are complementary in fostering fiscal responsibility and solidarity within the [EMU]'.[2] The fact that only euro area Member States which have correctly implemented the Fiscal Compact are eligible for ESM support is the strongest expression of this complementarity.[3]

Both treaties were publicly and politically very controversial. In various Member States one or both have been challenged in court. The procedural arguments lodged against the treaties relate to their hybrid character – half EU, half ordinary international treaty – while the substantive arguments in one way or another mostly regard an alleged loss of budgetary sovereignty or of budgetary prerogatives for the national Parliaments. European Council Decision 2011/199/EU has raised similar procedural and substantive constitutional issues.[4] That decision was the first taken under the simplified revision procedure of Article 48(6) of the Treaty on European Union (TEU) and has inserted a third paragraph into Article 136 TEU so as to remove any doubt as to the legality of the establishment of the ESM.

This contribution provides an overview and an analysis of the judgments. The structure is very simple. The first part deals with the procedural issues in the judgments on, respectively, the Decision 2011/199/EU, the ESM Treaty and the Fiscal Compact and is followed by a short interim conclusion. In the second part, the substantive issues are dealt with. The third part provides a contextual comparative analysis of several issues raised by the substantive parts of the judgments, such as the argumentative strategies used by the courts to limit the national

[2] ESM Treaty, Preamble, para. 5. [3] Ibid.; TSCG, Preamble, para. 25.

[4] European Council Decision of 25 March 2011 amending Article 136 of the Treaty on the Functioning of the European Union with regard to a stability mechanism for Member States whose currency is the euro (2011/199/EU) (OJ L 91, 6.4.2011, p. 1).

constitutional impact of the treaties and the legitimising effects of the judgments. Finally, some concluding remarks are presented.

2 Procedural Constitutional Issues

This part provides an overview of procedural constitutional issues that have arisen due to the hybrid character of the ESM Treaty, the Fiscal Compact and Decision 2011/199/EU. We start with the European Council Decision.

Decision 2011/199/EU: National Constitutional Perspectives on the Simplified Revision Procedure

European Council Decision 2011/199/EU inserted Article 136(3) into the Treaty on the Functioning of the European Union (TFEU), which provides that the euro area states may establish a stability mechanism à la the ESM to safeguard the stability of the euro area as a whole.[5] It was the first decision taken under the simplified treaty revision procedure in Article 48(6) TEU. That procedure has several distinctive features in comparison to the ordinary treaty revision procedure in Article 48(2)–(4) TEU. Two of these are relevant here. First, the content of an ordinary revision is decided upon by an (intergovernmental) conference of the governments of the Member States, that of a simplified revision by an EU institution, the European Council, with unanimity. In addition, an ordinary revision needs to be *ratified* by the Member States in accordance with their respective constitutional requirements, while a simplified revision merely needs *approval* in accordance with those requirements. These characteristics raise the question of the nature of the European Council decisions concerned.

The most common interpretation of the term 'approval' in Article 48(6) TEU, which is 'not a term of art of public international law',[6] is

[5] TFEU, Art. 136(3): 'The Member States whose currency is the euro may establish a stability mechanism to be activated if indispensable to safeguard the stability of the euro area as a whole. The granting of any required financial assistance under the mechanism will be made subject to strict conditionality'.

[6] B. de Witte and T. Beukers, 'The Court of Justice Approves the Creation of the European Stability Mechanism Outside the EU Legal Order: Pringle', *Common Market Law Review*, 50, 2013, 805–48, at 807 and n. 5.

undoubtedly that it concerns a simplified ratification requirement in the sense of Articles 11 and 14(2) of the Vienna Convention on the Law of Treaties.[7] In their judgments on the Treaty of Lisbon, the German Constitutional Court and the French Constitutional Council ruled that simplified treaty revisions have to be approved by their respective Parliaments in the same fashion as ordinary treaty revisions.[8] The same position is taken by the Polish Constitutional Tribunal, as we will see. In Ireland, however, a radically different reading was advocated in the case of *Doherty* v. *Referendum Commission*.

A. Ireland: On the Meaning of 'Approval' in Article 48(6) TEU

The hybrid nature of European Council Decision 2011/199/EU was at the basis of proceedings before the Irish High Court in the case of *Doherty* v. *Referendum Commission*.[9] At stake were statements by the Referendum Commission on the approval procedure for the decision; these statements were made in the context of the Irish referendum of 31 May 2012 on the constitutional bill for the approval of the Fiscal Compact. In the proceedings, the representative of the Irish Attorney General argued that Ireland was already bound by Decision 2011/199/EU because the Irish Prime Minister, as a member of the European Council, had agreed to it. By that, the Prime Minister had exercised the external affairs competences vested in the Irish government by Article 29.4.1 of the Irish Constitution,[10] and Irish approval in the sense of Article 48(6) TEU had been given. In the Attorney General's view, the only effect of the European Communities (Amendment) Act 2012, which inserted the European Council Decision in the definition of 'treaties governing the European Union' in the European Communities Act 1972, was to incorporate that decision in the internal (dualist) Irish legal order, not to have it approved by the Irish Parliament.[11] If I understand it well, this position is

[7] See M. Fitzmaurice, 'The Practical Working of the Law of Treaties', in M. Evans (ed.), *International Law*, 4th edn (Oxford University Press, 2014), pp. 66–200, at pp. 172–3.

[8] *Conseil Constitutionnel*, Decision No. 2007–560 DC of 20 December 2007, para. 26; *BVerfG*, Judgment 2 BvE 2/08 of 30 June 2009, point 312.

[9] *Doherty* v. *Referendum Commission* (2012), IEHC 21.

[10] Constitution of Ireland, Art. 29.4.1: 'The executive power of the State in or in connection with its external relations shall in accordance with Article 28 of this Constitution be exercised by or on the authority of the Government'.

[11] *Doherty*, paras. 60–1.

partly based on Irish constitutional law and partly on EU law (i.e. on a combined reading of Articles 48[6] TEU, 288[4] TFEU and 4[3] TEU [principle of loyal cooperation] in light of the autonomy of the EU legal order).[12]

To the extent that the Attorney General's position is based on an interpretation of the Irish Constitution, it cannot be easily refuted: at least, textually simplified treaty revisions in the sense of Article 48(6) TEU are not EU acts that, in accordance with Articles 29.4.7 and 29.4.8 of the Irish Constitution, require prior approval by both houses of the Irish Parliament. However, as far as her position is based on an interpretation of Article 48(6) TEU, it does not convince, as it deprives of any meaning the requirement of approval 'in accordance with the Member States' respective constitutional requirements, or in the words of Justice Hogan, reduces it to a 'pure formality'.[13] The Attorney General's position also seems to be at odds with the European Council's view of the approval requirement, since Article 2 of Decision 2011/199/EU requires the Member States to 'notify the Secretary-General of the Council without delay of the completion of the procedures for the approval of this decision in accordance with their respective constitutional requirements'.

The Referendum Commission's statements, whose factual accuracy was the real issue in *Doherty*, are not so easily brushed aside. The Commission, charged by law to provide fair and non-partisan information on issues submitted to referendum 'and related matters', made statements to the effect that, although the European Council Decision required the approval of the Irish Parliament, the government could not, given Parliament's consent, refuse to 'ratify' the decision of its own accord. In other words: the approval procedure would not consist of two political decisions (approval by Parliament, or by the people, if that is what the relevant national Constitution requires, and ratification by the executive), but of only one: approval by Parliament. The ratification/notification would merely be a notary act to let the other Member States know that Parliament had consented, not an expression or confirmation of the government's will to be bound.[14]

In my view, this is a defensible interpretation of the approval requirement in Article 48(6) TEU: The Member States' governments are already bound by simplified revision decisions, which require only the approval of the national Parliaments to enter into force. This interpretation is not

[12] Ibid., paras. 54–8. [13] Ibid., para. 58. [14] Ibid., para. 62.

incompatible with judgments of the French, German and Polish constitutional courts (*supra*), which are silent on the position of their governments after approval by the respective Parliaments. The High Court, in my view rightly, refused to declare the Referendum Commission's statements to be incorrect as they were not 'plainly wrong or inaccurate'.

Is a government's refusal to 'ratify' a 48(6) TEU decision of its own accord not merely a hypothetical issue? I do not think so. An individual who as member of the European Council has agreed to a decision may not necessarily be the same individual who has to 'ratify' it. It is not hard to imagine a situation in which a head of state is not a member of the European Council, but is the competent authority to ratify the decision and both opposes and refuses to ratify it. Although that problem did not arise in Ireland, it may well surface somewhere at some point in the future. In fact, something similar happened in the Czech Republic when President Klaus originally refused to ratify the Lisbon Treaty.

B. Poland: Article 136(3) TEU, No Transfer of Competences – Polish Style

In Poland, a group of *Sejm* deputies questioned the constitutionality of the act of Parliament of 11 May 2012 with which the *Sejm*, the Polish lower house, authorised the ratification of the decision. The procedure for approving ordinary treaties in Article 89(1) of the Polish Constitution had been followed, by which the *Sejm* may give its approval with simple majority and the Senate merely has a suspensive veto. The deputies contended that the decision, either alone or in conjunction with the ESM Treaty and/or the Fiscal Compact, amounted to delegating 'to an international organization or international institution the competence of organs of State authority in relation to certain matters' in the sense of Article 90(1) of the Polish Constitution. Therefore, it should have been approved with a two-thirds majority by both chambers of the Polish Parliament in the presence of at least half of the statutory number of their members, or, alternatively, by referendum, as prescribed respectively by Articles 90(2) and (3) of the Polish Constitution.

The Polish Constitutional Tribunal (*Trybunale Konstytucyjnym*), which qualified the decision as a 'special kind of an international agreement',[15]

[15] *Trybunale Konstytucyjnym*, Judgment K 33/12 of 26 June 2013, para. 6.1.1; see also para. 6.5.3, in which the decision is labelled 'an international agreement or an equivalent act'.

rejected the claim. One wonders if the Tribunal could not have taken a shortcut by referring to the *Pringle* judgment of 27 November 2012, in which the ECJ ruled that the decision does not increase the EU's competences.[16] Upon further consideration, however, one understands the Tribunal's approach: an 'increase of competences' in the sense of Article 48(6) TEU is not necessarily tantamount to a 'delegation of competences' in the sense of the Polish Constitution. By relying solely on the ECJ's decision, the Tribunal would have outsourced the 'competence' to interpret the Polish Constitution, something that it understandably did not want to do.[17] Therefore, it referred to the conclusions of the ECJ in *Pringle* only as 'corresponding' to those to which the Tribunal itself came after lengthy analysis of Article 90(1) of the Polish Constitution. The Tribunal also found support in the judgments of the German and Austrian Constitutional Courts.[18]

According to the Tribunal, a competence in the sense of Article 90(1) of the Polish Constitution concerns the authorisation given to a public institution 'to take certain actions, which, in principle, have legal effects and are related to issuing legally binding acts'.[19] The definition of 'delegation of competence', Polish style, thus appears to be *narrower* than that of an 'increase in competences' EU style: while the former, at least in principle, refers to competences to issue acts with legal effects, the latter refers to the ability 'to undertake any action which was not possible before the entry into force of amendment of the [TFEU]',[20] which may well be a competence to act without legal effects. Be that as it may, the challenged decision did not refer to any competence Polish style, let alone that it transferred one to an international organisation.[21] Instead, echoing *Pringle*, the Tribunal found that the decision merely *recognised* the competence of the euro area Member States to establish the ESM.[22]

[16] *Thomas Pringle* v. *Government of Ireland, Ireland and the Attorney General*, Case C-370/12, para. 75.

[17] The absence of preliminary questions of national courts on the ESM Treaty, with the exception of the Irish Supreme Court, has been explained by time pressure. See S. Bardutzky and E. Fahey, 'Who Got to Adjudicate the EU's Financial Crisis and Why?', in M. Adams, F. Fabbrini and P. Larouche (eds.), *The Constitutionalization of European Budgetary Constraints* (Oxford: Hart Publishing, 2014), pp. 341–8, p. 354. Two other explanations are that the constitutional issues that the courts had to decide were essentially national and that, after the procedure by the Irish Court, new questions were superfluous.

[18] *Trybunale Konstytucyjnym*, Judgment K 33/12, paras. 7.4–7.5.

[19] Ibid., para. 6.5.3.

[20] *Pringle*, para. 73.

[21] *Trybunale Konstytucyjnym*, Judgment K 33/12, para. 6.5.4.

[22] Ibid., paras. 7.3.2 and 7.3.3.

The Tribunal also dismissed the plaintiff's argument that, by ratifying Decision 2011/199/EU, Poland would have to become an ESM member once admitted to the euro area, as paragraph 7 of the Preamble to the ESM Treaty holds.[23] Legally, indeed, there is no connection between ratifying the European Council Decision and becoming an ESM member, as the latter requires separate ratification (Article 47 of the ESM Treaty).[24]

ESM and Stability Treaties: National Constitutional Perspectives on Their Relationship with EU Law

C. Austria, Germany, Hungary: The ESM Treaty and the Fiscal Compact – Ordinary Treaties or EU Amendment Treaties?

Several Member States have distinct procedures for parliamentary approval of ordinary treaties and EU amendment treaties; while the former may generally be approved by Parliament with a simple majority, the latter generally require qualified majorities. Austria, Germany and Hungary are among those states. In all three, the issue has arisen whether the ESM Treaty and/or the Fiscal Compact should be approved as an ordinary treaty, or as an EU amendment treaty.

The Hungarian Constitutional Court (*Magyarország Alkotmánybíróság*a) qualified the Fiscal Compact as an EU Treaty in the sense of Article E(2) of the (new) Hungarian Constitution, which entered into force on 1 January 2012. It held, on the basis of an interpretation of a similar provision in the previous constitution,[25] that every treaty that transfers competences specified in the Constitution, however minor, is an EU Treaty in the sense of Article E(2) on two conditions: first, that Hungary adheres to it as an EU Member State, together with other Member States, and second, that it leads to the exercise of the transferred competence by

23 ESM Treaty, Preamble, para. 7: 'As a consequence of joining the euro area, a Member State of the European Union should become an ESM Member'.

24 *Trybunale Konstytucyjnym*, Judgment K 33/12, paras. 7.3.4–7.3.9. See, further, K. Granat, 'Approval of Article 136 TFEU Amendment in Poland: The Perspective of the Constitutional Court on Eurozone Crisis Law', *European Public Law*, 21(1), 2015, 33–46, at 42. See also in this book Chapter 5, 'Differentiated Integration from the Perspective of Non-Euro Area Member States' by Thomas Beukers and Marijn van der Sluis.

25 *Magyarország Alkotmánybírósága*, Decision 22/2012 (V.11.) AB of 11 May 2012, paras. 47–9.

the Member States jointly, or by EU institutions. The Court added that the fact that the actual transfer does not take place at the moment of the entry into force of the treaty, but only at a later stage and under certain conditions, does not exempt the treaty from falling under Article E(2), because 'an international treaty can only be ratified once'.[26] The Fiscal Compact fulfilled the aforementioned conditions: it is concluded by the contracting parties as Member States of the EU, it interferes with budgetary competences of the Hungarian Parliament under the Hungarian Constitution and it bestows competences upon EU institutions.[27] It therefore required approval by the Hungarian Parliament with a two-thirds majority of its members.

In Austria and Germany, treaties that amend the EU's 'Treaty foundations' (*vertraglichen Grundlagen*) require approval by both houses of Parliament with two-thirds majority.[28] Despite the textual similarity, the ESM Treaty and the Fiscal Compact were treated differently in both states.

Although the German Constitutional Court qualified the ESM Treaty in its judgment of 19 June 2012 as an 'Angelegenheit der Europäischen Union' in the sense of Article 23(2) of the *Grundgesetz* (i.e. as an EU matter on which the German government should inform the *Bundestag* and the *Bundesrat* 'comprehensively and at the earliest possible moment'),[29] it never explicitly qualified it as an EU treaty amending the EU's treaty foundations.[30] Nevertheless, the political institutions decided that not only the ESM Treaty, but also the Fiscal Compact had to be approved by both houses of Parliament with the qualified majorities required for such treaties.[31]

In contrast to the German Court, the Austrian Constitutional Court (*Verfassungsgerichtshof*) explicitly decided the issue. As regards the ESM Treaty, it found that it did not amend Article 125 TFEU and therefore

[26] Ibid., paras. 50–1. The latter consideration refers to the fact that Hungary is not a euro area state yet and that the Fiscal Compact will only apply to it fully once the Hungarian derogation to belong to the euro area has been lifted by the Council, or earlier, if Hungary declares its intention to be bound by all or part of the provisions in Titles III and IV of the Fiscal Compact. See Fiscal Compact, Art. 14(5).

[27] *Magyarország Alkotmánybírósága*, Decision 22/2012, paras. 55–6.

[28] As per (Austrian) *Bundes-Verfassungsgesetz*, Art. 50(1)(2) jo.50(4) and (German) *Grundgesetz*, Art. 23(1)(3) jo. 79(2).

[29] *BVerfG*, Judgment 2 BvE 4/11 of 19 June 2012, point 144.

[30] Ibid., point 100.

[31] See C. Gröpl, 'Schritte zur Europäisierung des Haushaltsrechts', *Der Staat*, 52(1), 2013, 1–25, at 9–11.

was not an EU treaty in the sense of the Austrian Constitution. It did so relying on *Pringle*[32] and thus took the shortcut that the Polish Tribunal refused to take. In its judgment on the Fiscal Compact, the Court had no ECJ judgment on which it could rely. It based the assertion that Article 50(1)(2) of the *Bundes-Verfassungsgesetz* only relates to primary EU law – and not to treaties 'außerhalb des Unionsrechts' – on the text and the genesis of the provision. It underpinned its conclusion that the Compact is not primary EU law with references to Article 16 of the Fiscal Compact and to the fact that not all EU Member States are party to it.[33] Consequently, approval by only the *Nationalrat*, the Austrian lower house, with a simple majority sufficed.

Interestingly, the Austrian Court also ruled on the Interpretative Declaration on the European Stability Mechanism of 27 September 2012.[34] This Declaration, made by representatives of the ESM parties, was necessitated by the German Constitutional Court's judgment of 12 September 2012 and, inter alia, provides that the authorised capital stock of each ESM member cannot be raised without prior approval of each member's representative and with due regard to national procedures. The government of Corinthia alleged that the Declaration required the approval of the *Nationalrat* ex Article 50(1) *Bundes-Verfassungsgesetz*. Moreover, the ensuing 'illegality' of the Declaration would entail the illegality (of the approval) of the ESM Treaty, as the Declaration was a constitutive element of the will of the state parties to be bound by the ESM Treaty. The *Verfassungsgerichtshof*, however, found that it was a separate international agreement as well as a 'separate object of contestation' in the sense of Article 140a of the *Bundes-Verfassungsgesetz*. Therefore, even if the Declaration had been unconstitutional, it could not have taken the treaty down with it in its fall.[35] The Court subsequently found that the Declaration did not have to be approved by the *Nationalrat* at all, because – internally – it had no 'law changing or law increasing content' ('gesetzändernden oder gesetzesergänzenden Inhalt') in the sense of Article 50(1) of the *Bundes-Verfassungsgesetz*. That would only have been the case if the Declaration '[had] changed the meaning of

[32] *Verfassungsgerichtshof*, Decision SV 2/12–19 of 16 March 2013, para. III.B.3.4, point 52.

[33] *Verfassungsgerichtshof*, Decision SV 1/2013-15 of 3 October 2013, para. III. B.5.5.1, points 85–6.

[34] European Council, Interpretative Declaration, www.consilium.europa.eu/en/documents-publications/agreements-conventions/ratification/?v=decl&aid=2012002&pid=GR.

[35] *Verfassungsgerichtshof*, Decision SV 2/12–19, para. III.A. 3.3.3, point 28 and para. III.B, para. 3.2, point 48.

the affected provisions of ESM Treaty provisions to such an extent, that the *Nationalrat* could not have understood them in that way when the treaty was submitted to it for approval'.[36]

D. Interim Conclusion

The European Council Decision has raised an issue that, at some point in the future, may require adjudication by the ECJ or a national constitutional court, either separately or in conjunction: can governments, of their own accord, refuse to 'ratify' European Council Decisions ex Article 48(6) TEU? Moreover, the decision and the treaties have provided the Austrian and Hungarian Constitutional Courts and the Polish Constitutional Tribunal an occasion to clarify the terms 'single competence' in the Austrian Constitution, 'some of its competences' in the Hungarian Constitution and 'delegation of competence' in the Polish Constitution respectively. In addition, national court decisions on the dual nature of the treaties have clarified the concept of 'EU treaty' in the Austrian and Hungarian Constitutions. It is remarkable that, although Austria and Germany both require that treaties that affect the 'Treaty foundations of the EU' have to be approved by both houses of Parliament with qualified majorities, the ESM Treaty and Fiscal Compact were approved in that manner in Germany, while in Austria approval by the lower house with a simple majority sufficed.

3 Substantive Constitutional Issues

This second part provides an overview of the substantive elements of the national courts' judgments on the ESM Treaty and the Fiscal Compact. In the treatment of the German judgment, European Council Decision 2011/119 EU reappears.

The ESM Treaty

The ESM Treaty has been reviewed by the German *Bundesverfassungsgericht*, the Estonian Supreme Court (*Riigikohus*), the Irish Supreme Court and the Austrian *Verfassungsgerichtshof*. Before embarking upon their judgments, we examine a judgment of the Slovenian Constitutional

[36] Ibid., para. III.B.4.7.3.1, point 100.

Court (*Ustavno sodišče Republike Slovenije*) on the main precursor of the ESM, the European Financial Stability Facility (EFSF). In contrast to the ESM, the EFSF was designed as a temporary stability mechanism and as a *société anonyme* under Luxembourg law.[37]

A. Slovenia: Judicial Restraint, Limited Liabilities and Shared Responsibility

The judgment of the Constitutional Court of Slovenia on the act of Parliament providing the Slovenian guarantee for EFSF transactions heralds, in many respects, later decisions on the ESM Treaty by other national courts, inter alia, as regards the arguments lodged by the complainants. According to members of the National Assembly, the Slovenian lower house, various constitutional provisions were violated, boiling down to a loss of budgetary sovereignty (as the liability entered into was unclear and imprecise) and an infringement of Parliament's budgetary prerogatives (as Parliament's role was 'excessively reduced to merely being informed' of EFSF measures).[38] The Court dismissed all complaints.

Also, the rules that the Court inferred from the invoked constitutional provisions were a harbinger of later decisions made by the other courts: financial commitments must be limited, clear, and predictable, they may not be so huge as to deplete the national budget and they may not be raised without the approval of Parliament. The Court further pointed out that the contested act, by a reference to the act on the cooperation of the government and the National Assembly in EU affairs, did give the National Assembly rights to participate in the decision-making process of the 'Republic of Slovenia on a proposed funding programme'. Whether this implies that the act would have been unconstitutional if it had not provided these rights is unclear, but the emphasis that the Court

[37] The EFSF, the ESM Treaty and the Fiscal Compact were also the subject of judicial proceedings in Belgium and the Netherlands. For Belgium, see Grondwettelijk Hof (Constitutional Court), Judgments no. 111/2011 of 23 June 2011 (EFSF), no. 33/2012 of 1 March 2012 (EFSF), no. 156/2012 of 20 December 2012 (ESM) and 62/2016 of 28 April 2016 (Fiscal Compact). For the Netherlands, see Voorzieningenrechter (Summary Proceedings Judge), The Hague of 1 June 2012, LJN: BW7242. In all these cases, the complaints were dismissed for procedural reasons, for lack of interest, or for being outside the scope of competence of the relevant courts.

[38] *Ustavno Sodišče Republike Slovenije*, Judgment of 3 February 2011, Case U-I-178/10–18, paras. 2 and 4.

put on the government's duty to inform the National Assembly 'on all liabilities incurred' under the EFSF, may point in that direction.[39] Also invariably found in the judgments of other courts on the ESM Treaty is judicial restraint as one of the 'starting points for constitutional court review': the assertion of 'long-term economic impacts and their consequences on the stability of money' is a task 'for the government and legislature, not the courts [. . .] As a consequence, constitutional review of such issues is by necessity reserved'.[40]

Another review parameter formulated by the Slovenian Court regards the euro area Member States' shared responsibility to provide financial stability: 'in a case such as the case under consideration, which involves the interdependence of the Member States and their economies, concerted action among euro area Member States is required.'[41] The Estonian Supreme Court followed a similar line of reasoning.

B. Estonia: Instability as a Threat to 'Peoples' Income, Quality of Life and Social Security'

The Estonian chancellor of justice (*Õiguskantsler*), an independent institution that supervises compliance with the Estonian Constitution, alleged before the Supreme Court that the emergency voting procedure in Article 4(4) of the ESM Treaty was unconstitutional. While a decision to grant financial support generally requires unanimity within the Board of Governors,[42] consisting of the ministers of finance of the participating states, Article 4(4) allows the Board to grant support with a majority of 85 per cent of the votes if the Commission and the ECB both conclude that the economic and financial sustainability of the euro area is at stake. Because the number of votes a minister may cast under the provision is related to his state's contribution to the authorised capital stock of the ESM, and Estonia (originally) contributed only 0.186 per cent, the Estonian minister of finance lacks veto-power under the provision, along with many of his colleagues but excluding those of the three major countries. Article 4(4) therefore conflicted with the principles of parliamentary democracy and the budgetary powers of the Estonian Parliament (*Riigikogus*): it would not have 'the option to affect through the Government of the Republic the conditions of a financial assistance agreement'.[43]

[39] Ibid., resp. paras. 25, 29 and 30. [40] Ibid., para. 9. [41] Ibid., paras. 7–8.
[42] ESM Treaty, Article 5(6)(f) and Article 4(3).
[43] *Riigikohus*, Constitutional Judgment 3-4-1-6-1212 of July 2012, paras. 6–6.

In its judgment, the Estonian Supreme Court agreed with the chancellor that Article 4(4) infringed on fundamental constitutional principles: the right to decide on the budget is one of the core powers of the Parliament and cannot be delegated to the executive, not even temporarily.[44] This entails, if I understand it correctly, that the Estonian minister generally may only approve support measures if the Estonian Parliament consents to them.[45] Therefore, Article 4(4) infringes not only upon the budgetary prerogatives of the Estonian Parliament and consequently 'the principle of a democratic state subject to the rule of law and of the state's financial sovereignty', but also, indirectly, with the rights of the Estonian people, whose sovereignty lies at the basis of that of the state, to take their own decisions, irrespective of external influences.[46] The Court nevertheless, albeit with the smallest possible majority of 10 of the 19 judges, accepted the infringement of Estonian sovereignty by performing a proportionality test and interpreting the Estonian Constitution in a manner extremely favourable to international cooperation and European integration.

As regards sovereignty, which Article 1 of the Estonian Constitution describes as 'timeless and inalienable', the Court endorsed the position that 'membership of the EU and international organizations has become a natural part of sovereignty in this day and age'.[47] Since Estonia became a euro area member in 2011, as authorised by the Estonian people in the accession referendum in 2003, 'the economic and financial sustainability of the euro area is contained in the constitutional values of Estonia' and serves the duty of the legislative, executive and judicial institutions to guarantee the constitutional rights and freedoms of the Estonians (Article 14 of the Estonian Constitution). A threat to the stability of the euro area is therefore also a threat to the financial and economic stability of Estonia in general, and more particularly to the 'people's income, quality of life and social security'.[48]

Not only was the aim pursued by Article 4(4) legitimate, but the means employed were also appropriate, necessary and proportional *stricto sensu*. The emergency procedure gives no absolute guarantee that aid will be provided when necessary, but at least facilitates the decision-making

[44] Ibid., paras. 133–8. See also C. Ginter, 'Constitutionality of the European Stability Mechanism in Estonia: Applying Proportionality to Sovereignty' *European Constitutional Law Review*, 9(2), 2013, 335–54.

[45] *Riigikohus*, Constitutional Judgment 3-4-1-6-1212, paras. 150 and 133–8.

[46] Ibid., paras. 153 and 127. [47] Ibid., para. 130. [48] Ibid., paras. 154–69.

process. There is no other decision-making procedure that makes it equally plausible that threats to the euro area will be countered and that simultaneously interferes less with Estonian sovereignty: raising the qualified majority threshold to above 99.814 per cent would undo the infringement of Estonian sovereignty, but also devoid the procedure of any meaning.[49] Also, the balance between an infringement of Estonian financial sovereignty and democracy on the one hand and the protection of constitutional rights and freedoms by protecting the stability of the euro area on the other, worked out in favour of the latter. The Court downplayed the seriousness of the interference (it is implausible that Estonia will have to pay its full share of the capital stock, inter alia, because only states that have implemented the Fiscal Compact correctly qualify for financial support) and emphasised the importance of the emergency procedure: the stability of the euro can only be ensured in cooperation with the other euro area states, Estonia itself in the future might need to appeal to the fund for the protection of rights and freedoms of Estonians and cooperation within the EU and other international organisations provides the best way of 'guaranteeing the preservation of the Estonian people, the Estonian language and the Estonian culture'.[50]

The application of a proportionality test to justify the infringement of Estonia's sovereignty has been fiercely criticised by dissenters as some sort of *lèse majesté*: 'Sovereignty is not an object of trade'.[51] But if they had the chance to read the Irish Supreme Court's judgment before formulating their own opinions, they might have been inspired to subscribe to the dictum (not the reasoning) of the Estonian judgment. As it happens, the Irish Court applied the traditional concept of sovereignty wished for by the dissenters to the treaty – *and* approved it.

C. Ireland: No Abdication of Sovereignty

Thomas Pringle's name will forever be associated with the ECJ judgment of 27 November 2012, in which the European Court answered preliminary questions posed by the Irish Supreme Court on the validity of European Council Decision 2011/199/EU and the compatibility of the ESM Treaty with EU law. As is well known, the ECJ ruled that Decision 2011/199/EU is valid and that EU law does not preclude the conclusion of an agreement such as the ESM Treaty between the euro area states.[52]

[49] Ibid., paras. 176–84. [50] Ibid., paras. 186–203.
[51] The quote is from the dissenting opinion of Justice Jüri Ilvest. [52] *Pringle*.

Less well known is that the Irish Supreme Court, in its decision of 31 July 2012, for which the reasons were only delivered on 19 October 2012, not only decided to pose preliminary questions, but also ruled on Pringle's claim that the ESM Treaty involved a transfer of Irish sovereignty and required a constitutional amendment – and, thus, a referendum – in accordance with Article 46(2) of the Irish Constitution.

The Supreme Court dismissed the claims using the so-called Crotty-test, developed in the eponymous 1987 case. That case addressed whether ratification of the provisions of Title III of the Single European Act (SEA) on European Political (Foreign) Policy Cooperation necessitated a constitutional amendment. The contested SEA provisions required the Irish government to adapt its foreign policy positions to those of the other contracting states, thereby allegedly involving a transfer of sovereignty. The Supreme Court, with a three to two majority, agreed.[53]

Pringle, a member of the Irish lower house (*Dáil Éireann*), submitted that the ESM Treaty led to a similar abdication of sovereignty by allowing majority decision-making by the ESM institutions. The Court, in Justice Clarke's narrative, refused to apply a model of sovereignty which sees 'the ability of nations (and especially small nations) to achieve self-determination as being enhanced by a pooling of sovereignty so as to give greater practical leverage at an international level': that is not 'the model adopted by the Irish Constitution'.[54] But it nevertheless approved the treaty with a majority of six out of seven, including Clarke. Chief Justice Denham analysed that the ESM has two functions: to raise funds and to borrow money, and that neither function has the alleged effect. As regards the second function, he held that although the ESM institutions can take various decisions without the consent of Ireland, particularly also in the emergency procedure, these decisions do not *determine* the ESM's policy, but merely concern the implementation of the policy: the ESM's policy itself is defined by Ireland, together with the other members, in the ESM Treaty.[55] As regards the first function, he noted, as did the Estonian Court before him,[56] that a decision to raise the authorised capital stock requires a unanimous decision of the Board of

[53] Supreme Court, *Crotty* v. *An Taoiseach* (1987), IESC 4; (1987) IR 71, para. 62.

[54] Supreme Court, *Pringle* v. *Government of Ireland & ors* (2012) IESC 47, point 8.2. Judgment of J. Clarke.

[55] Ibid., para. 17viii–17xi. Judgment of C. J. Denham. J. Hardiman, dissenting, specifically opposed the emergency voting procedure: ibid., points 181–2.

[56] *Riigikohus*, Constitutional Judgment 3-4-1-6-1212, paras. 105–6. Understandably, a reference to the Interpretative Declaration of 27 September 2012 is missing in the Irish

Governors and, in Ireland, the approval of the *Dáil Éireann*.[57] The German Constitutional Court was not so sure about this.

D. Germany: No Violation of German Constitutional Identity

The *Bundesverfassungsgericht*'s decision of 12 September 2012 on the ESM Treaty is in line with those of the same Court on the Treaty of Lisbon of 30 June 2009 and on the so-called Euro rescue package, including the EFSF, of 7 September 2011. The decision is set in the key of the 'Verfassungsidentität des Grundgesetzes' (German constitutional identity), of which the right to vote in Article 38 of the *Grundgesetz* is part and parcel. It guarantees German citizens free and equal participation in the exercise of state power and is, in turn, connected to the budgetary prerogatives of the *Bundestag*, which are a central element of national democratic will formation. The *Bundestag* may not, therefore, relinquish its 'haushaltspolitische Gesamtverantwortung' (its overall budgetary responsibility).[58] This has consequences for the internal legal order as it can legitimise the introduction of a balanced budget rule that aims to safeguard Parliament's budgetary prerogatives in the future.[59] It also has consequences for Germany's participation in international and European integration: the *Bundestag* must remain 'Herr seiner Entschlüsse' (master of its own decisions), free from interference of EU institutions or EU Member States.[60]

The designation of the EMU as a 'stability community' is directly connected to this: the independence of the ECB, the objective of price stability, the prohibition of monetary financing, the 'no bailout' clause and the obligation of a sustainable budget all protect the budgetary prerogatives of the *Bundestag*. But although the design of the EMU as a 'stability community' is a *sine qua non* for Germany's participation, it is not immutable and may be changed to a certain extent to ensure the

judgment, the dictum was published on 31 July 2012 – i.e. before publication of reasoning of the Irish judgment on 19 October.

57 Supreme Court, *Pringle*, para. 17v. Judgment of C. J. Denham.

58 *BVerfG*, 2 BvR 1390/12 of 12 September 2012, paras. 104–8 (208–12 in English version; hence Engl.).

59 *BVerfG*, 2 BvR 1099/10 of 7 September 2011, para. 104; *BVerfG*, 2 BvR 1390/12, para. 120 (224 Engl.);

60 Ibid., para. 109 (213 Engl.).

proper functioning of the euro area. The German Court already stated as much in its *Maastricht* judgment.[61]

Regarding Decision 2011/199/EU, individual complainants argued that Article 136(3) TFEU constituted a fundamental shift in the EMU towards a 'transfer and liability union'.[62] To a certain extent the Court agreed: Article 136(3) brings about 'a fundamental reshuffling of the EMU'[63] by putting the principles of independence of the national budgets and of the euro area Member States' reliance on the financial markets for the funding of their debts, into perspective. However, it does so only to a limited extent, since the 'authorisation in Article 136(3) TFEU' ('die Ermächtigung des Art. 136 Abs. 3 AEUV') to establish a permanent assistance programme *à la* the ESM leaves the aforementioned fundamental elements of the EMU design essentially intact. Moreover, despite the threat to price stability it might bring about, the Court had to respect the legislature's decision to establish an ESM in view of the 'Einschätzungsspielraums der zuständigen Verfassungsorgane' (the latitude of assessment of the competent constitutional institutions).[64] This is one of the many expressions of judicial restraint that characterise the judgment of 12 September 2012.[65]

Here a fundamental difference of perspective between the German Court and the ECJ on Article 136(3) TFEU comes to light. While the latter found that the new provision did not affect the structure of the EMU and was thus merely declaratory,[66] the former qualified it as a game changer and as providing the authorisation to establish the ESM. It should be noted that this depiction of the German Court's reasoning is drawn from the summary proceedings judgment of 9 September 2012, which was rendered before the ECJ rendered *Pringle*. In its final judgment of 14 March 2014, the German Court stuck to its point, albeit with two subtle nuances: first, it added that the fundamental reshuffling was the consequence of Article 136(3) TFEU *in combination* with the establishment of the ESM and, second, that a fundamental reshuffling was

[61] Ibid., para. 118 (222 Engl.); BVerGE 89, 155 (Maastricht).

[62] *BVerfG*, 2 BvR 1390/12, para. 45 (149 Engl.).

[63] Ibid., para. 128 (232 Engl.): 'Art. 136 Abs. 3 AEUV bedeutet zwar eine grundlegende Umgestaltung der bisherigen Wirtschafts- und Währungsunion'.

[64] Ibid., para 130 (234 Engl.).

[65] See further M. Wendel, 'Judicial Restraint and the Return to Openness: The Decision of the German Federal Constitutional Court on the ESM and the Fiscal Treaty of 12 September 2012', *German Law Journal*, 14(1), 2013, 21–52.

[66] *Pringle*, para. 72.

taking place 'in the perspective of the understanding of the treaty that Germany had when it co-founded the EMU'.[67] However, the German Court agreed with the ECJ from the start that Article 136(3) TFEU does not concern a transfer of (budgetary) competences to the EU and merely 'confirms the sovereignty of the Member States' to establish a mechanism *à la* the ESM under certain conditions.[68]

Also, the ESM Treaty itself did not violate German constitutional identity. The *Bundestag* may agree to certain financial aid arrangements in a spirit of solidarity ('solidarische Hilfsmassnahme'), even if the financial consequences are of structural importance to the German budget,[69] on the condition that the financial commitments undertaken do not lead to a depletion of its budget authority and are quantitatively limited.

The constitutional review of the fulfilment of the first condition is very limited: the German Court allows German politics ample discretion. It only intervenes if the budget authority would run on empty for a considerable period of time.[70] The German government and the *Bundestag*'s assessment that this was not the case, although highly controversial in economic circles, had to be respected as it was not 'evidently erroneous'.[71]

As regards the second condition, the limitation of financial commitments, the German Court demanded an effective international reservation as a prerequisite for ratification, to preclude an interpretation of the ESM Treaty allowing the state parties' previously agreed-upon share in the stock capital to be raised without treaty amendment and, thus, without the consent of the *Bundestag*.[72] This was effected by the aforementioned Interpretative Declaration.[73]

The Court had yet another arrow in its quiver. To exercise its 'haushaltspolitische Gesamtverantwortung', the *Bundestag* should not only co-decide on every large-scale aid measure, as the ESM approval act and the

[67] *BVerfG*, Judgment of 18 March 2014 – 2 BvR 1390/12, para. 180: 'Zwar bedeuten die Aufnahme von Art. 136 Abs. 3 AEUV und die Errichtung des Europäischen Stabilitätsmechanismus – ausgehend von dem Vertragsverständnis, in dem Deutschland die Wirtschafts – und Währungsunion mitbegründet hat – durchaus eine grundlegende Umgestaltung der ursprünglichen Wirtschafts – und Währungsunion'.

[68] Ibid., para. 132 (236 Engl.); *Pringle*, paras. 72–3.

[69] *BVerfG*, 2 BvR 1390/12, para. 110 (214 Engl.); see also *BVerfG*, 2 BvE 2/08, para. 256.

[70] *BVerfG*, 2 BvR 1390/12, paras. 112–3 (216–7 Engl.).

[71] Ibid., para. 167 (271 Engl.).

[72] Ibid., paras. 147–9 (251–3 Engl.).

[73] See n. 35.

financial act on the ESM duly provided,[74] but also be fully informed: the 'core of the right of Parliament to be informed' is even part of German constitutional identity.[75] Consequently, the provisions declaring ESM documents inviolable (Article 30[5] of the ESM Treaty) and imposing a duty of professional secrecy on (ex)members of the Board of Governors (Article 34), ought not to be used to withhold information that Parliaments need to take their decisions. To effectively bar such an interpretation, the Court required yet another international reservation.[76] The Interpretative Declaration also accounts for this.[77] The Austrian Constitutional Court referred to it twice.

E. Austria: Only a 'Single Sovereign Right' Transferred by the ESM Treaty

On the substantive elements of the judgment of the Austrian *Verfassungsgerichtshof* on the ESM Treaty we can be very short. The treaty was allegedly unconstitutional because it transferred more than a 'single sovereign right' in the sense of Article 9(2) of the *Bundes-Verfassungsgesetz* to ESM institutions, to the Commission and to the ECJ. The treaty would also violate constitutional obligations to strive for a balanced budget and a thrifty, cost-effective and functional organisation of the national economy, inter alia, because the financial obligations entered into only aggravated the Austrian budgetary deficit and debt.

The Austrian Court rejected the complaints with arguments reminiscent of those used by the Irish Supreme Court and the German Constitutional Court. As regards the 'single sovereign right' complaint, it argued, on the one hand, referring to scholarship, that the phrase should not be interpreted too narrowly and, on the other, that the ESM had a limited objective and that the transferred competences merely regarded

[74] *BVerfG*, 2 BvR 1390/12, para. 111(215 Engl.). The emergency procedure under ESM Treaty, Art. 4(4) played no role whatsoever in the judgment, simply because Germany cannot be outvoted. We may assume that the *BVerfG* would have declared the ESM Treaty unconstitutional if it would have been different.

[75] Ibid., para. 111 (215 Engl.). These conditions were already formulated in the Euro Rescue Package/EFSF judgment of 7 September 2011: *BVerfG*, 2 BvR 987/10 of 7 September 2011. See A. von Ungern-Sternberg, 'Parliaments – Fig Leaf or Heartbeat of Democracy? German Federal Constitutional Court Judgment of 7 September 2011 – Euro Rescue Package', *European Constitutional Law Review*, 8(2), 2012, 304–22.

[76] *BVerfG*, 2 BvR 1390/12, paras. 150–5 (254–260 Engl.).

[77] See n. 35.

executive decisions.[78] As regards the financial and economic obligations imposed by the Austrian Constitution, the Austrian Court replied that it had to respect the decisions of the Austrian government and the *Nationalrat* to participate in the ESM to counter 'possible, unforeseeable economic and social damage', a decision that involved multiple 'general political and complex financial, monetary and economic assessments and considerations'. That options other than the one chosen by the political institutions remained open, as the complainant had argued, concerned a legal-political question ('rechtspolitische Frage') that was not for the Court to answer.[79]

Furthermore, it is noteworthy that the Austrian Court twice sought recourse to the Interpretative Declaration of 27 September 2012. First, to refute that the capital stock of the state parties could be raised without treaty amendment. Second, to rebut the argument that provisions of the ESM Treaty could frustrate the *Nationalrat*'s right to participate in ESM matters, as provided for in the Articles 50a–50d of the *Bundesverfassungs-Gesetz*.[80]

The Fiscal Compact

The most important provisions of the Fiscal Compact relate to national budgetary law. The treaty obliges the contracting parties to anchor a balanced budget rule in their national law and to install an automatic correction mechanism, to be triggered in case of a significant deviation from the budget rule. Moreover, the treaty assumes the existence of an independent national budgetary supervisor. Therefore, if not yet in place, this supervisor would have to be created (Article 3).

There are two sources of inspiration for this budgetary arrangement. The first is EU law. The budget rule in the treaty is conceptually similar to the balanced budget rule contained in Article 2bis of Regulation (EC) No 1466/97, as amended by Regulation (EU) No 1175/2011, albeit marginally stricter. The second source is the German *Grundgesetz*, which, since 2009, imposes a more-or-less similar budget rule.[81] For

78 *Verfassungsgerichtshof*, Decision SV 2/12–19, para. B. 3.6.3, point 61.
79 Ibid, para. B.3.5.3, point 57.
80 Ibid, resp. para. B.4.4.3, point 83, and para. B.4.6.3, points 93 and 94.
81 See A. Thiele, 'The 'German Way' of Curbing Public Debt', *European Constitutional Law Review*, 11(1), 2015, 30–54.

this reason, I first discuss the German judgment in which the Fiscal Compact was reviewed and only then the French one, even though it was rendered earlier. The Austrian *Verfassungsgerichtshof* also reviewed the treaty.

A. Germany: 'Weitgehenden Deckungsgleichheit' and the Democratic Nature of the Budget Rules

In its judgment of 7 September 2011 on the Euro Rescue Package/EFSF, the German Court already made clear that a balanced budget rule is not undemocratic *per se*. To the contrary, a limitation on the German Parliament's budgetary prerogatives may be necessary to protect the prerogatives of Parliament and its successors in the longer term, and thereby German democracy.[82] In its judgment of 12 September 2012, the Court added that a limitation on budgetary prerogatives may also be dictated by EU or international law and that it is up to the legislature, not the Court, to decide whether and to what extent a limitation is necessary. The Court's competence in this field is limited to safeguarding the 'openness of the democratic process' so that different majorities in the future can opt for another policy.[83]

In view of these considerations, and of the close resemblance ('weitgehenden Deckungsgleichheit') between the budget rules in the treaty, in EU law and in German constitutional law, the Court had no trouble dismissing the complaints against the treaty's budget rule.[84] It just as easily refuted the allegation that the absence of a termination clause in the treaty would deprive German politics for all eternity of the possibility to decide on another budgetary policy. It pointed out that any treaty may be ended with the consent of all contracting parties, and that a treaty also may be terminated unilaterally in the event of a fundamental change of the circumstances on which the will of the parties to be bound by the treaty is founded (*clausula rebus sic stantibus*; Article 62 of the Convention on the Law of Treaties): if Germany would withdraw from the EU or the EMU, the bottom would fall out of the Fiscal Compact.[85]

[82] *BVerfG*, 2 BvR 987/10, para. 104.
[83] *BVerfG*, 2 BvR 1390/12, paras. 120–4 (224–8 Engl.).
[84] Ibid., paras. 198–206 (302–310 Engl.).
[85] Ibid., paras. 214 and 215 (318 and 319 Engl.).

B. France: Avoiding Constitutional Amendment for the Incorporation of the Budget Rule

The decision of the French Constitutional Council, the *Conseil constitutionnel*, is short and scarcely reasoned, as is usual. The Council found the treaty's budget rule as such no more problematic than did the *Bundesverfassungsgericht*: it did not 'infringe upon the essential conditions for the exercise of national sovereignty any more than the earlier commitments of budget discipline' in EU law, which it 'copied and accentuated'.[86]

The greater part of the French decision is dedicated to the issue of how to implement the balanced budget rule into national law. The Council offered two alternatives derived from Article 3(2) of the Fiscal Compact, which requires that the budget rule should be written into national law 'through provisions of binding force and permanent character, preferably constitutional, or otherwise guaranteed to be fully respected and adhered to throughout the national budgetary processes'. The first option offered is based on the first part of the cited provision: prescribing the rule bindingly to government and the legislature. This would infringe the budgetary prerogatives of both government and Parliament and the principle of annual budgets and it would require a constitutional amendment.[87] The second option is based on the second part of the cited treaty provision: enacting an organic act establishing that (ordinary) 'acts on the multiannual guidelines for public finances' determine the French medium-term budgetary objective in conformity with the treaty's budget rule. This would *not* require a constitutional amendment, as neither the relevant organic act nor the ensuing acts on the multiannual guidelines for public finances would bind government and Parliament in the preparation and adoption of the national budget.[88]

The second option was chosen by the president of the Republic and his ruling majority through the enactment of the organic act 'on the multiannual guidelines for and governance of public finances'.[89] This organic act not only prescribes that acts 'on the multiannual guidelines for public finances' set France's medium-term budgetary objectives in line with the

[86] Conseil Constitutionnel, Decision 2012–653 DC of 9 August 2012, para. 16.
[87] Ibid., para. 21.
[88] Ibid., paras. 22–8. See also Conseil Constitutionnel, Decision 2012–658 DC of 13 December 2012, para 12.
[89] Organic Law of 17 December 2012 relative à la programmation et à la gouvernance des finances publiques.

treaty (Article 1), but also installs an Haut Conseil des Finances Publiques (HCFP),[90] which monitors whether draft budgets conform to the acts on the multiannual guidelines for public finances (Article 14).

The question as to how this arrangement – an organic act obliging an ordinary act to set fiscal parameters that do not bind the government and the budget legislature – can legally guarantee that the treaty's budget rule is 'fully respected and adhered to throughout' the budgetary process, as the second part of Article 3(2) of the Fiscal Compact requires, is a rhetorical one: it cannot. Politically, however, it will do the trick: any deviation from the budget rule will be immediately highlighted by the HCFP and will provide the parliamentary opposition with political dynamite. Moreover, the Constitutional Council pointed out that the budget rule binds the government and budget legislature thanks to the treaty's insertion into the monistic French legal order with supra-legislative (and infra-constitutional) status (Article 55 of the French Constitution). That entails, inter alia, that the French Parliament will have 'to comply with its provisions when enacting finance laws and social security financing laws'.[91] The Council also made clear that, if necessary, it would 'help' Parliament to comply, not on the basis of either the Fiscal Compact or the organic law, but relying upon Articles 14 and 15 of the Declaration of the Rights of Men and Citizens of 1789. It deduced from these provisions that 'the State's revenue and expenditure must be presented in a sincere manner'[92] and announced it would review whether budget laws have been 'genuinely' enacted, taking into account the opinions of independent institutions', amongst them the HCFP.[93] In short, the Council itself guarantees compliance with the treaty's budget rule.[94]

The decision (which was heaven-sent for the newly elected president François Hollande who, as a candidate for the presidency, had promised not to change the French Constitution on behalf of a balanced budget rule), has puzzled this commentator for some time. A binding national provision infringes upon the prerogatives of the budget legislature and requires a constitutional amendment, yet an equally binding treaty

[90] See in this book Chapter 4, 'Creation and Reform of Independent Fiscal Institutions in EU Member States: Incomplete and Insufficient Work in Progress?' by Diane Fromage for discussion of the creation and reform of Independent Fiscal Institutions through euro-crisis law.

[91] Conseil Constitutionnel, Decision 2012–653 DC, para. 18.

[92] Ibid., para. 13.

[93] Ibid., paras. 22 and 27.

[94] M. Lombard, 'Le Futur Rôle de Régulateur Financier du Conseil Constitutionnel', *L'Actualité Juridique. Droit Administratif*, 31, 2012, 1717–18, at 1717.

provision does not infringe upon these prerogatives and does not require a constitutional amendment. But what the Council means is this: there is, so to speak, nothing 'intrinsically' unconstitutional in binding the legislature to a budget rule. However, to do so in a purely national provision requires a constitutional amendment, because, apart from treaties, the budget authorities can only be bound by the Constitution.

C. Austria: Downplaying the Competences of the EU Institutions

Once again, the Austrian judgment will not detain us for very long, but it may coax a smile from the reader as the plaintiffs, members of the *Nationalrat*, got a taste of their own medicine. They submitted that Article 3(1)(b) of the Fiscal Compact unconstitutionally limited the Austrian budget legislature's manoeuvrability. The provision renders Article 3(1)(a), which states that contracting parties should have a balanced budget or run a surplus, less compelling, since it provides that a budget is deemed to be balanced or in surplus if the structural deficit is not higher than 0.5 per cent of GDP. A declaration of unconstitutionality of Article 3(1)(b) would have left the obligation under section (a) intact – the Austrian Court does not rule *ultra petitum*. In that case, the Austrian budget legislature would have had to enact *genuinely* balanced or in surplus budgets, instead of ones with slight deficits, and thus be even worse off. The Court therefore declared the complaint inadmissible.[95]

The plaintiffs also alleged that the Articles 5 and 8 of the Fiscal Compact overstepped the boundaries of allowable transfers under Article 9(2) of the *Bundes-Verfassungsgesetz*. The Court put the importance of the transfers into perspective, inter alia, by (implicitly) accepting the government's submission that the decisions of EU institutions on the basis of the Fiscal Compact lacked the legal effects attached to decisions of EU institutions on the basis of the EU treaties.[96] In other words, they are not endowed with direct effect and primacy. By downplaying the importance of the competence transfers in the treaty, the Austrian Court followed in the footsteps of its French and German brethren, as we shall see in the next part of this contribution.

[95] *Verfassungsgerichtshof*, SV 1/2013-15, para. 33. [96] Ibid., paras. 86–8.

4. A Contextual and Comparative Analysis

This third part consists of a contextual and comparative analysis of several issues raised by the national judgments previously discussed. We first deal with problems related to *ex post* treaty review and the predicament of the courts. After that, we analyse the national constitutional impact of the treaties and identify elements of the argumentative strategies used by the courts to take the heat out of them. Finally, we discuss the legitimising effects of the judgments and look at their consequences for the further reconstruction of the EMU.

A. *The Predicament of the Courts*

The ESM Treaty entered into force on 27 September 2012, the Fiscal Compact on 1 January 2013. In five states, constitutional review took place prior to ratification (Estonia, France, Germany, Ireland and Hungary), in Austria and Poland thereafter. Moreover, in Poland, an appeal against the Fiscal Compact is still pending.

In general, *ex post* review of EU treaties poses several problems. It places a burden on the functioning of the EU system and affects legal certainty: declaring a treaty unconstitutional years after its entry into force conjures all manner of known and unknown consequences for the EU and for (at least) 28 states. It also strains judicial review by placing courts in an almost untenable position: even if judges, in their heart of hearts, consider a treaty unconstitutional, they will think twice before passing judgment accordingly. This may affect the courts' reasoning, and thereby even the (perceived) legitimacy of their judgments. One is therefore tempted to subscribe to, and even extend, the president of the Austrian Constitutional Court's call for a constitutional amendment in Austria exchanging *ex post* for *ex ante* review.[97]

However, at least in the present case, these arguments need to be viewed in perspective. First, neither of the two treaties required ratification by all signatories, but only by 12 of them (Article 14[2] of the Fiscal Compact), or by as many signatories as was needed to pass the threshold of 90 per cent of the capital stock (Article 48[1] of the ESM Treaty). A Polish (or Belgian) finding that the Fiscal Compact is

[97] See the Report on Austria, Annex 1.1. prepared by D. Jaros for the Constitutional Change through Euro Crisis Law project of the EUI Law Department and available on its website: www.eurocrisislaw.eui.eu, http://eurocrisislaw.eui.eu/austria/.

unconstitutional would therefore not affect that treaty's functioning for the other signatories. Neither would an Austrian declaration of the unconstitutionality of the ESM Treaty have blocked that treaty's entry into force, at least not formally, as Austria represents no more than 2.7757 per cent of the capital stock. In this sense, the smaller states (ESM Treaty) and to some extent all individual states (Fiscal Compact) were 'legally insignificant'.[98] Second, the courts that reviewed the ESM Treaty and the Fiscal Compact *ex ante* were also under tremendous pressure to approve them, perhaps even more so because, at the time, the Eurocrisis was more virulent than it seems today and the consequences of a declaration of unconstitutionality would have been perhaps more profound.

Indeed, in view of the enormous financial, economic and political interests at stake, one wonders whether *any* court had an alternative to approving the treaties. I do not think so. Even if non-participation of the smaller states would not have prevented the ESM Treaty's into force, it would have broken the united front of the euro area states facing the Eurocrisis, isolated the relevant states in the EMU politically and perhaps even unleashed dynamics with unpredictable political (and possibly also financial and economic) consequences – who knows. On the other hand, the consequences of Germany's potential inability to take part in the ESM or France's refusal to ratify the Fiscal Compact were not unpredictable. In both instances, the euro area's united response to the Eurocrisis would have been aborted: in the latter instance, for political reasons and, in the former, for legal reasons as well (the ESM Treaty could not enter into force without Germany). It would be naïve to think that considerations of this kind were not in the back of the minds of the judges when they reviewed the treaties: constitutional law is not an abstract science and constitutional courts do not operate in a societal and political vacuum (and luckily so).

However, this does not mean that the judgments fail to convince. Actually, quite the contrary: The treaties did not pose as great a threat to the constitutional orders of the euro area Member States as thought at first, in part because the courts skilfully dismantled the potentially constitutionally explosive content of several treaty provisions, as will be argued in the next section.

98 Bardutzky and Fahey, 'Who Got to Adjudicate the EU's Financial Crisis and Why?', p. 346.

B. The National Constitutional Impact of the Treaties and Strategies Employed by the Courts

Although the Fiscal Compact has been fiercely criticised, also by the present author,[99] careful analysis shows that the limitations placed by its budget rule on the freedom of national budget authorities are only marginally stricter than those flowing from EU law proper. The courts could not have declared the Fiscal Compact's budget rule unconstitutional without at the same time bringing the constitutionality of the essentially similar budget rule in the Stability and Growth Pact into the discussion, and thereby the participation of their states in the EMU – and ultimately even in the EU.

Also, the competences transferred to the EU institutions were not the threats to the autonomy of the national budget authorities that they at first seemed to be, also because the French and the German courts have stripped the relevant provisions to the skin. Take Article 5 of the Fiscal Compact, which obliges euro area states subject to an excessive deficit procedure (Article 126 TFEU) to submit a 'budgetary and economic partnership programme' specifying detailed structural reforms meant to correct the deficit; the programme is 'defined' in EU law after approval by Commission and Council. The French Council ruled that these competences were not objectionable, as the relevant decisions do not 'have any binding consequences under national law'.[100] The German Court, referring to its French counterpart, stated that the provision does not give EU institutions a (direct) hold (*Durchgriff*) on the freedom of national legislatures to shape their budgets.[101] The French Council and the German Court also agreed that the Commission's competence to propose 'common principles' for the automatic correction mechanism (Article 3 [2] of the Fiscal Compact) does not give that institution the right to issue substantive budgetary directives.[102] Also as regards the ECJ's competence to rule on contracting parties' compliance with Article 3(2) (as per Article 8 of the Fiscal Compact) the French Council and German Court

[99] L. Besselink and J. H. Reestman, 'Editorial: The Fiscal Compact and the European Constitutions: "Europe Speaking German"', *European Constitutional Law Review*, 8(1), 2012, 1–7.

[100] *Conseil Constitutionnel*, Decision 2012-653 DC, paras. 13 and. 32.

[101] *BVerfG*, 2 BvR 987/10, para. 207 (311 Engl.).

[102] *Conseil Constitutionnel*, Decision 2012-653 DC, point 25; *BVerfG*, 2 BvR 1390/12, para. 211 (315 Engl.).

were in agreement: the ECJ is only allowed to check whether the budget rule has been correctly implemented, not whether the implemented rule is abided by.[103]

There remains the obligation to ensure compliance with the treaty's budget rule in national law, thereby indirectly also with the similar EU budget rule. The French Council took the sting out of this obligation by allowing its implementation in legal instruments which do not bind the budget legislature.[104]

The objections made against the ESM Treaty were, essentially, that it undermined national parliamentary democracy. It did so, allegedly, by the enormous liabilities undertaken, which – should they materialise – would prominently limit the room for manoeuvre of the national budget authorities, and by the loss of national Parliaments' grip on the disbursement of taxpayers' money by the ESM institutions (i.e. by the assembled national executives), on some occasions potentially even against the will of some of the participating states. Several elements of the argumentative strategies employed by the constitutional courts to take the edge off these arguments catch the eye.

A first element regards emphasising that the euro area states are all in the same boat, and that the stability of the euro area is somehow in the common interest. That argument is presented in various modalities: common responsibility (Slovenian Constitutional Court), solidarity (German Constitutional Court) and is sometimes mixed with arguments related to self-interest. This is best expressed by the Estonian Supreme Court, which stressed that the stability of the euro area can only be ensured in cooperation with the other euro area states and that Estonia itself might in the future need to appeal to the ESM for the protection of the rights and freedoms of Estonians.[105] And, although Poland is not yet an ESM contracting party, the Polish Constitutional Tribunal, leaving

[103] *Conseil Constitutionnel*, Decision 2012–653 DC, para. 30; *BVerfG*, 2 BvR 1390/12, para. 212; compare *Verfassungsgerichtshof*, SV 1/2013-15, para. 90.

[104] Also, for example, the Netherlands have implemented the rule in a formally non-binding way for the budget legislature, and arguably there is no need to do so in a binding way, at least not in monist states like France and the Netherlands. See J. H. Reestman, 'The Fiscal Compact: Europe's Not Always Able to Speak German', *European Constitutional Law Review*, 9(3), 2013, 480–500. Even in Ireland, where ratification of the Fiscal Compact required a constitutional amendment, the budget rule does not have constitutional force. See R. O'Gorman, 'An Analysis of the Method and Efficacy of Ireland's Incorporation of the Fiscal Compact', in Adams, Fabbrini and Larouche (eds.), *The Constitutionalization of European Budgetary Constraints*, pp. 273–95, pp. 278ff.

[105] *Riigikohus*, Constitutional Judgment 3–4-1–6-1212, paras. 186–203.

little doubt as to the fate of a future constitutional complaint against the ESM Treaty, expressed similar ideas in more general terms: it relativised the principle of sovereignty and stressed the importance of European and international cooperation for 'the fulfilment of the state's duties, and in particular those related to the protection of human rights'.[106] In the Austrian judgment, these sentiments are not clearly expressed, at least not by the *Verfassungsgerichtshof* itself, and the Irish Supreme Court is the odd man out, as its reasoning is, at least on the face of it, purely 'solipsistic'.

A second element of the strategies employed by the courts concerns judicial restraint *vis-à-vis* the economic and financial policy choices involved (or, in the case of Ireland, as regards foreign policy choices):[107] it is primarily up to the political institutions to make the 'general political and complex financial, monetary and economic assessments' which led to the decision to participate in the ESM, as the Austrian Court put it.[108] Of all the constitutional courts, it is probably the *Bundesverfassungsgericht* that keeps national politics on the shortest leash. Yet, in its ESM judgment(s), it displayed remarkable deference to the political process.

Subsequent strategic elements regard, respectively, the limitation of the subscribed liabilities to the inscribed stock capital and the requirement of, or the emphasis upon, the importance of information and participation rights for national Parliaments in ESM matters. These elements are already present in the EFSF judgments of the Slovenian and German Constitutional Courts of, respectively, 3 February 2011 and 7 September 2011, but here the German Court's judgment of 12 September 2012 with the reservations it required is dominant.

Actually, the reservation regarding the limitation of the subscribed stock capital seems somehow less important than the one regarding information rights. The former evidently concerns a pre-emptive strike against the ECJ, which may at some point be called upon to settle an interpretation or application dispute between ESM members, or between ESM members and the ESM-institutions (Article 37[3] of the ESM Treaty). As is well known, the ECJ favours the teleological method of interpretation, sometimes even at the expense of the text or the intentions of the state parties. The Interpretative Declaration effectively bars

106 *Trybunale Konstytucyjnym*, judgment K 33/12, para. 6.4.1.

107 Supreme Court, *Pringle* v. *Government of Ireland & ors*, para. 17.xiii. Judgment of C. J. Denham.

108 *Verfassungsgerichtshof*, Decision SV 2/12–19, para. B.3.5.3, point 57.

this route. But the Irish and Estonian Courts, which reviewed the ESM Treaty prior to the German Court, already presumed that the stock capital could not be raised without treaty amendment and this seems to have been the general presumption in political circles. Even without the required reservation and the ensuing Declaration, it would have been hard for the ECJ to find otherwise.

In contrast, the required reservation on information rights targets not so much the ECJ, but rather the national executives: it makes it very hard for them to withhold information regarding the ESM from Parliaments, despite their natural inclination to be secretive in international and European affairs. Indeed, national Parliaments in the plural: they all can benefit from it. In this respect, the *Bundesverfassungsgericht*, a *bête noire* in EU law circles, can only be applauded.

C. *EU Openness and Obstacles to Further Integration*

Fabbrini has contended that the provisions of the ESM and the Fiscal Compact could have been enacted as secondary EU law, that they would then have been immune from national judicial scrutiny and that this would have been the right way to proceed: although the EU political process is democratically deficient, involvement of the (national) courts, 'which by definition are non-democratic', provides no remedy for democratic deficits.[109] Fabbrini's implication is that the judgments discussed here have not enhanced the democratic legitimacy of the ESM and the Stability Treaties. Reality is, however, more nuanced.

Most of the Fiscal Compact's provisions could undoubtedly have been issued as secondary EU law, including its accentuation of the balanced budget rule. However, one wonders if EU secondary law could also have ordered the constituent powers to enshrine that budget rule in constitutional law (as proposed before the provision was toned down in hopes of preventing an Irish referendum, which, ironically, nonetheless had to take place). Of course, the ECJ's case law has, on more than one occasion, implicitly demanded constitutional adjustments from the Member States – think, for instance, of the second *Simmenthal*, the *Michaniki* and the

[109] F. Fabbrini, 'The Euro-Crisis and the Courts: Judicial Review and the Political Process in Comparative Perspective', *Berkeley Journal of International Law*, 32(1), 2014, 64–123, at 118.

Melloni judgments.[110] But in all these instances a change of interpretation of the relevant constitutional provisions sufficed to bring about the effect desired by the ECJ. Explicitly commanding the constituent powers of the euro area Member States to come into action by means of secondary EU law would seem to take things to an entirely different level. I seriously doubt whether the EU had or has the required political and constitutional authority. When it comes to the ESM, I have no doubt whatsoever. Even if it had been technically possible to establish the ESM by secondary EU law, for instance, on the basis of Article 122 or 352 TFEU, this would have been constitutional folly: the EU's authority is, at the moment, simply insufficient to force the national Parliaments to become the guarantors of such potentially enormous financial liabilities. This required a treaty, ratified in accordance with the relevant national constitutional requirements and thus the national Parliaments' (or peoples') consent. One sometimes forgets that treaties still provide the highest form of legal, political and democratic authority available in the EU.[111]

As regards the immunity of secondary EU law to national judicial scrutiny, we all know that no such immunity exists, at least not in Germany. And if the ESM had been established by an EU act it would probably have kindled constitutional resistance not only in Germany.

And as to effects of the judgments, they have not only *not* obstructed ratification of the treaties, but have rather helped to legitimise them, increasing their political and popular acceptance in ways that the political process on the national levels or on the EU level respectively were, or would have been, unable to provide. Thereby the judgments and, specifically, the ones on the ESM Treaty, have in various ways helped to legitimise a major shift in the functioning of the EMU.

First, they have ended the discussion on the constitutionality of the treaty or treaties reviewed in the states concerned. The legitimising effects of some judgments even seem to have worked cross-border. The rock-solid reasoning of the Estonian Supreme Court stands out in this respect: no matter how great the financial risks Estonia runs by participating in the ESM, the financial, economic and social risks of an instable or collapsing euro area are greater still. That message will have come across not only in Estonia. Similarly, that even the German Constitutional Court, the guardian of German democracy and statehood and thereby

[110] *Simmenthal II*, Case C-106/77; *Michaniki*, Case C-213/07; *Melloni*, Case C-399/11.

[111] W. T. Eijsbouts and J. H. Reestman, 'Editorial: In Search of the Union Method', *European Constitutional Law Review*, 11(3), 2015, 425–33, at 431.

indirectly also of national democracy and statehood in other Member States, accepted the treaties will have enhanced public and political acceptance not only in Germany. The openness towards the EU displayed by the judgments should provide no cause for amazement. That in all the states involved EU membership is enshrined in the national constitution and/or was approved by referendum, not only authorises, but also obliges the courts to interpret their constitutions in an EU-friendly manner. Indeed, with a variation on a well-known phrase dear to the *Bundesverfassungsgericht* one may say that the peoples and the constitutional legislatures are the masters of the (constitutional) courts. Again, this is most prominently expressed in the Estonian Supreme Court's ESM judgment, which is partly based on the Estonian people's approval of Estonia's accession to the EU and, consequently, to the euro area.[112]

But there are other ways too by which the judgments have conferred legitimacy on the treaties and have helped to increase their political and popular acceptance: by limiting the national constitutional impact of the treaties, as discussed above, and by indicating limits to further EMU integration, as will be discussed now. The latter may seem paradoxical, but is actually merely the other side of the medallion of openness towards Europe expressed by the judgments: the national constitutional authorities have indeed consecrated European integration, but not unlimitedly. For instance, a treaty that would give the EU institutions a direct hold on the national budgets seems to solicit a declaration of unconstitutionality in Germany and France in view of the vehemence with which the German Court and French Council denied that the Fiscal Compact did so. Similarly, the insistence of the Austrian, German, Irish and Slovenian Constitutional Courts on the need of limitation and predictability of the financial liabilities entered into, seems to indicate that the fully fledged introduction of Eurobonds will run into constitutional obstacles with them.

Even the Estonian Supreme Court found it necessary to give some thought to the matter of limits to further integration, probably also to appease the dissenters. The reasoning behind the proportionality review it performed – Estonia is better off in the EMU – can be very easily generalised: Estonia is anyway better off in the EU. The Court thus may appear to have issued a blank cheque enabling the further deepening of

[112] *Riigikohus*, Constitutional Judgment 3-4-1-6-1212, para. 163, 223. See also *Trybunale Konstytucyjnym*, Judgment K 33/12, para 6.6.3 and *BVerfG*, 2 BvE 2/08, para. 221.

European integration. But that is not the case. In an obiter dictum it stated that the constitutional amendment on EU membership, adopted by referendum in 2003,[113] has a limited reach. The amendment does 'not authorise the integration process of the European Union to be legitimised or the competence of Estonia to be delegated to the European Union to an unlimited extent': if future EU treaties provide for new transfers of competences 'and a more extensive infringement of principles of the Constitution ... it is necessary to seek the approval of the holder of supreme power, i.e. the people, and presumably amend the Constitution once again'.[114] We may safely assume that a treaty giving EU institutions the competence to intervene directly in the Estonian budget would fall into that category. It will undoubtedly be the same in Poland: the Polish Constitutional Tribunal reaffirmed that 'the constitutional identity of the Republic' should be respected, and that a transfer of 'core powers' that prevents Poland from functioning as a 'sovereign and democratic state' is not allowed.[115]

5 Concluding Remarks

The harvest of the judgments of the national courts on European Council Decision 2011/199 EU, the ESM Treaty and the Fiscal Compact, is rather diverse. From a procedural perspective, the judgments illustrate the diversity of the European constitutional landscape. At the same time, they express the still growing interconnectedness of the national and EU systems, economically, financially, politically and also constitutionally, as is symbolised by the references several courts made to their counterparts. Moreover, the judgments have legitimised and furthered the public and political acceptance of the treaties and thereby also a fundamental change in the functioning of the EMU: they provided a legitimacy that the political process was unable to provide on its own. Incidentally, the fact that the ESM emergency procedure was accepted by the Estonian Court, but would have been rejected by the German Court if Germany would have run the risk of being outvoted too, testifies that not all states are equally capable of protecting their constitutions in the external sphere.

[113] Constitution of the Republic of Estonia Amendment Act 2003, para. 1: 'Estonia may belong to the European Union, provided that the fundamental principles of the Constitution of the Republic of Estonia are respected'.

[114] *Riigikohus*, Constitutional Judgment 3-4-1-6-1212, para. 223.

[115] *Trybunale Konstytucyjnym*, Judgment K 33/12, resp. paras. 6.4.1 and 6.3.2.

Certainly, the legitimacy that the judgments provide came at a certain price. The judgments all somehow indicate that there is a point at which further EMU integration requires recourse to, and legitimation by, the constitutional authorities of the Member States. That is an expression of the very basic principles upon which also the European Union is built: democracy and the rule of law.

What consequences do the judgments entail for the reconstruction of the EMU that is on the agenda of the next decennium?[116] That is hard to tell. Much depends on the details of the reform proposals and on the inventiveness of the lawyers that design them. By now, they know where the constitutional sensibilities lie and they will try, if possible, to avoid them.[117] Moreover, the constitutional limits of reform have not yet been reached, at least judging by the 12 September 2012 decision of the *Bundesverfassungsgericht*, the court that has the most elaborated view on the EMU of all courts involved. According to the German Court, further adaptations may be made to the EMU, on the condition that it remains a stability community.[118] But nobody, not even the Court itself, knows exactly where the limits of the EMU as a stability community lie. In addition, courts do not always react as one would expect, as the following example from the same judgment may testify.

While allowing EU institutions a direct grip on the national budget would seem to be constitutional anathema in Germany, there is a good chance that 'arrangements of a contractual nature' between euro area Member States and Union institutions on national economic and budgetary policy, as proposed by the former president of the European Council, Herman van Rompuy, would meet with no constitutional objections there. As we have seen, Article 5 of the Fiscal Compact obliges euro area states under certain circumstances to negotiate a reform programme with the Commission and the Council that will be finalised in EU law. Such a programme also has a contractual nature, based as it is on 'offer and acceptance'. If such a programme is meant to apply for a longer period of time, thereby binding successive Parliaments, this is problematic from a

116 See the 'Five Presidents' Report': J. Juncker, D. Tusk, J. Dijsselbloem, M. Draghi and M. Schulz, 'Completing Europe's Economic and Monetary Union' (June 2015). See also J. Louis, 'The EMU After the Gauweiler Judgment and the Juncker Report', *Maastricht Journal of European and Comparative Law*, 23(1), 2016, 55–78.

117 C. Calliess, 'The Governance of the Eurozone and the Need for a Treaty Reform', in F. Fabbrini, E. Hirsch Ballin and H. Somsen, *What Form of Government for the Eurozone?* (Oxford: Hart Publishing, 2015) pp. 37–56, pp. 48ff.

118 *BVerfG*, 2 BvR 987/10, para. 118 (Engl. 222).

national democratic perspective.[119] Nonetheless, the German Court heartily welcomed the provision, reasoning that it would only strengthen the Member States' position in the excessive deficit procedure: instead of having to react to recommendations of Union institutions under the threat of sanctions, they now may propose and design their own reform programme.[120] This may be taking a very rosy view of Article 5, but it also indicates that there is room in the German constitutional context for what Pernice has called a 'moderate European framework' for tightening the autonomy of the national budget authorities.[121]

So, much depends on the details and on the lens through which the courts look at the concrete reform proposals. But, obviously, the possibility that EMU reform may run into constitutional obstacles in one or more Member States cannot be excluded. If it does, the obstacles can be overcome by the relevant constituent powers. Of course, that is easier said than done – changing a constitution to further EU integration is not an easy endeavour in these times of euro-scepticism and would require highly authoritative politicians with ample powers of persuasion. That might be regrettable from a financial, economic and perhaps even social perspective, as success is not guaranteed. But there is no sound alternative: Europe should not be constructed by stealth.

[119] As the complainants had argued. See *BVerfG*, 22 BvR 1390/12, para. 60 (Engl. 165).

[120] Ibid., para. 207 (311 Engl.).

[121] I. Pernice, 'Domestic Courts, Constitutional Constraints and European Democracy: What Solution for the Crisis?', in Adams, Fabbrini, Larouche (eds.), *The Constitutionalization of European Budgetary Constraints*, pp. 207–318, at p. 305.

11

Constitutions, Social Rights and Sovereign Debt States in Europe: A Challenging New Area of Constitutional Inquiry

CLAIRE KILPATRICK*

A cluster of cases decided by the constitutional courts of seven European bailout states dealing with the social implications of euro-crisis law present a rich new terrain for EU lawyers, for comparative constitutional lawyers and for scholars interested in the justiciability of economic and social rights alike. After outlining the backdrop of sovereign debt loan conditions and the social ambitions of the national constitutions, my analysis first describes several key features of this specific cluster of constitutional court rulings. I highlight, in particular, the fact that they have been brought largely by political institutions and actors rather than individuals or NGOs and that they focus on cuts to middle-class entitlements rather than the more traditional focus of socio-economic rights litigation, namely the poor. Second, I reflect on the sharp critiques which have been made of some of the constitutional court rulings, in particular of the Portuguese court, and suggest that the conventional framings of social rights and charges of 'middle-class' protection and juristocracy are inapposite in this context, for several key reasons. Third, I reflect on two curious features of this cluster of constitutional jurisprudence: first, the absence of the normal range of domestic judicial approaches to an apparent clash between national constitutional law and EU law and,

* Professor of International and European Labour and Social Law, EUI, Florence, claire.kilpatrick@eui.eu. I wish to thank Mark Dawson, Gráinne de Búrca, Bruno De Witte and Joanne Scott for exceptionally helpful comments. Earlier versions were presented at a workshop on *Constitutional Change through Euro-Crisis Law* held at the EUI in October 2014 and at the Hertie School of Governance in Berlin in April 2015. I am grateful to participants on both occasions for their comments. I wish also to thank Filipe de Brito Bastos and Viorica Viță for their research assistance, especially for responding to my further queries about Portugal and Romania respectively. This chapter was finalised in Summer 2016.

second, the fact that there is evidence of conscious judicial borrowing only across Eastern European states, despite the great similarity of context and issues arising. Finally, drawing on the case study of Hungary, I suggest that there may be links between the constitutional impact of euro-crisis law and other constitutional and democratic crises within European states.

1 The Backdrop – Sovereign Debt Loan Conditions and National Constitutions

A. *Sovereign Debt Loan Conditions*

This study concerns the interaction of constitutional orders in Europe with sovereign debt loan arrangements which have EU involvement. Sovereign debt loan assistance (bailouts) has been granted to seven EU Member States: Hungary, Latvia, Romania, Greece, Ireland, Portugal and Cyprus. It thus creates a new constitutional grouping of seven European states spanning East and West. Geographically, these states fall outside the typical focus of English-language constitutional social scholarship. That scholarship only exceptionally focuses on continental European countries other than (occasionally) Germany and almost exclusively focuses on the core Commonwealth states, as well as North and South America, Africa (especially the interesting case of the South African Constitution) and India. The flurry of interest in Eastern European constitution-making after 1989 largely dissipated after these states were urged not to include social rights in their constitutions as they transitioned to becoming market economies.[1]

Non-euro area states (Hungary, Latvia[2] and Romania) received the first wave of loans in 2008–10, while the euro area states entered into loans following the first Greek loan package in May 2010. Programmes have lasted for differing periods: well over five years in Greece (from May 2010 onwards), around three years for Ireland, Portugal and Cyprus (which entered into its programme in May 2013), and periods of one to two years in Hungary, Latvia and Romania (although this

[1] C. Sunstein, 'Against Positive Rights', *East European Constitutional Review*, 2(1), 1993, 35–9. The re-awakening of interest in Hungary and Romania as a result of constitutional crisis is discussed in the last section.

[2] Latvia subsequently joined the euro area as of 1 January 2014.

understates subsequent requests for assistance and the granting of precautionary financial assistance to some of these states following their exit from the initial bailout). Moreover, EU bailout states remain under post-programme surveillance until the loan has been substantially repaid.[3]

Sovereign debt loan assistance came with conditions that states had to meet. Those conditions prioritised rapid fiscal consolidation and structural reform, leading to dramatic changes to workplace and social rights and entitlements in bailout states. The EU institutions were for the first time involved in all these sovereign debt loans and some of the loans were provided from EU funding mechanisms. In what has been aptly dubbed 'The European Rescue of the Washington Consensus',[4] the EU institutions, sometimes with greater insistence and less flexibility than the International Monetary Fund (IMF), insisted on measures familiar from outside the EU in the 1980s and 1990s[5] and rolled out harsh austerity programmes in EU States requiring sovereign debt loans. There have been cuts to health, education, social security and social assistance, pay, pensions as well as an extensive deregulation of collective-bargaining structures and workplace protections. Never before has social loan

[3] See, for example, Ireland, where the Commission summarises as follows: 'Ireland is now subject to post-programme surveillance (PPS) until at least 75 per cent of the financial assistance received has been repaid. So barring any early repayments, PPS will last at least until 2031.The objective of PPS is ultimately to measure Ireland's capacity to repay its outstanding loans to the EFSM, EFSF and bilateral lenders. Under PPS, the Commission, in liaison with the European Central Bank, will (i) conduct regular review missions in the Member State to assess its economic, fiscal and financial situation; and (ii) prepare semi-annual assessments of Ireland's economic, fiscal and financial situation and determine whether corrective measures are needed'. European Commission, 'Post-Programme Surveillance for Ireland', http://ec.europa.eu/economy_finance/assistance_eu_ms/ireland/index_en.htm. Of the bailout states, only Latvia and Hungary have exited bailout governance (in January 2015), by repaying over 70 per cent of the loan.

[4] See S. Lütz and M. Kranke, 'The European Rescue of the Washington Consensus? EU and IMF Lending to Central and Eastern European Countries', *Review of International Political Economy*, 21(2), 2014, 310–38.

[5] R. W. Stone, 'The Scope of IMF Conditionality', *International Organisation* 62, 2008, 589 summarises well as follows: 'As late as the 1970s, only 26 percent of IMF loan disbursements involved substantial conditionality, but the Latin American debt crisis in the 1980s and the expansion of lending to Africa increased this figure to 66 percent by the end of the 1980s. In the subsequent decade … the number of conditions specified in an IMF program steadily climbed as the Fund sought to manage the transition from state planning to the market in former communist countries and grappled with the importance of financial-sector issues in the East Asian crisis'.

conditionality affected the states of Europe in such a far-reaching way.[6] It is unprecedented in its geographical scope with social loan conditionality applying to an array of Western European states. It is also remarkable in the range of socially relevant loan conditions, the length of time over which evolving social loan conditions have applied, and the far-reaching effects of the loan conditions on social and employment conditions.

Sovereign debt loan assistance is an important component of the broader category of euro-crisis law. By 'euro-crisis law', I mean the law governing sovereign debt loans as well as the overhaul of EMU governance following, in particular, the wave of euro area bailouts, which began with the first Greek bailout in May 2010. The term captures the unusual and multiple legal pedigree of euro-crisis law: it is used to encompass EU law relevant to the crisis as well as international agreements entered into by subsets of EU states and administered by EU institutions (such as some of the sovereign debt loan arrangements).[7] The structure of the legal space had important consequences for constitutional interactions, as we shall see. While keeping the focus on sovereign debt states, the interaction of bailout states with broader euro-crisis sources before and after bailout is of great interest,[8] as demonstrated later in the analysis of Hungary and Portugal. In this chapter, I refer to euro-crisis constitutional challenges and judgments as shorthand for cases concerning sovereign debt loan conditions.[9]

B. *The Social Ambitions of the Bailout Constitutions*

Comparative constitutional scholarship brings out the distinctive and expressive functions fulfilled by written constitutions. Although

6 Contrast D. Bilchitz, 'Socio-economic Rights, Economic Crisis, and Legal Doctrine', *International Journal of Constitutional Law*, 12(3), 2014, 710–39, who assumes an economic phenomenon resulting from the financial crisis, requiring states to make cuts in social expenditure. Yet, there is, in the EU, a *public multi-level governance phenomenon*, involving the EU and the IMF downgrading social spending and rights as a condition for obtaining sovereign debt loans. To leave this out is to overstate, and present as unmediated, the roles of both the state and the financial crisis in creating challenges for social rights.

7 It is not intended to indicate that it covers only euro area Member States.

8 During bailout, the application of much of the broader EMU regime is suspended.

9 On the different kinds of social loan conditions and for a set of arguments that almost all are challengeable as implementations of EU law, see C. Kilpatrick, 'Are the Bailout Measures Immune to EU Social Challenge Because They Are Not EU Law?', *European Constitutional Law Review*, 10(3), 2014, 393–421.

constitutions without social and labour rights are today quite exceptional, the social ambitions of constitutions differ widely.[10] From the perspective of their written constitutions, the seven EU bailout states constitute an interesting new grouping.[11] Euro-crisis law is brought into contact with very different constitutional sources, with wide variance in their social focus and ambitions. The Irish (1937) and Cypriot (1960) constitutions reflect both their age and their emergence from British rule. In Greece and Portugal the constitutions of 1975 and 1976 reflect their respective emergence from military dictatorship and fascism. Importantly, the EU bailout grouping contains three Eastern European states, which acceded to the EU in 2004 (Hungary and Latvia) and 2007 (Romania). This is especially interesting when reviewing the social ambitions of the original constitutional text, since an intense strand of the post-1989 constitutional debate concerned whether Eastern European constitutions should exclude social rights.

By the measure of the social ambitions and range of the constitutional text, Portugal tops the scale of EU bailout states. Although significantly amended, it is a constitutional text with a marked socialist focus: its Preamble speaks of 'opening up a path towards a socialist society'.[12] While this underpins multiple provisions about the organisation of the economy and worker management in Part II, it is also reflected in Part I, which is devoted to Fundamental Rights and Duties. The content of Part I is worth examining a little further, as it has been implicated in the controversy surrounding the Portuguese Constitutional Court's euro-crisis judgments. Preceded by a series of fundamental principles underpinning the Portuguese constitutional order (such as the Rule of Law in Article 2), Part I is divided into three Titles. While Title I covers General Principles, including the principle of universality (Article 12) and of equality (Article 13), Title II is divided into three chapters on rights, freedoms and guarantees. The first two deal,

[10] See D. Davies, 'Socio-Economic Rights', in M. Rosenfeld and A. Sajó (eds.), *The Oxford Handbook of Comparative Constitutional Law* (Oxford University Press, 2012), pp. 1020–35. See also the large dataset comparison of economic and social rights in constitutions in C. Jung, R. Hirschl and E. Rosevear, 'Economic and Social Rights in National Constitutions', *American Journal of Comparative Law*, 62(4), 2014, 1043–93.

[11] For discussions of 'families' as a focus of comparative constitutional law see V. Jackson, 'Comparative Constitutional Law: Methodologies' in Rosenfeld and Sajó (eds.), *The Oxford Handbook of Comparative Constitutional Law*, pp. 55–74.

[12] An English version of the Portuguese Constitution is made available on the Portuguese Constitutional Court's website: www.tribunalconstitucional.pt/tc/conteudo/files/constituicaoingles.pdf.

respectively, with civil rights and political rights and the third chapter is entitled 'Workers' Rights, Freedoms and Guarantees'. Five articles protect or institute respectively job security, workers' committees, freedoms concerning trade unions, trade union rights and collective agreements, the right to strike and prohibition of lockouts. Title III is devoted to economic, social and cultural rights and duties. Economic rights and duties concern the right to work (including the duty of the state to promote full employment policies) and a range of other workers' rights (such as to rest and leisure, wage protection measures, health and safety, social dignity), consumer rights, forms of enterprise ownership and management and private property. Social rights and duties concern social security and solidarity, health, housing and urban planning, environment, family, parenthood, childhood as well as protection for the young, the disabled and the elderly. Part of the controversy focused on the Court's use of Title I in its euro-crisis constitutional jurisprudence, as well as fundamental constitutional principles, rather than the specific labour and social provisions of Titles II and III.

Ireland and Cyprus lie at the other end of the constitutional scale, reflecting their age and their liberal common law constitutional origins. The Irish Constitution, apart from the right to education, contains no work or social rights. Its 'Directive Principles of Social Policy' (Article 45), which broadly direct the state to promote the welfare of the whole people are expressly framed for the political branch only and 'shall not be cognisable by any Court under any of the provisions of the Constitution'. For this, alongside a range of other reasons,[13] the Irish bailout was not subject to social constitutional challenge. Nor has (to date, at least) the Cyprus bailout[14] been challenged under a constitution[15] providing a limited range of social rights protection, mainly focused on work.[16]

[13] See A. Nolan, 'Welfare Rights in Crisis: The Case of Ireland', *European Journal of Social Law*, 4(1), 2014, 37–49 and A. Kerr, 'Social Rights in Crisis in the Eurozone: Work Rights in Ireland', *European Journal of Social Law*, 4(1), 2014, 50–62. However, it is worth noting that in late 2014 the largest scale mobilisations since the crisis began took place against water charges, with these being explicitly couched as infringements of human and constitutional rights to water. See www.right2water.ie/.

[14] See the report on Cyprus prepared by K. Pantazatou for the 'Constitutional Change through Euro Crisis Law' project of the EUI Law Department. All the country reports referred to in this paper are part of the same project and available on its website: http://eurocrisislaw.eui.eu.

[15] Available in English at: www.presidency.gov.cy/presidency/presidency.nsf/all/1003AEDD83EED9C7C225756F0023C6AD/$file/CY_Constitution.pdf.

[16] Art. 9 protects the right to a decent existence and to social insurance. Art. 26 provides the possibility of preventing contractual exploitation by those wielding economic power and

The Greek Constitution[17] has a similar work rights focus to that of Cyprus, but is somewhat more expansive. Article 22 provides that 'work constitutes a right and shall enjoy the protection of the State, which shall seek to create conditions of employment for all citizens'. It similarly enjoins the state to provide for the general working conditions of its people and to care for the social security of its working people. The right to unionise, collect union dues and to strike are also constitutionally protected.[18]

The Constitutions of the Eastern European bailout states turn out, in the event, not to have followed the advice not to protect social rights, with all of them providing significantly more protection than the liberal common law constitutions. Hence, the 1991 Romanian Constitution[19] protects the right to health and free state education.[20] As well as placing an obligation on the state to 'take measures of economic development and social protection, of a nature to ensure a decent living standard for its citizens', it provides citizens with the constitutional right to pensions, paid maternity leave, public medical care, unemployment benefit and other forms of social security.[21] Alongside protection of trade unions' freedom of association and the right to strike,[22] Article 41 protects the right to work, social protection at work, limitations of working hours and the right to collectively bargain. Special provisions protect people on account of age and disability. The Latvian Constitution[23] (which restores, with amendments, its 1922 text) has a smaller cluster of social rights covering the right to freely choose employment, an adequate wage guarantee, right to weekly and annual holidays and to social security, human

for the creation of collective labour contracts. Some protection of the right to strike is guaranteed in Art. 27. Art. 28(2) provides a broad non-discrimination clause, listing many grounds.

17 An official parliamentary translation of the Constitution of Greece (last revised 27 May 2008) is available at www.hellenicparliament.gr/UserFiles/f3c70a23-7696-49db-9148-f24dce6a27c8/001-156%20aggliko.pdf.

18 Art. 23.

19 An official parliamentary translation of the Constitution of Romania is available at www.cdep.ro/pls/dic/site.page?id=371.

20 Art. 34 ('Right to protection of health') and Art. 32 ('Right to education').

21 Art. 47 ('Living standards'). See also Art. 135 on various principles underpinning the economy including fair competition and improving quality of life.

22 Art. 9 ('Trade unions, employers' associations and vocational associations'), Art. 40 ('Right of association') and Art. 43 ('Right to strike').

23 An official parliamentary translation of the Constitution of Latvia is available at www.saeima.lv/en/legislation/constitution.

health and education, alongside a full freedom of association guarantee for labour (hence encompassing the right to bargain and strike).[24]

An overall sense of the social orientation of the constitutional text matters in assessing euro-crisis constitutional challenges. It matters both in a more textually focused sense and in a broader contextual sense. Textually speaking, it is noteworthy that the constitutional challenges on the whole have not fully exploited the constitutional space provided by most of the bailout constitutions. Moreover, euro-crisis constitutional judgments have not always been based on the social rights in constitutions, but have sometimes been based on other broader constitutional principles such as equality and the rule of law. Whether or not this is controversial and illegitimate partly depends on whether other more obviously suitable constitutional options exist. In a broader contextual sense, the life and spirit of the constitutional text, taken as a whole, may make certain readings and stances taken in euro-crisis constitutional judgments more understandable than a reading focused on specific constitutional provisions.

2 Key Features of Constitutional Court Challenges in Sovereign Debt States

Euro-crisis law provoked a series of significant constitutional judgments on the constitutional compatibility of changes to social rights required, more or less directly, to obtain sovereign debt loans. The key Greek constitutional judgments to date consist of a decision by the Greek Council of State (the highest administrative court) in 2012[25] and a decision with a different outcome and reasoning by the Greek Court of Auditors.[26] In Latvia, eight key constitutional

[24] See Arts. 106 to 112.

[25] Greek Council of State Pl. Decision 668/2012, 20 February 2012; see also Decisions 1285 and 1286/2012, 2 April 2012 and Cases 1283 and 1284/2012, 2 April 2012. See further Decision 2192/2014, 23 June 2014 (wage cuts for military service personnel unconstitutional because of their special role in defending the state) and Decision 2307/2014, 27 June 2014 (constitutional compatibility of almost all work measures in the second Greek Bailout). For a broader and more hopeful reading of the 2014 cases, see in this book Chapter 6 'Greece: Constitutional Deconstruction and the Loss of National Sovereignty' by Afroditi Marketou.

[26] Greek Court of Auditors, Proceedings of the 3rd and 4th special sessions of the plenary, 30 October 2012. Under Art. 73(2) Greek Constitution, the Court of Auditors delivers non-binding opinions on draft pension bills. See E. Psychogiopoulou, 'Welfare Rights in

challenges on social measures were decided, six in 2009[27] and two in 2010.[28] In Romania, a large number of emblematic decisions were taken between 2009 and 2011 on the constitutionality of a range of measures cutting pay, pensions and social benefits,[29] as well as collective bargaining and freedom of association rights[30] and employment protection,[31] although quantitatively the numbers of constitutional challenges were much higher.[32]

A significant series of Portuguese Constitutional Court decisions on social austerity measures have been taken as a result of loan

Crisis in Greece: The Role of Fundamental Rights Challenges', *European Journal of Social Law*, 3(1), 2014, 12–25.

[27] Latvian Constitutional Court, Case 2009-08-01 (cancellation of pension indexation); Case 2009–43-01 (reduction of pensions); Case 2009–44-01 (50 per cent cut to benefit for working parents); Case 2009–76-01 (cuts to pensions of Ministry of Interior staff); Case 2009–88-01 (cuts to retirement pensions for military personnel not yet in receipt of old-age pension); Case 2009-11-01 (cuts in judicial pay).

[28] Latvian Constitutional Court, Case 2010-17-01 (changes to incapacity for work benefits); Case 2010–21-01 (cuts to funding of occupational pensions). See the Report on Latvia prepared by Z. Rasnača.

[29] Romanian Constitutional Court: Decision 1415/2009 (constitutionality of capping salary additions and a new regime for compensating overtime); Decisions 872/2010 and 874/2010 (constitutionality of cuts to pensions, public-sector salaries, judges' salaries); Decision 873/2010 (constitutionality of cuts to judicial pensions); Decision 1237/2010 (constitutionality of changes to basis for calculating public pensions), Decision 1655/2010 (prolongation of salary cuts in 2011); Decision 1658/2010 (cap on bonuses for public employees); Decision 765/2011 (cut in maternity leave and monthly child-raising allowance); Decision 1533/2011 (compatibility of scheduling state compensation to those whose pensions had been unconstitutionally reduced).

[30] Romanian Constitutional Court: Decision 575/2011 (replacing collective bargaining on teachers' salaries to setting them by law); Decision 574/2011 (outlawing right of association, collective bargaining and industrial action for liberal professions and magistrates; repeal of certain rights of unions to formulate proposals to local authorities).

[31] Romanian Constitutional Court: Decision 1414/2009 (constitutionality of various measures concerning public-sector employment conditions); Decision 383/2011 (changes to labour code e.g. increase in probation period, possibility to suspend labour contract, dilution of unions' rights during elaboration of labour norms). See the Report on Romania prepared by V. Viţă.

[32] Note that these decisions are, quantitatively speaking, the tip of the constitutional challenge iceberg. They are the *ex ante* constitutional cases, while many measures were challenged *ex post* by questions of constitutionality raised in proceedings before other national courts, which can then refer them to the constitutional court. For instance, around one-third of the c.1,000 cases decided by the Court in 2012 concerned *ex post* social constitutional challenges triggered largely by euro-crisis measures.

conditionality: one in 2011,[33] one in 2012,[34] five in 2013,[35] one (very) politically resonant decision in May 2014[36] and further decisions following early bailout exit as a result of the May 2014 decision.[37] The range of successful constitutional challenges, the size of the bailout and the fact, unlike Romania and Latvia at the time of their bailout, of euro area membership combined to give these judgments and this Constitutional Court an exceptionally high political and media profile. A number of striking features immediately emerge from comparative analysis of euro-crisis constitutional jurisprudence.

First, the existence of constitutional judgments on social aspects of the bailouts does not necessarily point to civil society mobilisation. In fact, in all these states other than Greece,[38] constitutional legal challenges

33 Portuguese Constitutional Court: Judgment 396/2011, 21 September 2011 (Budget Law 2011: public-sector pay cuts. CONSTITUTIONAL).

34 Portuguese Constitutional Court: Judgment 353/2012, 5 July 2012 (Budget Law 2012: suspension of 13th and 14th month of salary for public-sector workers. UNCONSTITUTIONAL). Unconstitutional means at least one constitutional breach was found although not all provisions challenged may have been found to be unconstitutional.

35 Portuguese Constitutional Court: Judgment 187/2013, 5 April 2013 (suspension of holiday payments in public-sector; contributions obligations imposed on recipients of unemployment payments. UNCONSTITUTIONAL); Judgment 474/2013, 29 August 2013 (relaxing dismissal regime for public-sector workers. UNCONSTITUTIONAL); Judgment 602/2013, 20 September 2013 (relaxing private-sector employment protection. UNCONSTITUTIONAL); Judgment 794/2013, 21 November 2013 (increasing normal working hours of public sector. CONSTITUTIONAL); Judgment 862/2013, 19 December 2013 (cut in amount and calculation formula for public-sector pensions. UNCONSTITUTIONAL).

36 Portuguese Constitutional Court: Judgment 413/2014, 30 May 2014 (Budget Act 2014: pay reductions for public-sector workers; taxation of unemployment and sickness payments; suspension of occupational pension supplements for public-sector pensions. UNCONSTITUTIONAL).

37 Portuguese Constitutional Court: Judgment 572/2014, 30 July 2014 (Budget Act 2014: extraordinary solidarity contribution for pensions; transfer of public-sector employer contributions to general state funds. CONSTITUTIONAL); Judgment 574/2014, 14 August 2014 (norm providing for public-sector pay cuts in 2016–8 of unspecified amount. UNCONSTITUTIONAL); Judgment 575/2014, 14 August 2014 (Sustainability Contribution on all public pensions. UNCONSTITUTIONAL); Judgment 745/2014, 5 November 2014 (increase of public servants' contributions to health fund. CONSTITUTIONAL).

38 See, however, the challenge of measures upheld *ex ante* in Romania in numerous *ex post* challenges by individuals and their representatives. Moreover, unions in Romania and Portugal did challenge pay and pension cuts through other domestic courts, which made preliminary references to the European Court of Justice or which led to cases proceeding to the European Court of Human Rights. Romania and Court of Justice: C-434/11 *Corpul Național al Polițiștilor*, Order of 14 December 2011; C-134/12 *Corpul Național al*

occurred not through civil society mobilisation but rather through the use of political constitutional review mechanisms allowing designated politicians or other specially designated institutions to ask for ex ante or ex post review.

Second, while Portugal, Latvia and Romania have specialised constitutional courts, Greek constitutional challenges have been decided by a range of different courts. For some analysts, the absence of a specialised constitutional court in Greece has affected the robustness of constitutional review in the face of bailout demands.[39]

Third, the backdrop of euro-crisis and sovereign debt loans has meant that executive and legislative activity on social measures and resulting constitutional adjudication has been marked by arguments about what happens to social rights in a context of economic crisis or emergency.[40]

Perhaps the most striking comparative finding is the clustering of many of the constitutional challenges around cuts to pay, pensions and benefits. These cuts are often work-related and often concern public-sector workers, sometimes as a broad group and sometimes as a particular group, the most significant being judges. Although cuts may be expressed as suspensions, caps, freezes, in new calculation formulae or as the imposition of taxes or contributions on income, they all share the common feature of reductions (real or nominal) in the amount previously received. This is predominantly a constitutional jurisprudence of crisis-driven monetary cuts. However, there is also an important

Poliţiştilor, Order of 10 May 2012; C-462/11 *Cozman*, Order of 14 December 2012; C-258/14 *Florescu*, lodged on 26 May 2014. Portugal and Court of Justice: C-127/12 *Sindicato dos Bancários do Norte*, Order of 7 March 2013; C-264/12, *Sindacato Nacional dos Profissionais de Seguro* v *Fidelidade Mundial*, Order of 26 June 2014. European Court of Human Rights: Apps Nos 44232/11 and 44605/11 *Mihăieş v Romania*, Judgment (3rd section), 6 December 2011; Apps 45312/11, 45312/11, 45581/11, 45583/11, 45587/11, 45588/11 and 13902/11 *Frimu and others v Romania*, Judgment of 13 November 2012; Apps Nos 62235/12 and 57725/12 *Da Conceicão Mateus and Santos Januário* v. *Portugal*, Judgment (2nd section), 8 October 2013.

39 See the Report on Greece prepared by A. Marketou and M. Dekastros, Section III.8: 'despite the almost commonsensical character of the unconstitutionality of at least some of the statutes implementing euro-crisis law ... in Greece there is no strong and independent constitutional court that could annul these acts'. Similarly, G. Katrougoulos, 'The Greek Austerity Measures: Violations of Socio-Economic Rights', I.CONnect Blog, 29 January 2013, http://www.iconnectblog.com/2013/01/the-greek-austerity-measures-violations-of-socio-economic-rights/.

40 See the special focus in the four chapters in this book in *Part II National Constitutional Manifestations of Economic Emergency* focusing on emergency in Greece (Chapter 6), Spain (Chapter 7), Italy (Chapter 8) and Ireland (Chapter 9).

subsidiary focus on employment and labour rights. Hence, in Portugal, Romania and under the second Greek bailout, there is a broader set of employment-related constitutional challenges. For instance, both the Portuguese and Romanian constitutional courts and the Greek Council of State evaluated when law could set limits on collective bargaining as a source of norms,[41] as well as broader changes to employment protection in the public and private sector.[42]

What is missing, then, are broader social rights challenges on issues such as health, education and housing. A number of possible explanations for this absence can be discounted. It cannot be explained by reference to the social loan conditions, as these included interferences with health, education and housing. Nor can it be explained by reference to limits in the constitutional text: the bailout states in which constitutional challenges were brought provide clear opportunities in their constitutional texts for a much wider range of challenges than changes to work and welfare measures. Accordingly, the most striking absences in the sovereign debt states are challenges concerning precisely those rights central to contemporary constitutional social scholarship: rights to health, education and housing.[43] This means that a fuller and broader definition of the social[44] to encompass work-related rights and benefits is necessary to capture euro-crisis constitutional challenges. As Cécile Fabre notes, the European constitutional culture of social justice contrasts with the more typical commonwealth focus by being 'as it were, "complete", delineating as it does principles for individuals' status as citizens and workers'.[45]

[41] Portugal: Judgment 602/2013, above n. 35; Romania, above n. 30; Greece Council of State Decision 2307/2014 above n. 25.

[42] Portugal: Judgment 474/2013; 602/2013 and 794/2013, all above n. 35; Romania: Decision 1414/2009 and Decision 383/2011 above n. 31; Greece: Council of State Decision 2307/2014 above n. 25.

[43] K. Young, *Constituting Economic and Social Rights* (Oxford University Press, 2012); H. Alviar García, K. Klare and L. Williams (eds.), *Social and Economic Rights in Theory and Practice: Critical Inquiries* (Abingdon: Routledge, 2014). Tushnet instead investigates primarily the implications of doctrines on the application of constitutional rights between private parties for social and economic rights, see M. Tushnet, *Weak Courts, Strong Rights: Judicial Review and Social Welfare Rights in Comparative Constitutional Law* (Princeton University Press, 2008).

[44] See C. Kilpatrick and B. de Witte, *A Comparative Framing of Fundamental Rights Challenges to Social Crisis Measures in the Eurozone*, Swedish Institute for European Policy Studies (European Policy Analysis, November 2014), www.sieps.se/sites/default/files/2014_7epa_eng_A4_0.pdf.

[45] C. Fabre, 'Social Rights in European Constitutions', in G. de Búrca and B. de Witte (eds.), *Social Rights in Europe* (Oxford University Press, 2005), pp. 15–28, at p. 19. See also

3 Constitutional Court Critiques: Contextualisation and Questioning

The engagement of especially the Portuguese constitutional court with euro-crisis constitutional challenges has generated intense critique. Its use of equality and linked constitutional principles to evaluate cuts in governmental expenditure has been subject to intense, perhaps even unprecedented, criticism by Portuguese scholars. It has been accused in its euro-crisis jurisprudence of erring 'in virtually every dimension of its role' committing the errors of 'unfairness, unpredictability, illegitimacy and insularity' in the respective dimensions of the substance of its reasoning (unfair), the coherence and guidance of its reasoning (unpredictable), its inter-institutional relations (illegitimate) and its EU relations (insular).[46] The first three of these will be engaged with in this part of the analysis and the insularity critique will be considered in the third section, on EU constitutional interactions.

Euro-crisis constitutional challenges open questions about the current structure and points of focus of constitutional social scholarship. The current dominant normative paradigms are proportionality (the 'age of balancing') and a poverty-focused constitutionalism. When new developments occur, they generally come to be recognised and analysed within these dominant contemporary scholarly paradigms. I show below how this has shaped the debate on euro-crisis constitutional judgments and, by testing these paradigms against the reasoning of those judgments, I suggest they fail to effectively capture their nature.

W. Forbath for a suggestive argument that this is also part of the US constitutional heritage and possible futures: 'Social and Economic Rights in the American Grain', in J. Balkin and R. Siegel (eds.), *The Constitution in 2020* (Oxford University Press, 2009), pp. 55–68.

46 G. De Almeida Ribeiro, 'Judicial Activism Against Austerity in Portugal', I-CONnect blog (reproducing an essay), 3 December 2013, www.iconnectblog.com/2013/12/judicial-activism-against-austerity-in-portugal/. See also G. Coelho and P. Caro de Sousa, '"La Morte dei Mille Tagli": Nota sulla Decisione della Corte Costituzionale Portoghese In Merito Alla Legittimità del Bilancio annual 2013', *Giornale di diritto del lavoro e di relazioni industriali*, 139(3), 2013, 527–44; M. Nogueira De Brito, 'Putting Social Rights in Brackets? The Portuguese Experience with Welfare Rights Challenges in Times of Crisis', *European Journal of Social Law*, 4(1), 2014, 87–102. For a collection of constitutional critiques, see: G. de Almeida Ribeiro and L. Pereira Coutinho (eds.), *O Tribunal Constitutional e a Crise: Ensaios Críticos* (Almedina: Coimbra, 2014). For a counter-critique, see J. Reis Novais, *Em Defesa Do Tribunal Constitucional: Resposta aos Críticos* (Almedina: Coimbra, 2014).

Second, I show the neo-liberal default assumptions underpinning much of the analysis of euro-crisis constitutional judgments protecting public-sector workers and other 'middle-class' entitlements. I also consider why constitutional labour scholarship has neglected these issues.

Finally, this section turns to charges of judicial activism. During the crisis these have taken a traditional form by alleging that national constitutional courts that struck down measures taken to fulfil loan conditions were not sufficiently deferential to national Parliaments and executives. My claim is that, in a range of distinctive and interesting ways, this focus is misplaced. It understates which branches of government are involved when examining constitutional interactions with the judicial branch: as will clearly be demonstrated, these include the EU institutions in times of Eurocrisis. It under-examines the actions and evolving decision-making of the constitutional courts themselves and it assumes relationships between the branches of the state which do not prevail while the state is in bailout.

A. *Constitutional Social Scholarship Framings: Testing Their Euro-Crisis Utility*

Alongside robust critiques of euro-crisis constitutional judgments as illegitimate and unpredictable, crisis-driven constitutional social scholarship has, to date, focused on whether a proportionality or a 'minimum core' approach is best taken by courts when approaching such issues.[47] In what follows, I use euro-crisis constitutional judgments to test these framings.

Contiades and Fotiadou argue that proportionality can do all the judicial work of determining when social rights can or cannot be limited in times of crisis.[48] Among other merits, they suggest that proportionality

[47] A third distinctive argument, with links to minimum core arguments, is considered when we turn to critiques of protecting middle-class entitlements. See D. Landau, 'The Promise of a Minimum Core Approach: The Colombian Model for Judicial Review of Austerity Measures', in A. Nolan (ed.) *Economic and Social Rights After the Global Financial Crisis* (Cambridge University Press, 2014), pp. 267–98.

[48] X. Contiades and A. Fotiadou, 'Social Rights in the Age of Proportionality: Global Economic Crisis and Constitutional Litigation', *International Journal of Constitutional Law*, 10(3), (2012), 660–86. There is, in fact, very limited reference to EU bailout states' constitutional litigation in this analysis; just one of the Latvian decision (2009–43-01), see above n. 27.

shields judges more effectively from controversy than a minimum core approach. Bilchitz counters that a minimum core approach, whereby a baseline minimum for a right must always be secured by the state, is more fitting than a proportionality approach. More broadly, he argues for an approach that gives content to rights and gives proportionality a more circumscribed role as a mechanism for deciding when limitations on rights can be permitted.[49] Yet the assumption underpinning his analysis – that crisis-driven constitutional challenges are focused on meeting basic needs – is wrong in Europe. Contiades and Fotiadou rightly point out that the centre of gravity of Bilchitz's analysis is wrongly premised on crisis jurisprudence being about meeting basic needs (the minimum core) for food, health, shelter and income.[50] While increasing numbers of people may indeed be unable to meet their basic needs in EU bailout states, that is certainly not (to date) the focus of constitutional or human rights contestation in Europe. Cuts to existing entitlements are the main focus of challenge, rather than a failure to meet basic needs.

But the alternative proffered, proportionality as the one-size-fits-all solution to judicial management of social rights challenges in times of crisis, is also problematic. There are real differences in approach between courts in relating the economic crisis to fundamental rights. Each court decides which constitutional provisions are engaged, takes a specific position on how fundamental rights apply in times of economic 'emergency' and develops distinctive analyses of proportionality. In what follows, I distinguish the basis from the standard of review in a comparative analysis, in order to more fully review these framings and to evaluate whether equality and the rule of law as the basis for Portuguese constitutional review of cuts 'surely confirm that Court's resistance to review the austerity measures on the basis of the constitutionally entrenched social rights'.[51]

B. *Basis of Review*

The Portuguese reasoning is well set out in the official English summary of the first case in which public-sector salary cuts were found to breach

[49] Bilchitz, 'Socio-economic Rights'.

[50] X. Contiades and A. Fotiadou, 'Socio-Economic Rights, Economic Crisis and Legal Doctrine: A Reply to David Bilchitz', *International Journal of Constitutional Law*, 12 (3), 2014, 740–6.

[51] Nogueira de Brito, 'Putting Social Rights in Brackets'.

the constitutional equality guarantee in Article 13.[52] The Court first introduced the principle of equal sacrifice as a parameter.

The Court recalled that the principle of equality with regard to the just distribution of public costs, as a specific manifestation of the principle of equality, is a necessary legislative parameter which the legislator must consider when it decides to reduce the public deficit in order to safeguard the state's solvency. The sustainability of the public finances is of interest to everyone and, to the extent of their capacity to do so, everyone must contribute to the burden of the readjustments that are indispensable if that sustainability is to be ensured. The fact that the measures contained in the norms before the Court were not universal meant that they did not distribute the sacrifices equally between all citizens, in proportion to each one's financial capacity. They required an additional effort exclusively from certain categories of citizen.

Is this an unacceptable constitutional basis for evaluating monetary cuts? In fact, the constitutional basis for challenges to cuts differed on a broad East-West axis. Eastern European challenges were brought using distinctive constitutional *social* provisions; Western European challenges were not. Hence, in Latvia and Romania challenges to pension and benefit cuts were brought under the constitutional guarantee to social security.[53] Challenges to pay cuts, brought in Romania but not in Latvia, were brought on a different constitutional basis, the right to work (Article 41 Romanian Constitution). By contrast, cuts to both pay and pensions were dealt with on distinct but *non-social* constitutional bases in Greece and Portugal. In Greece this was the right to property (Article 17 Greek Constitution), the principle of proportionality (Article 25[1] Greek Constitution), equal participation of citizens in public burdens[54] (Article 4[5] Greek Constitution) and respect for human dignity (Article 2[1] Greek Constitution). In Portugal, the primary basis for the cuts jurisprudence was the Rule of Law in Article 2, used to underpin the principles of trust

[52] See Judgment 353/2012, above n. 34.

[53] Art. 47(2) Romanian Constitution: 'Citizens have the right to pensions, paid maternity leave, medical care in public health centres, unemployment benefits, and other forms of public or private social securities, as stipulated by the law. Citizens have the right to social assistance, according to the law.' Art. 109 Latvian Constitution: 'Everyone has the right to social security in old age, for work disability, for unemployment and in other cases as provided by law.'

[54] Art. 4(5) Greek Constitution: 'Greek citizens contribute without distinction to public charges in proportion to their means'.

and legitimate expectations,[55] and the principle of equality in Article 13 (1): 'All citizens possess the same social dignity and are equal before the law'. That is to say, the use of equality as a basis for reviewing monetary cuts is shared by some other, but not by all, European constitutional courts. Although this substantially blunts the criticism of the use of equality as exceptional, it leaves the question of whether those courts that used equality and related broad constitutional principles to evaluate monetary cuts 'mis-used' their constitutional text. This depends on whether one thinks there is an obviously better-suited provision available in constitutional texts for evaluating such cuts. Is the right to work, used in Latvia to evaluate pension cuts, an obviously better fit?

Moreover, the trenchant critique of avoiding the social rights basis in the constitution is based only on a partial assessment of the Portuguese Constitutional Court's record. It ignores a substantial body of its jurisprudence applying specific constitutional labour and social provisions, especially in Part 1, Title II of the Constitution dealing with workers' rights, to constitutionally review a significant range of other changes driven by the bailout programme. Take, for instance, the integrity of collective bargains, protected in all the bailout constitutions other than Ireland. The Portuguese Constitutional Court took the following starting point as the basis for careful examination of a series of legislative interventions into collectively agreed norms:

> under the Constitution workers are the holders of the right to enter into collective labour agreements, albeit they can only exercise it via trade unions. This exercise is guaranteed 'under the terms laid down by law'. Because this guarantee is founded in the Constitution, the fact that the details are left to "the terms laid down by law" cannot mean that the guarantee itself is placed in the hands of the ordinary legislator.[56]

Portuguese constitutional jurisprudence has leant towards an interpretation that the right to collective agreements is a right which the ordinary law must format, but that in doing so the latter can neither empty the right of its content, nor itself decide every aspect of labour law in ways that

[55] Art. 2 Portuguese Constitution: 'The Portuguese Republic is a democratic state based on the rule of law, the sovereignty of the people, plural democratic expression and political organisation, respect for and the guarantee of the effective implementation of the fundamental rights and freedoms, and the separation and interdependence of powers, with a view to achieving social, economic and cultural democracy and deepening participatory democracy.'

[56] Judgment 602/2013, above n. 35. Taken from the official English summary of the judgment by the Portuguese Constitutional Court.

cannot be opted out of by collective agreements. The ordinary law cannot delimit the untouchable core of the right to enter into collective labour agreements, because otherwise one would be inverting the normative hierarchy and emptying the constitutional precept of its legal force.

Compare this to the Romanian Constitutional Court's position that prohibiting collective bargaining for teachers to deviate from law was not a breach of the constitutional right to collectively bargain as:

> The Constitutional Court has consistently held that the right to collective bargaining and the binding nature of collective agreements are guaranteed by the Constitution, under the provisions of Article 41(5), but that the conclusion of collective agreements must be subject to the law. These agreements are a source of law, but their legal force cannot be superior to the law. Consequently, collective agreements are guaranteed insofar as they do not go against the law in force. To hold otherwise, 'would violate a fundamental principle of the rule of law, namely the primacy of law in regulating social relations'.[57]

The constitutional basis for reviewing monetary cuts varied across Europe. Rather than providing simple answers about the 'right' basis for review, it raises further questions about the criteria by which that might be ascertained. By focusing constitutional social evaluation and analysis only on the basis of monetary cuts, the scholarly evaluation of the courts is skewed and an important constitutional hinterland of jurisprudence on other social issues remains unexplored.

C. *Standard of Review*

Portuguese and Greek constitutional review show just how much the standard of review can vary despite their reliance on very similar constitutional provisions as the basis for review. Greece placed much more emphasis on exceptional fundamental rights protection in extreme situations, with the assumption that responding to the economic crisis defines the public interest; while Portugal placed constitutional commitments in a more central position and used them to develop more extensive guarantees of review of the distribution of the burdens of adjustments. This raises the question of whether it is, in fact, primarily the standard (strict vs. deferential) rather than the basis of review (equality, rule of law) that is the subject of attack.

[57] Decision 575/2011, above n. 30. Personal unofficial translation. See also Greek Council of State Decision 2307/2014, above n. 25.

Take the key judgment of the Greek Council of State which was in turn heavily relied upon by the European Court of Human Rights (ECtHR) in the decisions of both courts on the same case: *Koufaki*, decided in Greece in February 2012 and by the ECtHR in May 2013.[58] These courts reasoned that the monetary cuts were in the general interest and also coincided with those of the euro area Member States, in view of the requirement under EU legislation to ensure budgetary discipline and preserve the stability of the euro area. It only remained to determine whether Ms. Koufaki's pay cut struck a fair balance between this general interest and protection of her fundamental rights. Both courts dismissed several arguments that the salary cuts breached the proportionality principle. The fact these cuts were not temporary was justified, since the legislature's aim had been not only to remedy the acute budgetary crisis at that time but also to consolidate the State's finances on a lasting basis. Nor did Ms. Koufaki risk falling below the subsistence threshold.

Unlike the Greek Council of State, but like the Latvian and Romanian Constitutional Courts, the Portuguese Constitutional Court found that the extremely serious economic/financial situation and the need for measures that are adopted to deal with it to be effective cannot serve as grounds for dispensing the legislator from being subject to the fundamental rights and key structural principles of the state based on the rule of law. While the Constitution clearly cannot distance itself from economic and financial reality, it does possess a specific normative autonomy that prevents economic or financial objectives from prevailing in an unlimited way over parameters such as that of equality, which the Constitution defends and with which it must ensure compliance. Such a *prima facie* breach of the constitutional equality principle required therefore evaluation of the legislator's justification.

The Court considered that the only justification, that it could deem proven, for the public-sector salary cuts included in the budget law for 2012 was the measure's efficacy, given that it was certain to produce effects and to do so quickly in the search for a result that would be of important public interest. However, the Court also recalled that even within the framework of a serious economic/financial crisis, the legislator's freedom to resort to cutting the remuneration and pensions of persons who receive them from public funds, with a view to achieving a budgetary balance, cannot be unlimited. The difference between the

[58] See above Decision 668/2012 at n. 25 and ECtHR, Decision of 7 May 2013, Joined Cases 57665/12 and 57657/12, *Koufaki and Adedy* v. *Greece.*

degree of sacrifice undergone by those who are affected by this measure and that of those who are not must be subject to limits.

Legal equality is always a proportional equality, so any inequality that is justified by a difference in situations cannot be immune from a judgment of proportionality. The Court said that the difference in treatment in the case before it was so substantial and significant that the efficacy-related reasons advanced for the measure were not valid enough to justify such a large difference, all the more so in that it was possible to resort to alternative solutions.[59]

Further comparison shows there are still other ways to structure constitutional reasoning on cuts. The Romanian Constitutional Court decided that pay cuts should be subject to a different constitutional regime than pension cuts. It is possible for the Romanian Constitutional Court to choose which constitutional guarantees can be subject to public interest restrictions. Pay cuts, including judicial pay cuts, were constitutional because they were found to be subject to the public interest provision in Article 53 the Romanian Constitution.[60] However, pension cuts were unconstitutional because they were not subject to the public interest provision: being pre-constituted rights based on the contribution principle such limitations were not permitted in the Romanian constitutional order.[61] Where the public interest provision applied, however, it provided an easy path towards constitutionality. The Court found that the reference to the 'defence of national security' in the public interest provision covered not just military but also economic and social security. It was possible to restrict rights on this basis without it being necessary to officially declare a state emergency (under Article 93 Romanian Constitution) and it was easy to establish proportionality, especially given the temporary nature of the cuts:

[59] Case 353/2012 above n. 34.

[60] Art. 53 Romanian Constitution provides: (1) The exercise of certain rights or freedoms may only be restricted by law, and only if necessary, as the case may be, for: the defence of national security, of public order, health, or morals, of the citizens' rights and freedoms; conducting a criminal investigation; preventing the consequences of a natural calamity, disaster, or an extremely severe catastrophe.

(2) Such restriction shall only be ordered if necessary in a democratic society. The measure shall be proportional to the situation having caused it, applied without discrimination, and without infringing on the existence of such right or freedom.

[61] Special Magistrates' pensions were not pre-constituted in this way but were instead found unconstitutional on the basis of breaching the constitutional principle of judicial independence, in Art. 123(3) Romanian Constitution. See Decision 873/2010, n. 29.

> The Court finds that there is a proportionality between the means employed (25% reduction pay/benefits) and the legitimate aim pursued (reducing budget expenditures/rebalancing the state budget) and that there is a fair balance between the requirements of the general interest of the community and the protection of fundamental rights of the individual. The Court also notes that the challenged legislative measure is applied without discrimination, in the sense that the 25% cut applies to all categories of public sector staff in the amount and method.[62]

The Latvian Constitutional Court subjected each interference with specified social rights to proportionality analysis. This required asking whether the constitutionally suspect measure was duly established by law, pursued a reasonable and legitimate objective and was proportionate (in the double sense of being the least restrictive alternative and balancing). The reasoning turned on the last of these, as securing the sustainability of social insurance by balancing its budget was a reasonable and legitimate objective contributing to societal welfare.

As far as the least restrictive limb of proportionality was concerned, the Court examined carefully the time and effort expended by the other branches of the state on investigating alternatives commensurate with both the financial crisis and the interests affected by the challenged measures. Hence, a reduction of pensions by 70 per cent for those in employment failed the least restrictive test, as the other branches had failed to carry out an adequate analysis of alternatives, while non-indexation of pensions satisfied this limb as the alternatives (reduction of pensions or an increase in contributions) were less favourable.

The last part of the analysis is balancing the benefits to society against the detriments to those affected. Here again, the 70 per cent pensions reduction failed this limb on both procedural (insufficient time given to those affected to assess how to respond to their change in position and an inadequate transitional period) and substantive (insufficiently differentiated approach applied to all those affected and no subsequent compensation envisaged for the cuts), while the non-indexation of pensions was found to strike a constitutional balance. Given that the measures involved a non-increase and were temporary, the benefit gained by society from the contested norm outweighed the infringement of rights of those affected.

While the Portuguese Constitutional Court's reasoning and standard of review is certainly not beyond reproach or critique, it is best viewed in

[62] Decision 872/2010, n. 29.

the company of its fellow bailout constitutional courts, not as in a constitutional corner of shame on its own, as much of the exceptionally critical commentary asserts. The blunt and non-textually evident distinction operated by the Romanian Constitutional Court to sharply differentiate the standard of review on pay and pensions can certainly be questioned as much as the comparison between public-sector workers and others not affected by measures operated by the Portuguese Constitutional Court in applying the equality principle. The Latvian Constitutional Court was criticised for the coherence of its judgments when it found pension cuts unconstitutional but cuts to benefits for working parents to be constitutional. The very light-touch review operated by the Greek Council of State can be seen as providing insufficient constitutional restraint. These examples also underline that analysis and evaluation of the standard of review is not best served by a global proportionality analysis in which one common method or basic tool, a 'constitutional Esperanto' in Contiades and Fotiadou's language, is and should be applied everywhere.[63] As can be seen, the differences between the standards developed and applied are at least as significant as their similarities. Moreover, the particular issue of how to accommodate constitutional review of social measures with economic crisis or emergency, or even entry into sovereign debt loans, merits specific attention and analysis.

D. *Unfair and Ill-Advised to Protect the 'Middle-Class'?*

The real nub of the constitutional critique of Portuguese cuts jurisprudence is the unfairness of constitutional protection of public-sector workers.[64] Taking a telling 'imaginary example' of a state tripling public-sector salaries while placing the burden of debt adjustment solely on tax increases, De Almeida Ribeiro argues that the Portuguese Constitutional Court's position means that 'private sector employees are expected to subsidize excessive earnings in the public sector'. This underpins his other assertions grounding the unfairness charge: that those

[63] X. Contiades and A. Fotiadou, 'Social Rights in the Age of Proportionality: Global Economic Crisis and Constitutional Litigation'.

[64] See Nogueira de Brito, 'Putting Social Rights in Brackets': 'the Court is engaged in a judicial activist path . . . [which] . . . has little to do with the enforcement of social or work rights but is specially aimed at the protection of public-sector employees'.

public-sector workers with greater job security than private-sector workers should bear the burden of adjustment and that the Court should have proceeded on the assumption (without the need for careful data) that private-sector workers have already suffered wage cuts in the crisis and therefore public-sector workers needed, too, to suffer in a roughly similar way.[65] There is much to be said about this line of constitutional attack. My goal here is simply to open some profitable lines of further inquiry and debate.

First, it fits comfortably into a series of current 'common-sense' positions in European elite discourse, which decry cushioned public-sector jobs and over-protected labour market 'insiders'. It also fits the shift in European social policy from social protection in work to a minimal safety net for the avoidance of social exclusion and to encouraging states to invest in labour market–enhancing skills acquisition.[66]

Second, as noted above, cuts to public-sector workers' pay and pensions and to labour protections differ from the typical focus of traditional constitutional social scholarship on rights for those in poverty. Consequently, constitutional social scholarship has scant ammunition to respond to attacks on the constitutional protection of those with – albeit, typically, modest – resources. Yet this is the central group at issue in euro-crisis constitutional challenges.

Third, two very different strands, one 'neo-liberal' and one 'critical', of constitutional social scholarship expressly warn against conflating constitutional social victories with the protection of those in need, rather than 'the middle-class'. Many expressly state that the only viable judicial social constitutionalism is the protection of a minimum core for the least advantaged. Accordingly, the critique of the Portuguese Constitutional Court draws on an established set of positions in constitutional social scholarship. The key sites for this discussion to date have been judgments of the Hungarian Constitutional Court in the mid-1990s on the sovereign debt loan conditions set by the IMF and judgments of the Colombian Constitutional Court around the millennium.

The closest antecedent of contemporary critique is undoubtedly Andras Sajó's robust attack on the Hungarian Constitutional Court in

65 De Almeida Ribeiro, 'Judicial Activism'.

66 See, for a recent example, European Commission, *Social Agenda*, EU Economic Policy in the Making, No 40 4/2015 (April 2015), http://ec.europa.eu/social/main.jsp?langId=en&catId=89&newsId=2198.

the mid-1990s.[67] It struck down, as unconstitutional, Hungarian laws cutting pensions and sick pay and means-testing maternity support, passed at the IMF's behest, by relying on legal certainty as the most important conceptual element of the Rule of Law.[68] These decisions were bad, in his view, because:

(a) They created fierce and destabilizing conflict between the branches of government;
(b) The Court took a hasty and populist stance, obstructing vital economic modernization, behaving in a fiscally irresponsible fashion, shoring up an unaffordable welfare state and undermining the market economy;
(c) The status quo protected by the Court was inefficient (ill-suited to a free-market economy) and unfair (middle-class oriented to the detriment of the poor and the victims of transition).[69]

A much less red-blooded neo-liberal critique, albeit coming up with the same policy outcomes, is provided by Landau. He contrasts two waves of Colombian Constitutional Court jurisprudence. In the first wave, the Court protected pensioners and mortgagees without carrying out an assessment of whether the measure affected their minimum level of subsistence. Similarly, it also protected all public-sector workers against real wage cuts, when the government proposed protecting only those earning less than twice the minimum wage. Landau argues that, like the Hungarian decisions in the mid-90s, such decisions are vulnerable to charges that they have substantial budgetary effects, overstep the judicial

[67] A. Sajó, 'How the Rule of Law Killed Hungarian Welfare Reform', *East European Constitutional Review*, 5(1), 1996, 31–42. See also his similar arguments a decade later: 'Social Rights as Middle-Class Entitlements in Hungary: The Role of the Constitutional Court' in R. Gargarella, P. Domingo and T. Roux (eds.), *Courts and Social Transformations in New Democracies. An Institutional Voice for the Poor?* (Hampshire: Ashgate, 2006), pp. 83–106.

[68] K. Scheppele, 'A Realpolitik Defense of Social Rights', *Texas Law Review*, 82(7), (2004), 1921–61 provides an analysis of these decisions some of which (No. 43/1995, No. 56/1995) are found in English translation in L. Sólyom and G. Brunner (eds.), *Constitutional Judiciary in a New Democracy: The Hungarian Constitutional Court* (University of Michigan Press, 2000). The Court found inter alia that abrupt changes to social security payments violated the Rule of Law clause in the Constitution.

[69] Note the telling detail (providing a clear dividing line with progressive critical critiques) that he criticises the distributive outcome whereby to comply with the judgments, without further increasing the budget deficit, the socialist majority in Parliament increased the personal income tax for the highest income bracket (48 per cent for the top 10 per cent of tax-payers).

role and raise substantial equity concerns where they protect pensions and other assets owned by the relatively affluent, rather than the poor. He contrasts this first wave unfavourably with the second wave,[70] in which the Court upheld public-sector wage cuts which protected the lowest paid and focused its constitutionality assessment on whether measures harmed the poorest and most vulnerable members of the population. The overall prescription for courts everywhere dealing with austerity is to cleave to a minimum core approach.

While the careful and rigorous analysis of the distributive effects of social rights, including the judgments of constitutional courts, more often urged in the critical strands of this literature, is certainly to be fully embraced, used without care this kind of analysis is deeply problematic, not least because its 'easy' arguments regarding the unfairness of protecting the entitlements of workers in general, or public-sector workers in particular, are at risk of becoming 'common-sense'.

First, there is a risk that *default neo-liberal assumptions* take the place of searching analysis of distributive effects.[71] Indeed, contrary to those assumptions, it seems highly unlikely that appropriate enforcement of constitutional safeguards for workers is a straightforward zero-sum trade-off with appropriate constitutional safeguards for the least advantaged. While the relationships between these differing social components certainly deserve further investigation, it may well often be the case that protecting both is mutually beneficial and promotes an overall package lessening societal inequalities. Arguments that it is unfair to protect workers *rather than* the poor are often therefore simply arguments that a constitutional court is obstructing the author's preferred economic model: a free-market economy in which social protection is restricted to a means-tested minimum.

[70] By which point an effective attack by neo-liberal economists in prominent official positions in Colombia (notably by Salamon Kalmanovitz of the Colombian Central Bank) had fed into a change of judicial personnel and approach by the Colombian Constitutional Court. See Landau, 'The Promise of a Minimum Core Approach', pp. 279–81. García, *Socio and Economic Rights in Theory and in Practice*, p. 70 notes that this powerful neo-liberal opposition led, in 2011, to constitutional reform geared towards forcing courts to take into account budgetary restrictions.

[71] For an interesting account of this phenomenon see David Kennedy's analysis of Deepak Lal's work and its influence on the policies of international financial institutions: D. Kennedy, 'Political Choices and Development Common Sense', in D. Trubek and A. Santos (eds.), *The New Law and Economic Development: A Critical Appraisal* (Cambridge University Press, 2006), pp. 95–173, pp. 133–7.

Second, there is a risk of *default neo-liberal assumption extension* in which one moves from criticism of carefully focused examples of constitutionally adjudicating particular wage/benefits cuts for public-sector workers to assuming that all constitutional protection of workers is so fraught with difficulties of judicial role, empirical assessment and obstructing macro-economic adaptation that it is best not undertaken. Hence, Landau moves directly from applauding new-found judicial deference to monetary cuts to endorsing the deference shown by the Colombian Constitutional Court to 'sweeping changes to the laws governing workers' rights . . . the law made the hiring, firing and regulation of workers more flexible by, for example, making workers easier and less expensive to terminate and altering the definition of a working day'. Such measures 'require courts to undertake difficult line-drawing exercises', to confront 'the empirical difficulty of determining the effect of the changes in question on the economy. . .', to avoid creating 'political pushback' and 'threaten[ing] to leave petitioners with either no protection or rigid protection that makes it impossible for the State to respond to changing macro-economic circumstances'.[72]

Third, there is also an important question of *constitutional integrity*. A question is raised about the meaning of the extensive constitutional commitments relating to workers, which – as we have seen earlier – are a hallmark of many European constitutions. Should the 'poverty-only' role of social constitutional review be endorsed, the outcome is that the extensive social constitutional commitments relating to work, including work-related benefits, are to be denied any autonomous constraining effect.[73] Yet this puzzling and surely controversial constitutional outcome is never justified by the proponents of the 'poverty-only' social constitutional reading.

Fourth, one might imagine that the field could be occupied, or contested, by *constitutional labour law* scholars. Yet the focus of this scholarship lies elsewhere. One strand lies in emphasising collective autonomy

[72] Landau, 'The Promise of a Minimum Core Approach', pp. 284–5.

[73] See, extra-judicially, Portuguese Constitutional Court judge Ana Guerra Martins, 'Constitutional Judge, Social Rights and Public Debt Crisis', *Maastricht Journal*, 22(5), 2015, 678–705, at 695, to this effect: 'In our opinion, according to the [Portuguese Constitution], corroborated by a consistent constitutional jurisprudence . . . the social rights are genuine fundamental rights, not merely principles of social policy, and consequently, in a constitutional state, the law shall respect these rights . . . Furthermore the [Portuguese Constitution] was not suspended. By contrast, despite the financial and debt crises, it was in force'.

and worker democracy. On this understanding, the 'labour constitution' democratizes capitalist economies by providing for the collective regulation of the economy through unions, works' councils, employers and their associations.[74] Another part of the scholarship focuses on constitutional adjudication hampering legislative introduction of labour and social protection by use of federal/state boundaries or constitutional protections.[75] Others engage cautiously and sceptically with judicial constitutional rights protection of (mainly) freedom of association rights.[76] Although bridges can certainly be built from these concerns to the euro-crisis constitutional jurisprudence, extensive building work is needed especially in relation to the specificities of social loan conditionality and the role of constitutional courts, economic crisis and social constitutionalism and the position to be taken in relation to monetary cuts for workers, especially in the public sector.

E. The Traditional Juristocracy Critiques Are Not Compelling in Times of EU Sovereign Debt

Examining the inter-institutional dimension provides an opportunity to consider another of the charges levelled against the Portuguese Constitutional Court: that of illegitimacy or juristocracy or judicial activism. Its judgments certainly attracted exceptional media coverage and analysis. One *Financial Times* example from 24 October 2013, headlined 'Portugal's constitutional court threatens bailout', gives the flavour. It begins:

> Robed in black and accustomed to the quiet of their Lisbon Chambers, the 13 judges of Portugal's constitutional court have found themselves propelled unexpectedly into the cut and thrust of high European politics.

[74] For a highly interesting recent analysis developing this collective democracy reading, see R. Dukes, *The Labour Constitution: The Enduring Idea of Labour Law* (Oxford University Press, 2014).

[75] An exemplary comparative analysis developing such themes is O. Kahn-Freund, 'The Impact of Constitutions on Labour Law', *Cambridge Law Journal*, 35(2), 1976, 240–71.

[76] See, for example, H. Arthurs, 'Labour and the 'Real' Constitution', *Cahiers de Droit*, 48(1–2), 2007, 43–63, for whom the economic structure (the 'real' constitution) matters more than the formal constitution which is vague and leaves ample room for challenge and for change. A recent intense focus on such discussions has been a series of Canadian Supreme Court decisions on freedom of association rights. See, for example, J. Fudge, 'Constitutional Rights, Collective Bargaining and the Supreme Court of Canada: Retreat and Reversal in the Fraser case', *Industrial Law Journal*, 41(1), 2012, 1–29.

> Defenders of the inviolability of national laws for some, enemies of reform to others, the seven men and six women have become critical to the success or failure of Portugal's 78 billion euro bailout programme and, by implication, the resolution of the Eurozone crisis.[77]

Charges of judicial activism during the crisis have taken a traditional focus by sustaining that national constitutional courts that struck down measures taken to fulfil loan conditions were not sufficiently deferential to national Parliaments and executives.

A key purchase of constitutional social scholarship is its inter-institutional awareness. It is alert to whether and how courts attract constitutional and political controversy when they accept constitutional challenges to social rights and when and how they can take steps to diminish such controversy. The argument is made that courts carrying out constitutional review of social rights can weaken objections of judicial over-reach by engaging in forms of constitutional review other than strong-form review. This can exist through formalized constitutional mechanisms which combine constitutional judicial review with giving the final word to the legislature[78] or through constitutional review practices developed by specialised constitutional courts which engage in a more dialogic fashion with the parties to the case or other branches of government.[79] My analysis builds on such work in the specific European sovereign debt context to claim that, in a range of distinct and interesting ways, the traditional focus is misplaced. It under-specifies the branches of government when examining constitutional interactions with the judicial branch: as will clearly be demonstrated these must be expanded in the context of Eurocrisis to include the EU institutions. It under-examines the actions and evolving decision-making of the constitutional courts themselves. It assumes relationships between the branches of the state that do not prevail while a state is in bailout.

[77] 'Portugal's Constitutional Court Threatens Bailout', *Financial Times* (24 October 2013), www.ft.com/cms/s/0/884f61d2-3bfb-11e3-b85f-00144feab7de.html#axzz43iW7rcSB.

[78] See M. Tushnet, *Weak Courts, Strong Rights: Judicial Review and Social Welfare Rights in Comparative Constitutional Law* (Princeton University Press, 2008). He distinguishes between weak-form and strong-form judicial review, arguing that the former weakens certain objections to constitutional enforcement of social rights.

[79] K. G. Young, *Constituting Economic and Social Rights* (Oxford University Press, 2012); W. Forbath, 'Cultural Transformation, Deep Institutional Reform, and ESR Practice: South Africa's Treatment Action Campaign' in L. E. White and J. Perelman (eds.), *Stones of Hope: How African Activists Reclaim Human Rights to Challenge Global Poverty* (Stanford University Press, 2011), pp. 51–90.

F. *Expanding the Relevant Branches*

A first unusual development signalling expansion of the relevant branches, as well as a surely abnormal EU constitutional interaction, is the explicit interaction between the judgments of the Portuguese Constitutional Court and EU legislative sources. Hence, the Council Implementing Decisions setting out the changing loan conditions for the Portuguese bailouts cite these constitutional court judgments and note the budgetary 'gap' they create. The decisions addressed to Portugal after these decisions consider how to manage 'political and legal risks in the implementation process'.[80] Similar references in EU sources can be found in the third Greek bailout commencing in August 2015.[81] National constitutional court decisions on fundamental constitutional principles have accordingly explicitly become for the EU legislature 'legal risks' to be managed.

The Portuguese Constitutional Court decision of 30 May 2014 provoked a series of *multi-level* institutional and political communications and consequences.[82] The most important consequence was the Portuguese government's early exit from the loan assistance programme. This can be framed, as in the troika statement set out below, as a decision by the Portuguese government not to seek an extension of the programme. It can also be read as a failure by the Portuguese state to meet the loan conditions required by the EU (and IMF) for disbursement of the final tranche of the loan (€2.6 billion). In any event, the troika statement also urged the government to press on regardless with reform and to bridge the gap created by its constitutional court:

> The European Commission, the European Central Bank and the International Monetary Fund take note of the Portuguese government's intention to await the pending Constitutional Court rulings concerning adopted budgetary measures before formulating a comprehensive response. These rulings are not expected before the IMF and EU programme expires at the end of June. We take note of the government's decision not to seek an extension of the program and to allow its

[80] Council Implementing Decision 2013/323/EU of 21 June 2013 amending Implementing Decision 2011/344/EU on granting Union financial assistance to Portugal (OJ L 175, 27.6.2013, p. 47).

[81] Council Implementing Decision 2015/1411 of 19 August 2015 approving the macroeconomic adjustment programme of Greece (OJ L 219, 20.9.2015, p. 12), Art. 2(2) states: 'The Greek government shall monitor fiscal risks, including court rulings, and shall take offsetting measures as needed to meet the fiscal targets'.

[82] Judgment 413/2014, n. 36.

> expiration without completing the 12th and final review and without receiving the associated final tranche.
>
> We welcome the government's firm commitment to identify the measures needed to fill the fiscal gap created by the Constitutional Court rulings, in order to reach the budgetary targets agreed under the programme. We encourage the government to continue with the ongoing process of structural reform. Sound economic policies for the medium term will be essential to reinforce the economic recovery and ensure sustainable growth and job creation. We remain ready to assist the authorities and the Portuguese people as they continue in this effort.[83]

A further triangular institutional interaction was also provoked between the Portuguese government, the Constitutional Court and the troika. As the troika statement notes, the Portuguese government had cited its supposed need for clarification from the constitutional court – before tabling alternative savings to replace those struck down by the court in May 2014 – as one of the justifications for forgoing the last tranche of the euro area bailout.[84] Yet the constitutional court in a subsequent judgment rejected the government's request to clarify its decision on the 2014 state budget. It dismissed the idea that its original ruling had contained any obscurity or ambiguities – the two words used by the government in justifying its request for clarification. It was not up to the constitutional court to clarify to other state organs the terms on which these other branches must exercise their legislative or administrative competences.[85]

While this notable inter-institutional episode certainly underlines the multi-level branches of public authority that need to be modelled in EU sovereign debt episodes, it may also seem to give considerable force to the charge of illegitimacy or judicial activism or juristocracy levelled against the Portuguese Constitutional Court. Yet other elements must be considered and evaluated before any assessment can be made.

G. *Expanding Consideration of Constitutional Courts and Their Interactions*

The measuring and mapping of inter-institutional relations can also usefully be traced in a range of ways inside the constitutional courts themselves. Such

[83] European Commission, 'Statement by the European Commission, European Central Bank, and International Monetary Fund on Portugal' (12 June 2014), http://europa.eu/rapid/press-release_STATEMENT-14-191_en.htm?locale=en.

[84] Portuguese News Agency, 19 June 2014. [85] Judgment 468/2014, 18 June 2014.

analysis can include qualitative and quantitative analysis of the judgments,[86] tracking the evolution of dissent within the court across the arc of euro-crisis challenges,[87] or across different issues or between different judges.[88]

These courts did not ignore the difficult situation in which their decisions placed the political branches. The Portuguese Constitutional Court had earlier, at the cost of significant internal dissent, introduced a constitutional innovation to accommodate the difficult position of the Portuguese government. Indeed, its jurisprudence can be read as a series of warnings followed by action. Its first Budget Law judgment found the 2011 pay cuts to be constitutional but made clear the delimited boundaries making that finding possible. Its second Budget Law judgment found the 2012 pay cuts to fall outside the constitutional limits set out in 2011. However, it exceptionally suspended the effects of its judgment to protect the execution of the budget, which had already been implemented for over six months, as not to do so could, it explicitly reasoned, put in danger the continued financing of the Portuguese State by the troika.[89] The Latvian Constitutional Court acted similarly.[90]

Moreover, in considering the juristocracy charge, it is important to underline again that these cases were brought before the Portuguese Constitutional Court (and the others) using political constitutional review mechanisms. Hence, it is the President of the Portuguese Republic, Portuguese elected representatives and the Ombudsman who maintain that the challenged measures fail to respect the Portuguese

86 For example, if we look at the length of the judgments there are two clear peaks in the Portuguese Constitutional Court's euro-crisis judgments: while most of the judgments range between 20 to 30 pages the two most controversial (187/2013 and 413/2014) are both over 90 pages long, with dissenting opinions making up between 20 to 30 pages of the total length.

87 Dissents in the Portuguese Constitutional Court bailout decisions had three peaks: in Judgment 187/2013, its first decision finding unconstitutionality (with 11 out of a possible 13 judges dissenting), in Judgment 602/2013 on relaxing private-sector employment protection (12 out of a possible 13 judges dissenting) and in Judgment 413/2014, which prompted early bailout exit (each judge dissented on at least one issue).

88 Because of expiring mandates, 19 different constitutional court judges participated in the Portuguese Constitutional Court decisions and only 6 judges participated in all 12 decisions listed above. Of these, dissents ranged from 3 out of 12 (Judge Guerra Martins) to 8 out of 12 (Judge Cunha Barbos).

89 Judgment 353/2012, n. 34, para. 6.

90 In Judgment 2009-11-01 the Latvian Constitutional Court temporarily suspended (until 1 January 2011) its finding that cuts of 15 per cent to judicial pay were unconstitutional on the basis that their immediate repeal would endanger budget stability and societal welfare.

Constitution. That is to say, constitutional review operates in these challenges as national politics by other means framed and channelled by the constitutional text. Such review is to ensure that the legislature acts within its constitutional limits.

H. The Assumptions of Juristocracy in Times of Sovereign Debt

Much of the force of the juristocracy charge derives from the argument that courts are interfering with more legitimate and democratically accountable choices within a state. But this, it is important to stress, is a state of affairs which does not prevail while a state is in bailout. During bailout, a wide range of national democratic choices become suspended as external lenders set the terms for loan disbursements. Indeed, one of the primary characteristics of the national measures in response to euro-crisis loan conditionality is the use of emergency procedures such as special executive powers and the shortcutting of normal Parliamentary procedures and debates.[91] Hence, constitutional court judgments *can* become a new resource for governments in dealing with lenders to argue for renegotiations of terms in order to maintain constitutionality.[92] Yet this does not seem to be a feature of national government responses to successful euro-crisis constitutional challenges. Empowerment of the national vis-à-vis the EU/IMF is not a discernible outcome of findings of unconstitutionality. Rather than re-opening the global figure of cuts required to the national budget in return for loans, the outcome was a governmental search for alternative acceptable measures delivering equivalent savings to satisfy the EU Commission, the IMF and (for euro area states) the European Central Bank.

4 A Structured EU, and a Shared European, Constitutional Space?

A. A Structured EU Constitutional Space?

The loan conditions directly clashed with constitutional commitments related to social rights in both EU and national constitutional law. On the

[91] See, for example, Romania the use of emergency delegated legislation under Art. 115(5)–(8) of the Constitution, as well as extensive use of a special legislative procedure under Article 114 Constitution, relying on a confidence vote before Parliament, rather than the normal processes of parliamentary debate and amendment: see, further, the Report on Romania prepared by Viță, Section III.9. See also the four country case studies of emergency in this book in *Part II National Constitutional Manifestations of Economic Emergency*.

[92] See further Kim Lane Scheppele, 'A Realpolitik Defense of Social Rights'.

basis of the existing paradigms of EU constitutional law, this should have led to one of two established paths for mediating such EU constitutional conflict being followed, one based on unmediated acceptance of EU primacy, the other based on national constitutional mediation of EU primacy. This can be referred to as 'the structured EU constitutional space'. Yet neither of these paths was taken by constitutional courts. I consider what actually happened and a good explanation for why it did so.

Given that the loan conditions emanated from the EU,[93] an important question is raised as to how these national constitutional decisions mesh with EU law. Assume that the loan conditions are straightforwardly EU law, bracketing doubts which exist on this issue, to which we return below.[94] Loan conditions based on EU law sources make its national execution an implementation of that EU law. Although those EU sources are often acknowledged in these national constitutional court decisions, and the specific instructions of the MoUs are often referred to in constitutional judgments, the legal implications of that EU connection are entirely ignored. To see how this matters we need to consider the bases for EU law supremacy over national constitutions. We shall see that neither of the two key characterisations of the foundations of EU-national constitutional interactions explains what happened in the national decisions finding national laws implementing EU loan conditions to be unconstitutional. Departing from this interesting and puzzling finding, we consider other possible explanations.

B. *Characterisation 1: National Constitutional Review Courts Accept the EU Account of Supremacy*

From the Court of Justice's perspective, as Stephen Weatherill states, 'even the most minor piece of technical Community legislation ranks above the most cherished constitutional norm'.[95] Central for fundamental rights or constitutional principles is *Internationale Handelsgesellschaft*[96] in which the Court of Justice had to deal with a challenge to

[93] The cases of Greece and Cyprus are more complex, as the primary loan sources were agreed by the Member States acting inter-governmentally. However, this does not straightforwardly preclude EU review for a series of reasons, as explored in Kilpatrick, 'Are the Bailout Measures Immune to EU Social Challenge?'.

[94] Ibid.

[95] Stephen Weatherill, *Law and Integration in the European Union* (Oxford University Press, 1995), p. 136.

[96] Case 11/70, [1970] ECR 1125.

a Community Regulation which conflicted with the German Basic Law. The Court found that 'the validity of a Community measure or its effect within a Member State cannot be affected by allegations that it runs counter to either fundamental rights as formulated by the constitution of that state or the principles of a national constitutional structure'. If the national court has doubts about the legality *under EU law* of the EU norm the Court of Justice's supremacy jurisprudence requires it to apply, it cannot evaluate or set aside the dubious EU norm but is required by the Court of Justice to make a validity reference.[97]

On this characterisation the EU bailout norm should be applied even if it conflicts with the national constitution because of full and unmediated acceptance of the EU understanding of EU supremacy. However, national constitutional courts finding the loan conditions to raise concerns should consider whether EU bailout norms complied with *EU norms.* This should have led to preliminary references to the Court of Justice from national constitutional review courts on the validity under EU law, including the social commitments in the Treaties and the EU Charter of Fundamental Rights, of the bailout sources as well as more general constitutional principles such as the principle of equality or of legitimate expectations, both of which are key features of the national constitutional decisions. Yet this clearly did not happen.

C. Characterisation(s) 2: Nationally Mediated Reception of Supremacy and Its Implications

An alternate characterisation, when we speak of constitutional courts in Europe contesting EU sources, is based on analysis of an inter-court relationship with the Court of Justice asserting different bases for EU law supremacy from some national constitutional courts.[98] It is well-known that many, indeed most, national constitutional systems do not accept the Court of Justice's asserted monopoly on the nature of validity and primacy. National courts by and large have not accepted the EU version of primacy whereby it is inherently supreme as a matter of EU law but

[97] Case 314/85 *Foto-frost* [1987] ECR 4199.

[98] For an extended analysis, see De Witte, 'Direct Effect, Primacy and the Nature of the Legal Order', in P. Craig and G. de Búrca (eds.), 2nd edn, *The Evolution of EU Law* (Oxford University Press, 2011), pp. 323–62.

rather have given effect to primacy via a *national constitutional basis*.[99] While this works straightforwardly when the primacy of EU law is asserted over conflicting national legislation, the national constitutional basis for EU law primacy clearly means constitutional incompatibilities are more difficult to resolve when this characterisation is adopted. As Bruno De Witte notes, 'If the national courts (and other national authorities) think that European law ultimately derives its validity in the domestic legal order from the authority of the constitution, then they are unlikely to recognize that EU law might simply prevail over the very foundation from which its legal force derives'.[100] Constitutional courts have often allowed small modifications to the national constitutional settlement but not allowed EU law to override essential elements of the national constitution. These typically include fundamental rights but also national constitutional identity and competence limits. Hence while the first characterisation espouses a hierarchical view of supremacy, on this characterisation it is best seen as a heterarchical relationship, raising questions about how to manage these competing views when concrete conflicts arise.

Because the loan conditions are found unconstitutional on a range of grounds, including constitutionally protected rights and principles, it is extremely interesting to try to place these national constitutional cases inside this kind of analysis. Yet they do not fit the prototypical manifestations of this characterisation of EU constitutional interactions. It is difficult to convincingly read these cases as an instance of explicit constitutional interaction through dialogue, co-operation or conflict.

We can underline the contrast by setting these euro-crisis constitutional interactions against the most highly developed national constitutional model for managing such EU-national constitutional tensions on fundamental rights, that of Germany.[101] Imagine if these cases concerning constitutional breaches of fundamental rights or principles had

[99] For a relevant recent example see the Romanian Constitutional Court's rejection of a constitutional amendment in 2014 (Decision 80/2014, 16 February 2014) which would have had the effect of making EU law prevail over all Romanian law, including its constitution, on the basis that this would breach Art. 152 of the Romanian Constitution: 'no revision shall be made if it results in the suppression of the citizens' fundamental rights and freedoms, or of the safeguards thereof.'

[100] De Witte, 'Direct Effect, Primacy and the Nature of the Legal Order', p. 352.

[101] For a useful recent overview of the German Federal Constitutional Court's position, see E. Vranes, 'German Constitutional Foundations of, and Limitations to, EU Integration: A Systematic Analysis', *German Law Journal*, 14(1), 2013, 75–122.

come before German courts. Those courts would have found themselves inside a richly developed and highly nuanced national constitutional jurisprudence on how to manage possible conflicts between national constitutional requirements and EU legislation. It is an extensively elaborated and evolving jurisprudence on constitutional dialogue, co-operation and review in an EU-national constitutional system for protecting fundamental rights. According to that jurisprudence, national courts should first make references to the Court of Justice to check compliance of the suspect EU norm with EU fundamental rights and principles. The national constitutional court retains a reserve review power to change this system should EU Fundamental Rights protection depart radically from the level in place when this constitutional jurisprudence was put in place.

By contrast, although our cases involve a conflict between EU-authored loan conditions and national constitutions, there is no open conflict or dialogue with the Court of Justice and indeed no consideration of how such fundamental rights tensions should be judicially managed. Because the Portuguese, Latvian and Romanian Constitutional Courts base their decisions on assessing the constitutionality of the national laws rather than their EU foundations, they avoid any open EU conflict. They do not say, for example, that the national constitution cannot permit EU law containing loan conditions to operate because that EU law fails to respect fundamental elements of the national constitution, and that the basis for EU law supremacy requires EU law to so respect its constitution. Nor do they consider whether their constitution requires a different reading in light of E(M)U developments: indeed some of the invective directed at the Portuguese Constitutional Court decisions was to the effect that it had failed to understand that its constitutional settlement needed 're-reading' to adjust and re-orient itself to the commitments of euro area membership,[102] or as part of the constitutional duty to

[102] This was a feature of some of the dissenting judgments in the Portuguese Constitutional Court. See, for example, Judge Pedro Machete in Judgment 187/2013, n. 35: national constitutional commitment to European integration demands heed to euro area integrity, respect for the principle of loyal cooperation, and constraints resulting from measures adopted under Arts. 122(2), 123 and 125 TFEU. See also Judge Lúcia Amaral's dissent in Judgment 353/2012, n. 34, stating that the challenged measures have to be read in light of the constitutional mandate to participate in European integration (Art. 7[5] and [6] Portuguese Constitution) and, in particular, respect for the obligations resulting from membership of the euro area that came with the financing of the Member States in debt.

participate in EU integration,[103] leading to different outcomes on these constitutional challenges. Yet none of these constitutional courts read the bailout sources through either classical EU constitutional or 'euro area' EU constitutional lenses.

D. *Alternative Readings – Avoiding Undesired EU Judicialization of Constitutional Conflict*

We now need to unbracket discussions about the nature of these sources. Consider two possible ways of characterising them:

1. International 'bailout' sources/national engagement with those international sources
2. EU 'bailout' sources/national implementation of those EU sources

What is most significant is that the bailout measures are never fully articulated in national constitutional challenges as either an implementation of EU law or as acts of EU institutions. Either explicitly, as in the case of Latvia,[104] or implicitly and partially, as in the cases of Portugal[105]

[103] See Judge Lúcia Amaral's dissent in Judgment 574/2014, n. 37, in which she argues that the balancing test nested in the constitutional equality principle should incorporate the constitutional value of EU integration. This duty was arguably strengthened by the inclusion of 'EU integration' clauses in some constitutions as a consequence of various Treaty developments: the Maastricht Treaty and following ratification in some countries of the (ultimately abandoned) Treaty for a Constitution for Europe. Hence, the Portuguese constitution was amended in 2004 to add a new basis for EU integration, Art. 8(4): 'The provisions of the treaties that govern the European Union and the rules issued by its institutions in the exercise of their respective responsibilities shall apply in Portuguese internal law in accordance with Union law and with respect for the fundamental principles of a democratic state based on the rule of law'.

[104] See Latvian judgment 2009–43-01, n. 27 (finding 10 per cent and 70 per cent pension cuts unconstitutional), which notes that the MoU of 13 July 2009 contains a pledge by the Latvian government to make these cuts but appears to consider that it is not legally binding: 'the fact that the above documents contain the pledge of the government to adopt the challenged provisions does not mean that the international creditors have stipulated these particular conditions ... The Constitutional Court did not receive any information attesting that the international creditors stipulated the adoption of the impugned provisions as a prerequisite for granting the loan ... The measures in the [MoU] are to be characterised as an action of the State with the aim to reduce budget expenditure and, consequently, to be eligible for the international loan'.

[105] In Portugal the bailout sources, and broader EU commitments to fiscal limits, are acknowledged and their EU nature and compliance are seen as an element of the public interest. See, for example, Judgment 413/2014, n. 36, para. 30. In Judgment 574/2014, n.37, perhaps not coincidentally, post-bailout exit, the Court develops its views further.

and Romania,[106] the non-EU characterisation of the bailout sources is adopted, clearing the way for national constitutional review.

The complex and variegated legal nature of the bailouts, both their hybrid EU/international nature and the prominent position given to Memoranda of Understanding (MoUs) as a bailout component, may indicate that national actors did not consider that the normal regime for considering EU sources in their national legal order applied to these sources.[107] Yet there are overwhelming arguments in the case of the bailout sources applied to Latvia, Romania and Portugal that the loan conditions were contained in EU sources.[108] Accepting this as the sole reason for the exit from EU constitutional interactions accordingly raises questions about the grasp of EU law by national constitutional courts.[109]

Yet there is an alternative, and also complementary, explanation. This is that not addressing the EU nature of the bailouts may have served to avoid what promised to be an open and highly charged conflict with the EU institutions and legal order, including the Court of Justice, by taking validity challenges against the EU components of bailout programmes. While the Portuguese Constitutional Court's findings that national

It takes the view that the Fiscal Compact Treaty, as a non-EU law source, cannot be read in light of the Portuguese Constitution's European Integration clause (Art. 8[4]) and that the Stability and Growth Pact Recommendations are subject to a similar reading on the basis that they set only ends, not means. It further states that national legal norms must comply with the Portuguese Constitution as recognised by Art. 4(2) TEU, which provides for respect of the national identity of the Member States, including their fundamental political and constitutional structures. Finally, it finds that the reasoning used in its bailout jurisprudence on cuts (on equality, proportionality and legitimate expectations) is part of the hard core of the Rule of Law and constitute part of a common legal heritage, to which the Union is also bound (para. 12).

106 The Romanian Constitutional Court barely elaborates on the legal nature of the bailout measures, limiting itself to noting the government was responding in a timely manner to the IMF.

107 For other reasons, see C. Kilpatrick, 'On the Rule of Law and Economic Emergency: The Degradation of Basic Legal Values in Europe's Bailouts', *Oxford Journal Legal Studies*, 35 (2), 2015, 325–54.

108 See, for further analysis, Kilpatrick, 'Are the Bailout Measures Immune to EU Social Challenge?'. The situation in relation to Greece is more complex.

109 There are reasons to doubt such an explanation, particularly in relation to the Portuguese Constitutional Court, where, for example, the President of the Constitutional Court until late 2012, Rui Moura Ramos, was a judge of the Court of First Instance (now the EU's General Court) from 1995 to 2003. One Portuguese Constitutional Court judge, Ana Guerra Martins, writing extra-judicially (n. 73 at 702) explains that the MoUs left too much freedom to the national legislature to be considered as EU obligations; for extensive counterarguments and examples see Kilpatrick, 'Are the Bailout Measures Immune to EU Social Challenge?'.

bailout measures were unconstitutional provoked intense national and EU institutional responses, the nature of the conflict and controversy would have been very different had it been openly framed by that constitutional court as EU (bailout) sources breaching fundamental rights and principles in the Portuguese Constitution.[110] Hence these constitutional court responses to bailout sources are perhaps better viewed as efforts to avoid an *undesired EU judicialization* of the conflict between bailout sources and national constitutional rights. Failure to fully and legally characterise the bailout sources as EU sources allowed a space for national constitutional review to occur without such an undesired EU judicialization of the conflict between bailout sources and national constitutional guarantees.

If this is an insular response, the last of the charges levelled at the Portuguese Constitutional Court by its critics, then it is an insular response taken by every single constitutional review court in the EU faced with euro-crisis constitutional challenges. In any event, a closer comparative reading suggests quite the opposite characterisation: the judgments are carefully cosmopolitan, involving an astute analysis of the consequences for EU judicial-constitutional interactions of alternate readings and a determination to avoid those consequences. Of course, at the same time it surely demonstrates that a robust and open constitutional judicial dialogue between national constitutional courts and the Court of Justice of the European Union is far from guaranteed to occur even when it is an acutely needed input into the legality of the EU's social constitutional crisis.

5 A Shared European Constitutional Space?

How could we measure whether those euro-crisis states in which constitutional challenges occurred are a shared European constitutional space? At one end of the spectrum one could identify mere *commonalities* that is to say *separate and apparently uncoordinated but similar* legal and

110 See M. Pires, 'Private versus Public or State versus Europe? A Portuguese Constitutional Tale' *Michigan Journal of International Law Emerging Scholarship Project* (2013), 101–7, who maintains that deciding the cases on a purely internal basis 'was very typical of Portuguese constitutional thought, which avoids open confrontation with European law' (102) and that 'The Court did not want to enter a battle, which it does not feel comfortable fighting, preferring to deal with the issue in a national perspective' (106). Contrast Pires' view with the Portuguese Court's more robust engagement with EU sources post-bailout exit in Judgment 574/2014, above n. 37, discussed above at n. 103.

political dimensions to constitutional challenges, reasoning and responses to euro-crisis demands. More intensely, and involving active sharing, would be *horizontal sharing and utilisation* by courts (or those appearing before them) of relevant constitutional judgments and arguments. More intense still would be evidence of *active transnational coordination of strategies* by constitutional litigants or courts towards relevant EU and international institutions.

Euro-crisis constitutional judgments provide some exceptional examples of commonalities, the most interesting of which is the approach by constitutional courts to managing potential EU constitutional conflict, explored above. There is no evidence of the most intense form of sharing: transnational co-ordination by constitutional litigants or courts.

The reasoning of constitutional courts is traditionally a central focus of those seeking signs of a shared transnational constitutional space, in the sense of horizontal borrowing and inspiration. I look first at horizontal inspiration of constitutional courts by each other's judgments in euro-crisis or related episodes of constitutional jurisprudence and, second, at recourse by constitutional courts to relevant shared norms: from the Council of Europe, the ILO or UN instruments.

The crisis prompted a new reaching out to constitutional courts of other Member States. In Decision 872/2010 the Romanian Constitutional Court decided that a reduction of 15 per cent in pensions was unconstitutional. To underline this idea, the Court looked at '*some considerations made by other Constitutional Courts with regard to the right to pension*'. This recourse by the Romanian Constitutional Court to comparative constitutional law was truly exceptional: out of around 13,000 decisions issued by the Romanian Constitutional Court from 1991 only 14 have referred to foreign jurisprudence. Four of these 14 judgments concern euro-crisis law.[111] This makes it an interesting example of new kinds of transnational judicial communications provoked by the bailouts. It is equally noteworthy that the Romanian Constitutional Court's comparative constitutional interpretation came *almost exclusively* from Central and Eastern European EU Member States: the Hungarian decisions from the mid-1990s discussed earlier,[112] a number of euro-crisis judgments of

[111] See also Decision 873/2010, Decision 874/2010 and Decision 1533/2011, all at n. 29. See further E. Tanasescu and S. Deaconu, 'Romania: Analogical Reasoning as a Dialectical Instrument', in T. Groppi and M-C. Ponthereau (eds.), *The Use of Foreign Precedents by Constitutional Courts* (Oxford: Hart, 2013), pp. 321–46.

[112] See nn. 67–8.

the Latvian Constitutional Court[113] and decisions of the Czech and Lithuanian Constitutional Courts on cuts to judicial benefits.

The single example to date of use by Eastern European constitutional courts of Western euro-crisis constitutional jurisprudence is also instructive. The Romanian state, responding to those constitutional judgments finding pension cuts unconstitutional, had scheduled compensation payments amounting to over 1 per cent of Romanian GDP to public-sector workers. When the scheduling of these payments was constitutionally challenged the Romanian Constitutional Court operated a constitutional control limited to obvious infringements of the constitutional text in order to leave Parliament an appropriate margin of appreciation in the area of budgetary policy. This was backed up by reference to the German Constitutional Court's first euro-crisis judgment of 7 September 2011 on the package of measures on financial aid granted to Greece and funds made available for saving the euro.[114] At the same time, there was no use by Western European bailout courts (Portugal, Greece) of the first wave of Eastern European constitutional court bailout jurisprudence. Although it is possible that Eastern bailout courts looked to Western bailout courts without citing them, the difference in which courts they cite is relevant. As we move through the second decade of EU Eastern enlargement this is a new and interesting strand of analysis. It raises questions about the existence of two rather separate European spheres of comparative constitutional influence.

The use of international human rights sources in these judgments is also an interesting point of comparison. The Latvian Constitutional Court quotes extensively from the General Comments issued by the UN Economic and Social Rights Committee. All the constitutional review courts bar Portugal drew extensively on the ECHR and Strasbourg Court jurisprudence while the Portuguese Constitutional Court drew on the EU Charter of Fundamental Rights.[115] There is scarce invocation of ILO or European Social Charter text or supervisory bodies' findings.[116] Hence, while constitutional social scholarship increasingly mingles human and constitutional rights, euro-crisis constitutional jurisprudence does not follow this pattern.

113 Latvian Judgments 2009–43-01 and 2009-11-01 (at n. 27).

114 Decision 1533/2011 (at n. 29).

115 See, for example, Judgment 474/2013 citing Art. 30 EUCFR (protection of unjustified dismissal).

116 See, for example, Judgment 474/2013 Portuguese Constitutional Court invoking Art. 24 European Social Charter.

6 Connecting Constitutional Crises with Eurocrisis and Social Rights: The Example of Hungary under Orbán

While much has been written about the rule of law, constitutional revision and constitutional crisis in Hungary under the Orbán government in power since 2010[117] and about Eurocrisis, these discussions remain separate.[118] My claim is that placing such changes within the context of euro-crisis law adds important new dimensions to the analysis. Focusing on constitutional reform, euro-crisis and social rights show linkages between these phenomena deserving further exploration as part of broader discussions of the causes, channels and consequences of democratic crisis in Hungary. Although I limit myself to a preliminary exploration of one central example, Romania would be an obvious further candidate for this kind of analysis.[119] I do not claim that sovereign debt loan assistance or the related broader context of EMU constraints are necessarily dominant or unvarying explanations for constitutional crisis. However, I do suggest that this entirely overlooked aspect really deserves focused attention as it suggests certain important linkages between economic instability, sovereign debt management and constitutional crisis in Europe.

The Hungarian bailout took place under the post-1989 constitutional settlement which amended but did not replace the 1949 Constitution. Hungary obtained an EU loan in November 2008.[120] Hungary under the

117 For two recent collections, see A. von Bogdandy and P. Sonnevend (eds.), *Constitutional Crisis in the European Constitutional Area; Theory, Law and Politics in Hungary and Romania* (Oxford: Hart, 2015); C. Closa and D. Kochenov (eds.), *Reinforcing Rule of Law Oversight in the European Union* (Cambridge University Press, 2015).

118 See, for example, Jan-Werner Müller's analyses of both phenomena with no links drawn between them: 'Europe's Perfect Storm: The Political and Economic Consequences of the Euro-crisis', *Dissent*, 59(4), 2012, 47–53 and 'Hungary and the EU', *Aspen Review*, 2(4), 2013, 46–9.

119 In mid-2012 the Romanian government tried to oust the President and dismissed the Ombudsman, while its constitutional court rejected as unconstitutional a law amending its organisation and functioning. See Venice Commission, Opinion CDL-AD(2012)026-e, www.venice.coe.int/webforms/documents/CDL-AD(2012)026-e.aspx#. Although Bogdan Iancu notes that there was no link between popular protest in 2012 and the drastic cuts to public servants' salaries in 2010, he stresses the contested role of sovereign debt programmes in pushing through privatisations, 'Separation of Powers and the Rule of Law in Romania: The Crisis in Concepts and Contexts' in von Bogdandy and Sonnevend (eds.), *Constitutional Crisis in the European Constitutional Area*, pp. 153–70, at pp. 153–4.

120 Council Decision of 4 November 2008 granting mutual financial assistance for Hungary (2009/103/EC) (OJ L 37, 6.2.2009, p.7) under what is now Art. 143 TFEU. The EU

post-1989 Constitution had a strong constitutional court,[121] easy to directly access. It had developed a strong constitutional jurisprudence including on social rights which had fairly extensive protection in the constitution.[122] Importantly, that social rights constitutional jurisprudence had been forged in the crucible of a wave of challenges to social cuts imposed by IMF austerity lending policies to Hungary in 1995 in the transition period.[123] Despite this, it appears that no constitutional challenges were brought to the measures introduced to comply with sovereign debt loan conditions.[124]

However, austerity and the focus on levels of public debt played a role in highly significant constitutional, social and political developments since entry into bailout in November 2008. A technocrat government was installed in April 2009, to be replaced by the Fidesz government of Viktor Orbán in April 2010 with 52 per cent of the vote and, as a result, over two-thirds of Parliamentary seats. This constitutionally significant parliamentary majority provided it with a platform to alter the constitutional revision rule from one requiring a four-fifths vote in favour to one requiring a two-thirds vote in favour. It subsequently replaced the post-1989 constitution with a Fundamental Law which entered into force on 1 January 2012, although it has been amended in highly significant ways since then.[125] There are links worth exploring between the timing, conditions and politics of the 2008 bailout and the election of Fidesz in 2010.[126] There are connections between the demands of EU macro-

balance of payments loan was up to €6.5bn (while the IMF's was up to €12.5bn). The actual loan amount was lowered (€5.5bn out of €6.5bn from the EU and €9.1bn out of €12.5bn from the IMF) and the loan period (November 2008–October 2010) was shortened by one year.

121 See the 'Tavares Report' of the European Parliament which notes that 'since the start of the democratic process in Hungary the Constitutional Court has been recognised as an outstanding constitutional body throughout Europe and the world'. European Parliament, 'Report on the situation of fundamental rights: standards and practices in Hungary (pursuant to the European Parliament resolution of 16 February 2012)' (2012/2130 [INI]), 25 June 2013, www.europarl.europa.eu/sides/getDoc.do?type=REPORT&reference=A7-2013-0229&language=EN.

122 See especially Arts. 70A-J of the 1949 Constitution (as amended), including the right to: work, time off work, freely associate and strike, wage income protections, health, social security and education.

123 See above nn. 67–8.

124 See the Report on Hungary prepared by D. Dojcsák.

125 The Fundamental Law of 2012 is very different in content and tone from its predecessor. Although it continues to protect, albeit in extensively redrafted terms, a similar range of social and work rights, the overall detail is highly important.

126 Note, further, that in 2011, Hungary requested further precautionary financial assistance. This was made politically conditional by the EU on the Orbán government committing to central bank independence and the judicial reforms recommended by

economic governance (particularly the Excessive Deficit Procedure [EDP] with its headline reference values of 3 per cent deficits and 60 per cent debt)[127] and the budgetary measures inserted in the Fundamental Law. One of the central constitutional changes introduced by the 2012 Fundamental Law is to lower the public debt below 50 per cent[128] and a key political priority of the newly elected Orbán government was to reduce public debt and deficit without resorting to typical austerity measures.

The abnormal deficit reduction measures taken had dramatic effects on social rights. They entailed, inter alia, suspension of transfer payments from the state to the mandatory private pension pillar (reducing deficit), a 2010 law requiring individuals to transfer to the state their private pension assets (again to reduce its deficit, by over 10 per cent in 2011) or face penalties although the latter were subject to extensive amendment over time. It also entailed special taxes, including exceptionally high (98 per cent) and retroactive taxation of severance payments for public-sector employees alongside a constitutional amendment aiming to protect the measure from constitutional challenge. When the Constitutional Court condemned this first iteration from July 2010, Parliament promptly reintroduced the tax with a much longer period of retroactive effect accompanied by a much more extensive constitutional amendment excluding full review. With these more restricted powers, the Constitutional Court found that the five-year retroactivity of the taxation of

the Venice Commission. See European Commission, 'Commission Decides to Enter into Negotiations on Precautionary Financial Assistance with Hungary' (IP/12/407), 25 April 2012, http://europa.eu/rapid/press-release_IP-12-407_en.htm. This financial assistance was not taken up.

127 For the functioning of the EDP, see especially Art. 126 TFEU, Protocol 12 TFEU and Regulation 1467/97 of 7 July 1997 on speeding up and clarifying the implementation of the excessive deficit procedure (OJ L 209, 2.8.1997, p. 6), which is part of the Stability and Growth Pact, as amended in 2011 to include public debt as well as public deficit in the EDP. Note, also, the veto power on the budget given by the Hungarian Fundamental Law to a Budget Council: Art. 44(3).

128 See Art. 36(4): 'The National Assembly may not adopt an Act on the central budget as a result of which state debt would exceed half of the Gross Domestic Product'; Art. 36(5): 'As long as state debt exceeds half of the Gross Domestic Product, the National Assembly may only adopt an Act on the central budget which provides for state debt reduction in proportion to the Gross Domestic Product'; Art. 36(6): 'Any derogation from the provisions of Paras (4) and (5) shall only be allowed during a special legal order and to the extent necessary to mitigate the consequences of the circumstances triggering the special legal order, or, in case of an enduring and significant national economic recession, to the extent necessary to restore the balance of the national economy'.

public servants severance payments contravened the constitutional right to human dignity but that it was unable to review the taxation itself.[129]

One apparent goal of such measures was to exit the EDP by taking the deficit below 3 per cent. Hungary was in an EDP from its EU accession in May 2004 until June 2013.[130] Yet this goal failed. The EU refused to accept the budget surplus in 2011 resulting from pension nationalization as compliance with the EDP. Noting that the pensions' nationalization meant Hungary recorded a surplus in 2011, this was regarded as only 'formal respect' of the 3 per cent excessive deficit value and still a breach of the EDP because it was not respected on the basis of a structural and sustainable correction.

Indeed, this Hungarian action provoked a very different EU response as it became the only state to date to have the clause in the European Structural and Investment Funds from 1994 permitting suspension of payments because of excessive deficit invoked against it. In March 2012, the maximum amount (0.5 per cent GDP) of ESI funds was suspended from Hungary from January 2013 onwards, although this suspension was lifted before coming into effect.[131]

At the same time, parallel reforms curtailed the possibility of successfully mounting constitutional challenges to these social rights changes driven by political budgetary goals. The Constitutional Court's composition has been changed and its role dramatically restricted in the new constitutional settlement. No longer can cases easily be brought before it. More specifically its fundamental rights jurisdiction is expressly constitu tionally limited in the area of budgetary reforms. Under the Fundamental Law, the Constitutional Court's powers of ex post review of the constitutionality of budget-related laws from a substantive point of view have been substantially limited to violations of an exhaustive list of rights,[132] thus obstructing the review of constitutionality for breach of other fundamental

[129] Subsequently found by the ECtHR to breach the right to property in the ECHR in Decision of 14 May 2013, Case 66529/11, *NKM* v. *Hungary*, 14 May 2013: taxation level constituted a breach. Although the Hungarian authorities had a wide margin of discretion in tax matters, especially in times of economic instability, and therefore had a legitimate aim, the tax imposed was not proportionate.

[130] Council Decision 2013/315/EU of 21 June 2013 abrogating Decision 2004/918/EC on the existence of an excessive deficit in Hungary (OJ L 173, 26.6.2013, p. 43).

[131] The suspension was lifted in June 2012. See Council Implementing Decision of 13 March 2012 suspending commitments from the Cohesion Fund for Hungary with effect from 1 January 2013 (OJ L 78, 17.3.2012, p. 19).

[132] Art. 37(4) Hungarian Fundamental Law: 'As long as the state debt exceeds half of [GDP], the Constitutional Court may . . . review the Acts on the central budget, the implementation of

rights such as the right to property, the right to a fair trial and the right not to be discriminated against.[133] Moreover, its jurisprudence under the post-1989 Constitution, including its important judgments on austerity and social rights, is expressly repealed by the Fundamental Law.

Although the Constitutional Court continued, while adapting when required to its reduced mandate, to issue judgments condemning the constitutionality of central measures, the pensions' reforms were not the subject of a constitutional ruling. Kim Lane Scheppele, who has closely followed the changing constitutional situation in Hungary comments:

> The Constitutional Court then never issued the decision it had said it would publish on the effective nationalization of Hungarian's private pensions. The pension law, passed last spring, eliminated the state-provided pensions that Hungarians had paid into all of their working lives, in a move equivalent in the US to the abolition of social security. But the law abolished social security payments only for those who refused to transfer their private pension funds into state hands. Given that prior decisions of the Constitutional Court had said that people had a property interest in the payments they had made into the state pension system, the new pension law was surely unconstitutional under the standards that the Court had previously set. But rather than reiterate its previous arguments, the Court simply said nothing.[134]

Challenges to the new pension regime therefore went instead to the ECtHR. Close to 8,000 complaints were lodged, prompting the Registrar to require all new applications to be lodged via trade unions.[135]

the central budget, central taxes, duties and contributions, customs duties and the central conditions for local taxes for conformity with the rights to life and human dignity, to the protection of personal data, to freedom of thought, conscience and religion, or the rights related to Hungarian citizenship, and it may annul these Acts only for the violation of these rights'. It is also, and quite astonishingly, provides that such review is excluded for any Act passed while state debt exceeded 50 per cent even when state debt goes below that figure. That is to say, a perpetual restriction on constitutional review for budgetary Acts passed during times of excessive debt: Art. 37(5) Hungarian Fundamental Law.

133 See 'Tavares Report' (at n. 121); see also K. Lane Scheppele, 'Hungary's Constitutional Revolution', The Conscience of a Liberal, *New York Times* (19 December 2011), http://krugman.blogs.nytimes.com/2011/12/19/hungarys-constitutional-revolution.

134 K. Lane Scheppele, 'The Unconstitutional Constitution', The Conscience of a Liberal, *New York Times* (2 January 2012), http://krugman.blogs.nytimes.com/2012/01/02/the-unconstitutional-constitution/#more-27941. And id 'Constitutional Revenge' 1.3.2013 http://krugman.blogs.nytimes.com/2013/03/01/guest-post-constitutional-revenge/?_r=0.

135 'Human Rights Court inundated with Hungary complaints', *Euractiv* (16 January 2012). The Court found an application by an individual opting to stay in the private system, and claiming breach of her right to property under the ECHR, manifestly unfounded: Decision of 15 January 2013, Case 34929/11, *E.B.* v. *Hungary*. It is worth noting that the

This outline has certainly not identified or sufficiently analysed all the issues or linkages. Yet I hope it suffices to demonstrate that reading the new Hungarian constitutional settlement and politics through the twin lenses of euro-crisis law and social rights adds new perspectives to both the study of comparative and EU constitutionalism in times of Eurocrisis and the 'abusive constitutionalism' of which Hungary is a significant European example.[136]

7. Conclusion

This chapter has shown the rich new sources and questions raised by considering the interaction of constitutions, sovereign debt and social rights in Europe today. Through its four areas of inquiry (key features of euro-crisis constitutional judgments, testing the frames and critiques of euro-crisis constitutional judgments, assessing the puzzles of EU and European constitutional interaction and linking European constitutional crisis and Eurocrisis) it aims, above all, to evidence what a rewarding and challenging new area of constitutional inquiry this is. It uses this new area of constitutional inquiry to reorient its emphases towards, for example, a broader definition of the social, a focus on European states and the specific circumstances of sovereign debt states. It deepens analysis in relation to some issues such as the light shed by this inquiry onto EU constitutional interactions and evidence of a shared East and West European constitutional space. It critiques some dominant critiques and develops alternative readings of, to give two examples, judicial activism and 'middle-class' protection. Its objective overall is to use these sources to broaden, deepen and question the sources and debates to which it can be connected.

However, at best, the analysis hints at the very substantial strains placed on the deep structure of the constitutional settlements of bailout states. The quantity and nature of the gaps opened between constitutional commitments and lived political and social reality means that no matter how significant some constitutional courts' interventions may be

Hungarian government had, by then, made modifications to the pension regime applied to the 2 per cent of citizens retaining their private pension (98 per cent having moved to the state regime) so that they could obtain entitlements based on both their private and state-sector contributions.

136 D. Landau, 'Abusive Constitutionalism', *UC Davies Law Review*, 47(1), 2013, 189–260.

in addressing some of these constitutional gaps in the EU bailout states, overall they have a very limited role. The role of the EU institutions in creating such constitutional gaps is an important theme of this chapter. By April 2016, only one state, Greece, remained in a sovereign debt programme. For most of the states analysed here, the sovereign debt episode is, for now, complete, and hopefully not to be repeated. Barring fresh sovereign debt episodes, other than further Greek challenges, the euro-crisis constitutional judgments analysed in this chapter constitute a complete set from this group of seven states. However, the wider constitutional story of sovereign debt in Europe has certainly not yet run its course. How the peoples of Europe and their representatives and institutions interpret and respond to this exceptional turn in European and EU economic, social and constitutional history is a matter of no small importance.

INDEX